KJE 10 EUR

THE EUROPEAN UNION
AN ONGOING PROCESS OF INTEGRATION

LIBER AMICORUM ALFRED E. KELLERMANN

T.M.C. ASSER INSTITUUT
The Hague

THE EUROPEAN UNION
AN ONGOING PROCESS OF INTEGRATION

LIBER AMICORUM ALFRED E. KELLERMANN

Edited by

Jaap W. de Zwaan
Jan H. Jans
Frans A. Nelissen

Steven Blockmans
Managing Editor

T·M·C·ASSER PRESS

Published by T·M·C·ASSER PRESS
P.O.Box 16163, 2500 BD The Hague, The Netherlands
www.asserpress.nl

T·M·C·ASSER PRESS English language books are distributed exclusively by:

Cambridge University Press, The Edinburgh Building, Shaftesbury Road,
Cambridge CB2 2RU, UK,
or
for customers in the USA, Canada and Mexico:
Cambridge University Press, 40 West 20th Street, New York, NY 10011-4211, USA

www.cambridge.org

ISBN 90-6704-187-4

T.M.C. Asser Instituut - Institute for Private and Public International Law, International Commercial Arbitration and European Law
Institute Address: R.J. Schimmelpennincklaan 20-22, 2517 JN The Hague, The Netherlands; P.O. Box 30461, 2500 GL The Hague, The Netherlands; Tel.: (31-70)3420300; Fax: (31-70) 3420359; URL: www.asser.nl.
Over thirty years, the T.M.C. Asser Institute has developed into a leading scientific research institute in the field of international law. It covers private international law, public international law, including international humanitarian law, the law of the European Union, the law of international commercial arbitration and increasingly, also, international economic law, the law of international commerce and international sports law. Conducting scientific research either fundamental or applied, in the aforementioned domains, is the main activity of the Institute. In addition, the Institute organizes congresses and postgraduate courses, undertakes contract-research and operates its own publishing house, T·M·C·ASSER PRESS. Because of its inter-university background, the Institute often cooperates with Dutch law faculties as well as with various national and foreign institutions. The Institute organizes Asser College Europe, a project in cooperation with East and Central European countries whereby research and educational projects are organized and implemented.

FOREWORD

Hero worship is culturally hardwired into our psyche and cultivated in our early development by our experience of our parents – a daddy and mommy who are all powerful, all beautiful, all everything. Our eventual awakening to their frailty only intensifies our searches elsewhere for other heroes – both in private and public life.

And so it is, too, in our intellectual life: St Sigmund, St Karl, St Jurgen *et cetera* – *Chacun a son Saint*... For many, history is still a story of kings, and prime ministers, and generals, and statesmen (and stateswomen). And so it is, too, in our little puddle of European law. For many it is a story of a hero, the European Court of Justice: A St George, armed with constitutional hermeneutics, who slaughtered the dragon of national protectionism, pettiness and what else. The spillover from all of this is that awful, ubiquitous culture of celebrityship which has also invaded, indeed conquered, the long-desecrated halls of academia.

But there are, too, other kinds of heroes. In the world of letters, this it most memorably found in the opening chapters of Stendhal's *Chartreuse de Parme* in the epoch-making description of the battle of Waterloo. The hero is not Napoleon or Wellington but the magnificent foot soldier Fabrizio del Dongo (who naturally admires Napoleon and is totally modest about his own bravery and achievements), through whose eyes the real tale is told. And so, just as History discovered social history and High Culture discovered popular culture, so did we discover that in, say, the heroic story of Van Gend en Loos, the *Tariefcommissie*, and the Commission legal service, and the lawyers for Van Gend en Loos were, alongside the Court, the true movers and shakers of that legal Waterloo. And that hard sought, carefully sifted and systematically organised legal data is the true foundation on which this or that fancy theory must rely and rest.

So let us take our hat of to a magnificent Fabrizio of European law – Alfred Kellermann. Born just before the War and fortunately escaping the ignoble fate of most Dutch Jews, there is something noble and historically appropriate in a life commitment to an institution named for his co-religionist and Nobel Peace Prize winner, Tobias Michael Carel Asser, and to an academic pursuit in a field inspired by, and historically committed to, the messages of reconciliation, tolerance and respect for Others.

Modest to a fault, Kellermann, year in and year out, with his collaborators identifies the intellectual challenge, drafts the plan, sets the scaffolding, and then withdraws whilst others step into the limelight. An unerring eye to what was essential, important, and a dogged way of insisting on the detail, the technical, the seemingly unimportant – all of which are the poetry of law.

A tribute to Alfred Kellermann is inevitably and necessarily a tribute to that equally admirable Institution he serves – indispensable in the study of European law (and not only European law); and it is inevitably and necessarily a tribute to the culture whence he grew – the Netherlands – exemplified by the list of contributors to this volume. They will never say so themselves, indeed, never think it themselves. But who can contest that in terms of specific gravity, Dutch legal science has been the leaven in the European legal dough? So, *chapeau* to all these unsung heroes.

J.H.H. Weiler*

* J.H.H. Weiler, University Professor and Jean Monnet Chair, Director of the Global Law School Program, NYU School of Law.

ALFRED E. KELLERMANN:
ACADEMIC COMMUNITY ORGANISER

For almost forty years, Alfred E. Kellermann has been one of the pillars of the T.M.C. Asser Instituut in The Hague. Whoever thinks about the Asser Instituut thinks about Kellermann. In his capacity as General Secretary, he has represented the institute on countless occasions both in the Netherlands and abroad. No wonder that many have mistakenly called him the Secretary General of the Asser Instituut.

Born in The Hague on 9 November 1937, raised in Switzerland during the Second World War and trained at Leiden University and at the European Commission's Legal Service in Brussels in the early years of the European integration process, Alfred Kellermann is a European by nature and vocation.

When joining the interuniversity Asser Instituut in 1966, at a time when European law was scarcely taught at Dutch law schools, Kellermann considered it his task to raise awareness for this new and important discipline. Perhaps his finest accomplishment in this respect is the organisation of the so-called 'Asser Colloquia' on EC (later EU) law. The first-ever Asser Colloquium was held in The Hague in 1972 and dealt with the application of EC law in the legal order of the Netherlands. Since then, conferences on European law have been held annually and quickly gained a reputation as a major event in the European Union law calendar at which Dutch-speaking legal experts meet to discuss topics of varying nature. Some of the more noteworthy colloquia concerned aspects of the external relations of the European Communities, Economic and Monetary Union and the decentralisation of European competition law. Every four or five years, a session of the Asser Colloquium on European law is held in English. Memorable events have included the 1995 Asser Colloquium on 'Reforming the Treaty on European Union', the 2000 Colloquium concerning 'EU Enlargement: The Constitutional Impact at EU and National Level' and of course the 2004 Colloquium on 'The EU Constitution: The Best Way Forward?'

As conference organiser and secretary of the so-called 'Commission of European Law', composed of the professors of EU law at Dutch universities and/or their deputies, Kellermann has been instrumental in the creation of a network of EU law experts in the Netherlands, and indeed across Europe. Thanks to his involvement in the very fruitful cooperation in the framework of the biennial Hague-Zagreb-Ghent Colloquium on International Trade Law (since 1971), Kellermann has also managed to involve scholars from Eastern Europe in the exchange of ideas on the development of European law. With the publication of the Asser Colloquia's proceedings, as well as the compilation of joint student readers and case materials, Kellermann has contributed greatly to the education of students and scholars in European law.

As a follow-up to the successful Hague-Zagreb-Ghent Colloquium on International Trade Law, Asser College Europe (ACE) was established in September 1989 as a framework involving several academic institutions from Central and Eastern European countries and the T.M.C. Asser Instituut to improve education, research and the sharing of information in the fields of international trade law and European law. Thanks to the financial backing of the Dutch Government, and particularly the Ministry of Foreign Affairs, ACE has become one of the most important academic ventures between Eastern and Western Europe. Alfred Kellermann was one of the key figures in the development of this pan-European interuniversity collaboration scheme, even before the collapse of the Berlin Wall in 1989.

Thanks to his fantastic networks, Alfred Kellermann was able to develop many other scientific, training and consultancy projects. One of the larger spin-offs of Asser College Europe was a PHARE-sponsored project through which a comprehensive needs analysis on European Integration Studies was carried out in eleven Central and Eastern European countries (1998). As a consultant and senior lecturer in EU law, Kellermann has served in countless short and long-term projects all over Europe, including Russia. Also worth mentioning are his positions as team leader in the TACIS-sponsored project on 'Harmonisation of Environmental Standards in Russia' (2002-2004) and as director of the MATRA-sponsored multi-country project in Central and Eastern Europe on 'The Impact of Accession on the National Legal Orders of (pre-)Candidate Countries' (2002-2004). A little-known but nonetheless important feature of Kellermann's impressive track record of projects concerns the classification of official documents adopted by the Community's institutions. This pioneering project was first carried out in 1967 and formed the precursor to the *Guide to EEC Legislation* (first published in 1979). This guide proved a useful source at a time when the CELEX search engine was only available to *fonctionnaires* of the Community.

On 6 November 2002, Alfred Kellermann's unabated efforts in raising awareness for the European integration process and building bridges across Europe in order to organise the academic community in this field were officially recognised by the New Bulgarian University, which awarded him the title of *Doctor Honoris Causa*. On 29 April 2003, Kellermann received a royal decoration as a Knight in the Order of Orange-Nassau for his work and contributions to Dutch society as secretary, treasurer and member of the board of the Jewish Community of The Hague (1965-1970), as chairman of the Dutch branch of the International Association of Jewish Lawyers and Jurists (1972-2002), and as member of the board and legal advisor of the Fashion Fair of Amsterdam (1973-1998).

The European Union: An Ongoing Process of Integration contains 27 original contributions authored by prominent EU lawyers from academia and practice and concentrates on the three main areas of European integration that mark the path of the career of *Alfred E. Kellermann*: institutional and constitutional aspects (Part I), general principles and substantive aspects (Part II) and new Member States and Eastern Europe (Part III). The contributions included in this *liber amicorum* vary from thematic in-depth studies to studies of a comparative nature. Their themes cover, *inter alia*, the structure of the Union according to the Constitution for Europe, the changes and challenges with which the Union's institutions are faced, including the newly created positions of the President of the European Council and the Union Minister for Foreign Affairs, future paths of flexibility (enhanced cooperation, partial agreements and pioneer groups), the role of national competition authorities and national courts under Regulation 1/2003, the constitutional preparation for EU accession in the new Member States and the influence of European integration on the development of law in Russia. Where possible, last-minute updates of the contributions have been made to take account of the changes introduced on 18 June 2004, when the Heads of State and Government gave their agreement to the text of the Treaty establishing a Constitution for Europe.

Finally, we owe many thanks to Daniel Stephens and Inge van Dun-van den Bosch, who worked with great zeal throughout the short course of the preparation of this *liber*. They are the ones who made the timely publication of this tribute possible.

On behalf of many, and regardless of his recent retirement, we have the pleasure of wishing Fred lots of success in his ongoing quest to raise awareness of the importance of the European integration process.

The Editors

TABLE OF CONTENTS

ABBREVIATIONS

AB	Administratiefrechtelijke beslissingen, Rechtspraak Bestuursrecht
ADD	Addendum
AFDI	Annuaire Français de Droit International
AJIL	American Journal of International Law
BAT	Best Available Technologies
BiH	Bosnia-Herzegovina
Bull. EC	Bulletin of the European Communities
CDE	Cahiers de Droit Européen
CDU	Christlich Demokratische Union Deutschlands
CEE	Communauté économique européenne
CEES	Common European Economic Space
CESR	Committee of European Securities Regulators
CFI	Court of First Instance
CFSP	Common Foreign and Security Policy
CIE	Committee of Independent Experts
CIG	Conférence intergouvernementale
CIS	Commonwealth of Independent States
CLR	Cyprus Law Reports
CMEA	Council for Mutual Economic Assistance
CMLRep.	Common Market Law Reports
CMLRev.	Common Market Law Review
Coll.	Collection of laws
Coll. CC	Collection of decisions and opinions of the Constitutional Court
COM	European Commission document
Comecon	Council for Mutual Economic Assistance
CONV	Convention
COR	Committee of the Regions
Coreper	Comité des Représentants Permanents (EU)
CS	Common Strategies
CSCE	Commission on Security and Cooperation in Europe
CSDP	Common Security and Defence Policy
CSES	Common Space of External Security
CSREC	Common Space of Research and Education, including Cultural Aspects
CSU	Christlich Soziale Union in Bayern

EAEC	European Atomic Energy Community
EC	European Community
ECB	European Central Bank
ECHR	European Convention for the Protection of Human Rights and Fundamental Freedoms
ECJ	European Court of Justice
ECN	European Competition Network(s)
Ecofin	The Council of Economics and Finance Ministers of the European Union
ECPR	European Consortium for Political Research
ECR	European Court Reports
ECSC	European Coal and Steel Community
EEA	European Economic Area
EEC	European Economic Community
EEZ	Exclusive Economic Zone
EFARev.	European Foreign Affairs Review
EFFC	European Federation of Professional Football Clubs
EIPA	European Institute of Public Administration
ELR	European Law Review
EMSA	European Maritime Safety Agency
EMU	Economic and Monetary Union
EP	European Parliament
EPC	European Policy Centre
ESC	European Securities Committee
ESC	Economic and Social Committee
ESDP	European Security and Defence Policy
ETS	European Treaties Series
EU	European Union
EUI	European University Institute, Florence
Eurojust	European Judicial Cooperation Unit
Europol	European Police Office
EuZW	Europäische Zeitschrift für Wirtschaftsrecht
FCC	Federal Constitutional Court
FIFA	Fédération Internationale de Football Association
FRY	Federal Republic of Yugoslavia
FYROM	Former Yugoslav Republic of Macedonia
GAERC	General Affairs & External Relations Council
GASP	Gemeinsame Außen- und Sicherheitspolitik der Europäischen Union
GDP	Gross Domestic Product
GSP	Generalised System of Preferences

HR	High Representative
ICAO	International Civil Aviation Organisation
ICC	International Chamber of Commerce
ICJ Rep.	International Court of Justice, Reports of Judgments, Advisory Opinions and Orders
ICSID	International Centre for the Settlement of Investment Disputes
ICTY	International Criminal Tribunal for the former Yugoslavia
IGC	Intergovernmental Conference
ILO	International Labour Organisation
IMCO	Intergovernmental Maritime Consultative Organisation
IMO	International Maritime Organisation
IOC	International Olympic Committee
IPO	Initial Public Offering
ISLJ	The International Sports Law Journal
IT	Information Technology
JAT	Jugoslovensko Aviontransport
JB	Jurisprudentie Bestuursrecht
JHA	Justice and Home Affairs (EU)
JT	Journal des tribunaux (Belgium)
KEDO	Korean Peninsula Energy Development Organisation
LL.M.	Legum Magister, Master of Laws
MARPOL	International Convention for the Prevention of Pollution by Ships
MBA	Master of Business Administration
MEP	Member of the European Parliament
MEPC	Marine Environment Protection Committee
MGIMO	Moscow State Institute of International Relations
MNR	Ministry for Natural Resources (Russia)
MSC	Maritime Safety Committee
NATO	North Atlantic Treaty Organisation
NCA	National Competition Authority
NGO	Non-governmental Organisation
NJ	Nederlandse Jurisprudentie
NJCM	Nederlands Juristen Comité voor de Mensenrechten
NTER	Nederlands Tijdschrift voor Europees Recht
nyr	not yet reported

OJ	Official Journal of the European Communities/Union
OUP	Oxford University Press
PCA	Partnership and Cooperation Agreement
PESC	Politique étrangère et de sécurité commune
PHARE	originally: Poland Hungary Assistance for the Reconstruction of the Economy
PJCC	Police and Judicial Cooperation in Criminal Matters
PM	Prime Minister
QMV	qualified majority voting
R&D	Research and Development
RF	Russian Federation
RSCAS	Robert Schuman Centre for Advanced Studies
SAC	Supreme Arbitration Court
SaM	Serbia and Montenegro
SAP	Stabilisation and Association Process
SC	Supreme Court
SCIFA	Strategic Committee on Immigration, Frontiers and Asylum
SEW	Sociaal Economische Wetgeving
SOLAS	International Convention for the Safety of Life at Sea
SPS	Socijalisticka Partija Srbije (Socialist Party of Serbia)
TACIS	Technical Assistance to the Commonwealth of Independent States
TEU	Treaty on European Union
UEFA	Union Européenne de Football Association
UK	United Kingdom
UMFA	Union Minister for Foreign Affairs
UN	United Nations
UNCITRAL	United Nations Commission on International Trade Law
UNFCCC	UN Framework Convention on Climate Change
UNMIK	United Nations Interim Administration Mission in Kosovo
US	United States
USA	United States of America
USSR	Union of Soviet Socialist Republics
WADA	World Anti-Doping Agency
WEU	Western European Union
WG	Working Group

WHI   Walter Hallstein-Institut, Berlin
WPNR   Weekblad voor privaatrecht, notariaat en registratie
WTO   World Trade Organisation

YBEL   Yearbook of European Law

PART I

INSTITUTIONAL AND CONSTITUTIONAL ASPECTS

THE STRUCTURE OF THE UNION ACCORDING TO THE DRAFT CONSTITUTION FOR EUROPE

Koen Lenaerts*

1.   INTRODUCTION

Inspired by the *acquis jurisprudentiel* of the Court of Justice of the European Communities (hereinafter, the 'Court of Justice'), it was acknowledged by many, well before the release of the draft Treaty establishing a Constitution for Europe (hereinafter, the 'draft Constitution' or 'Constitution'), that the Union already had a constitution in the form of a conglomerate of Treaties forming 'the constitutional charter of a Community based on the rule of law'.[1] The legal notion of 'constitution' can be generally defined as the organisational text shaping the institutional design of a polity and laying down the fundamental principles upon which government is to exercise its powers and which form a limitation to the exercise of such powers.[2] The basic Treaties of the Union display those minimalist features since they contain the organisational rules structuring the exercise of public authority, state the foundational values of the EU legal order/polity and refer to fundamental rights that limit any legitimate exercise of public authority.[3] Moreover, adding to these formal constitutional features, the Court of Justice has referred in its case-law to the principles of supremacy and direct effect of Community law,[4] to the hierarchy of norms underlying the concept of the rule of law inasmuch as some rules necessarily take precedence over others,[5] or else to the judicial enforceability of the rules contained in the EC Treaty as limits to be

---

* Prof. Koen Lenaerts, Judge of the Court of Justice of the European Communities and Professor of European Law, Leuven University. All opinions expressed are personal to the author. This paper is based on the draft Treaty establishing a Constitution for Europe, adopted by consensus by the European Convention on 13 June and 10 July 2003, submitted to the President of the European Council in Rome on 18 July 2003, *OJ* 2003 C 169 of 18 July 2003.

[1] Opinion 1/91 *European Economic Area* [1991] *ECR* I-6079.

[2] For a more elaborate 'neutral' definition, see *Black's Law Dictionary* (St. Paul, Minn., West Publishing Co. 1990) p. 311.

[3] K. Lenaerts and M. Desomer, 'New Models of Constitution-Making in Europe: The Quest for Legitimacy', 39 *CMLRev.* (2002) p. 1217 at p. 1220.

[4] Opinion 1/91 *European Economic Area* [1991] *ECR* I-6079, para. 21.

[5] Case 294/83 *Les Verts* v. *Parliament* [1986] *ECR* 1339, para. 23; [1987] 2 *CMLR* 343.

observed in any exercise of public authority at the level of the Community or the Member States.[6] Those developments were supplemented by the recognition of the exclusive competence of the Court of Justice to rule on the validity of acts of the Community institutions and thus to determine the limits of the competences of the Community.[7]

The crisis of legitimacy of the European Union rooted in the opacity of the structure inherited from Maastricht and in a lack of political vision to convince the peoples of Europe of the added value of integration, as well as the perspective of the biggest enlargement in EU history, prompted the European Council, under pressure from across Europe, to convene a Convention in order to re-issue the Union's Constitution through a bottom-up approach.[8] The outcome of the Convention thus represents an attempt to 'reconstitutionalise' the Treaties on which the Union is founded, at a moment of intense political significance. One of the most powerful achievements of the Convention has been the shaping of a new structure for the Union, simplified, but more importantly, unified. Indeed, following the suggestion of the Laeken Declaration, the draft Constitution achieves the merger of the European Community and Union into a single European Union,[9] endowed with legal personality,[10] the legal acts of which take precedence over Member States' laws,[11] must be in the form of a defined set of instruments[12] and are commonly adopted under a unified procedure.[13] As a corollary of the merger, the jurisdiction of the Court of Justice as the ultimate umpire of the European legal order, and thus judicial review of the acts adopted by the Union, has been extended.[14] Coupled with a clear vertical division of competences,[15] this structure establishes for good an autonomous political authority, i.e. a constitutional regime in its own right, co-existing with the Member States.

---

[6] Ibid.

[7] Reference is made here to the so-called *judicial Kompetenz-Kompetenz,* as to 'who decides who decides'. See Case 314/85 *Foto-Frost* v. *Hauptzollamt Lübeck-Ost* [1987] *ECR* 4199, para. 15; [1998] 3 *CMLR* 57.

[8] See Lenaerts and Desomer, loc. cit. n. 3.

[9] Draft Constitution, Article 1.

[10] Ibid., Article 6.

[11] Ibid., Article 10.

[12] Ibid., Articles 32 to 36.

[13] Ibid., Articles 33 and III-302 for legislative acts and Articles 35 and 36 for non-legislative acts.

[14] Principally in the area of freedom, security and justice (which combines the current third pillar with the Community competences presently contained in Title IV of Part III of the EC Treaty) where the draft Constitution consecrates the principle of full jurisdiction of the Court of Justice.

[15] Draft Constitution, Articles 9 to 17.

2.   THE MERGER OF THE TREATIES

Three Treaties – the Treaty on European Union, the Treaty establishing the European Community and the Treaty establishing the European Atomic Energy Community – co-exist today to give the Union its contours,[16] a situation that renders the current structure of the Union extremely complex and its working procedures inherently opaque. The draft Constitution merges the existing Treaties, but imperfectly, since Euratom will last as an independent legal entity with the sole modification of its institutional and financial rules, as laid down in the protocol attached to the Constitution.[17] Still, the combination of the EU Treaty and the EC Treaty into a single supreme instrument is essential to rationalise the objectives, powers and policy instruments of the Union and to create a single public authority. Most of the other features introduced by the draft Constitution and analysed hereinafter are moreover logical consequences of this combination.

As a corollary to the merger between the Community and the Union, the Maastricht 'pillars' structure is abolished. The common foreign and security policy – the so-called second pillar – is included in Title V of Part III of the Constitution, entitled 'The Union's External Action'. Police and judicial cooperation in criminal matters – the so-called third pillar – is grouped with the current EC competences on visas, asylum, immigration and other policies related to free movement of persons,[18] in Chapter IV of Title III of Part III of the Constitution, under the denomination of 'area of freedom, security and justice'. This important methodological shift entails the extension of the Community (i.e. supranational) method to police and judicial cooperation in criminal matters, while the common foreign and security policy (hereinafter, the 'CFSP'), because of its integration within the constitutional structure, cannot be classified as purely intergovernmental anymore. If the intergovernmental nature of the second and third pillars is often pointed to as the insuperable obstacle to the emergence of a substantive constitution at the Union level,[19] this proposal of the draft Constitution certainly represents a major breakthrough.

Concretely, the draft Constitution proposes that police and judicial cooperation in criminal matters be carried out by means of Europeans laws and

---

[16] The fourth historic Treaty establishing the European Coal and Steel Community expired on 23 July 2002.

[17] See Article 3 of the protocol amending the Euratom Treaty, which states: 'The institutional and financial provisions of the Treaty establishing a Constitution for Europe … shall apply to this Treaty…'.

[18] See Title IV of Part III of the EC Treaty, which includes judicial cooperation in civil matters (see Article 65 EC).

[19] C. Franck, 'Traité et constitution: les limites de l'analogie', in P. Magnette, ed., *La constitution de l'Europe* (Brussels, Editions de l'Université de Bruxelles 2000) p. 36.

framework laws,[20] like policies on border checks, asylum and immigration and judicial cooperation in civil matters.[21] According to Article 33(1), European laws and framework laws are adopted, on the basis of proposals from the Commission, jointly by the European Parliament and the Council of Ministers under the ordinary legislative procedure,[22] which requires the Council to decide by qualified majority.

The CFSP remains a peculiar field, especially due to its inherently political nature, which makes it an executive prerogative, the exercise of which tradition-ally escapes judicial scrutiny.[23] Its integration within the draft Constitution as one among other competences in external relations, and the consecutive imposition of fundamental principles, such as primacy, to the measures adopted at Union level, illustrate nonetheless a desire to consider this policy area as an integral part of the Union's sphere of activity, and not as a domain regulated by an exceptional *modus operandi* out of the general structure of the Union. This is further clarified by various attempts through the text of the draft Constitution to guarantee a greater consistency of the Union's external action, especially with the creation of a Union Minister of Foreign Affairs, elected by the European Council but also Vice-President of the Commission, and whose nomination will thus be subject to the approval of the European Parliament.

3.   A SINGLE LEGAL PERSONALITY

If the European Community has long been recognised as a subject of international law, an ambiguity remains as to the European Union's legal capacity. Hence, if the wish to simplify the structure of the Union implied merging the Treaties and the pillars, ensuring its effectiveness and guaranteeing its autonomy required the grant of legal personality to the Union. Article 6 of the draft Constitution thus states unequivocally that 'the Union shall have legal personality'. The direct consequences of this development are numerous, ranging from the ability to act on behalf of the Member States and sign treaties in all Union fields of activity, to

---

[20] Draft Constitution, Articles III-171 to III-178.

[21] Ibid., Articles III-166 to III-170, i.e. the current Title IV of Part III EC Treaty.

[22] Ibid., Article III-302.

[23] Because of this, rather than on the basis of a specific organisational choice, Article III-282(1) of the draft Constitution reaffirms the general exclusion of the Court of Justice's jurisdiction with respect to CFSP. In the United States, foreign policy decisions are also conferred the status of inherently 'political questions', which are hence only susceptible to be scrutinised by federal courts in a limited manner. See K. Lenaerts, *Le Juge et la Constitution aux Etats-Unis d'Amérique et dans l'ordre juridique européen* (Brussels, Bruylant 1988) pp. 12-13, 541-542, 632-634, and the references provided there.

legal standing before courts, membership of international organisations or participation in international conventions.

The Convention Working Group on Legal Personality rightly argued that a single legal personality for the Union was fully justified for reasons of effectiveness, legal certainty, transparency and the building of a higher profile for the Union 'not only in relation to third States, but also *vis-à-vis* European citizens'.[24] While increasing input and output legitimacy, the grant of legal personality to the Union brings it further into conformity with a constitutional regime that is able to exercise rights and undertake obligations in relation to both its own constituents and other international subjects.

4.   PRIMACY

The principle of primacy of European law provides a good example of the process of reconstitution of the Union operated by the Convention. First articulated by the Court of Justice in its 1964 judgment in *Costa/ENEL*,[25] and despite being well affirmed and respected, this principle remains a judicial construct until now, i.e. it has never been introduced within any European Treaty. This implies, for instance, that in the area of the CFSP, where the Court of Justice is deprived of any jurisdiction, it remains up to each Member State to determine the status, in its internal legal order, of EU measures adopted in that area.[26]

Article 10 of Part I of the draft Constitution[27] clearly states that the Constitution and law adopted by the Union's institutions – without limitation (i.e. including CFSP decisions) – 'shall have primacy over the law of the Member States'. Primacy of European law is however restricted by the principle of conferral (Article 9(2) of the Constitution): only those acts adopted by the Union 'in exercising the competences conferred on it' will take precedence over conflicting rules of national law. No general subordination of the Member States' constitutional order is thus at stake. The principle of primacy is first of all a rule of conflict of laws. Hence, the Union's Constitution co-exists with the constitutions of the Member States – as a complementary constitutional instrument that European citizens can precisely identify as the supreme law that they have in common – to form a *Verfassungsverbund*[28] or 'cooperative constitutional order' at the European level.

---

[24] Final report of Working Group III on Legal Personality, CONV 305/02 – WG III 16, p. 15 at (2).

[25] Case 6/64 *Costa* v. *ENEL* [1964] *ECR* 585 at 594; [1964] *CMLR* 425.

[26] K. Lenaerts and P. Van Nuffel, *Constitutional Law of the European Union* (London, Sweet & Maxwell 1999) p. 666 at para. 19-005.

[27] Like the Supremacy Clause contained in Article VI(2) of the Constitution of the United States.

[28] The expression is borrowed from I. Pernice, 'Multilevel constitutionalism and the Treaty of Amsterdam: European constitution-making revisited?', 36 *CMLRev.* (1999) p. 707. The translation of

5.   A UNIFIED SET OF INSTRUMENTS

A powerful development proposed by the draft Constitution lies in the rationalisation of the instruments through which the Union may exercise the competences
conferred upon it.[29] The Union currently uses no less than fifteen different
instruments, some having the same appellation but entailing different legal
effects, others being rarely used.[30] This diversity has contributed to the development of an obscure patchwork of norms with ill-defined scope, legal effects and
institutional origin. This situation consequently limits democratic control over
governance at the European level.

The Convention proposes to reorganise the Union's instruments, under Title V
of Part I, inspired by the crucial distinction, common to all Member State legal
systems, between legislative and executive acts. The concern underlying this
division lies in a better definition and separation of powers at the European level,
enabling the setting up of a true hierarchy of norms.[31] Due to the peculiarities of
the Union's institutional system, the draft Constitution proposes an innovative
distinction between legislative[32] and non-legislative acts.[33]

5.1   Legislative acts

The Union's legislative action is to be conducted through two set of instruments,
European laws and European framework laws. The former are defined as legislative acts of general application, binding in their entirety and directly applicable in
all Member States. The latter are conceived as legislative acts binding as to the
result to be achieved but leaving the national authorities free to choose the form
and means of achieving that result.[34] In this new typology, European laws are to

---

Verfassungsverbund into 'cooperative constitutional order' is derived from the idea of 'closely
intertwined' and interdependent legal orders showing mutual respect for each other, developed
recently in Lenaerts, 'Interlocking legal orders in the European Union and comparative law', 52
International Comparative Law Quarterly (2003) p. 873. See also Lenaerts and Desomer, loc. cit. n.
3, at p. 1221.

[29] Because specific adoption procedures are linked with each instrument and because the draft
Constitution has proposed to merge the EU and EC Treaties, such rationalisation has constituted a
particularly sensitive issue for the Convention.

[30] See the executive summary of the report of the Working Group on Simplification, presented
to the plenary session of the European Convention on 5-6 December 2002, CONV 424/02.

[31] Although not defined as such in the Constitution, the hierarchy of norms would then read as
follows (top down): the Constitution; European laws and framework laws; European regulations
adopted as delegated acts; European regulations and decisions adopted directly under the Constitution; European regulations and decisions adopted as implementing acts.

[32] Draft Constitution, Article 33.

[33] Ibid., Article 34.

[34] Ibid., Article 32.

replace current EC regulations and 'third pillar' decisions where these instruments are used to enact legislation (i.e. to lay down rules based on a Treaty provision and containing basic policy choices in the field concerned),[35] whereas European framework laws are to replace the current EC directives and 'third pillar' framework decisions (again when they are used as legislative instruments). The common denominator of legislative acts lies in the fact that the adoption of both instruments should be subject to the 'ordinary' legislative procedure, i.e. joint adoption by the European Parliament and the Council of Ministers by qualified majority,[36] on the basis of a proposal from the Commission.[37] This method best incarnates the double democratic legitimacy of the Union's legislative process, as a common expression of Europe's citizens through the Parliament and of the Member States through the Council. The expansion of the scope of co-decision is nevertheless balanced by the maintenance of special legislative procedures 'in the specific cases provided for by the Constitution',[38] which entails adoption of laws or framework laws by the Council of Ministers alone by unanimity voting, after mere consultation of the Parliament.[39] This choice reflects a rather realist and pragmatic approach which certainly tends to suffer from a lack of democratic legitimacy, but which simply testifies to the particular sensitivity of those matters to some, if not all, Member States.[40]

5.2 Non-legislative acts

The use of acts of a non-legislative nature is also significantly rationalised by the draft Constitution, which limits them to two types of instruments: European regulations and European decisions. A European regulation is of general application

---

[35] The category of European laws should also cover the current decisions of a *Beschluß*-type which have no particular addressees and are used for the adoption of financing programmes or supporting actions.

[36] Draft Constitution, Article 22.

[37] Ibid., Article 33(1).

[38] Ibid., Article 33(2).

[39] See, for example, Articles 53(3) (setting the limits of the Union's own resources), III-10 (right to vote and to stand as a candidate in municipal and European elections), III-62 (harmonisation of turnover taxes, excise duties and other forms of indirect taxation), III-64 (approximation of legislation), III-68 (setting up centralised Union-wide authorisation, coordination and supervision of intellectual property rights protection), III-104(3) (various matters in the field of social policy), III-175(1) (measures combating serious crime with cross-border dimension), III-176(3) (operational police cooperation), III-178 (measures setting the conditions under which police authorities of one Member State can operate in the territory of another Member State), etc.

[40] See K. Lenaerts and M. Desomer, 'À la recherche d'un équilibre pour l'Union: répartition des compétences et équilibre institutionnel dans le projet de Traité établissant une Constitution pour l'Europe', in O. De Schutter and P. Nihoul, eds., *Une Constitution pour l'Europe* (Brussels, Larcier 2004) p. 75.

and can be either binding in its entirety and directly applicable, or binding only as regards the result to be achieved on all Member States to which it is addressed. A European decision is binding in its entirety, either generally or only for those to whom it is addressed if it specifies them.[41] This particularly broad definition enables the replacement, in the field of the CFSP, of all instruments of a deci-sional nature, i.e. the current 'common strategies', 'joint actions' and 'common positions',[42] by European decisions.[43] It has also, regrettably, enabled certain political trade-offs to take place, moving the adoption of some specific measures provided for by the Constitution to the non-legislative side, thereby escaping the 'ordinary' legislative procedure. Recourse can be had to those non-legislative acts when a provision of the Constitution directly calls for it,[44] when a law or frame-work law delegates to the Commission the power to enact delegated regulations to supplement or amend them (delegated acts), or when it is necessary to ensure the uniform implementation of binding European acts at the national level (imple-menting acts).[45]

The Union's legal arsenal is completed by two non-binding instruments, namely recommendations and opinions, like Article 249 EC already provides today.

The introduction of a category of 'delegated regulations' within the Union nomenclature of normative instruments is aimed at limiting the level of detail of basic legislation, which can affect its ability to respond promptly to changes in circumstances in specific regulatory environments, while guaranteeing the democratic legitimacy of the Union's action. Pursuant to Article 35(1) of the draft Constitution, legislative acts, including those adopted on the basis of special legislative procedures, may delegate to the Commission the power to enact delegated regulations to supplement or amend certain non-essential elements of those acts. It belongs to the legislature to define the objectives, content, scope and duration of the delegation, provided that the enactment of measures dealing with essential elements of an area are reserved for legislative action. Given the novelty of this ability for the legislature to delegate its power, Article 35(2) also offers a list of 'conditions of application' through which the European Parliament and the Council of Ministers may control the execution of the delegation by the Commis-sion. Under a 'call back' provision, the legislature might thus revoke the delegation, in the case of excess of authority by the Commission or because of the political sensitivity of some technical aspects of a particular issue, for instance,

---

[41] Draft Constitution, Article 32.

[42] Article 12 EU.

[43] Draft Constitution, Articles III-195(3) and III-201.

[44] This type of non-legislative acts may be adopted either by the Commission, the Council of Ministers, the European Council or the European Central Bank, depending on what the Constitution provides for.

[45] Draft Constitution, Articles 34, 35 and 36.

and decide to enact measures on its own.[46] The legislature might also explicitly determine that delegated regulations may enter into force only if no objection is expressed by the Parliament or the Council of Ministers within a specific period of time. It is worth underlining two important aspects of the delegation process, and of its monitoring in particular, which denote the concern of the drafters of the Constitution for a better clarification of the separation of powers at Union level. First, the power to enact delegated regulations is reserved to the Commission, thereby reinforcing its status of European executive.[47] Hence, neither the Council of Ministers, nor a specialised agency, nor any comitology committee might be empowered with that capacity. Second, acknowledging that it would be improper to endow a comitology committee with the ability to monitor the execution of the delegation,[48] Article 35(2) stresses that the 'conditions of application' to which the delegation is subject must be explicitly determined in the habilitating law or framework law, which normally enables the European Parliament to participate fully in the designing of the monitoring process (at least in the overwhelming number of cases where the ordinary legislative procedure applies).[49]

As far as the executive sphere as such is concerned, the draft Constitution, while conceding to Member States the primary competence to implement European measures,[50] nonetheless grants executive powers to the Union 'where uniform conditions for implementing binding Union acts are needed'.[51] These implementing powers will be conferred by the act in question primarily to the Commission and 'in specific cases duly justified', as well as in the field of the

---

[46] A comparable form of review already exists nowadays in the regulation of financial services (including banking and insurance activities), under the so-called Lamfalussy procedure. If the Commission is authorised to adapt technical aspects of financial services regulation in order to respond quickly to market situations, this procedure also allows for a recall of this early form of delegated regulation to the European legislature, i.e. the European Parliament and Council of Ministers.

[47] Except in the field of the CFSP.

[48] See contra M. Dougan, 'The Convention's Draft Constitutional Treaty: bringing Europe closer to its lawyers?', 28 ELR (2003) p. 763 at p. 786.

[49] This is not to say, though, that the Commission could not involve advisory and technical committees in the exercise of the powers it has received by delegation. Consider for instance the role played by the European Securities Committee (ESC) and by the Committee of European Securities Regulators (CESR) under the Lamfalussy procedure, which prepares opinions for the Commission with market participants, end-users and consumers and monitors the Member States' regulatory practices to ensure consistent implementation and application of EU financial regulations. The IGC 2003's first addendum to the Presidency proposal document (Addendum 1 to the Presidency proposal, CIG 60/03 ADD1, Annex 14) expressly proposed to introduce a declaration in the Final Act of the Conference taking note of the 'Commission's intention to continue to consult experts from the Member States in the preparation of delegated regulations in the financial services area, in accordance with its established practice.'

[50] Draft Constitution, Article 36(1).

[51] Ibid., Article 36(2). The terms 'binding acts' in this provision encompasses laws, framework laws, regulations – including delegated regulations – and decisions.

CFSP,[52] to the Council of Ministers. Article 36(3) then provides that the mechanisms for control by Member States of the Union's implementing acts (comitology) must be laid down in European laws, to be adopted according to the ordinary legislative procedure and no longer by the Council of Ministers acting alone and unanimously as is currently the case.[53]

5.3 A better hierarchy of norms?

The new architecture of the Union instruments is thus built around the pivotal notion of 'legislation', against which the other acts are defined. The breakdown between legislative and non-legislative acts may nevertheless be questioned to some extent, with a direct impact on the hierarchy of norms the draft Constitution aims to introduce. Although Article 32(1) does not expressly mention it, a careful reading of Article 35 and of Part III of the draft Constitution suggests that the allotment between legislative and non-legislative acts has been realised in agreement with the jurisprudential *acquis*, in particular by saving the qualification of 'legislative acts' for those laying down the 'basic elements of the matter to be dealt with'[54] and containing fundamental political choices. It is not clear, however, to what extent certain non-legislative acts adopted directly on the basis of the Constitution will really deal with less basic or fundamental regulatory choices, especially when adoption procedures are comparable to special legislative procedures.[55] Hence, one may wonder why those important measures should escape a truly legislative debate with full involvement of the European Parliament and, as a corollary, whether the introduction of a somewhat shaky hierarchy of norms will really reach its intended objectives in terms of clarity, transparency and legitimacy.

It remains that with the proposed clarification of the Union's instruments, and as the consequence of a better separation of powers,[56] the draft Constitution presents a first attempt to define a clearer hierarchy of norms, albeit with the necessary nuances that dealing with sensitive matters at the European level

---

[52] Ibid., Article 39. Since foreign policy resorts primarily to the State's 'diplomatic function', it is inherently susceptible to be carried out through executive measures.

[53] Article 202 EC.

[54] See notably Case 25/70 *Köster* [1970] *ECR* 1161, para. 6; [1972] *CMLR* 255.

[55] See, for instance, Article III-52(1) of the draft Constitution, which confers to the Council of Ministers the power to adopt European regulations in order to give effect to the rules on competition after consultation of the European Parliament. For a comment on this issue, see Dougan, loc. cit. n. 48, at pp. 783-784.

[56] It is the functional separation of powers, clearly distinguishing between the legislative, executive and judicial functions, each of them being carried out in accordance with proper procedures, which is at stake here. See K. Lenaerts, 'Some Reflections on the Separation of Powers in the European Community', 28 *CMLRev.* (1991) p. 11.

entails. Separation of powers is itself a guarantee of democracy; a clear hierarchy of norms is a guarantee of transparency and of democratic control. With such restructuring of the tools to design and implement its policies, and of the procedures and institutions responsible for their adoption, the Union is endowed with a political system comparable to those of the Member States and thereby reaffirms its autonomy as a political authority based on the rule of law.

6.   A UNIFIED SYSTEM OF DIVISION OF COMPETENCE

The existence of any political entity entails the exercise of certain competences. In a multilevel structure like the European polity, or any federal structure, the issue of vertical division of competence is crucial to guarantee the autonomy of each level and to achieve a balance in governance. A 'clear' division of competence is also essential to ensure that citizens can identify and understand the role of each political entity they belong to and thus to enhance input legitimacy[57] at each level of government. The Laeken Declaration forcefully emphasised the need to 'clarify, simplify and adjust the division of competence between the Union and the Member States', which the completion of the internal market had obscured, in order to make it 'more transparent' and avoid the 'impression that the Union takes on too much in areas where its involvement is not always essential'. Called upon to address this legitimacy concern, the Convention has devised a response by means of a move towards a unified system of division of competence, inspired by the *acquis jurisprudentiel* of the Court of Justice[58] and doctrinal comments,[59] between the Union, on the one hand, and Member States and the other levels of government within their own political structures, on the other. This unified system thus contributes to the strengthening of the Union as a political authority in its own right, with the Court of

---

[57] Input legitimacy addresses the question of direct legitimisation of political power through the democratic participation of the citizens or their elected representatives in transparent decision-making and constitution-making procedures. See E. Stein, 'International integration and democracy: No love at first sight', 95 *AJIL* (2001) p. 489.

[58] For early case-law, see e.g. Opinion 1/75 [1975] *ECR* 1355; Case 804/79 *Commission* v. *United Kingdom* [1981] *ECR* 1045; Case 22/70 *Commission* v. *Council (AETR)* [1971] *ECR* I-263; Joined Cases 3, 4 and 6/76 *Kramer* [1976] *ECR* 1279; and Opinion 1/76 *Inland Waterway Vessels* [1977] *ECR* I-741.

[59] See, for example, S. Weatherill, 'Competence', in De Witte, ed., *Ten reflections on the Constitutional Treaty for Europe* (Florence, EUI/RSCAS 2003) p. 45; A. Von Bogdandy and J. Bast, 'The European Union's Vertical Order of Competences: The Current Law and Proposals for its Reform', 39 *CMLRev.* (2002) p. 227; K. Boskovits, *Le juge communautaire et l'articulation des compétences normatives entre la Communauté européenne et ses Etats members* (Brussels/Athens, Bruylant/Sakkoulas 1999); and C. Sasse and H.C. Yourow, 'The Growth of Legislative Power of the European Communities', in E. Stein and T. Sandalow, eds., *Courts and Free Markets: Perspectives from the United States and Europe* (Oxford, Clarendon Press 1982).

Justice as the ultimate umpire to ensure, through the exercise of its *Kompetenz-Kompetenz*, that each level of the European constitutional order does not encroach upon the domain of the others.

6.1   Fundamental principles

The division of competence proposed by the Convention is effectuated in accordance with four core principles: conferral,[60] subsidiarity,[61] proportionality[62] and loyalty.[63]

The principle of conferral – the formulation of which is currently encapsulated in Article 5(1) EC – entails that Union action is limited to the spheres of activity bestowed on it by the Member States in the Constitution. As a corollary, the Convention stresses that 'competences not conferred upon the Union in the Constitution remain with the Member States'. This provision, which can be found in a similar wording in the constitutions of various federal States, like the United States[64] and Germany,[65] vests residual powers, i.e. those not conferred to the Union, in the Member States, as the holders *ab initio* of plenary powers. The exercise by Member States of their so-called 'retained competences' nonetheless implies the respect of Community law in line with the principle of primacy and the duty of loyalty.[66] Nowadays, the principle of conferral is mitigated by the flexibility clause of Article 308 EC, which gives the Council, acting unanimously, the ability to 'take appropriate measures' in case action is necessary to attain one of the objectives of the Community and the Treaty has *not* provided the necessary powers therefore. Following the deep concerns expressed towards the use of this provision, which is supposedly responsible for the creeping invasion of the Union into Member State competences, the draft Constitution has reframed, but not abolished,[67] this possibility. The flexibility clause is circumscribed by Article 17

---

[60] Draft Constitution, Article 9(2).

[61] Ibid., Article 9(3).

[62] Ibid., Article 9(4).

[63] Ibid., Articles 10(2) and 5(2).

[64] See 10th Amendment to the US Constitution, which reads as follows: 'The powers not delegated to the United States by the Constitution, nor prohibited by it to the States, are reserved to the States respectively, or to the people.'

[65] Article 30 of the German Basic Law reads as follows: 'The exercise of governmental powers and the discharge of governmental functions is incumbent on the *Länder* insofar as this Basic Law does not otherwise prescribe or permit.'

[66] For examples of judicial applications of those principles, see Case C-165/91 *van Munster* [1994] *ECR* I-4661; Case C-262/97 *Engelbrecht* [2000] *ECR* I-7321; and Case C-157/99 *Smits and Peerbooms* [2001] *ECR* I-5473.

[67] Some members of the Convention nonetheless defended 'that Article 308 was inherently open to misuse and should therefore be deleted', as stated in the final report of Working Group V on Complementary Competencies, CONV 375/1/02 – WG V 14, p. 14.

to the attainment of policy objectives defined in Part III of the draft Constitution, while unanimity voting in the Council is supplemented by the necessary consent of the European Parliament. The Commission is also required to draw national Parliaments' attention to proposals based on the flexibility clause, and the Constitution expressly excludes harmonisation through this provision in areas where specific provisions of the Constitution prohibit harmonisation of national laws,[68] so that it cannot become an indirect way to amend the Constitution.[69]

Article 1 of the Constitution states that the competences conferred upon the Union shall be exercised 'in the Community way', while Article 9(3) and (4) emphasises respect for the principles of subsidiarity and proportionality, found in current Article 5 EC, the first of which is applicable only 'in areas which do not fall within [the Union's] exclusive competence'. Besides the application of the principle of proportionality to the form of Union action and no longer only to its content, the Constitution also provides, in a specific protocol, a system for monitoring the application of those principles by the institutions in the decision-making process. Since the system is aimed at being preventive, it is up to the Commission, as the sole initiator of Union action in most fields, to undertake obligations in order to ensure their respect. First, it is proposed that the Commission includes a detailed statement in all legislative proposals to appraise compliance with the subsidiarity and proportionality requirements.[70] Secondly, the Commission is invited to send all its legislative proposals to the national Parliaments at the same time as it sends them to the Union legislator.[71] Any national Parliament, after consulting with regional Parliaments where appropriate, might then send to the Presidents of the European Parliament, the Council of Ministers and the Commission, which should take it into account, 'a reasoned opinion stating why it considers that the proposal in question does not comply with the principle of subsidiarity.'[72] The Commission would also be required to review its proposal if reasoned opinions emanate from one third of the votes attributed to national Parliaments.[73] *Ex post* judicial control of the principle of

---

[68] Examples of such 'exclusion' of harmonisation can be found in the areas of non-discrimination policy (Article III-8(2)), employment policy (Article III-101), social policy (Article III-104(2)(a)), immigration policy (Article III-168(4)), public health policy (Article III-179(5)), industrial policy (Article III-180(3)), culture (Article III-181(5)(a)), education (Articles III-182(4)(a) and III-183(4)), civil protection (Article III-184(2)) and administrative cooperation (Article III-185(2)).

[69] In Opinion 2/94 *Opinion pursuant to Article 228(6) of the EC Treaty* [1996] *ECR* I-1759, the Court of Justice had already made clear that Article 308 EC could not be used to that effect.

[70] Protocol on the Application of the Principles of Subsidiarity and Proportionality, para. 4.

[71] Ibid., para. 3.

[72] Ibid., para. 5.

[73] Under this system, national Parliaments of Member States with unicameral parliamentary systems are said to have two votes, while each of the chambers of a bicameral parliamentary system would have one vote. The threshold of one third is lowered to a quarter in the case of an

subsidiarity would also be reinforced by the recognition to Member States, acting on behalf of their national Parliament, of a specific cause of action for infringement of this principle by a legislative act. The same right would be recognised to the Committee of the Regions regarding legislative acts for the adoption of which the Constitution provides that it be consulted.[74]

The exercise of their respective competences by the Union and Member States is also regulated by the respect of the principle or duty of loyalty, which is reinforced in the draft Constitution compared to current Article 10 EC. Articles 10(2) and 5(2)(2) of the Constitution deal respectively with the positive obligation for Member States to 'ensure fulfilment of the obligations flowing from the Constitution or resulting from the Union Institutions' acts' and with the negative obligation to 'refrain from any measure which could jeopardise the attainment of the objectives set out in the Constitution'. Those provisions, which mimic current Article 10 EC, are reinforced by Article 5(2)(1), which introduces a bilateral duty of cooperation, in line with the case-law of the Court of Justice.[75] The Union would thus also be required to assist the Member States 'in carrying out tasks which flow from the Constitution'.

6.2   Three main categories of competences

One of the single most important features of the draft Constitution lies with the reshuffling of the Union competences into three categories: exclusive competences, shared competences and supporting, coordinating or complementary competences. These categories, presented in Article 11 and explained further in Articles 12, 13 and 16 of the Constitution, do not depart radically from the current division of competences, as shaped by the case-law of the Court of Justice. The Convention has not carried out a purely formal restatement of the present situation though. Rather, it provides a true reconstitution of current principles and fixes the system of division of competences, whereas the identification of the nature of Community competences nowadays requires a very tortuous mind that is able to play with various Treaty provisions and Court of Justice decisions.[76]

---

initiative of the Commission, or of a group of Member States under the provisions of Article III-165 of the Constitution. Protocol on the Application of the Principles of Subsidiarity and Proportionality, para. 6.

[74] Ibid., para. 7.

[75] Case C-2/88 Imm., *Zwartveld e.a.* [1990] *ECR* I-3365.

[76] D. Hanf and T. Baumé, 'Vers une clarification de la répartition des compétences entre l'Union et ses États membres? Une analyse du projet d'articles du Presidium de la Convention', 39 *Cahiers de droit européen* (2003) p. 135 at pp. 141-142. Categorising competences is of course high politics and the debates that were held as to where to place a certain competence led to unfortunate shortcomings in the constitutional text. Social policy for instance was included within the category of shared competences. The Declaration for incorporation in the final act concerning Article III-107 (the

In the case of exclusive competence, only the Union may legislate and adopt legally binding acts, except when it allows Member States to do so.[77] In other words, exclusive competence entails that 'full responsibility in the matter ... [is] transferred to the [Union]'[78] and, if not expressly consented to by the Union, 'excludes any competence on the part of Member States which is concurrent' with that of the Union.[79] Pursuant to Article 36 of the draft Constitution, Member States nevertheless retain their general power to implement those legally binding Union acts. Article 12(1) contains an exhaustive list of policy areas resorting to the Union's exclusive competence: the establishment of competition rules necessary for the functioning of the internal market,[80] monetary policy for the Member States that have adopted the euro, common commercial policy, customs union and the conservation of marine biology. The Union's exclusive external competence is limited to the realm of Article 12(2), which constitutes a sub-category of Article III-225. Pursuant to Article 12(2), the Union is thus exclusively competent to conclude international agreements when their conclusion is provided for in a legislative act of the Union, is necessary to enable it to exercise its internal competence,[81] or affects an internal Union act.[82] Article III-225(1) adds that the Union may also conclude such agreements 'where the Constitution so

---

'social policy' article of Part III of the Constitution), proposed by the Italian Presidency (see Addendum 1 to the Presidency proposal, 9 December 2003, IGC 60/03 ADD1, p. 41), clearly states, however, that the policies described in this provision fall essentially within the competence of the Member States, that measures taken at Union level shall be of a complementary nature, and that they are aimed at providing encouragement and promoting coordination rather than harmonising national systems. Taking this Declaration into account makes it almost impossible to maintain that social policy is a shared competence, and yet the IGC did not relocate social policy to the list of 'complementary competences'. Such an occurrence is of course problematic in terms of transparency, especially as the latter was the main objective pursued by this exercise of constitution making.

[77] Draft Constitution, Article 11(1).

[78] Case 41/76 *Donckerwolcke e.a.* [1976] *ECR* 1921, para. 32.

[79] Opinion 2/91 *ILO* [1993] *ECR* I-1061, para. 8.

[80] It is worth noting the careful wording of the Union competence to enact competition *rules*, intended to be compatible with the decentralisation of the enforcement of European competition law, as provided in Regulation 1/2003 of 16 December 2002 on the implementation of the rules on competition laid down in Articles 81 and 82 of the Treaty, *OJ* 2003 L1/1.

[81] See Opinion 1/76 *Inland Waterway Vessels* [1977] *ECR* 741, para. 3, where the Court of Justice held that 'whenever Community law has created for the Institutions of the Community powers within its internal system for the purpose of attainting a specific objective, the Community has authority to enter into the international commitments necessary for the attainment of that objective even in the absence of an express provision in that connexion.'

[82] What is at stake here is the uniform application of internal Community law, as the Court of Justice pointed out in Case 22/70 *Commission* v. *Council (AETR)* [1971] *ECR* 263, para. 31. Consequently, when the Union adopts provisions laying down common rules, whatever form they may take, the Member States no longer have the right, acting individually or even collectively, to undertake obligations with third countries which affect those rules or alter their scope.

provides'[83] and if entitled to do so by a binding but non-legislative act of the Union.[84] In those latter cases, the Union's external competence will be either shared (e.g. environment) or of a supporting nature (e.g. culture).

Shared competence means that the Union and Member States have concurrent power to legislate and adopt legally binding acts in the area in question, provided that Member States may exercise that competence only if the Union has not exercised it, or has decided to cease exercising it.[85] Member States are thus submitted to the pre-emption of Union acts, which is a particular application of the principle of primacy of Union law, with the effect of depriving Member States of their shared competences to the extent that the Union exercises them.[86] Article 13(3) and (4) of the draft Constitution nevertheless introduces an exception to the pre-emption principle in the fields of research, technological development and space, development cooperation and humanitarian aid, where the exercise by the Union of its shared competence 'may not result in Member States being prevented from exercising theirs'.[87] This provision is arguably the result of a compromise between the supporters of a limitation of Union competences in those areas to supporting action and those who favoured a shared competence in the sense of Article 11(2).[88] Considering the principle of primacy and the duty of loyalty, however, it is argued that the choice of a shared competence without pre-emption still prevents Member States from enacting norms that are contrary to Union law in those fields of activity. Article 13(1) of the draft Constitution also provides that the category of shared competences has been conceived as the residuary category,

---

[83] See, for example, Article 7(2) concerning accession to the European Convention for the Protection of Human Rights and Fundamental Freedoms, Article III-129(4) in the field of environmental policy or Article III-181(3) in the sphere of culture.

[84] Binding but non-legislative Union acts consist of European regulations or decisions, as provided in Article 32(1). This possibility cannot be induced straight from the wording of Article III-225, in its *English version*. However, whereas the English version of Article III-225 mentions the ability for the Union to conclude agreements with third countries based on a 'binding Union *legislative* act' (emphasis added), the French version simply refers to 'acte juridique obligatoire', whether legislative *or not* (the Dutch version also refers generally to 'bindende rechtshandeling van de Unie'). Despite the fact that this notable difference has not been revised in the 'cleaned-up' text of the draft Constitution (see Doc. IGC 50/03, available at: <http://ue.eu.int/igcpdf/en/03/cg00/cg00050.en03.pdf>), it would arguably be illogical to deny the possibility for the Union to conclude agreements with third countries based on enabling European decisions, i.e. a non-legislative European act, for instance in the area of the CFSP, but also to collaborate with international institutions in the framework of the Union's monetary policy (Article III-90) or to set up joint R&D undertakings with third countries (Article III-154).

[85] Draft Constitution, Article 11(2).

[86] See K. Lenaerts and P. van Ypersele, 'Le principe de subsidiarité et son contexte: étude de l'article 3B du Traité C.E.', 30 *Cahiers de droit européen* (1994) p. 3.

[87] Draft Constitution, Article 13(3) and (4).

[88] The final report of Working Group V on Complementary Competencies, CONV 375/1/02, p. 8, recommended classifying research and development policies among the areas of Union supporting action.

i.e. all competences are shared if they do 'not relate to the areas referred to in Articles 12 [exclusive competences] and 16 [supporting, coordinating or complementary competences]'. The list of matters displayed in Article 13(2) may thus only be non-exhaustive[89] and aimed at providing some insight into the content of this category without limiting it further.

Article 16(2) enumerates the Union's supporting, coordinating or complementary competences. They correspond to actions taken in the fields of industrial policy, protection and improvement of human health, education, vocational training, youth and sport, culture and civil protection. Contrary to some suggestions made throughout the Convention process, the draft Constitution does not exclude, fortunately,[90] the possibility for the Union to exercise its supporting competences through legally binding acts,[91] including legislative acts.[92] However, the principle of pre-emption has been excluded from this category of competences.[93] Again, the principles of primacy and loyal cooperation nonetheless require Member States to refrain from any measure which could jeopardise the uniform application of any supporting action or coordinating programme. If legally binding acts are allowed, the Union is precluded from harmonising Member States' laws or regulations on the basis of the provisions of Part III of the Constitution dealing with the areas specified in Article 16(2). This prohibition should not, however, affect the ability for the Union, pursuant to Article III-65 (current Article 95 EC) of the draft Constitution, to take measures for the approximation of Member State laws 'which have as their object the establishment and functioning of the internal market' and which could have side-effects on one of the policy areas listed as areas of supporting, coordinating or complementary action. It is a pity, though, that the Convention did not insert in Article III-65 the *acquis jurisprudentiel* of *Germany* v. *Parliament and Council* ('Tobacco Directive'),[94] in order to prevent any creeping expansion of Union law. Just to recall, this case requires the Union to identify precisely the obstacle(s) to free movement or distortion(s) of competition that the action taken on the basis of that provision seeks to eliminate, and whether the obstacle(s) or distortion(s) at stake is/are appreciable.

---

[89] The text of Article 13(2) refers to 'principal areas'.

[90] It would have been regrettable to limit Union action in the fields listed in Article 16 to the adoption of non-binding measures, since it is sometimes necessary to lay down the conditions of implementation of a Community complementary action through a generally applicable legislative act. See V. Michel, '2004: le défi de la répartition des compétences', 39 *Cahiers de droit européen* (2003) p. 17 at p. 51.

[91] Draft Constitution, Article 16(3).

[92] See, for instance, Article III-181(5) of the draft Constitution in the sphere of culture.

[93] Draft Constitution, Article 11(5).

[94] Case C-376/98 *Germany* v. *Parliament and Council* [2000] *ECR* I-8419.

6.3   The coordination of economic and employment policies and the CFSP

Article 11(3) and (4) of the draft Constitution treats two specific areas of Union competence separately, namely the promotion and coordination of Member States' economic[95] and employment policies[96] and the definition and implementation of a common foreign and security policy, including the 'progressive framing of a common defence policy' (former second pillar). Despite the specific treatment they are subject to, the wording of Article 13(1) leads to the conclusion that those areas should be classified as shared competences, which is the residuary category, with the consequence that the principle of pre-emption of Union action is applicable to them. Any fears of the Member States to the effect that they will lose their say in those sensible matters should nevertheless be set aside, due to the limited scope of the Union's legislative power resulting from Part III provisions dealing with economic policy, employment and the CFSP. More precisely, economic[97] and employment[98] policies call for the Union to give the necessary impulses to the development of coordinated strategies through non-binding measures (guidelines, recommendations, etc.) or at least through non-legislative acts (European decisions). Recourse to legislative acts (European laws and framework laws) in CFSP matters is, moreover, squarely prohibited.[99]

7.   CONCLUSION

The draft Constitution lays down a novel structure for a unified Union endowed with its own body of institutions, a specific set of instruments to exercise its powers, legal personality to exercise rights and undertake obligations and an attribute – the principle of primacy of European law – which enables it to exercise effectively its limited sovereignty over the entirety of its assigned territory. The Convention has not carried out a purely formal reconstitution of the Union however. Combined with the incorporation of the Charter of Fundamental Rights in Part II of the Constitution and Titles I and II of Part I, which synthesise the values, principles and goals which underlie the European project, as well as the strengthening of the limits to the legitimate exercise of its sovereign powers by the Union, the new structure proposed by the draft Constitution gives an additional dimension to the Union through

---

[95] See current Article 99 EC.
[96] See current Article 128 EC.
[97] Draft Constitution, Articles III-70 to III-76.
[98] Ibid., Articles III-97 to III-102.
[99] Ibid., Article 39(3). More generally, see Articles 39-40 and III-195 to III-215.

a complete re-foundation of its legitimacy as an autonomous political authority. The new structure indeed envisions increasing the democratic participation of citizens in the decision-making process, both directly and through their Member States' governments, improving the transparency of 'who does what by which means' at the Union level, and contributing, hence, to a better identification of citizens with the European design.

RETHINKING THE INSTITUTIONAL SYSTEM

Tim Koopmans[*]

1. INTRODUCTION

Institutional reform has been on the European agenda for quite a while now. The considerable enlargement of the European Union, as currently taking place after lengthy negotiations, seems to make such a reform unavoidable. So far, however, little if anything has been realized. The situation may even be worse: there is a noticeable lack of ideas on the future of the institutional system. For example, the recent draft Treaty establishing a European Constitution fails to tackle the problem, by proposing only limited amendments to the existing rules.[1] The moment may have come for a reassessment of the way the European institutions have been working, or have failed to work, in the framework of the European Union. It is my submission that nothing short of a complete overhaul of the existing institutional system can help the Union to operate properly.

In this paper, I propose to analyze briefly the present institutional difficulties before trying to develop some new ways of thinking on the evolution of the institutions of the Union, in the short term as well as in the long run.

2. DEVELOPMENTS

The institutional system was devised for a European Community of six Member States in the 1950s. Later, it was applied to a Community of nine, then ten, then twelve, then fifteen Member States, without any major adjustment. From now on, it will have to work in a European Union consisting of twenty-five Member States. The obvious question is whether this quantitative change is not of such an importance that it will turn into a qualitative change: the very character of the institutions will be affected by the quantitative leap. A Commission or a Court of twelve or fifteen members may still work as a commission or a court, but a Commission or a Court of twenty-five will act more like a public meeting or a

---

[*] Judge of the Court of Justice of the European Communities, 1979-1990; President of the Board of the Asser Institute, 1991-1998. This paper reflects the situation on 1 April 2004.

[1] Arts. I-18 to I-28 of the draft Constitution.

The European Union: An Ongoing Process of Integration – Liber Amicorum Alfred E. Kellermann
© 2004, T.M.C. Asser Instituut, The Hague, and the authors

diplomatic conference. The existing rules are not adapted to the new situation. Drastic decisions may be necessary and, as there is no popular pressure towards institutional change, some political courage will be required to draw the consequences from the growth of the European Union. Rightly or wrongly, this growth was approved unanimously and without reserve by the old Member States of the Union.

There is a second factor that makes institutional reform infinitely more difficult. The initial institutional rules were drafted for the European Economic Community, whose main purposes were to establish a common market and to coordinate the economic policies of the Member States.[2] Since then, many important areas of public activity have been added to the responsibilities of the European institutions: monetary union, environmental problems, the coordination of foreign affairs, military collaboration and certain aspects of criminal law, to mention only a few. The decision-making process remained more or less the same: a mixture of independent research-based Community initiatives, diplomatic negotiations in the Council and a certain amount of parliamentary influence. These procedures are aimed at achieving a certain consensus between Member State administrations and European institutions. A process of this kind can work very well for regulations on the common agricultural market for wheat, pork or flatfish, or for directives on the protection of wild birds or on equality of treatment in employment, but it is a bad solution for matters of foreign affairs and military collaboration. It lacks the degree of decisiveness that is required for taking a stand at the right moment.

Moreover, the purpose of establishing a common market or protecting the environment lends a certain direction and a certain cohesiveness to the activities to be performed by the institutions, but military collaboration and the coordination of foreign affairs lack any kind of precision of this kind. Finally, Member States can hardly be regarded as equals in military matters: some are neutral, some still play a military role of a certain importance in world affairs and some are merely disinterested.[3] At the executive level, the same problems occur in aggravated form: the implementation of EC rules on matters like agricultural markets, anti-competitive behaviour of enterprises and State subsidies is left to an independent Community institution, the Commission, but military powers like the United Kingdom or France would not dream of granting any decision-making capability in that area to such an autonomous institution. This statement not only reflects the current situation, but also, in all likelihood, at least that of the near future. For some Union matters, thinking in terms of the initial EC procedures is

---

[2] Art. 2 of the original EC Treaty.
[3] See J.P.H. Donner, ed., *Europa, wat nu?*, Report V91 (Wetenschappelijke Raad voor het Regeringsbeleid 1995) ch. 2.3.

not a viable option. The true choice is between not collaborating at all or collaborating according to other institutional rules and procedures than those of the initial Community treaties.

A third factor that tends to add to the existing uncertainties is the fact that the decision-making system has changed significantly during the last twenty years, although these changes happened tacitly and have not always been discussed in terms of institutional modifications. In particular, the elevation of the conference of Heads of State and Government to the rank of a Union institution, under the confusing name of 'European Council', and the definition of its task in the treaties on European Union, has profoundly modified the institutional balance brought about by the initial Community treaties. The political role of the Commission has been considerably reduced by the admission, in the Union treaties, that there is only one institutional framework and that, in this framework, the European Council provides the necessary leadership ('impetus') and determines the general political guidelines.[4] The traditional role of the Commission as the initiator of steps in the integration process may thus have been severely limited, although much will of course depend on actual practice. The literature on this redefinition of the Commission's responsibilities is scant.[5]

A fourth factor is the incredible complexity of the present system. Decision making with four or five institutions is already difficult in itself. The gradual increase of the powers of the European Parliament has given rise to a certain number of new procedures, covering different possibilities between mere advice and co-decision of the Parliament.[6] The Council often decides by qualified majority, but the way such a majority is calculated – a result of very serious negotiations between ministers of foreign affairs – baffles the imagination.[7] Only a true specialist can find his way through this labyrinth. The estrangement of many European citizens from EU matters may be partly due to the incomprehensibility of its decision-making system.

There is a fifth and somewhat exasperating factor to complete this gloomy picture. The linguistic regime is gradually giving rise to a considerable growth of bureaucracy. The basic principle that all the official languages of the Member States are the official languages of the Union can probably not survive in the long run. The European Economic Community of six Member States had four official languages; the European Union now has something like twenty. This not only means that many interpreters will be necessary, but also that twenty versions of the Official Journal and the European Court Reports will have to be published,

---

[4] Arts. 3-4 EU.

[5] But see Deirdre M. Curtin, 'The constitutional structure of the Union: a Europe of bits and pieces', *CMLRev.* (1993) p. 17.

[6] See Arts. 251-252 (ex Arts. 189b-189c) EC.

[7] Art. 205 (ex Art. 148) EC.

that there will be as many translation services and that new multilingual personnel will be required for the libraries, the press services, the registry of the European courts, and so forth. The whole idea has something nightmarish about it. At present, debates in the Commission are actually conducted in English and French, while in the European courts they are conducted only in French. The generally accepted axiom is, however, that the direct effect of important parts of EC law, in particular of regulations, requires that the citizens of the Union can examine the applicable texts in their own language.[8] Similarly, national courts should be able to interrogate the Court of Justice, under the system of preliminary rulings, in their own language, and receive an answer in the same language.[9] This system certainly has its merits, but its effects on staff numbers and working space render the institutions more and more unwieldy. From this point of view, a quick look at the increase in the number of the office buildings in Brussels or Luxemburg is more convincing than many a theoretical consideration.

3.   BASIC ASSUMPTIONS

When the EEC institutional system was established in the late 1950s, it was variously described as 'supranational', 'pre-federal' or 'confederal'. This – admittedly loose – terminology was intended to express the conception that the European Community was not just an international organization like any other. In particular, it was assumed to have institutions that, passing over the national governments and administrations, could issue rules and decisions directly binding upon citizens and business corporations. It is clear that this characteristic still subsists, but with an important proviso: increasingly, negotiations between the members of the European Council determine what kind of rules or decisions will be imposed by the other political institutions of the Union.[10] The autonomy of these institutions, once a matter of pride among the governments of the participating States, is thus gradually threatened by those same governments. A simple extrapolation of this line of development will ultimately roll back the originality of the European institutional system and replace it by a traditional form of diplomatic decision making, albeit at a high level. In a certain sense, Europe would then return to the times of the Holy Alliance of the early 19th century, when the ministers of foreign affairs of the great powers of the day settled issues

---

[8] See Art. 249 (ex Art. 189) EC.

[9] See Art. 234 (ex Art. 177) EC.

[10] See also J.H.H. Weiler, 'Fin-de-siècle Europe: On Ideas and Ideologies in Post-Maastricht Europe', in D.M. Curtin and T. Heukels, eds., *Institutional Dynamics of European Integration*: *Essays in Honour of Henry G. Schermers*, Vol. II (Dordrecht, Nijhoff 1994) p. 23.

of European importance by unanimity (and decided simultaneously where to send troops in case of revolutionary disturbances).[11]

There are, however, two reasons why such an evolution is not very likely. First, the Commission and its administration have been able to accumulate a lot of know-how on problems that Heads of State and of Government dislike discussing, such as trade negotiations, mergers between major airline companies, restructuring the steel sector or organizing intervention systems for agricultural products. The second reason is that it would be difficult, and also contrary to European practice as it has developed so far, to renounce entirely the institutional originality of the early days. The difficulty will be to define and to circumscribe the areas where the original Community decision-making practice is to be safeguarded. This idea may provide us with a *'clou'* for devising a new point of departure when shaking up the institutional system. There is an important *acquis* (set of achievements) in the area of economic law and policy that could be managed by autonomous Union institutions, under parliamentary scrutiny and judicial supervision, rather than by diplomatic negotiations. This conclusion does not imply at all that matters of foreign affairs and military collaboration could be managed in the same way.

This idea immediately raises a problem that has often been evoked without ever leading to a real debate. It is indeed one of the main unanswered questions concerning the European integration process: is it a single process, or is it so differentiated that it actually consists of different integration processes, and would such a differentiation be desirable and practicable in the long run? The Schengen Agreement on the free movement of persons, the monetary union with its single currency, the special arrangements adopted for some Member States, most notably for Denmark, and the use of 'opt-in' and 'opt-out' clauses since the Maastricht treaty reveal a degree of differentiation that is hardly compatible with the basic idea of one institutional framework, but this differentiation exists and has been recognized in the treaties.[12] It might be that the European Union is heading for an *'Europe à géométrie variable'*. The problem is then whether this evolution should be reversed and, if not, what kind of institutional consequences are to be drawn from it.[13] We cannot continue to pretend that there is only one institutional framework when, in fact, we have been quietly creating a number of different frameworks, each with its own rules and procedures. The monetary procedures clearly illustrate this point.[14]

---

[11] See Henry Kissinger, *A World Restored: Metternich, Castlereagh and the Problems of Peace 1812-1822* (Boston, Houghton Mifflin 1957) ch. X-XV.

[12] See the contributions of John Usher and Jaap de Zwaan to the *Cambridge Yearbook of European Legal Studies*, Vol. 1, 1998 (Oxford, Hart 1999) ch. 4 and 6.

[13] See also Edouard Baladur, 'Combien d'Europes?', *Le Monde*, 5 March 2004.

[14] See, in particular, Arts. 122-123 (ex Arts. 109k-109l) EC.

The next problem is that any major institutional reform is liable to come into collision with the concept of continuity of the European integration process. It is true that the initial dynamism of this process, which seemed to imply that every step on the road to further integration would necessarily require a next step, appears to have lost its momentum. According to the more recent literature, there is nothing 'automatic' or 'necessary' in the integration process, and political practice confirms this idea.[15] This is of course a relief to those who, like the British conservatives, regularly complain that things should be left as they presently are and that any further step on the path towards integration might cause serious trouble. In order to accept such a view, however, we ought to be sure that the full consequences of the monetary union, for example, have been considered, but the recent conflicts surrounding the so-called Stability Pact demonstrate that this is not the case. Similarly, the existing treaty provisions hold out the prospect of a European 'internal market' that guarantees free movement of goods, persons, services and capital within the territory of the Union.[16] It would, however, be an exaggeration to pretend that such an internal market has been completely realized, or that new economic or political developments could never compel the Union's institutions to broach new areas of activity. Problems such as the extent of border controls, the relationship between government involvement and free trade in sectors such as the shipbuilding industry or aircraft construction, and the relationship between patent law and access to pharmaceutical products are very far from being solved. In other words, even the most conservative politician on European matters has to admit that the time for blocking any new initiative has not yet arrived.

The concept of continuity is particularly important for the new Member States of the Union. For most Central and East European countries, the Union is a permanent European home where they will finally occupy their rightful place. That Union is the Union as they know it and as it has developed over the past forty or fifty years – not an organization changed beyond all recognition.[17] In this sense, the perspectives for a thorough change of the institutional system have their own limits, which are more guided more by political and psychological considerations than by economic logic or by legal argument.

This conclusion also has repercussions for the problem of the official languages. It is not impossible to reform the Union in such a way that it will be relieved of the risk of being bogged down by translation problems. Community

---

[15] See C.-D. Ehlermann, 'Increased Differentiation or Stronger Uniformity', in J.A. Winter et al., eds., *Reforming the European Union: The Legal Debate* (The Hague 1996) p. 27.

[16] Arts. 14-15 (ex Arts. 7a-7c) EC.

[17] See Maurits Coppieters, 'De visie van het Europees Parlement op Oost-Europa (1989-1993)', in P. De Meyere et al., eds., *Oost-Europa in Europa, eenheid en verscheidenheid, Essays in honour of Frits Gorlé* (Brussels 1996) ch. 8.

rules could be issued in the form of directives rather than regulations (with some exceptions, for example, for internal rules such as staff regulations), and these directives could be issued in English and French. Similarly, the linguistic regime applicable to the European Court of Human Rights could be followed for the Union's Court of Justice and Court of First Instance.[18] This may well be an aim that is worth pursuing, but it is, to all appearances, an inappropriate subject of institutional change in the short term.

4.   BLUEPRINTS

The first thing to be done, from the point of view of institutional reform, is to leave the monetary union for the moment as it presently operates and then to make a further distinction between matters of the common market and matters closely connected to it, on the one hand, and foreign affairs and military collaboration, on the other. For the first category of subjects, the typical Community system of decision making should be preserved in full. Important rules that are to be applied to the citizens of the Union, either directly or after transposition into national law by national parliaments, should be established on the basis of a Commission proposal and co-decision of the European Parliament and the Council acting by qualified majority. The definition of the qualified majority should of course be simplified, for example in the sense indicated by the 2003 draft Constitution.[19]

In contrast, a new system of decision making should be devised for military matters and foreign affairs: one that is closer to the procedures followed in NATO and by the United Nations than to Community procedures. It has been argued, not without some foundation, that Europe may need its own 'Security Council' with a limited membership, for example ten or eleven members, and with a specific and permanent role for the three 'great powers' of the Union: France, Germany and the United Kingdom.[20] Majority voting would apply, but a right of veto for the three great powers could be envisaged.

In this dual system, it would be possible to give their original roles back to the European Council and the Commission. In common market matters, the Commission should fully recover its initiating task, while the role of the European Council would henceforth be limited to participating in appointment procedures. In matters of defence and foreign affairs, however, the European Council should

---

[18] The European Convention of Human Rights has no parallel to Art. 290 (ex Art. 217) EC, but the general regime of the Council of Europe applies. See the European Court of Human Rights' judgment of 21 February 1986 in *James* v. *United Kingdom*, Series A, No. 98.

[19] Art. I-24 of the draft Constitution.

[20] In this sense, see Antonio Missiroli and Martin Ortega in *NRC-Handelsblad*, 17 February 2004.

retain and develop its power to determine the general lines of the policy to be pursued, while daily problems would be left to the above-mentioned European 'Security Council'. The present Council Secretariat and its legal service could then act as secretariat and research department. The Commission should keep aloof: it is an autonomous institution, not a secretariat or supporting service of any intergovernmental body. Members of the Commission should be selected on the basis of their opinions, not their nationality. For this reason, some form of intervention of the European Parliament in the appointment procedures would be required.[21] In such a dual system, it would also be possible to limit the number of members of the Commission, for example to eleven or thirteen. New treaty rules should explicitly provide that members of the Commission do not in any way 'represent' their Member State or its government. However, the members of a European 'Security Council' would do so, as they would be acting as the mandatories of their governments.

In military matters, it appears that a European 'Security Council' could only function if a European supreme command is established. It would not be necessary for all Member States to participate in this form of military integration, but the three 'great powers' would need to come to an agreement before anything else could be arranged. The conception that the Union is only a 'civil power' that can do without any form of military involvement, though popular during the 1980s, cannot be maintained any more, and the Maastricht Treaty already formally put an end to it.[22] If the Union is involved in peacekeeping operations, for example, it should be able to act with the necessary speed and efficiency.

The powers of the European Parliament should be adapted to the dual structure. Its powers of control cannot be identical for matters left to the autonomous institutions and for those placed in the care of intergovernmental bodies. In matters of foreign policy and military collaboration, the European Parliament should remain a forum of advice and debate. Apart from such a general parliamentary activity, it should also have powers of investigation, organized more or less along the lines of those of the US Senate. In common market matters, however, the Parliament should have regulatory powers in co-decision with the Council and be able to hold a no-confidence vote against the Commission as in the present situation.[23] Moreover, the general powers of the European Parliament should include full budgetary powers as recently proposed in the draft Constitution.[24] For important appointments, such as the appointment of members of the Commission, the Court of Justice, the Court of First Instance and the Court of Auditors, it might be possible to follow the example of the procedure for appointing

---

[21] See also, for example, Art. I-26 of the draft Constitution.
[22] See Art. 17(1) EU.
[23] Art. 201 (ex Art. 144) EC.
[24] Art. III-310 of the draft Constitution.

judges at the European Court of Human Rights. There, each government nominates three candidates and the Parliamentary Assembly makes the selection.[25] In the European Union, the European Council could nominate the candidates and leave the final decision to the European Parliament.

For collaboration in the area of home affairs, justice and criminal law (the former 'third pillar' of the Union), a choice has to be made: it should either retain its specific character from an institutional point of view or be integrated into the general common market model.[26] If the latter option is made, some additional institutional arrangements may be necessary. As the scope of measures to be taken is not dictated by the logic of the common market but by the political will to extend Union activities to new areas, the European Council should determine the working program for these activities. A similar argument might be applied to questions of direct taxation, which some Member States regard as the very heart of their national sovereignty. However, direct taxation is so closely linked to the operation of the common market that a different choice could be justified. On these specific issues, it would also be possible, though perhaps not advisable, to provide for a right of veto by national parliaments. It seems to me that safeguarding the principle of subsidiarity, which governs the division of powers between national and Union authorities, should be the task of the Union institutions. Of course, choices of this kind should be made at the political level, not by the judiciary, as proposed by the authors of the draft Constitution in a moment of flagging inspiration.[27] Courts are in a position to supervise procedures that must be followed. They can also decide that no reasonable institution could have come to a certain interpretation of the concept of subsidiarity, but they cannot decide by themselves whether or not a proposed action can be 'sufficiently' achieved by national authorities, in accordance with the definition of subsidiarity that currently governs Union activities.[28] That is a matter for political decision making, which should be organized accordingly.

The Court of Justice should consist of eleven or thirteen judges and six or seven advocates general. No such limitation is required for the Court of First Instance, which sits in chambers of three or five judges and whose judgments are subject to appeal. The Court of First Instance can have as many judges as there are Member States, or even twice that number. Specialized Union courts should be established for staff cases and for the interpretation of the common customs tariff. With regard to staff cases, it might be possible to provide immediately that litigation will only be conducted in English or French.

---

[25] Art. 22(1) of the European Convention on Human Rights.

[26] See, respectively, Arts. 29-34 EU and Art. III-158 of the draft Constitution.

[27] See Art. 7 of the Protocol on the Application of the Principles of Subsidiarity and Proportionality attached to the draft Constitution.

[28] Art. 5 (ex Art. 3b) EC; Art. I-9(3) of the draft Constitution.

5.   CONSEQUENCES

The admission that Union activities cover several integration processes, rather than just one, can constitute a point of departure for institutional reform. There is no legal or political necessity for compelling Ireland and Sweden to participate in military collaboration for the sole reason that they are partners in economic integration. It may be difficult, in certain cases, to draw a clear line of distinction, but that is not a new problem.[29] The history of social policy in the European Community, including equal treatment in employment, illustrates this abundantly.

Moreover, a flexible approach will diminish the pressure of many Member States to have one of their own nationals in every Union institution. The various institutions will all be governed by their own particular rules and procedures. Discussion and decision-making methods that may be appropriate for Council meetings or for the European Council are patently unsuitable for bodies such as the Commission, a European 'Security Council' or the Court of Justice. The experience of the European Court of Human Rights, with its ever-increasing membership combined with an ever-increasing caseload, can serve as an example of how not to do things.[30]

Abandoning, for the moment, the idea that there is one single process of European integration will probably have a profound psychological effect. The conception that there is only one way forward, that of extending existing European mechanisms to more and more areas of activity, cannot be sustained any longer. On the other hand, the model I have tried to sketch can nevertheless be regarded as what the French would call *un modèle évolutif* – it is so constructed that it leaves room for alternative developments, in particular for further steps on the path to integration. The model has the advantage of being practicable, but the disadvantage of leaving little room for any kind of European idealism. In this respect, it suffers the consequences of an evolution that started a long time ago and found its provisional apogee in the appalling scenes of haggling in Nice and Rome at the beginning of the new millennium. President De Gaulle and Prime Minister Thatcher could perhaps be regarded as 'anti-Europeans' in their day, but it is difficult to define at present what 'pro-European' and 'anti-European' is supposed to mean. The general lukewarmness towards European integration exhibited by politicians and political parties can be seen as symbolic of the change of heart that has taken place during the last twenty or twenty-five years. In the population and the media in many Member States, lukewarmness is some-times close to downright hostility. It is not difficult to lay part of the blame on the

---

[29] See also B. Meyring, 'Intergovernmentalism and supranationality: two stereotypes for a complex reality', *ELR* (1997) p. 221.

[30] See Paul Mahoney, 'An insider's view of the reform debate (how to maintain the effectiveness of the European Court of Human Rights)', 29 *NJCM-Bulletin* (2004) p.170.

shoulders of the politicians. After all, it is not only their role to translate the general public's feelings of uneasiness into political action; they have also been elected (or, occasionaliy, appointed) to help direct the development of public opinion in one direction rather than another. Being a politician presupposes that one has a certain view of the future and that one tries to win support for that view.

This conclusion, unassailable though it may be, does not provide us with guidelines for institutional reform. Opinions may change, and nobody knows exactly what the future holds in store for our continent. External pressures of an unknown nature may again force European politics in the direction of further integration, but it is also possible that a creeping rebirth of nationalist feelings will put a stop to any further 'Europeanization'. The European Union of 2005 will differ significantly from the European Community of 1962. We can regret that situation, but it is like crying over spilt milk, albeit perhaps a lot of milk. However, we should try to organize decision-making procedures in such a way that a more clear-cut institutional structure can be constructed on that basis, either in the near or in the distant future. The Charter of Human Rights will, of course, immediately be part of such a unique institutional structure that covers the entirety of the European integration processes.[31] The 'umbrella' of the Union can be expanded as time grows ripe for it. In the long run, there is no logical or political necessity to give the dual structure a permanent character. For the moment, the main problem is to keep what we have and to make it workable again. Unfortunately, this seems to be impossible without profound changes in rules and procedures. Failing to recognize the importance of the institutional problems will indisputably contribute to immobility. If that is what some European politicians have in mind, they should say so explicitly and try to convince their voters.

It is my conviction that, presently, institutional problems constitute the hard core of the European debate. As interested academics, we should try to contribute to it. Alfred Kellermann, to whom this paper is dedicated, and I are both 'past our dancing days', as Shakespeare puts it, and we may both be unqualified 'to breathe life into a stone', to quote the same author.[32] However, as spectators of the European scene rather than players on it, we can still participate in the discussions that help to shape the future of the European adventure. That future will almost certainly be developed step by step, as Robert Schuman so rightly predicted more than half a century ago.[33] Continuing to take these steps is currently more important than devising grand designs, but the infrastructure for doing so ought to be in a better shape than it is now.

---

[31] See also Part II of the draft Constitution.
[32] Respectively: *Romeo and Juliet*, I-5, and *All's Well That Ends Well*, II-1.
[33] In his famous declaration of 9 May 1950.

DISTURBING OR REBALANCING POWERS WITHIN THE EUROPEAN UNION?

Laurence W. Gormley*

INTRODUCTION

The carefully arranged balance between the institutions of the European Communities has long been the object of academic study, and no less an authority than Pescatore has delivered an impressive explanation of why the classic separation of powers in the Montesquieu model appears inadequate in the Community context.[1] Advocate General Saggio saw that balance in the following terms:

'Concerning the principle of institutional balance, suffice it to say that a general rule of law of that sort essentially concerns the relationship between the institutions, and more particularly compliance with the reciprocal powers of the institutions. Whilst it is true that the exercise of functions by an institution that does not have the competence to perform them in itself constitutes infringement of the balance between the institutions, it is in precisely the opposite case, namely where whilst remaining within the powers conferred upon it an institution has in one way or another limited the exercise of the powers of the others,[2] that that principle really becomes relevant.'[3]

Yet, as will be explained below, the institutional balance established by the Treaties also concerns the relationship between the institutions of the Community,

---

* Professor of European Law and Jean Monnet Professor, University of Groningen (Jean Monnet Centre of Excellence); Barrister; Professor at the College of Europe.

[1] See P. Pescatore, 'L'Executif Communautaire: Justification du Quadripartisme Institué par les Traités de Paris et de Rome', *CDE* (1978) p. 387 at p. 394.

[2] The learned Advocate General referred at this point in a footnote to, *inter alia*, Case C-329/95 *European Parliament* v. *Council* [1997] *ECR* I-3213 at 3246 ('due consultation of the Parliament in the cases provided for in the Treaty constitutes an essential formal requirement breach of which renders the measure void' and 'effective participation of the Parliament in the legislative process ... represents an essential factor in the institutional balance intended by the Treaty.' This picks up the points made in earlier cases discussed below. J.P. Jacqué, 'The principle of institutional balance', 41 *CMLRev.* (2004) pp. 383-384 refers to the principle being one aspect of the rule that the institutions have to act within the limits of their competences, a rule presently expressed in Art. 7(1) EC.

[3] Case C-159/96 *Portugal* v. *Commission* [1998] *ECR* I-7379 at 7399.

The European Union: An Ongoing Process of Integration – Liber Amicorum Alfred E. Kellermann
© 2004, T.M.C. Asser Instituut, The Hague, and the authors

now the Union, and the Member States. The delicate balance now appears to be threatened if the proposed Constitution is adopted.[4]

INSTITUTIONAL BALANCE IN THE CASE LAW

The phrase 'institutional balance' in Community law has a considerable heritage in the case law of the Court. It first surfaced there specifically in the celebrated opinion of Advocate General Dutheillet de Lamothe in the classic series of cases on the system of agricultural deposits – *Internationale Handelsgeselleschaft, Köster, Henck* and *Scheer*[5] – in the context of the legality of the Management Committee procedure in the adoption of delegated legislation. The argument ran that the procedure was contrary to the Treaty for three reasons: it conferred on the Management Committee a right to take part in the legislative work of the Commission; it permitted the Member States to obtain from the Council a decision effectively quashing that of the Commission; and it infringed the prerogatives of the European Parliament. The learned Advocate General had little difficulty in pointing out the fallacy of those claims,[6] and in *Köster* and *Scheer*, in particular, the Court also expressly rejected those claims.[7]

Although there has hardly been a period in which the relationships between the political institutions of the Community could be said to have been tranquil, it was only ten years later that the actual phrase 'institutional balance' reappeared in the case law, in the celebrated isoglucose litigation in 1980.[8] Here, the Court saw the consultation of the European Parliament in the legislative process of the Community as 'an essential factor in the institutional balance intended by the Treaty' and thus, 'although limited, … it reflects the fundamental democratic principle that people should take part in exercise of power through the intermediary of a representative assembly.' It followed therefore that 'due consultation of the Parliament in the cases provided for by the Treaty … constitutes an essential formality disregard of which means that the measure concerned is void.'

---

[4] Clearly this will depend on whether, if at all, it ever passes the ratification hurdles, particularly those involving a referendum.

[5] Respectively, Cases 11, 25, 26 and 30/70 [1970] *ECR* 1140 at 1142-1144 (Opinion).

[6] Much of his analysis was based on the Jozeau-Marigné Report (European Parliament Session Docs. 1968-69, No. 115) and on the Resolution adopted by the Parliament on 3 October 1968 (*OJ* 1968 C 108/37).

[7] Case 25/70 *Einfuhr- und Vorratsstelle für Getreide und Futtermittel* v. *Köster, Berodt & Co.* [1970] *ECR* 1161 at 1172; and Case 30/70 *Scheer* v. *Einfuhr- und Vorratsstelle für Getreide und Futtermittel* [1970] *ECR* 1197 at 1208-1209.

[8] Case 138/79 *SA Roquette Frères* v. *Council* [1980] *ECR* 333 at 3360; and Case 139/79 *Maizena GmbH* v. *Council* [1980] *ECR* 3393 at 3424. In the context of rates of exchange for calculating remuneration, see also the staff cases decided on 4 February 1982, e.g. Case 817/79 *Buyl* v. *Commission* [1982] *ECR* 245 at 262.

Sometimes, of course, the concept of balance between the institutions appears in slightly other phrasing: 'In accordance with the balance of powers between the institutions, the practice of the Parliament cannot deprive the other institutions of a prerogative granted to them by the Treaties themselves.'[9] This is clearly the 'more relevant' situation to which Advocate General Saggio referred. On myriad occasions, relating to the seat of the Parliament, its budgetary rights and the immunity of its members, the theme of institutional balance has been very much to the fore. The institutional balance in fact features heavily in fundamental case law, irrespective of the phrase used. The relationship between the Commission and the Council has often been the occasion for disputes,[10] as has the extent to which powers may be delegated to bodies outside the institutional structure of the Communities or, by extension, the Union. Already in the early judgment in *Meroni*,[11] the Court emphasized that the balance of powers that characterizes the institutional structure of the Community constitutes a fundamental guarantee granted by the Treaty. Nevertheless, the Court found subsequently that this guarantee does not provide a remedy in the absence of an express creation of a remedy in the Treaty.[12] In its opinion on the proposed minor amendment of the ECSC Treaty,[13] the Court referred to the 'balance between the institutions of the Community provided for by the Treaty'. Recently, the European Central Bank had to be reminded rather clearly that, although it is independent in the exercise of its functions, it is nevertheless part of the Community structure and subject to the rules and accountability provided for by Community law.[14] The Ombudsman too has found that his decisions are not immune from judicial review.[15]

In institutional disputes, the rights of the Parliament have frequently held centre stage. Frequently, this has been in the context of disputes about budgets and about the seat of the Parliament.[16] Parliament has ingeniously found ways of

---

[9] Case 149/85 *Wybot* v. *Faure* [1986] *ECR* 2391 at 2409 (sessions of the European Parliament, in the context of an MEP's immunity).

[10] E.g. Case 22/70 *Commission* v. *Council* [1971] *ECR* 263 (ERTA).

[11] Case 9/56 *Meroni* v. *High Authority* [1957 & 1958] *ECR* 133 at 152.

[12] Case C-345/00 *FNAB et al.* v. *Council* [2001] *ECR* I-3811. Jacqué, loc. cit. n. 2, at pp. 385-386 notes the distinction now drawn by the Court in relation to those rules which concern the institutional balance in general and those which more specifically protect private individuals. While infringement of either group may lead to the annulment of a measure, only in the case of the infringement of the latter would the Community be liable in damages for disregard of a superior rule of law protecting individuals: Case C-282/90 *Industrie- en Handelsonderneming Vreugdenhil* v. *Commission* [1992] *ECR* I-1937 at 1968.

[13] Opinion of 17 December 1959 [1959] *ECR* 266 at 273.

[14] Case C-11/01 *Commission* v. *European Central Bank* [2003] *ECR* I, nyr (10 July 2003).

[15] Case C-234/02 P *European Ombudsman* v. *Lamberts* [2004] *ECR* I, nyr (23 March 2004).

[16] E.g. Case 23/86R *United Kingdom* v. *European Parliament* [1986] *ECR* 1085; Case 34/86 *Council* v. *European Parliament* [1986] *ECR* 2155; Case C-41/95 *Council* v. *European Parliament* [1995] *ECR* I-4411 (budgets) and Case 230/81 *Luxembourg* v. *European Parliament* [1983] *ECR*

formally respecting the requirements of intergovernmental decisions about its seat, while essentially moving the axis of its political operations from Luxembourg and Strasbourg to Brussels. In fact, the circus of moving for part-sessions is one of the most publicized examples of money wasting affecting the institutions; another is abuses (or permitted uses) of expense allowances by MEPs.

Another important forum for the development of the Parliament's rights has been the Parliament's right to seek the annulment of Community acts. After an initial rebuff,[17] the Court finally succumbed, recognizing that hitherto there was no guarantee that a measure adopted by the Council or the Commission in disregard of the Parliament's prerogatives could be reviewed. The Court acknowledged that:

> 'Those prerogatives are one of the elements of the institutional balance created by the Treaties. The Treaties set up a system for the distribution of powers among the different Community institutions, assigning to each institution its own role in the institutional structure of the Community and the accomplishment of the tasks entrusted to the Community.
>
> Observance of the institutional balance means that each of the institutions must exercise its powers with due regard for the powers of the other institutions. It also requires that it should be possible to penalize any breach of that rule which may occur.
>
> The Court, which under the Treaties has the task of ensuring that in the interpretation of application of the Treaties the law is observed, must therefore be able to maintain the institutional balance and, consequently, review the observance of the Parliament's prerogatives when called upon to do so by the Parliament, by means of a legal remedy which is suited to the purpose which the Parliament seeks to achieve.'

Although the Court recognized that it could not confer standing on the Parliament without the requirement of demonstration of an interest in bringing an action, it also recognized that it was its duty to ensure that the provisions of the Treaties concerning the institutional balance were fully applied and to see to it that the Parliament's prerogatives, like those of the other institutions, could not be breached without it having available a legal remedy, among those laid down in

---

255; Case 108/83 *Luxembourg* v. *European Parliament* [1984] *ECR* 1945; Case 39/89 *Luxembourg* v. *European Parliament* [1991] *ECR* I-5643; Cases 358/85 & 51/86 *France* v. *European Parliament* [1988] *ECR* 4821; and Case C-345/95 *France* v. *European Parliament* [1997] *ECR* I-5215 (seat). See also R.G. Corbett, F.B. Jacobs and M. Schackleton, *The European Parliament*, 4th. edn. (London, Harper 2000) pp. 27-32; and K. Bradley and A. Feeney, 'Legal Developments in the European Parliament', 14 *YBEL* (1994) p. 401 at p. 430.

[17] Case 302/87 *European Parliament* v. *Council* [1987] *ECR* 5615 (comitology).

the Treaties, that may be exercised in a certain and effective manner. Accordingly, it found that:

'The absence in Treaties of any provision giving the Parliament the right to bring an action for annulment may constitute a procedural gap, but it cannot prevail over the fundamental interest in the maintenance and observance of the institutional balance laid down in the Treaties establishing the European Communities.'[18]

Thus, the Parliament was given standing to protect its prerogatives, an approach which was taken up in the Treaties at Maastricht: it became a semi-privileged litigant, although very quickly learned that having standing is not the same thing as winning an action.[19] As the Parliament has gained in strength in terms of judicial review, so too has the pressure increased on it to behave responsibly: the interinstitutional dialogue is subject to the same mutual duties of sincere cooperation as govern relationships between the Member States and the Community institutions.[20] Finally, at Nice, the European Parliament was raised to the status of a privileged litigant, no longer required to show an interest in actions for annulment of acts of political institutions. This is a most interesting development, as it means that Parliament can appeal against acts of which it is the co-adopter. While that may at first sight appear strange, it parallels the right of the Member States to appeal against acts, irrespective of how they voted on their adoption.[21] Moreover, the Council could always appeal. Parity between the Parliament and the Council is thus restored.[22] Where the power of the Parliament is most likely to bite in practice, however, is in relation to delegated legislation adopted in accordance with comitology procedures. Parliament's hand is undoubtedly strengthened: it is no longer confined to the crumbs of the Comitology Decision[23] and of the Modus Vivendi.[24]

---

[18] Case C-70/88 *European Parliament* v. *Council* [1990] *ECR* I-2041 at 2072-2073.

[19] See e.g. Case C-316/91 *European Parliament* v. *Council* [1994] *ECR* I-625 (financing under Lomé, application inadmissible); Case C-65/93 *European Parliament* v. *Council* [1995] *ECR* I-643 (GSP, Parliament's own refusal to cooperate, application dismissed); Case C-417/93 *European Parliament* v. *Council* [1995] *ECR* I-1185 (TACIS, discussions in Council before Parliament's opinion was delivered, application dismissed) which the Parliament lost; Case C-388/92 *European Parliament* v. *Council* [1994] *ECR* I-2067 (road passenger transport cabotage, reconsultation obligation); Case C-21/94 *European Parliament* v. *Council* [1995] *ECR* I-1827 (road tolls, reconsulatation obligation); and Case C-392/95 *European Parliament* v. *Council* [1997] *ECR* I-3213 (visas for third country nationals, reconsultation obligation) which the Parliament won.

[20] Case 65/93 *European Parliament* v. *Council* [1995] *ECR* I-643 at 668.

[21] Case 166/78 *Italy* v. *Council* [1979] *ECR* 2575 at 2596.

[22] The European Parliament and the Council may well be co-defendants, e.g. Case C-378/00 *Commission* v. *European Parliament & Council* [2003] *ECR* I-937 (Comitology II/LIFE).

[23] Council Decision 1999/468/EC, *OJ* 1999 L 184/23.

[24] *OJ* 1996 C 102/1.

OPINIONS ON ENVISAGED INTERNATIONAL AGREEMENTS

Another major forum within which the institutional balance has been examined judicially is opinions on the compatibility of envisaged international agreements with Community law.[25] Here the Court has often been concerned with its own dignity and status.[26] Thus, in the absence of amendment of the founding Treaties, the proposed establishment of judicial mechanisms which could lead to conflicting interests in relation to the judiciary, or to the Court of Justice not being the final instance charged with ensuring that the law is observed, has been found to be incompatible with Community law. Perhaps this approach in part explains the reluctance of the Member States to permit the Court of Justice a really significant role in the Third Pillar of the Union, with *à la carte* access to justice and a firm approach of *forum non conveniens* in relation to operational matters as the consequences.[27]

THE INSTITUTIONS AND THE MEMBER STATES

Although questions of institutional balance have often concentrated on the relationship between the political institutions of the Community, the frequent disagreements concerning fisheries policy demonstrate that the institutional balance may also very much concern the relationship between those institutions and the Member States. While, in the face of the failure of the Council to take action required of it, the Court has permitted Member States to take certain action, this has been as trustees of the common interest, on an interim basis only and as part of a process of collaboration with the Commission;[28] the Court has however not permitted unilateral proposals from the Commission in the face of political inaction to be attributed legal effect, otherwise mere proposals would themselves become binding acts.[29] Advocate General Da Cruz Vilaça firmly rejected an attempt by the Commission to argue that, instead of a standstill approach (extending the validity of existing measures for as long as there was no formal renewal or alteration by the Council), an 'exceptional circumstances'

---

[25] Interinstitutional disputes or disputes with institutional implications in the context of external relations are of course also well-known in ordinary cases, e.g. Case 22/70 *Commission* v. *Council* [1971] *ECR* 263; and Case C-25/94 *Commission* v. *Council* [1996] *ECR* I-1469.

[26] Opinion 1/76 (Draft Agreement establishing a European laying-up fund for inland waterway vessels) [1977] *ECR* 741; Opinion 1/91 *EEA I* [1991] *ECR* I-6079; Opinion 1/92 *EEA II* [1992] *ECR* I-2821; and Opinion 2/94 (Accession of the Community to the ECHR) [1996] *ECR* I-1759.

[27] See Art. 35 EU.

[28] Case 804/79 *Commission* v. *United Kingdom* [1981] *ECR* 1045 at 1073.

[29] Case 325/85 *Commission* v. *Ireland* [1987] *ECR* 5041 at 5087-5088.

approach of permitting the Commission to enforce its proposals unilaterally was appropriate and justifiable.[30] The Court had no hesitation in following the learned Advocate General in this rejection of the Commission's somewhat novel arguments.

It is very much the Member States that are called upon to play a part in the functioning of the institutions: the Court has resisted the siren calls of autonomous regions at sub-State level seeking to place themselves on the same footing as Member States.[31] This remains true even since the establishment of the Committee of the Regions and the possibility that a Member State might be represented in the Council by a person of ministerial rank (authorized to commit the Member State in question) who is not actually a minister at national level. This national orientation is also reflected in the attitude of the Commission. The Commission deals with Member States, not with regions, although the problem is sometimes solved (for example in relation to discussions on individual regional policy matters) by a mixed composition of the delegation from the Member State concerned, where a particular dossier is clearly not a matter of federal competence. Nevertheless, in Community law, the Member State carries the can at the end of the day.

EVOLUTIONARY NATURE OF THE INSTITUTIONAL BALANCE

An important aspect of the institutional balance in the Communities, and indeed in the Union, is its evolutionary nature. The original structure of the Spaak Report has been developed and built on, not merely through every substantive amendment of the Treaties, but also through the case law of the Court and through soft law developments. In practice, the latter offer a practical way of resolving issues, which Member States and Parliamentarians see as useful instruments for the achievement of political goals without the political dangers of having to put hard law changes out as hostages to fortune in national fora. However, soft law can sometimes transmute into hard law at the flick of a switch. Thus, the Edinburgh and Birmingham declarations on subsidiarity and proportionality[32] were raised to the status of a protocol to the EC Treaty at Amsterdam.

The evolutionary nature of the institutional balance has become a *leitmotif* in Community law in general. The balance of influence, and to a somewhat lesser extent also power, has over the years very much shifted in favour of the Parliament,

---

[30] Ibid., at 5064-5065.

[31] Case C-95/97 *Région wallonne* v. *Commission* [1997] *ECR* I-1787; and Case C-180/97 *Regione Toscana* v. *Commission* [1997] *ECR* I-5245.

[32] See *Bull. EC* 10-1992, point I.8; and *Bull. EC* 12-1992, point I.15.

so that the people of Europe are indeed called upon to play an increasing part in the activities of the Communities, but still only rather indirectly in those of the Union. The reporting obligations in the EU Treaty itself are terse, but they are respected; more useful perhaps is the classification of Second and Third Pillar expenditure as non-compulsory expenditure in the Community budget. This ensures that, via the power of the purse, the Parliament can have some more influence on these largely intergovernmental pillars of the Union than might at first seem possible. Pernice and Thym have rightly observed that institutional design and political convergence go hand in hand, and that it has always been a characteristic feature of European integration that procedural reform facilitates political progress – and *vice versa*.[33] It is not surprising then, that the balance between the institutions of the Community, now of the Union, will be revisited from time to time.

THE CURRENT SITUATION

At this stage, it seems that while the Member States collectively remain the most important aspect of the Union's structure, the Council increased its importance at the expense of the Commission, largely symbolically, but firmly, at Nice. Thus, the appointment of Commissioners is no longer the preserve of the common accord of the governments of the Member States (albeit with involvement of the Parliament): the Council proceeds by qualified majority and by common accord with the nominee for President, expressly in accordance with the proposals made by each Member State; the final appointment is made by the Council, acting by qualified majority.[34] The Commission maintains its key power base, the exclusive right of initiative in the Community system, but the Parliament has been given a right of quasi-initiative (to request the Commission to submit a proposal), an approach which is often also used by the European Council. In relation to the inappropriately named Second and Third Pillars[35] of the Union, while the Commission formally merely has the joint right of initiative with the Member States, appearing to be intended to play second fiddle in these essentially intergovernmental aspects of the

---

[33] I. Pernice and D. Thym, 'A New Institutional Balance for European Foreign Policy?', 7 *EFARev.* (2002) p. 369 at pp. 374-380.

[34] Art. 214(2) EC, codifying and strengthening a long-standing practice of not vetoing each other's nominees.

[35] See L.W. Gormley, 'Reflections on the architecture of the European Union after the Treaty of Amsterdam', in D. O'Keeffe and P.M. Twomey, eds., *Legal Issues of the Amsterdam Treaty* (Oxford, Hart 1999) p. 57 at pp. 57-58; and L.W. Gormley, 'The Judicial Architecture of the European Union after Nice', in A. Arnull and D. Wincott, eds., *Accountability and Legitimacy in the European Union* (Oxford, OUP 2003).

Union's activities, the vast majority of the initiatives taken in the Second Pillar nevertheless come from the Commission.

A few observations seem appropriate in response to Jacqué's recent article on the institutional balance.[36] He explains that the institutional balance between the three political actors (European Parliament, Council and the Commission) has shifted to the disadvantage of the Commission because the Commission only retains authority *vis-à-vis* the Council insofar as it expresses the general interest in an independent manner. By way of reaction to this point, it may be observed that the Commission is supposed to do this in presenting its proposals to the Council or to the European Parliament and the Council jointly.[37] Jacqué sees the Commission, to the extent that it has been placed largely in the hands of the Parliament, as having lost credibility as far as the Council is concerned: the Council prefers to negotiate directly with the Parliament, rather than with the Commission, which has become the spokesman for the Parliament's arguments. The latter part of this proposition seems, with respect, very much to reflect matters as seen from the Council's point of view, and underplays the Commission's own rights and honest broker role (particularly, for example, in conciliation) in the legislative procedure. Jacqué further observes that the search for agreement with the Parliament in the first or second reading reduces the Commission's powers, as it can hardly hang on to its proposal when the other two institutions have reached agreement on a different text. Certainly, this may often be the political reality, although the Commission may occasionally prefer to withdraw a proposal rather than see an emasculated proposal adopted.[38] Finally, Jacqué sees the formal significance of the Commission's right of initiative as being increasingly hollowed out, given the obligation (which he suggests may be contrary to the Treaty) that is increasingly frequently imposed by Community legislation on the Commission to submit proposals, and the fact that the instructions in question frequently indicate what the content of those proposals should be. Frequently, however, these instructions may be to work out implementing measures, and the Commission itself will have proposed such a construction; on other occasions, there may indeed be more to Jacqué's observation.[39]

As has already been demonstrated above, the Parliament's importance has increased in relation to judicial review. In addition to its considerable budgetary

---

[36] Jacqué, loc. cit. n. 2, at p. 390.

[37] Hence the simple qualified majority (in cases where qualified majority voting applies) when the Council acts on a proposal from the Commission, and the double qualified majority when it does not, see Art. 205(2) EC.

[38] See P.J.G. Kapteyn and P. VerLoren van Themaat, ed. and further rev. by L.W. Gormley, *Introduction to the Law of the European Communities*, 3rd. edn. (London/The Hague, Kluwer Law International 1998) pp. 203 (discussing the controversy on this point) and 416.

[39] See the discussion in ibid., pp. 409-411.

powers (which were conferred long ago), it has increased its influence and power significantly over the years with the expansion of qualified majority voting and with the invention of new decision-making procedures. The Parliament is much more of a true legislature (albeit a co-legislature) than it was.

The Court of Justice has achieved a higher profile and steps have been prepared in the Treaty of Nice to streamline the administration of justice.[40] Nevertheless, the arrangement of responsibilities and powers would still largely be familiar to the authors of the Spaak Report, at least as far as the Community system is concerned; they would approvingly note the increased profile of the Parliament and the extension of qualified majority voting and the improvements in decision-making procedures. They might be less pleased with the development of the European Council and the fact that the Member States have adopted and maintained the intergovernmental approach in the supporting Second and Third Pillars of the Union. Finally, the newest, fifth institution, the Court of Auditors, has seen its headline influence and status increase, but still its recommendations and criticisms often do not receive sufficient follow-up for it to capitalize on its potential.

THE CONSTITUTION

There seems to be a rather strange anomaly relating to the institutional framework of the Constitution:[41] In Article I-19(1), the institutional framework is said to comprise the European Parliament, the European Council, the Council of Ministers, the European Commission and the Court of Justice. While the European Central Bank and the Court of Auditors are later listed as 'other institutions', they are clearly outside the framework. The logical reason for this approach is unclear.

A number of interesting features stand out in the Constitution as far as institutional balance is concerned.[42] The institutions will (unsurprisingly in view of the case law) be obliged to practise 'mutual sincere cooperation'.[43] This codifies the

---

[40] As to the judicial architecture of the Union after Nice, see L.W. Gormley, 'The Judicial Architecture of the European Union after Nice', in Arnull and Wincott, op. cit. n. 35, at p. 133.

[41] The phrase 'the Constitution' refers to the final renumbered text published as CIG 87/04; CIG87/04 ADD 1 deals with the Protocols and Annexes and CIG87/04 ADD 2 deals with Declarations to the Final Act of the Intergovernmental Conference and the Final Act itself. This text is due to be signed at Rome on 29 October 2004. The expression 'the draft Constitution' refers to the draft presented in the version of 18 July 2003, adopted by the European Convention on 13 June and 10 July 2003.

[42] See further 'Editorials', 28 ELRev. (2003) pp. 449 and 761; M. Dougan, 'The Convention's draft Constitutional Treaty: Bringing Europe closer to its lawyers?', 28 ELRev. (2003) p. 763; and Føllesdal, 'Achieving Stability?', Federal Trust Online Paper 06/04. For this and other Federal Trust papers, see <http://www.fedtrust.co.uk/eu_constitution>.

[43] Constitution, Art. I-19(2).

existing obligation under Article 10 EC, but is undoubtedly politically reinforced by being expressed at Treaty level.

The responsibility of the Parliament to elect the President of the Commission, set out in Articles I-20(1) and I-27(1) of the Constitution, emphasizes more clearly the Commission's accountability to Parliament. However, the personal accountability of the President, in particular, for the actions of his Commissioners proposed in Article I-25(5) of the draft Constitution has not been retained. As far as the Commission is concerned, the changes will be quite dramatic, although not all the suggestions of the draft Constitution have been taken on board by the IGC. The proposed system of rotation has undergone some changes: the first Commission to be appointed under the provisions of the Constitution will still consist of one national from each Member State, including its President and the Union Minister of Foreign Affairs (UMFA), who will be one of its Vice-Presidents.[44] Given that the members of the Commission in office on the date of entry into force of the Treaty establishing a Constitution for Europe will remain in office until the end of their terms of office,[45] this means that it will be a good number of years before a reduction in the size of the Commission will be achieved. The draft Constitution had envisaged a smaller Commission from 1 November 2009, with a President, the UMFA as Vice-President, and thirteen European Commissioners on an equal rotation system to be worked out in accordance with two principles in a European Decision.[46]

The Constitution retains these twin principles. First, Member States must be treated on a strictly equal footing as regards the determination of the sequence of, and the time spent by, their nationals as members of the Commission; thus the difference between the total number of offices held by nationals of any given pair of Member States may never be more than one.[47] Secondly, subject to the first principle, each successive Commission must also be so composed as to reflect satisfactorily the demographic and geographical range of all the Member States of the Union.[48] However, the above-mentioned date has been dropped in favour of the end of the term of office of the first Commission appointed under the provisions of the Constitution, after which the number of members of the reduced-size Commission, including its President and the UMFA, will correspond to two-thirds of the number of Member States, unless the European Council, acting

---

[44] Constitution, Art. I-26(5). This latter office is considered below. The draft Constitution had envisaged the UMFA as being the only Vice-President.

[45] Protocol 34 on transitional provisions relating to the institutions and bodies of the Union, Art. 4. On the day of appointment of the UMFA, the term of office of the sitting member of the Commission who is of the same nationality as the UMFA will end, ibid.

[46] Draft Constitution, Art. I-25(3).

[47] Constitution, Art. I-26(6)(a).

[48] Constitution, Art. I-26(6)(b).

unanimously, decides to alter this figure.[49] The IGC rightly rejected the draft Constitution's idea of non-voting Commissioners; these would have been be a consolation prize for those Member States that did not at any given moment have a full European Commissioner, but it may be wondered what self-respecting politician would have rushed to fill such a junior position.

There is still, strangely, no provision for what happens if the Parliament fails to approve the College of Commissioners. This is a mystifying oversight, in particular because there *is* provision for putting forward a new candidate if the candidate for President is not approved.[50] Perhaps the obvious approach would be for another suggestion to be made and the proposed Commission to be resubmitted for approval. The draft Constitution's idea of those Member States that were to have voting Commissioners[51] submitting a list of three persons from which the President-elect would choose one[52] has rightly not been retained in the Constitution. It would have caused an unacceptable amount of rather public bloodletting and would have placed far too much power in the hands of the President-elect.

Jacqué[53] has argued that having one Commissioner per Member State does not strengthen the Commission, but merely turns it (despite the independence of its members) into an intergovernmental institution that is in competition with the Council. However, this is far from what was intended by the Spaak Report and the founding Treaties; it is also alien to the approach in the Constitution. The Commission is *not* an intergovernmental institution but a supranational institution with its own powers and duties to act in the Community interest. Jacqué argues that it is necessary to restore the Commission's independence and that even if the issue of size is settled, there must be a counterweight to ensure the Commission's independence as regards the Council and the Parliament. The Commission's independence has most often been seen in terms of independence from influence by the Member States or private parties, but it is clear that it must be equally independent from the other two political institutions. The ultimate guarantor of independence is the Court, but it would have to be prepared to expedite cases in which interference is alleged.[54] In any event, it will be important for the Commission to make it clear that even though it will be appointed by the European

---

[49] Constitution, Art. I-26(6).

[50] Constitution, Art. I-27(1).

[51] Whom it referred to as European Commissioners, as opposed to the non-voting Commissioners.

[52] Draft Constitution, Art. I-26(2).

[53] Jacqué, loc. cit. n. 2, at pp. 390-391.

[54] It can decide to do so under Art. 62a of the Rules of Procedure, as (in a different context) in Case C-27/04 *Commission* v. *Council* [2004] *ECR* I, nyr (13 July 2004) on the excessive deficit procedure. As to the consolidated Rules of Procedure, see <http://europa.eu.int/cj/en/instit/txtdocfr/index.htm>.

Council,[55] it is certainly no poodle and will continue to maintain its own institutional responsibilities: a strong, independent and active Commission will be as essential in the future as it was in 1958! The decision to have the Commission appointed by the European Council (rather than by the Council as at present) at least reinforces the notion that the Commission is not the servant of the Council, but rather a full partner with the Council and the European Parliament in the decision-making process. Similarly, although the Commission is politically responsible to the European Parliament, it is neither its servant nor its poodle.

The Constitution rightly recognizes that at least in time a Commission composed of one member per Member State will be somewhat unwieldy to say the least, and that it would be better to work with a smaller Commission. The precise working of the system of equal rotation is something of an evil day, postponed for a future European Decision. It is submitted that this Decision should be constructed to represent each time a balance of large and small State interests, as well as reflecting the old and the new membership. However, in view of the fact that the Union is composed of large, medium-large, medium, medium-small and small Member States in terms of population size and physical size, it has not proved possible simply to provide that every Member State would have a member every other mandate. Although the draft Constitution's approach would have at least allowed every Member State to have 'eyes and ears' at all Commission meetings, it did reinforce the (erroneous) perception that the Commission is somehow the property of the Member States, a form of intergovernmentalism. A solution whereby some Member States would be permanently represented in the Commission, with others having a rotating membership, would have been too much at odds with the idea of equality of membership of the Union to deserve serious consideration.

The IGC has in fact taken account of the need to continue to ensure that the Commission is properly able to take account of the interests of all the Member States. Thus, a Declaration has been incorporated into the Final Act of the Treaty establishing a Constitution for Europe noting that the IGC considers that the reduced-size Commission 'should pay particular attention to the need to ensure full transparency in relations with all Member States.' Accordingly, it 'should liaise closely with all Member States, whether or not they have a national serving as Member of the Commission, and in this context pay special attention to the need to share information and consult with all Member States.' Moreover, the IGC considered that the Commission ought to 'take all the necessary measures to ensure that political, social and economic realities in all Member States, including

---

[55] Constitution, Art. I-27(2). Candidates will be suggested by the Member States in accordance with Constitution, Art. I-26(4) and (6), second subparagraph, and proposed by the Council in common accord with the President-elect, subject as a body (including the President and the UMFA) to a vote of consent by the European Parliament.

those which have no national serving as Member of the Commission, are fully taken into account.' Such measures ought to include 'ensuring that the position of those Member States is addressed by appropriate organisational arrangements.'[56] It remains to be seen what form this will take in practice; it is unlikely that the Commission will invite representatives of those Member States that have no national represented in its composition to send an observer to its meetings, as such an approach would reinforce an intergovernmentalist impression in terms of Jacqué's argument. More likely is that in the preparation of legislative proposals and other positions, informal soundings will be taken on a more systematic basis than hitherto.[57]

It has rightly been decided not to endow the European Council with legislative functions. The fact that the President of the European Council may not hold a national mandate[58] emphasizes the full-time nature of the responsibilities of the position. The length of his mandate (two and a half years) mirrors that of the President of the European Parliament. There may thus be two presidencies of the European Council per parliamentary term, although the President of the European Council may have his term renewed once.[59]

With the last few Treaty revisions, the Council has become a strange animal. Legally it is one institution, but the notion of a hierarchy of Councils has been given credence and some support by the establishment of a Council that meets in the composition of Heads of State or Government. References to the Council in this formation will disappear if the Constitution enters into force, and even the very limited role of the governments of the Member States meeting at the level of Heads of State or Government envisaged in the draft Constitution[60] has not survived the IGC. The creation of a Union Minister for Foreign Affairs (UMFA), who will chair the Foreign Affairs Council, departs significantly from the six-monthly rotation scheme which has hitherto prevailed and which will continue for other Council formations, albeit within pre-established groups of three Member States covering an eighteen-month period.[61] This seems to be modelled to an extent on the present Troika arrangements for the Presidency.

---

[56] Declaration on Art. I-26.

[57] Even now, before the Commission adopts proposals or other measures, it will usually have consulted widely, both at the level of civil servants of the Member States and the EEA, with both sides of industry and with civil society.

[58] Constitution, Art. I-22(3).

[59] Constitution, Art. I-22(1). He or she may also be dismissed in the case of an impediment or serious misconduct, ibid.

[60] Draft Constitution, Art. III-84(2)(b) (appointment of the members of the Executive Board of the ECB). Instead, the European Council will appoint the Executive Board: Constitution, Art. III-382(2), second subparagraph; Statute ESCB/ECB, Art. 11.

[61] Draft Decision of the European Council on the exercise of the Presidency of the Council, attached to the Declaration on Art. I-24(7). A European Decision is to be adopted by the European

As far as qualified majority voting (QMV) is concerned, the compromise achieved in Article I-25 of the Constitution is remarkable.[62] The Nice arrangements will apply until 31 October 2009,[63] with the new arrangements applying thereafter. Of particular interest is the extension of QMV in the Common Foreign and Security Policy; moreover, by virtue of Article III-300(3), the European Council may by unanimity permit the Council to act by qualified majority in cases other than those set out in Article III-300(2). This is a logical application of the system of taking major decisions by unanimity prior to the use of QMV.[64] Apart from decisions having military and defence applications,[65] there would appear to be no logical limit to this *passerelle* provision – it is not limited to specific types of measures or actions, or areas of activity, within Common Foreign and Security Policy. Interestingly, QMV may also be extended in relation to the use of enhanced cooperation.[66] Thus, if such an extension has taken place, latecomers to that particular instance of enhanced cooperation will automatically sign up for it. If, finally, all Member States sign up, QMV still applies in the area concerned.[67] Returning to the Second Pillar and QMV, the status of the UMFA also deserves note. His or her proposals (in the areas in which he or she is competent) will, for the purposes of QMV, be treated on the same footing as proposals of the Commission: the simpler qualified majority applies.[68] This is logical, as he or she takes account of the political interests of all the Member States in presenting proposals.

This Union Minister is a strange animal. He or she will be appointed by the European Council, acting by qualified majority, with the agreement of the President of the Commission; the European Council may dismiss him or her by means of the same procedure.[69] Yet the UMFA is also one of the Vice-Presidents of the Commission and, as such, is subject to the collective approval of the

---

Council, acting by a qualified majority, establishing the list of other Council formations: Constitution, Art. I-24(4). As to configurations prior to the adoption of this European Decision, see the Protocol on transitional provisions relating to the institutions and bodies of the European Union, Art. 3. The draft Constitution had provided for a rotation period for the other Council formations of at least a year: Draft Constitution, Art. I-23(4).

[62] See also the Draft Decision on the implementation of Constitution, Art. I-25, which reflects the concepts of the Ioannina Compromise.

[63] This is achieved by repeating them in the Constitution, in Protocol on transitional provisions relating to the institutions and bodies of the European Union, Art. 2.

[64] See Art. 23 EU.

[65] Excluded from the possible application of QMV by Constitution, Art. III-300(4).

[66] Constitution, Art. III-422.

[67] For further discussion of the institutional balance in relation to foreign policy, see D. Thym, 'The New Institutional Balance of European Foreign Policy in the Draft Treaty establishing a Constitution for Europe', WHI Paper 12/03 (Berlin, Walter Hallstein Institute 2003).

[68] Constitution, Art. I-25(1) and (2).

[69] Constitution, Art. I-28(1).

Commission by the European Parliament.[70] In respect of his or her handling of external relations and coordination of other aspects of the Union's external action within the Commission, the UMFA is bound by Commission procedures to the extent that this is consistent with what is required to fulfil mandates laid down by the Council.[71] Like other members of the Commission, the UMFA must resign (as a Commissioner) if required to do so by the President of the Commission,[72] yet it is only the European Council that may dismiss him or her in his or her capacity as the UMFA. The President of the Commission would surely need to be sure of the political support of a qualified majority in the Council (having taken soundings) in order to ensure that no political impasse resulted.

Much will ride on the synergy or lack of it between the President of the Commission and the UMFA. If the latter finds that there is a huge gulf between the wishes of the Council and the mood of the Commission, his or her position will become untenable. A major break is clearly made with the separation of powers between the Council and the Commission, and there is bound to be the perception of the UMFA as a potential fifth column, whereas he or she will have to be a facilitator and conciliator if the holder of the position is to command confidence in the institutions concerned. While this is a *novum* compared with the present Community pillar within the Union, double or triple hats are not unknown: the present Secretary-General of the Council is also the High Representative for Foreign and Security Policy and the residual Secretary-General of the WEU. The advantage over the present system of these new arrangements from the point of view of accountability will be that, in relation to his or her (prospective) functioning within the Commission, the European Parliament will be able to question the UMFA extensively and could, if it were dissatisfied, vote down the whole Commission on the ground of the UMFA's role. Indeed, if a censure motion on the Commission is passed in the European Parliament, the UMFA must resign as a member of the Commission (which is required to resign as a body).[73] The European Parliament will also be able to question the UMFA about his or her activities as President of the Foreign Affairs Council. Wearing several hats permits the UMFA to be attacked from several angles at once.

The creation of the UMFA does not in fact answer Kissinger's single telephone number problem of who speaks for Europe. The UMFA's remit does not extend to commercial policy matters (which remain with the Commission and in particular its member with the external trade portfolio), and specific policy areas are likely to remain within the remit of the members of the Commission dealing

---

[70] Constitution, Art. I-27(2).

[71] Constitution, Art. I-28(4).

[72] Constitution, Art. I-27(3). This provision says he must resign in accordance with the procedure in Constitution, Art. I-28(1), but the latter provides for dismissal, not for resignation.

[73] Constitution, Art. I-26(8); see also Art. III-340 (for the censure vote procedure).

with the portfolio concerned. Furthermore, the President of the European Council may also be expected to want to play a significant role, and specific reference is made to external representation at his or her level, without prejudice to the UMFA's powers.[74] It is submitted that this means that the President of the European Council would meet with the President of the United States, and the UMFA would meet with the American Secretary of State, at the annual US-EU summits and on other occasions. Correspondingly, the latter two would meet independently or accompany the former two.

As far as the Court of Justice is concerned, it and its workload, like Topsy, just grows and grows: the Court of Justice will become the European Court of Justice; the Court of First Instance is clearly meant to be transferred into the new High Court; and specialized courts can be annexed to the latter.[75] A significant invention is the panel to advise on the suitability of candidates for the European Court of Justice and the High Court, composed of seven former members of the European Court of Justice and the High Court, members of national supreme courts and lawyers of recognized competence, one of whom is nominated by the European Parliament.[76] The way in which the panel will operate will be laid down by a European Decision and the appointment of its members will be laid down by a European Decision taken by the Council on the initiative of the President of the European Court of Justice.[77] The appointment remains an act by common accord of the governments of the Member States, but after consultation of the panel. At the moment the nomination of candidates is a purely national process, the degree of transparency varying widely.[78] The panel may well be empowered to hold hearings and must inevitably be influenced by the political hue of the candidates, even if indirectly, and particularly in relation to perceived federal, intergovernmental or economic strategy preferences. This is bound to happen even if it is instructed to have regard only to legal qualities. Whether this system will produce a competent and balanced court is as open a question, as is whether the present system produces a competent and balanced court.

CONCLUDING REMARKS AND SALUTATION

To return to the title of this paper – disturbing or rebalancing – it appears that the institutional balance in the Constitution represents a significant shift from the

---

[74] Constitution, Art. I-22(2).

[75] Constitution, Arts. I-29(1) and III-359(1).

[76] Constitution, Art. III-357.

[77] Ibid.

[78] Some Member States (such as the United Kingdom and the Netherlands) now advertise for applicants, but the degree of transparency remains lamentably low.

visions of the Spaak Report and a considerable shift from the present arrangements. In particular, there is a distinct blurring of the line between the
Commission and the Council, and even, it may be sensed, a devaluation of the
Commission. The solution for the membership of the Commission when it
becomes smaller is decidedly complex. Moreover, the position of the UMFA
seems a most unhappy compromise: he or she will attempt to be all things to all
people, with a very good chance of being torn asunder like the veil of the Temple.
All in all, the Constitution is not a particularly positive document as far as
institutional questions are concerned. Those who are content with what is on offer
might prefer to speak of a natural rebalancing and can rightly point to the fact that
the balance between the institutions is not written in stone. Yet, it can certainly be
argued that in reality there is such a disturbance of the fundamental concepts of
institutions with their own clear responsibility and (functional and legal) independence that the Constitution's approach represents a dramatic and undesirable
departure from the vision of European integration that preceded it. In view of the
unseemly spectacle of Giscard d'Estaing presenting the draft Constitution to
Silvio Berlusconi, and its decidedly *Europe des Nations* approach,[79] the draft
Constitution's image is that of a less than ideal blueprint for the future of Europe
– it was certainly not a set of tablets brought down from the Mount. Although the
Constitution as settled on 18 June 2004 (Waterloo Day) is an improvement on the
draft, it might perhaps be unwise for the people of Europe to embrace this
somewhat Trojan horse without looking it very firmly in the proverbial mouth. It
is unlikely to catch the hearts and minds of Europe's citizens in the way that the
US Constitution occupies an important place in every American's mind.

Fred, you have worked tirelessly for the Asser Institute and for European law
and European integration; your contacts are legendary and your energy unabated.
Your career has recently been crowned with an Honorary Doctorate, and European law is unlikely to let you hang up your travelling boots just yet: *ad multos
annos*.

---

[79] Vernon Bogdanor pointed out at a conference celebrating thirty years of Community law in
the United Kingdom (London, May 2004) that Eurosceptics really ought to be rather pleased with the
draft Constitution!

THE ROLE OF THE EUROPEAN COMMISSION OVER THE YEARS: CHANGES AND CHALLENGES

Jaap W. de Zwaan*

The subject of this contribution is inspired by the skills and capacities of Fred Kellermann, whose enthusiasm and endeavours to create a European law network in the Netherlands have made him a unique person. Without Fred, the spread, at least in the Netherlands, of knowledge and interest regarding European law and, more generally, the process of European integration would certainly have been less. For several years, Fred has also been active in the new and applicant Member States of the European Union, undertaking similar activities. Perhaps his finest accomplishment concerns the establishment and organisation of the famous Asser Colloquia in The Hague, bringing together – in September of each year – representatives of all sectors and circles, private and public, who in their daily activities are occupied with European law. We therefore pay tribute to Fred as a wonderful activist and promoter of the European cause!

1. INTRODUCTION

In this contribution, attention will be paid to the role of the Commission in the process of European integration.[1] First, the original characteristics of the Commission's role as developed at the beginning of the 1950s will be discussed. Then the changes that these characteristics have undergone over the years will be analysed. After looking at the reforms regarding the position of the Commission as introduced by the draft Constitutional Treaty, finally, some observations will be made regarding the challenges to its future role.

---

* Prof. Dr. Jaap W. de Zwaan, Professor of the Law of the European Union at the Law School of Erasmus University Rotterdam; Vice-President of the Executive Board and Member of the Governing Board of the T.M.C. Asser Institute.

[1] For recent and general publications on this subject, see also G. Edwards and D. Spence, eds., *The European Commission* (London, Cartermill Publishing 1994); G. Majone, 'The European Commission: The Limits of Centralization and the Perils of Parliamentarization', 15 *Governance: An International Journal of Policy, Administration and Institutions* (2002); A. Michalski, *Governing Europe: The Future Role of the European Commission* (The Hague, Clingendael Institute 2002). Reference may also be made to handbooks such as P. Craig and G. de Búrca, *EU Law: Text, Cases and Materials*, 3rd edn. (Oxford, Oxford University Press 2003), in particular pp. 54-65.

The European Union: An Ongoing Process of Integration – Liber Amicorum Alfred E. Kellermann
© 2004, T.M.C. Asser Instituut, The Hague, and the authors

2.   THE ORIGINALITY OF THE COMMISSION'S ROLE AND
         RESPONSIBILITIES

The Commission is the most original and most supranational institution of the
European Union. As an autonomous organ created at the international level, the
Commission acts independently from the Member States, and its main mission is
to protect and serve the general interest of the European Union.[2]
     The most significant roles of the Commission are the following:[3]

-    **Initiator:** The Commission has the exclusive right of initiative regarding
     legislation to be adopted at Union level.
-    **Guardian of the Treaties:** The Commission has the competence to monitor
     whether Member States and undertakings are respecting their treaty obligations.
-    **Executive:** The Commission has the competence to take decisions implement-
     ing earlier framework decisions of the Council and/or European Parliament.
-    **Representative:** Although not specifically referred to in Article 211 EC, the
     Commission is the natural representative of the Community in external fora
     and negotiations.[4]

In view of the nature of these responsibilities, the Commission is traditionally
referred to as the initiator and motor of the process of European integration.
     On the other hand, it must be acknowledged that the Commission does not
possess a very precise and recognisable position within the institutional framework of the European Union. Indeed, the Commission cannot be regarded as the
'government' or, as commonly stated in the media, the 'executive board' (in
Dutch: *'dagelijks bestuur'*) of the Union. Certainly, the originality of the prerogatives of the Commission has something to do with this phenomenon.
     In this context, it should be remembered that under the former ECSC Treaty,
and also under the EAEC Treaty, the Commission had and has a more precise role
to play. In fact, at the time it was referred to as the 'High Authority', the Commission, was the central organ of the European Coal and Steal Community,
holding far-reaching decision-making, administrative and executive powers.[5] In a

---

  [2] This key responsibility of the Commission will be fully reflected in the European Constitution.
According to Art. I-25(1) of the draft Constitutional Treaty, the European Commission shall promote
the general European interest and take appropriate initiatives to that end. In the present EC Treaty, a
reference to 'the general interest of the Community' is found in Art. 213(2) EC, which states that the
members of the Commission shall be completely independent in the performance of their duties.

  [3] See, notably, Art. 211 EC.

  [4] Art. 300(1) EC.

  [5] See, for example, former Art. 8 ECSC, according to which the Commission had the duty to
ensure that the objectives set out in the Treaty were attained. See also former Arts. 14 (instruments),
58(2) (quota) and 60 (prices) ECSC. The general responsibility of the Council was to harmonise the

way the same is true for the European Atomic Energy Community.[6] However, these characteristics no longer correspond to the functioning of the Commission under the EC Treaty.

3. WEAKNESSES

One of the main weaknesses of the Commission's position in the institutional framework of the Union is that, while exercising its prerogatives, the Commission is hardly visible to the ordinary citizen. In fact, this is true for all activities undertaken by the Commission. For example, the ordinary public is not aware when and where the Commission meets. The Commission's meetings are not open to the public. Then, when the Commission presents a proposal, the text is normally published on the Internet and in the *Official Journal* of the European Union. In practice, however, proposals will only be read by experts. In the course of the legislative process, the Commission appears at sessions of the parliamentary committees and in the plenary of the European Parliament. The Commission also participates in all meetings of the Council.[7] The President of the Commission is even a full-fledged member of the European Council.[8]

However, all these activities do not result in an active and visible public appearance of the Commission. In fact, they only reflect its participation in sessions of other institutions involved in the decision-making process of the Union.

Moreover, once a Commission proposal is adopted by the Council (and the European Parliament),[9] the responsibilities regarding implementation, application and enforcement of the decision concerned rest with the Member States. In these stages, the involvement of the Commission is restricted to its role, as important as it may be, as the 'guardian of the Treaties'.[10]

It must thus be concluded that the Commission is hardly present in the public debate and not visible to the ordinary citizen. It should therefore not come as a surprise when the public does not regard the European Commission as an important international layer of government. This lack of identity on the part of

---

action of the Commission and that of the governments, which – as stated in Art. 26(1) ECSC – were responsible for the general economic policies of their countries.

[6] See, for example, Art. 4 EAEC, according to which the Commission shall be responsible for promoting and facilitating nuclear research and for complementing it by carrying out a Community research and training program. See also Arts. 12 (dissemination of information) and 53 (the Agency which shall be under the supervision of the Commission) EAEC.

[7] At working group, COREPER or ministerial level. On the legal basis of the participation of the Commission in Council meetings, see Art. 5(2) of the Council's Rules of Procedure, *OJ* 2002 L 230/7.

[8] Art. 4(2) EU.

[9] The reference here is to the co-decision procedure of Art. 251 EC.

[10] In this context, see Arts. 226 (infringement procedure) and 228 (penalty payments) EC.

the Commission, which is still the most supranational institution of the Union, is one of the defects of the European construction and one of the reasons why a citizens' Europe is so difficult to achieve.

4.   RECENT DEVELOPMENTS

Over the years, the Commission's exercise of its powers and prerogatives has been influenced by many factors and developments.

4.1   **Right of initiative**

Thus, the emergence of the *European Council* in 1974 and its functioning since[11] have clearly had an impact on Commission's exercise of its right of initiative. Indeed, major political processes at European level have been stimulated not so much by the Commission, but by the European Council. Famous examples in this respect are EMU (Economic and Monetary Union) and JHA (Justice and Home Affairs) cooperation.[12] The impact of the European Council on the day-to-day activities of the Union is furthermore illustrated by the regular invitations to the Commission (and the Council) in its conclusions to prepare appropriate proposals in certain policy fields.

Later, when it was decided to introduce the *pillar structure* in the Maastricht Treaty, the Commission was not granted a right of initiative in Second and Third Pillar cooperation, like the one it already had in First Pillar cooperation. On the contrary, until today, the Commission holds a shared right of initiative in these areas,[13] on the same footing as the Member States. Under the Maastricht version of Third Pillar cooperation, the Commission's right of initiative was even restricted to certain subject areas.[14] The Treaty of Amsterdam subsequently even introduced a shared right of initiative, which the Commission is expected to exercise on the same footing as the Member States, in relation to First Pillar cooperation. The reference here it to the substance of Title IV of Part Three of the EC Treaty, concerning visas, asylum, immigration and civil law cooperation.[15] This was obviously a unique, but also bad, precedent. Now, of course, a connec-

---

[11] See Art. 4 EU.

[12] The EMU modalities have been elaborated in the Treaty of Maastricht. Those of JHA have been elaborated in the Treaty of Maastricht and the Treaty of Amsterdam. A JHA working program was laid down in the conclusions of the Tampere European Council of October 1999.

[13] Respectively, the Common Foreign and Security Policy and Police and Judicial Cooperation in Criminal Matters.

[14] Former Art. K.1(1)-(6) EU, to be read in conjunction with former Art. K.3(2), first indent, EU.

[15] Arts. 61-69 EC. However, as of 1 May 2004, the right of initiative in this domain lies exclusively with the Commission. This is a consequence of the rule included in Art. 67(2), first indent, EC.

tion can be made between Second and Third Pillar cooperation and Title IV of the EC Treaty, on the one hand, and the politically sensitive character of the policy fields concerned, on the other. This apparently made the Member States reluctant to apply the traditional supranational procedures and rules in these domains.

In the context of the Commission's right of initiative, it is furthermore worth mentioning that the strong position the Commission holds in the decision-making process, notably because of the principle according to which its proposals can only be amended by the Council by unanimous decision,[16] is weakened once the *co-decision procedure* applies, especially when, in the framework of the so-called second reading negotiations between the Council and the European Parliament, a conciliation committee meeting is convened.[17] This is because the principle of Article 250(1) EC Treaty no longer applies at this stage. In this case, the priority has clearly been to reinforce the role of the European Parliament in the European legislative process. Thus the institutional position of the Commission has been sacrificed in favour of an increase in the democratic character of the decision-making process of the Union.

4.2   Guardian of the Treaties

As to the Commission's role as the 'guardian of the Treaties', it should be observed that the infringement procedure of Articles 226 to 228 EC does not apply to *Second and Third Pillar* cooperation.[18] Regarding the Third Pillar, in particular, this may easily affect the effectiveness of the cooperation, in view of the interests that are at stake and the fact that legally binding decisions can be taken in this field. Another striking phenomenon in this respect emerged in the autumn of 2003, when the non-compliance of France and Germany with certain EMU criteria was discussed in the Council. Because of the fact that the Member States refused to entrust the Commission with the responsibility to enforce the rules and criteria of EMU and the Stability and Growth Pact at the time when these rules and criteria were negotiated, the decision making in the Council ended in deadlock.[19]

---

[16] Art. 250(1) EC. The full text reads: 'Where, in pursuance of this Treaty, the Council acts on a proposal from the Commission, unanimity will be required for an act constituting an amendment to that proposal, subject to Article 251(4) and (5) EC.'

[17] Art. 250(1) EC, to be read in conjunction with Art. 251(4) and (5) EC.

[18] A reference to these treaty provisions is lacking in Art. 28(1) (Second Pillar) and Art. 41(1) (Third Pillar). That being said, the Court has jurisdiction to rule on any dispute between Member States and the Commission regarding the interpretation or the application of conventions established under Art. 34(2)(d) EU: see Art. 35(7) EU.

[19] And even lead to the introduction by the Commission of a case against the Council: see Case C-27/04 *Commission* v. *Council, OJ* 2004 C 35/5.

4.3   Executive

Furthermore, it is often said with regard to the Commission's role as 'executive' that the willingness of the Council to *delegate implementing powers* to the Commission is limited. Indeed, whereas in Article 202, third indent, EC the Treaty obliges the Council to delegate implementing powers to the Commission as a rule,[20] in practice the Council reserves the right to exercise these implementing powers directly relatively often. It goes without saying that this attitude of the Council does not contribute to the efficiency of the decision-making process of the Union and can only increase the workload of the Council itself.

4.4   Representative

The nature and characteristics of *Second and Third Pillar* cooperation also have implications for the role of the Commission as the natural 'representative' of the European Union. Indeed, because of the non-supranational character of the cooperation in these policy domains the responsibility to represent the Union lies not with the Commission but in the hands of the Presidency.[21] A recent example illustrating the reluctance of the Member States and the Council to present the Commission as its representative to third countries and other international organisations is the appointment by the Justice and Home Affairs Council of 19 March 2004 of a terrorism coordinator.[22] Indeed, whereas the Commission has over the years developed a broad infrastructure as well as broad expertise in all areas of JHA cooperation,[23] the new position was attached not to the Commission, or the JHA Commissioner, but to the High Representative for the CFSP who, as is well known, also serves as the Secretary-General of the Council.[24]

5.   THE DRAFT CONSTITUTIONAL TREATY

Having considered these developments over the years, it is now time to analyse the innovations proposed by the European Convention to the extent that they are

---

[20] For the modalities of this process of delegation, see Decision 1999/468 ('Comitology') of the Council, *OJ* 1999 L 184/23.

[21] Arts. 18 and 19 EU (Second Pillar), to be read in conjunction with Art. 37(2) EU (Third Pillar).

[22] See Council Doc. 7555/04 (Presse 94) of 19 March 2004, p. 6. Here the new position is referred to as 'counter-terrorism coordinator'.

[23] JHA covers both the substance of Title IV of the EC Treaty (Visa, asylum, immigration and civil law cooperation) and the substance of Title VI of the EU Treaty (Police and judicial cooperation in criminal matters).

[24] Art. 26 EU.

relevant to the Commission.[25] Some of these innovations are of direct importance for the position of the Commission, while others are only relevant in an indirect manner. Reference will be made to reforms concerning:

- the scope of the right of initiative of the Commission;
- the composition of the Commission;
- the way in which the President and the other members of the Commission are appointed;
- the role of the European Council;
- the role and prerogatives of the President of the European Council; and
- the creation of a Union Minister of Foreign Affairs.

A number of observations can be made regarding all these innovations.

5.1 Scope of the right of initiative

Although this aspect has hardly been mentioned in the discussions about the European Constitution, the Commission will gain a lot as regards the scope of its right of initiative once the Constitution – as currently drafted – enters into force. In principle, all legislation to be adopted by the Council (and the European Parliament) has to be based on a proposal from the Commission. In the area of freedom, security and justice,[26] in particular, the Commission's position will be strengthened in this regard. This is true, for example, for policies regarding internal and external frontiers, visas, asylum and immigration policy, as well as civil law cooperation.[27] Until 1 May 2004, the Member States and the Commission held a right of initiative in these fields, but from this date forward only the Commission possesses such a right.[28] In the area of criminal law and police cooperation,[29] where the Member States in future will keep a right of initiative alongside the Commission, the position of the Commission has also reinforced. This is because, instead of disposing of an individual right, which is the situation at present,[30] the Member States' right of initiative in this area can in future only be exercised by at least a quarter of the Member States.[31]

---

[25] For the draft Constitutional Treaty, the reference is to CONV 850/03.

[26] The EU objective referred to in Art. I-3(2) of the draft Constitutional Treaty.

[27] Title IV of Part Three of the EC Treaty. For the draft Constitutional Treaty, the reference is to Part III, Title III, Chapter IV, Sections 1-3.

[28] See Art. 67(2), first indent, EC.

[29] Title VI of the EU Treaty. For the draft Constitutional Treaty, the reference is to Part III, Title III, Chapter IV, Sections 4-5.

[30] Art. 34(2) EU.

[31] Art. I-41(3) of the draft Constitutional Treaty, to be read in conjunction with Art. III-165 of the draft Constitutional Treaty.

In connection with the Commission's right of initiative, it is worth mentioning that the principle of *Article 250(1) EC* – unanimity in the Council is required for amending a Commission proposal – will be maintained after the entry into force of the European Constitution.[32] Although at first sight this is of course positive news, the question arises what the significance of this principle will be in practice after 1 May 2004, the date of the accession of ten new Member States to the European Union, because it is hard to imagine that unanimity to amend a Commission proposal can ever be achieved in a situation of twenty-five Member States. However, if this is a correct assumption, the unanimity rule of Article 250(1) EC will in future have no practical meaning and can therefore no longer be regarded as a credible principle. In this context, it should be recalled, that in practice the Commission is often prepared to amend its proposals on the request of only one or a couple of Member States. The Commission itself is thus apparently not aware of the importance of the principle of Article 250(1) EC as an instrument to protect its right of initiative. That being said, for the purpose of credibility and practicality, it would have been better to replace the principle of unanimity in Article 250(1) EC with a form of (super-)qualified majority in the Council.[33]

5.2   Composition

Before 1 May 2004, the date of the entry into force of the Treaty of Accession, the Commission consisted of twenty members. The Commission included at least one national each Member State, but could not include more than two nationals from the same Member State.[34] According to the modalities of the Treaty of Nice,[35] as amended by the Treaty of Accession,[36] the Commission will include – as of 1 November 2004 – one national from each of the Member States. However, when the European Union consists of twenty-seven Member States, the number

---

[32] See Art. III-301 of the draft Constitutional Treaty. Apart from (the second reading in) the co-decision procedure, additional exceptions have been made for the establishment of the multi-annual financial framework (Art. I-54) and the budget procedure (Art. III-310).

[33] At present, the modalities of the 'qualified majority' are to be found in Art. 205(2) EC. As to the size of a super-qualified majority in the Council, inspiration may be drawn from the size of the qualified majority as laid down in the European Constitution: a majority of the Member States and three-fifths of the population of the Union: see Art. I-24(1) of the draft Constitutional Treaty. For example, a super-qualified majority in Council might require the votes of two-thirds of the Member States and four-fifths of the population of the Union.

[34] Art. 213(1) EC. At present the five biggest Member States (France, Germany, Italy, the United Kingdom and Spain) are entitled to present two candidates and the other Member States are entitled to present one.

[35] Art. 4(1) and (2) of the Protocol on the Enlargement of the European Union, attached to the Treaty of Nice.

[36] Art. 45(2)(d) of the Treaty of Accession.

of Commissioners will be decreased, and will thus be less than the number of Member States. When this happens, the members of the Commission will be chosen according to a rotation system based on the principle of equality, the implementing arrangements for which will be adopted by the Council, acting unanimously. From 1 May 2004 to 1 November 2004, the Commission will be composed of thirty members.[37]

On the other hand, according to the proposals of the draft Constitutional Treaty, the Commission will consist of a college comprising its President, the Union Minister of Foreign Affairs/Vice-President, and thirteen European Commissioners selected on the basis of a system of equal rotation between the Member States. The Commission President will then appoint non-voting Commissioners from all the other Member States, who will be chosen according to the same criteria as those applying to the members of the College.[38] These arrangements are supposed to take effect on 1 November 2009.[39] This means that, at this time, the Commission will consist of as many members as there are Member States.[40]

Although perhaps understandable from a political point of view,[41] these proposals obviously do not provide the best solution. Indeed, a Commission composed of so many members cannot function properly and efficiently. On the contrary, these ideas can only contribute to further bureaucracy at European level. It is also highly questionable whether proper portfolios may be created for twenty-five (or more) people. In this respect, it should be noted that individual Commissioners are already served by competent Directors-General. Moreover, in practice, the fact that certain Commission members will have voting rights while others will not, will create differences in status. The question thus arises, for example, whether suitable candidates will be interested in being appointed as non-voting Commissioners.

For all these reasons, it is clear that the number of Commissioners must be limited. The objectives of efficiency and effectiveness require us to do so. In this context, it must be remembered that the Commission has as its mandate to serve

---

[37] Art. 45(1) and 45(2)(a) and (b) of the Treaty of Accession. During this period, the Prodi Commission (twenty members) will be supplemented by one Commissioner per new Member State.

[38] It appears that these additional members will have responsibilities similar to 'staatssecretaris-sen' in the Dutch constitutional system.

[39] For these arrangements, see Art. I-25(3) of the draft Constitutional Treaty.

[40] The Prodi Commission had different ideas concerning its composition. In the European Convention, the Commission proposed a formula according to which each Member State would have a Commissioner. Decision making would in the first instance take place in the framework of 'groups' of Commissioners.

[41] For example, the new Member States, in particular, insisted on having their own Commissioner during the negotiations in the European Convention and at the IGC preparing the draft Treaty establishing a Constitution for Europe.

the general interest of the European Union[42] and not the interests of all the individual Member States. Another suggestion could be to link the number of Commissioners to the number of policy fields – all of equal weight and importance – in which the European Union is active. Still better, however, would simply be to stick to the number of fifteen Commissioners. On the basis of this principle, a rotation system should be developed according to which all Member States rotate on the basis of full equality and in fixed order.

5.3   Appointment procedures

At present – and this is the result of amendments introduced by the Nice Treaty – the President and the other members of the Commission are appointed by the Council, acting by qualified majority, after having been subjected as a body to a vote of approval by the European Parliament. In fact, the Council first nominates the person it intends to appoint as President of the Commission. This nomination has to be approved by the European Parliament. Then, acting by qualified majority and by common accord with the nominee for President, the Council adopts the list of other persons that it intends to appoint as members of the Commission. After this, the European Parliament must lend its approval to the whole college. In the end, however, it is the Council that appoints the Commission.[43]

In the draft Constitutional Treaty, a clear distinction has now been made between the President and the other members as to the appointment procedure. For example, Article I-26(1) states that the European Council, taking into account the results of the elections for the European Parliament and after appropriate consultations, shall put to the European Parliament its proposed candidate for the Presidency of the Commission. This decision of the European Council is taken by qualified majority. The candidate concerned shall be elected by the European Parliament by a majority of its members. Thereafter, it is up to each Member State, determined by a system of rotation,[44] to produce a list (in which both genders have to be represented) of three persons whom it considers qualified to be a European Commissioner. By choosing one person from each of these lists on the basis of his or her competence, commitment and independence, the President then selects the thirteen Commissioners. The President and the other candidates, including the future Union Minister of Foreign Affairs as well as the persons

---

[42] Art. I-25(1) of the draft Constitutional Treaty.

[43] On these issues, see Art. 214(2) EC.

[44] A relationship exists here with the other proposal included in the draft Constitutional Treaty, namely, to limit the number of (voting) Commissioners, apart from the President and the Union Minister of Foreign Affairs, to thirteen (see Art. I-25(3)).

nominated as non-voting Commissioners, will in the end be submitted collectively to a vote of approval by the European Parliament. The Commission's term will be five years.

Obviously, these proposals result in a more democratic procedure for the appointment of the Commission. On the other hand, it is not really the European Parliament that appoints the President or the other members of the Commission. In fact, the Parliament only confirms the choice(s) of the European Council, the Member States and the President-elect. Apart from that, the more fundamental question arises whether it is in fact absolutely necessary for the President and the other members of the Commission to be (directly) elected by the European Parliament. Indeed, the members of the Parliament are the representatives of their Member States and have been elected by their own citizens. In other words, they have a national mandate. It may therefore be argued that the (direct) election of the President (and the other members) of the Commission by the European Parliament does not necessarily serve the general interest of the European Union. A more neutral procedure might therefore even be more appropriate. In the past, for example, all the members of the Commission were appointed by representatives of the governments of the Member States.[45] Now, to the extent that national Parliaments really can influence the selection of the candidates, it cannot be argued that this procedure is no less democratic than the one that now appears in the draft Constitutional Treaty.

5.4 European Council

As is well known, the European Council referred to in Article 4 of the Treaty on European Union is at present not formally an institution.[46] On the other hand, it clearly is an important political organ. Indeed, as noted earlier,[47] the European Council has acquired great influence on the development of the process of European integration since it was convened for the first time at the beginning of the 1970s.

The Treaty of Amsterdam has further strengthened the position of the European Council by giving it specific decision-making powers in several domains.[48] The Constitution will further reinforce this tendency. Indeed, as appears from the draft text, the European Council will be formally recognised as an institution of the Union[49] and will have decision-making power in several sensitive policy

---

[45] In essence, this was the procedure that was in force before the Treaty of Maastricht.
[46] For the list of institutions, see Art. 7 EC.
[47] See section 4.1 *supra*.
[48] For example, in the area of the CFSP: see Arts. 17 (defence) and 23 (decision making) EU.
[49] Art. I-18(2) of the draft Constitutional Treaty.

areas, including, for example, the area of freedom, security and justice,[50] the Common Foreign and Security Policy[51] and, more generally, the Union's external action.[52] Once the Constitution as currently drafted enters into force, the European Council will be the institution that takes the politically most sensitive and important decisions. It will then be up to the Commission and the 'ordinary' Council to implement its framework decisions.

That being said, it is equally clear that the way the European Council operates in practice may constitute a serious threat to the Commission's exercise of its most vital prerogative, namely, its exclusive right of initiative.

As long as the European Council respects the terms and objectives of the Constitution and limits itself to issuing (purely) political guidelines[53] for implementation by the ordinary legislator of the Union, its approach can hardly be criticised. In fact, such an approach could be looked upon as the first selection, by the highest political leaders of the Member States, of the priorities laid down in the Treaty. Apart from this, it is important to recall that the President of the Commission is a full-fledged member of the European Council. He or she is therefore in a position to influence the actions of the European Council. Thus, to the extent that the further implementation – as it were in the second instance – of the treaty priorities selected by the European Council will be carried out by means of traditional, supranational procedures, a strong role of the European Council in the policy making of the Union can be accepted. Such a situation would at any rate leave the Commission with a substantial margin of discretion to secure a proper exercise of its right of initiative.[54]

5.5   President of the European Council

According to Article I-21(1) of the draft European Constitution, the European Council shall elect a President, by qualified majority, for a term of two and a half years, which is renewable once. Although the idea to appoint a President of the European Council seems at first sight a revolutionary innovation, the responsibilities of the President are modest. In this respect, it is stated that the President shall:[55]

---

[50] Art. III-159 of the draft Constitutional Treaty.

[51] Art. III-196(1) of the draft Constitutional Treaty.

[52] Art. III-194 of the draft Constitutional Treaty.

[53] See the wording in Art. 4(1) EU.

[54] In fact, a similar idea is found in the Commission's Communication 'European Governance – A White Paper', COM (2001) 428 final of 25 July 2001, *OJ* 2001 C 287/1 at p. 4.

[55] Art. I-21(2) of the draft Constitutional Treaty.

- chair the European Council and drive forward its work;
- ensure its proper preparation and continuity;[56]
- facilitate cohesion and consensus within the European Council; and
- present a report to the European Parliament after each of its meetings.

Furthermore, the President of the European Council shall ensure the external representation of the Union on issues concerning its Common Foreign and Security Policy without prejudice to the responsibilities of the Union Minister of Foreign Affairs.[57] As regards incompatibilities, it is made clear that the President of the European Council may not hold a national mandate.[58]

Based on this formulation, the position of President of the European Council may be looked at as a further contribution to the intergovernmental dimension of EU cooperation. In particular, it poses an additional threat to the institutional role of the (President of the) Commission. Indeed, by creating a permanent chair within the group of Heads of State and Government, and by not conferring this role on the President of the European Commission, the intention was apparently to reinforce the influence of the Council and the Member States over the course of the integration process. Moreover, the prerogative of the President of the Council to represent the Union on issues concerning the Common Foreign and Security Policy is at first sight contrary to the main responsibility of the Union Minister of Foreign Affairs to represent the Union in this policy area.[59] In addition, the President of the European Council may in practice easily overshadow the (activities of the) President of the Commission, who is – and will remain – a member of the European Council.[60] If this happens, it may even have a negative impact on the Commission's general performance of its tasks and duties.

5.6   Minister of Foreign Affairs

According to Article I-27(1) of the draft Constitutional Treaty, the European Council shall, acting by qualified majority and with the agreement of the President of the Commission, appoint a Union Minister for Foreign Affairs. The Minister shall conduct the Union's Common Foreign and Security Policy and will chair the Foreign Affairs Council.[61] The position of High Representative for the

---

[56] According to Art. I-21(2) this has to be done in cooperation with the President of the Commission and on the basis of the work of the General Affairs Council.

[57] Art. I-21(2), second indent, of the draft Constitutional Treaty.

[58] Art. I-21(3) of the draft Constitutional Treaty.

[59] See Art. I-27(1) and (3) of the draft Constitutional Treaty. For a discussion of this other new position, see section 5.6.

[60] For the composition of the European Council, see Art. I-20(1) of the draft Constitutional Treaty.

[61] Art. I-23(2) of the draft Constitutional Treaty.

CFSP[62] will thus be abolished. As already noted, the Union Minister will be one of the Vice-Presidents of the Commission. In the Commission, the Minister will be responsible for handling external relations and for coordinating other aspects of the Union's external action.[63]

The idea to introduce this 'double-hatted' personality represents a good innovation. Indeed, this reform reconciles a number of interests. First, it reflects the connection between economic and foreign policy issues, a relationship that is often experienced when the Community acts externally, for example, in the framework of the Common Commercial Policy or the EC cooperation policy. Second, it confirms the need for coherence and consistency in the Union's overall policies. On the other hand, where a single person is simultaneously a member of two institutions that have different responsibilities, problems may arise in the exercise of both functions. The division of responsibilities between the President of the European Council and the Minister of Foreign Affairs regarding the Common Foreign and Security Policy[64] may in practice also give rise to frictions. The success of this new position will therefore largely depend of the personality of the person appointed as Union Minister of Foreign Affairs.

6.   ANALYSIS

In the light of the innovations contained in the draft Constitutional Treaty, certain conclusions may be drawn as to the traditional role and responsibilities of the European Commission.[65]

6.1   **Initiator**

Because the supranational characteristics of EU cooperation will be strengthened as a consequence of the abolishment of the pillar structure, the Commission's role as an 'initiator' will also be reinforced. As explained earlier, this phenomenon will, *inter alia*, widen the scope of the Commission's (exclusive) right of initiative. In fact, apart from initiatives taken by a quarter of the Member States in the areas of police and criminal law cooperation, a 'joint' right of initiative, to be exercised by the Commission or a Member State, will only continue to exist in the

---

[62] Art. 26 EU.

[63] Art. I-27(3) of the draft Constitutional Treaty. The paragraph is completed by a sentence according to which the Minister, in exercising these responsibilities within the Commission, 'and only for these responsibilities', shall be bound by Commission procedures.

[64] Cf., the task of the President of the European Council, as reflected in Art. I-21(2), second indent, of the draft Constitutional Treaty.

[65] See section 2 *supra*.

areas of the Common Foreign and Security Policy and the Common Foreign and Defence Policy. In view of the politically sensitive character of these areas, this situation is acceptable, at least for a transitional period. On the other hand, the ever-stronger position of the European Council may easily overshadow the Commission's responsibility to initiate new developments and will strengthen the intergovernmental dimension of the Union's cooperation.

6.2   Guardian of the Treaties

The fact that, in future, more impetus will be given to the supranational character-istics of the Union's cooperation will also reinforce the Commission's role as the 'guardian of the Treaties'. For example, as a result of the abolishment of the pillar structure, the scope of application of the 'infringement procedure'[66] will be widened.

6.3   Executive

As to the responsibility of the Commission as the 'executive' of the Union, it is difficult to make precise predictions about future developments. That being said, the enlargement of the Union as of May 2004 obliges the Council to exploit fully the possibility of delegating implementing powers to the Commission. Indeed, in a situation where the Union is composed of twenty-five (or more) Member States, new legislative instruments should only take the form of global norms. They should have the character of framework decisions[67] that grant national authorities a sufficient margin of discretion with regard to their implementation. Their further refinement at European level should be left to the Commission.

6.4   Representative

Finally, it seems that the 'representative' role of the Commission will be strength-ened as a consequence of the creation of the position of Union Minister of Foreign Affairs, who will at the same time serve as Vice-President of the Com-mission. On the other hand, a weakening of the Commission's representative role may result from the creation of the position of President of the European Council.

The overall results are therefore mixed. However, with regard to the most vital element of the Commission's responsibilities – its initiating role – it may be

---

[66] Arts. 226-228 EC. See also 'European Governance – A White Paper', loc. cit. n. 54, at p. 21.

[67] To be distinguished from the framework decision in the sense of Art. 34(2)(b) EU, which is the Third Pillar equivalent of the Community directive. See also 'European Governance – A White Paper', loc. cit. n. 54, at p. 19.

concluded from the foregoing that, on balance, the results of the European Constitution are positive. In this context, it is worth emphasising once more that the fact that the Commission, when presenting proposals for acts of legislation, has to respect the priorities periodically set by the European Council on the basis of the Treaty objectives is acceptable. This is because, as explained earlier,[68] a prominent role of the European Council is inherent to the present stage of the European integration process and may even, to the extent that the European Council's priorities will be implemented according to the traditional supranational procedures,[69] strengthen the democratic character of overall EU cooperation.

7.   THE COMMISSION PRESIDENT AS PRESIDENT OF THE EUROPEAN COUNCIL?

The position of the President of the Commission has been strengthened by the reforms introduced by the Treaty of Amsterdam. For example, Article 217 EC states that the Commission shall work under the political guidance of its President. Furthermore, it is the President who shall decide on the internal organisation of the Commission, and the responsibilities incumbent upon the Commission shall be structured and allocated among its members by the President. It is also the President who appoints Vice-Presidents. Last but not least, a member of the Commission has to resign if the President so requests.[70]

However, the draft Constitutional Treaty introduces several innovations which, once adopted, can easily weaken the position of the President. Indeed, although the President of the Commission still is – and will remain – a full-fledged member of the European Council, his or her role may be negatively affected, on the one hand, by the activities of the President of the European Council and, on the other, by those of the Union Minister of Foreign Affairs. In view of the fact that, in future, three persons – the President of the European Commission, the President of the European Council and the Union Minister of Foreign Affairs – will potentially have a responsibility with regard to the external representation of the Union, the effectiveness of this representation will in practice largely depend of the personalities of the persons appointed to these jobs.

---

[68] See section 5.4 *supra*.

[69] This notion refers to elements such as the exclusive right of initiative of the Commission, qualified majority voting in the Council and co-decision of the European Parliament and the Council as the ordinary procedure for legislation, as well as full jurisdiction for the Court of Justice. See also 'European Governance – A White Paper', loc. cit. n. 54, at p. 6. For some Commission ideas regarding the improvement of the 'Community method', see its Communication on the Future of the European Union: 'European Governance – Renewing the Community Method, COM (2001) 727 final of 5 December 2001.

[70] For these elements, see the paragraphs of Art. 217 EC.

Therefore, and because of the nature of the Commission's responsibilities as the 'guardian' of the general interest of the European Union, an interesting option might be to formally appoint the President of the Commission as the President of the European Council. The President of the Commission could then give up his or her seat on the European Council. Such an approach would reflect the gradual increase in the initiating and representative roles of the Commission. Moreover, the idea to appoint the President of the Commission as the President of the European Council corresponds with the existence of the European Union as an autonomous organisation possessing own powers and institutions. The idea is also not contrary to the text of the Constitution, because Article I-21(3) of the draft Constitutional Treaty only states that the President of the European Council may not hold a national mandate. Furthermore, such a combination of responsibilities would strengthen the supranational character of EU cooperation as a whole. Last but not least, it would contribute to the coherence of overall EU policy.

8.   FINAL REMARKS

In summary, the mission and role of the Commission as the most original element of the European Union's institutional framework should be organised in such a way that:

- The Commission is composed of fifteen members. For the composition of the Commission a rotation system has to be developed in the framework of which all Member States rotate on the basis of complete equality.
- The Commission is chaired by a President who at the same time serves as President of the European Council.
- The Commission has an exclusive right of initiative in all EU policy domains, with the exception of the CFSP and the ESDP, where – for a transitional pe- riod – a joint right of initiative exercised by the Member States and the Commission is acceptable.
- The Commission is in a position to control the compliance of the Member States (and undertakings) with their treaty obligations in all EU policy domains.
- The Commission is exclusively competent to adopt implementing measures for framework decisions adopted by the Council and the European Parliament.
- The Commission is the natural representative of the European Union in its relations with third countries and international organisations.

On the basis of these conclusions, there is no fundamental objection to amending the principle laid down in Article 250(1) EC – unanimity in Council is required for an act constituting an amendment of a Commission proposal – in such a way that a Commission proposal may be amended by a (super-)qualified majority decision of the Council.

A Commission thus organised will not only be able to perform its roles as initiator, guardian of the Treaties, executive and representative in a decent manner. It will also be well prepared to serve a European Union that will continue to enlarge and may, at a certain moment, be composed of more than thirty Member States.

THE PRESIDENT OF THE EUROPEAN COUNCIL: THE BEGINNING OF A EUROPEAN GOVERNMENT?

Richard H. Lauwaars*

1.   INTRODUCTION

In the middle of January 2003, the French and German Governments presented a proposal regarding the institutional architecture of the European Union. This presentation occurred within the framework of the Convention that had been established to prepare a draft constitutional treaty for the European Union.[1] The most spectacular part was the suggestion to provide the Union with a full-time President, who would be chosen by the European Council for a period of five years or a renewable period of two and a half years. In essence, the President would exercise a long-term Presidency of the European Council, instead of the half-yearly Presidencies that characterise the Union as it is today.[2]

According to the Franco-German proposal, the President of the European Council would fulfil the following two functions:

- preparation, chairmanship and stimulation of the activities of the European Council and supervision of the execution of its decisions; and
- representation of the Union at international level on the occasion of meetings with Heads of State or Government, without intruding upon the powers of the Commission and its President and conscious of the fact that the day-to-day responsibility for the Common Foreign and Security Policy (CFSP) rests with the European Minister of Foreign Affairs, a post that was also proposed in the Franco-German proposal.

The draft European Constitution that was submitted by Mr Giscard d'Estaing to the European Council of Thessaloniki on 19 June 2003 dealt with the responsibilities of the President of the European Council in Article I-21 (2). This paragraph has been repeated more or less literally in the draft European Constitution that was agreed upon by the Heads of State and Government in Brussels on

---

* Member of the Dutch Council of State.
[1] *Agence Europe*, Document No. 2311, 17 January 2003.
[2] See my 'Editorial', 2 *SEW* (2003) p. 41.

The European Union: An Ongoing Process of Integration – Liber Amicorum Alfred E. Kellermann
© 2004, T.M.C. Asser Instituut, The Hague, and the authors

25 June 2004.[3] According to the first subparagraph, which concerns responsibilities that do not fall under the CFSP, the President is responsible for chairing the European Council as well as for the preparation and continuity of the work of the European Council, in cooperation with the President of the Commission and on the basis of the discussions of the General Affairs Council. The President's special responsibilities in respect of the CFSP are defined in the second subparagraph. According to this provision, the President is responsible, in this capacity and 'at his or her level', for the external representation of the Union in matters that fall within the ambit of the CFSP, without prejudice to the powers of the European Minister of Foreign Affairs.

In the aforementioned editorial of February 2003, I already expressed myself positively regarding the Franco-German proposal and, in particular, the suggestion to appoint a more or less permanent President. One of my arguments for this was that a European government, or at least a number of European government posts, cannot be found exclusively at the Commission; the governments of the Member States also have to be involved in the process, either by delegating one or more of their members or by means of the creation of a European 'hybrid' such as a European Minister of Foreign Affairs.[4] I stand by this positive judgment as far as the above-mentioned provisions of the draft European Constitution are concerned. In this article, in honour of Fred Kellermann and as a token of gratitude for so many years of friendship, I will elaborate my arguments, particularly as regards the following two aspects:

a. theory: the relationship between a permanent Presidency and the supranational model, nowadays referred to as the Community model;[5] and
b. practice: the need for a permanent Presidency and the possibility of the birth of a full-fledged European government in the future.

---

[3] Article I-21, second paragraph, reads as follows:
'The President of the European Council:
(a) shall chair it and drive forward its work,
(b) shall ensure its preparation and continuity in cooperation with the President of the Commission, and on the basis of the work of the General Affairs Council,
(c) shall endeavour to facilitate cohesion and consensus within the European Council,
(d) shall present a report to the European Parliament after each of the meetings of the European Council.
    The President of the European Council shall at his or her level and in that capacity ensure the external representation of the Union on issues concerning its common foreign and security policy, without prejudice to the powers of the Union Minister for Foreign Affairs.'
[4] 'Hybrid' because the person concerned will have to combine the functions of the High Representative for the CSFP and the Commissioner for External Relations.
[5] See R. Barents, 'Hoe constitutioneel is de Grondwet voor Europa?', 1 *SEW* (2004) p. 8, left-hand column: Because the term 'supranational' has become rather suspect in some Member States, the term 'Community model' serves as a fashionable replacement.

2.	INTERGOVERNMENTAL v. SUPRANATIONAL
	(OR COMMUNITY) METHOD

The contrast between these two methods is as old as the hills. In general, the intergovernmental method is characterised by the maintenance by each of the participating States of its own sovereignty. In supranational organisations, the participating States transfer some of their powers to the organisation.[6] Thus, the organisation should have the power to take binding decisions, decision making should take place by means of a majority vote or an organ consisting of independent individuals and the organisation should have some financial authority.[7] There is no organisation that is fully supranational, and the term should therefore be used in a relative sense. The consequence is that the distinction between supranational and intergovernmental has become 'blurred'.[8] In fact, the line between intergovernmental and supranational should be drawn along a sliding scale.

It is on this sliding scale that we have to place the European Council. The question is whether the Council comprises so many intergovernmental features that the EC can no longer be qualified as a supranational organisation or, in other words, as an organisation that is based on the Community method.[9] Timmermans answers this question in the negative. According to him, the European Council is 'since many years part of the Community method, to the extent that it operates as catcher in the back or as forerunner, where decision making according to the normal Community decision-making model fails'.[10] Drijber, too, poses the question whether the European Council detracts from the Community method.[11] His conclusion is 'that the European Council and the Community method are related to each other in a symbiotic rather than in an antagonistic way'.[12] In this connection, he also cites Jean Monnet, who after the establishment of the European Council in December 1974, wrote 'la Communauté avait à nouveau un organe moteur qui la conduirait jusqu'à l'étape du gouvernement européen...'.[13]

---

[6] H.G. Schermers and N.M. Blokker, *International Institutional Law*, 3rd rev. edn. (The Hague/London/Boston, Nijhoff 1997) p. 42.

[7] Ibid., p. 41.

[8] Ibid., p. 42.

[9] Leaving the European Union as such (i.e. the second and third pillars) out of account, the question is whether (a permanent President of) the European Council is compatible with the supranational model.

[10] 'Editorial', 9 *SEW* (2002) p. 301 (author's translation).

[11] B.J. Drijber, 'De Communautaire methode: Een noodzakelijk goed?', in *Liber Amicorum Bernard Bot* (2003) pp. 133-148.

[12] Ibid., p. 139, with an explicit reference to the opinion of Timmermans quoted above.

[13] B.J. Drijber, loc. cit. n. 11, at p. 140, referring to Jean Monnet, *Mémoires* (Paris, Fayard 1976) p. 778.

Finally, Barents has recently written that 'the view that the European Council does not "fit" in the Community model should at least be called into question'.[14]

I endorse the views of the above-mentioned authors, but I would like to add that the situation has not always been like this. On the one hand, the European Council initially placed itself right outside the Community model.[15] It was only in the so-called Declaration of Stuttgart of 19 June 1983 that the Council began to retreat from the intergovernmental model.[16] On the other hand, in order to accommodate the views of these authors, one has to broaden the concept of the supranational/Community method to a certain extent in order to take account of the fact that the European Council sometimes acts as an intergovernmental organ, for example when dealing with amendment of the Treaties.[17]

Having established that the European Council is compatible with the Community model – that it could even be described as a *part* of that model – a permanent Presidency will not add to or detract from this. This Presidency, as provided for in the Franco-German proposal and in essence maintained in the draft Constitution,[18] aims at increasing the effectiveness of the meetings of the European Council. In my view, a permanent Presidency is therefore wholly compatible with the Community model.

3.   THE NEED FOR A PERMANENT PRESIDENT AND THE POSSIBILITY OF A FULL-FLEDGED EUROPEAN GOVERNMENT IN THE FUTURE

The need for a permanent President can be justified on the following two grounds. In the first place, a Union of twenty-five Member States and about 450 million inhabitants requires a stable administration. Such an administration cannot be provided via the old-fashioned method of half-yearly Presidencies. It is here that the requirements of thorough preparation and continuity mentioned in the first subparagraph of Article I-21 (2) of the draft Constitution have to demonstrate their full advantage. Second, a permanent President is needed because in

---

[14] R. Barents, loc. cit. n. 5, at p. 9, left-hand column.

[15] See R.H. Lauwaars, 'The European Council', 14 *Common Market Law Review* (1977) pp. 25-44 at p. 42.

[16] See the Solemn Declaration on European Union adopted by the Stuttgart European Council on 19 June 1983, *Bull. EC* 6-1983, pp. 26 ff. On this occasion, the European Council declared that, when acting in respect of matters that would fall under the EC, it would do so 'as the Council within the meaning of the Treaties' (para. 2.1.3).

[17] Cf., Timmermans, text at n. 9 *supra*.

[18] The only points of difference are that the supervision of the execution of the decisions of the European Council has been deleted from the first subparagraph and that the order to respect the powers of the Commission in the second subparagraph has not been repeated, but in my view this is a matter of course.

this way the right person can be selected for the job. He or she has to be an incorruptible, more or less generally accepted politician who is able to represent the Union internally and externally in the proper way. This brings us to the second subparagraph of Article 1-21 (2) regarding the CFSP and relations with third countries, without prejudice to the powers of the European Minister of Foreign Affairs.

When writing about the permanent President and the European Minister of Foreign Affairs, are we dealing with the beginning of a European government? Let me state from the outset, as I already did in the aforementioned editorial, that such a government, if it ever arrives, cannot be formed exclusively by the Commission, because the latter deals mainly with the first pillar. Past and present members of the national governments of the Member States – the masters of the second and third pillars – should also be part of such a government. But conversely, and to this extent I disagree with Eijsbouts,[19] a future European government should also not consist exclusively of (former) members of the national governments of the Member States or, in particular, of the European Council. According to Eijsbouts, removing the powers of the European Council and upgrading the Commission to a parliamentary government could never be taken seriously.[20] However, one cannot ignore the Commission in those areas where it possesses exclusive powers, such as, for example, the Common Commercial Policy. The same applies to areas that fall either wholly or partly within the scope of its activities.

Because it finds its roots in both the European Council and the Commission, the combination of a permanent President of the European Council and a European Minister of Foreign Affairs can therefore be regarded in a very positive way and at the same time be described as the beginning of a European government.[21] The first subject of substantive Union policy that will be covered by this government is the Common Commercial Policy, which as remarked earlier[22] will be part of the job of the new EU Foreign Minister. Other areas that could be entrusted to European ministers include Economic and Monetary Union (as the personification of the Ecofin Council, which to a certain extent already operates as a separate institution), justice (as the political counterpart of the proposed European Public Prosecutor) and defence (in the framework of the Common Defence Policy). In this way, each pillar would have its 'own' minister: the first for EMU, the second for defence and the third (police and justice cooperation in criminal matters) for European criminal law, while the area that belongs jointly to the first and the

---

[19] W.T. Eijsbouts, 'Presidenten, parlementen, fundamenten. Europa's komende constitutie en het Hollands ongemak', 13 *NJB* (2003) pp. 662-673.

[20] Ibid., p. 667, right-hand column.

[21] Cf., M. Jorna, Europese wetgeving volgens de ontwerp-grondwet, preadvies voor de Nederlandse Vereniging voor Wetgevingsjuristen (April 2004) p. 5 et seq.

[22] See n. 4 *supra*.

second pillars (external relations) will be covered by the new EU Foreign
Minister and general coordination will be in the hands of the President of the
European Council.

4.   FINAL OBSERVATIONS

The above considerations, in particular those concerning the possibility of the
formation of a European government, may seem rather far-fetched. Especially as,
at the present moment, there is only a draft Constitution and, even after the
conclusion of the Treaty establishing a Constitution for Europe, there are still
many potential pitfalls that have to be negotiated. However, Europe cannot make
progress by satisfactorily looking back upon what has been achieved until now. In
the mid 1960s, when the integration process seemed to be completely stuck (at
the time of France's 'empty chair' policy), one of my former teachers said to me:
'Who will defend the unmistakable advantages of the integration process if we,
the Europeans, don't do it ourselves?'

I am sure that Fred will agree with this statement.

Almost forty years later, I have nothing to add to this remark by my former
teacher.

THE UNION MINISTER FOR FOREIGN AFFAIRS: EUROPE'S SINGLE VOICE OR TROJAN HORSE?

Jan Wouters[*]

'L'Europe verra ses institutions renforcées avec un président stable du Conseil européen, avec un ministre des affaires étrangères de l'Union qui amplifiera le rôle de chacune de nos nations'.[1]

This is one of the statements with which, on 19 June 2004, French President Jacques Chirac illustrated the 'historic' nature of the deal struck at the Brussels European Council the previous day, in which the European Heads of State and Government, after many months of protracted negotiations, reached agreement on the Draft Treaty establishing a Constitution for Europe (hereinafter, 'the Constitution').[2] The present contribution, written to celebrate Fred Kellermann in warm friendship and esteem, takes a brief look at the provisions of the Constitution concerning the Union Minister of Foreign Affairs (hereinafter usually referred to as 'the Minister') and tries to find out a bit more about the idea's origins and the nature and functions of the Minister. Will the establishment of this position lead to a Europe that speaks with one voice in the world, or could he/she be a Trojan horse for the Community method in the EU's external relations?

1. THE ORIGINS OF THE UNION MINISTER FOR FOREIGN AFFAIRS

The idea to create the position of Union Minister for Foreign Affairs emanated from the Convention's Working Group VII on External Action. One finds it floated for the first time in November 2002 in a note by Mr Gunter Pleuger, an alternate member of the Convention, with the telling title 'Double hat'.[3] The note

---

[*] Professor of International Law and the Law of International Organisations, Leuven University; *Of Counsel*, Linklaters De Bandt, Brussels.

[1] *Le Monde*, 19 June 2004.

[2] The text of the Constitution to which reference will be made in this contribution is the one laid down in CIG 86/04 of 25 June 2004, i.e. the provisional consolidated version of the draft Treaty establishing a Constitution for Europe.

[3] Working Document 17 of 5 November 2002.

The European Union: An Ongoing Process of Integration – Liber Amicorum Alfred E. Kellermann
© 2004, T.M.C. Asser Instituut, The Hague, and the authors

makes a good diagnosis of the current institutional imbroglio and the challenges ahead, and in this regard speaks for itself:

> 'Greater demands will be placed on an enlarged Union, especially in the field of external relations. The Union must enhance its capability to act in this area in order to meet these increased demands. For this it is vital that the Union speaks with one voice to the outside world on external relations issues. Moreover, the Union must strive for greater coherence in the formulation and implementation of foreign policy decisions. The relationship between the External Relations Commissioner and the High Representative for the CFSP is a key issue here. The current good cooperation due to the personal qualities of the present office holders should not blind us to the rivalry inherent in the current system. We must overcome these structural weaknesses.'

Since the maintenance of the status quo was untenable and a full merger of the two offices not realistic, the note proposed a 'necessarily less perfect compromise which would generate the maximum degree of synergy possible at present', this being 'the exercise of the two offices by one person (so-called "double hat"). The apparatuses would remain separate, also the different decision-making procedures for the different competences would remain unchanged.'

This idea did not fall on deaf ears. In the final report of the Working Group on External Action of 16 December 2002,[4] one finds the following passage in paragraph 5 (Enhancing coherence and efficiency between institutions and actors):

> 'In order to ensure better coherence between foreign policy decisions on the one hand, and deployment of instruments in the field of external relations on the other hand, the Group was of the opinion that the current roles of the HR for CFSP and the Commissioner responsible for external relations should be reconsidered. ... Notwithstanding the different positions, a large trend emerged in favour of a solution which would provide for the exercise of both offices by a "European External Representative".

> This person, who would combine the functions of HR and Relex Commissioner, would
> -   be appointed by the Council, meeting in the composition of Heads of State or Government and acting by a qualified majority, with the approval of the President of the Commission and endorsement by the European Parliament;

---

[4] CONV 459/02 of 16 December 2002.

- receive direct mandates from, and be accountable to, the Council for issues relating to CFSP. In his/her capacity as HR, he/she would have the formal, but not exclusive, right of initiative. When he/she exercised his/her right of initiative on CFSP, the Commission will abstain from taking a competing initiative. His/her initiatives on CFSP and decisions to put them into effect would not be subject to prior approval by the College of Commissioners. Decisions on CFSP matters would continue to be taken in the Council according to relevant procedures. He/she would not have the right to vote in the Council;
- be a full member of the Commission and preferably its Vice-President. In his/her capacity as External Relations Commissioner, he/she would put proposals to the College and fully participate in its decisions for matters falling under current Community competence, which would follow the normal procedures;
- ensure the external representation of the Union, replacing the current Troika.

A number of members made their agreement on this suggestion dependent on a satisfactory solution on the whole institutional setting. The Group agreed that this issue has important institutional implications, and thus has to be examined in the wider context.'

When re-reading this passage, one cannot help being struck by the level of detail of the proposal and by the fact that the Constitution's final text does not deviate terribly much from this original blueprint.

It is worth mentioning that the aforementioned final report added a footnote to the notion 'European External Representative', which reads: 'Other titles have also been put forward in the course of discussion, notably "EU Minister of Foreign Affairs" and "EU Foreign Secretary". The prevailing view was that the title of "European External Representative" had the advantage of not corresponding to a title used at national level.' The Convention's final text is, in this respect, more audacious than the one of the Working Group. The fact that the name issue was not yet resolved at the time the intergovernmental conference (hereinafter, 'IGC') took off follows, *inter alia*, from the UK Government's report 'A Constitutional Treaty for Europe' of September 2003, which mentions as outstanding issues not just 'how to ensure that the new post is properly accountable to Member States in the Council, and its relationship with the Commission', but also 'an issue as to how exactly he is described'.[5]

---

[5] Secretary of State for Foreign and Commonwealth Affairs, *A Constitutional Treaty for the EU. The British Approach to the European Union Intergovernmental Conference 2003* (September 2003) p. 29, para. 52.

2.   THE UNION MINISTER FOR FOREIGN AFFAIRS IN THE
        CONSTITUTION

Only a combined reading of a great number of provisions of the Constitution, scattered over Parts I and III, enables one to obtain a reasonable overview of the Minister's role and position.

In the context of Part I of the Constitution, the Minister appears for the first time in Article I-20, which deals with the European Council. Paragraph 2 of this article states *in fine* that the Minister 'shall take part in its [i.e. the European Council's] work'. This provision indicates, on the one hand, that the Minister shall always be there and take part fully in the European Council meetings; he or she therefore enjoys a more privileged position than the ministers or European Commissioner who, pursuant to Article I-20(3), *may* assist the European Council when the agenda so requires and the members of the Council so decide. On the other hand, the provision makes clear that, unlike the Heads of State or Government, the President of the European Council and the President of the Commission, the Minister is not a 'member' of the European Council. He or she therefore does not take part in the actual decision making of the latter.

Article I-21 on the European Council President immediately raises the problem of the demarcation of tasks between the newly-created function of President of the European Council and the Minister and thereby the more general problem of the coherent external representation of the Union. As follows from Article I-21(2), second paragraph, the President of the European Council is *inter alia* given the task to 'at his or her level and in that capacity ensure the external representation of the Union on issues concerning its common foreign and security policy, without prejudice to the powers of the Union Minister for Foreign Affairs'. Like the Minister, the President of the European Council is a new position provided for by the Constitution; unlike the Minister though, this position was not proposed by the Convention's Working Group on External Action but by France and Germany in January 2003.[6] It is interesting to reflect for a moment on the relationship between the Minister and the European Council President: one may indeed wonder whether, now the 'rivalry inherent in the current system' (see section 1 *supra*) has been dealt with pragmatically by introducing the 'double hat', the Constitution has not created a new type of rivalry. For what does external representation by the President of the European Council 'at his or her level and in that capacity' mean other than that it is this person who is supposed to meet with the Heads of State and Government of non-EU countries and do business with them? As the European Parliament has stressed, the election of the President of the European Council 'could entail unforeseeable consequences for the institutional balance of the Union'. For this

---

[6] See the contribution of Richard H. Lauwaars to the present volume.

reason, the Parliament recommended that 'the role of the President must be strictly limited to that of a chairperson in order to avoid possible conflicts with the President of the Commission or the Union Minister for Foreign Affairs and not endanger their status'.[7]

A following article in which the Minister appears deals with the definition of the qualified majority within the European Council and the Council. Pursuant to Article I-24(2) – one of the provisions on which there was tough bargaining until the last moment – when the Council is not acting on a proposal from the Commission or from the Minister, the qualified majority shall be defined as 72 per cent of the members of the Council, representing Member States comprising at least 65 per cent of the population of the Union. This provision also applies to the European Council when it is acting by qualified majority.[8] However, as unanimity remains the general rule in the area of the common foreign and security policy (hereinafter, 'CFSP') and the common security and defence policy (hereinafter, 'CSDP'), this provision does obviously not imply that each time the Minister makes a proposal, the Council shall adopt a decision by qualified majority voting (hereinafter, 'QMV'). To be fair, in the chapter on the CFSP, the Constitution provides, by way of derogation from the unanimity rule for European decisions, that the Council shall act by qualified majority 'when adopting a European decision defining a Union action or position, on a proposal which the Union Minister for Foreign Affairs has presented following a specific request to him or her from the European Council made on its own initiative or that of the Minister' (Article III-201(2), first paragraph, subparagraph b).[9] That being said, the general non-suppression of the unanimity requirement in the case of a proposal by the Minister with the Commission's support has been criticised by the European Parliament.[10]

Article I-25 of the Constitution, which deals with the European Commission, refers to the Minister as one of the Vice-Presidents of the Commission[11] and stipulates that, if a censure motion on the Commission is carried by the European Parliament, 'the Members of the Commission shall resign as a body and the Union Minister for Foreign Affairs shall resign from the Commission'[12] (see also

---

[7] European Parliament resolution of 24 September 2003 on the draft Treaty establishing a Constitution for Europe and on the convening of the Intergovernmental Conference (IGC) (11047/2003 - C5-0340/2003 - 2003/0902(CNS)) para. 20.

[8] Article I-24 (2)(a) of the Constitution.

[9] The Minister also has a role to play if a Member State intends to oppose the adoption of a European decision based on QMV: he or she 'will, in close consultation with the Member State involved, search for a solution acceptable to it'. If he or she does not succeed, the Council may, by QMV, request the matter to be referred to the European Council (Article III-201(2), second paragraph).

[10] European Parliament resolution of 24 September 2003, loc. cit. n. 7 *supra*, para. 29, last indent.

[11] Article I-25(5) of the Constitution.

[12] Article I-25(8) of the Constitution. This provision is further elaborated in Article III-243 of the Constitution.

section 3 *infra*). The Minister also appears in Article I-26, which deals with the President of the Commission. This article makes clear that the President of the Commission, the Minister and the other Members of the Commission 'shall be subject as a body to a vote of approval by the European Parliament'[13] and, significantly, that the Minister 'shall resign, in accordance with the procedure set out in Article I-27(1), if the President so requests'.[14] It is interesting to note that this provision uses the term 'resign' and not 'resign from the Commission', as in Article I-25(8) (see *supra*). The reference to Article I-27(1) (see *infra*) seems to imply that although the President of the Commission can force the resignation of the Minister – in the same way that he or she can also veto the latter's appointment[15] – the actual decision on ending his or her term of office is taken by the European Council, acting by qualified majority.

The cornerstone provision on the Minister is Article I-27 of the Constitution, which merits a quotation in full:

'1. The European Council, acting by a qualified majority, with the agreement of the President of the Commission, shall appoint the Union Minister for Foreign Affairs. The European Council may end his or her term of office by the same procedure.

2. The Union Minister for Foreign Affairs shall conduct the Union's common foreign and security policy. He or she shall contribute by his or her proposals to the development of that policy, which he or she shall carry out as mandated by the Council. The same shall apply to the common security and defence policy.

3. The Union Minister for Foreign Affairs shall preside over the Foreign Affairs Council.

4. The Union Minister for Foreign Affairs shall be one of the Vice-Presidents of the Commission. He or she shall ensure the consistency of the Union's external action. He or she shall be responsible within the Commission for responsibilities falling to it in external relations and for coordinating other aspects of the Union's external action. In exercising these responsibilities within the Commission, and only for these responsibilities, the Union Minister for Foreign Affairs shall be bound by Commission procedures to the extent that this is consistent with paragraphs 2 and 3.'

Further down in Part I of the Constitution, it is worth pointing to Articles I-39 and I-40, which contain specific provisions relating to the CFSP and the CSDP, respectively. Pursuant to Article I-39(4) '[t]he common foreign and security

---

[13] Article I-26(2), second paragraph, of the Constitution.

[14] Article I-26(3), second paragraph, of the Constitution.

[15] See Article I-27(1) of the Constitution ('with the agreement of the President of the Commission').

policy shall be put into effect by the Union Minister for Foreign Affairs and by the Member States, using national and Union resources.' Article I-39(7) states that, in the field of the CFSP, the European Council and the Council 'shall act on an initiative from a Member State, on a proposal from the Union Minister of Foreign Affairs or on a proposal from that Minister with the Commission's support'. Article I-40(4) makes clear that European decisions on the implementation of the CSDP, including those initiating a mission within the meaning of that article (i.e. missions outside the Union for peacekeeping, conflict prevention and strengthening international security[16]), shall be adopted by the Council acting unanimously 'on a proposal from the Union Minister for Foreign Affairs or an initiative from a Member State. The Union Minister for Foreign Affairs may propose the use of both national resources and Union instruments, together with the Commission where appropriate.'

In Part III, Title V, of the Constitution, which concerns the Union's external action, references to the Minister are obviously rife and we will not go through all of the provisions concerned. However, the core provision, Article III-197, merits to be quoted in full:

'1. The Union Minister for Foreign Affairs, who shall chair the Council for Foreign Affairs, shall contribute through his or her proposals towards the preparation of the common foreign and security policy and shall ensure implementation of the European decisions adopted by the European Council and the Council.

2. The Minister for Foreign Affairs shall represent the Union for matters relating to the common foreign and security policy. He or she shall conduct political dialogue with third parties on the Union's behalf and shall express the Union's position in international organisations and at international conferences.

3. In fulfilling his or her mandate, the Union Minister for Foreign Affairs shall be assisted by a European External Action Service. This service shall work in cooperation with the diplomatic services of the Member States and shall comprise officials from relevant departments of the General Secretariat of the Council and of the Commission as well as staff seconded from national diplomatic services of the Member States. The organisation and functioning of the European External Action Service shall be established by a European decision of the Council. The Council shall act on a proposal from the Union Minister for Foreign Affairs after consulting the European Parliament and after obtaining the consent of the Commission.'[17]

---

[16] See Article I-40(1) of the Constitution.

[17] A declaration on this article will be incorporated in the Final Act, in which the IGC declares that, as soon as the Constitution is signed, the Secretary-General of the Council, the High Representative for the Common Foreign and Security Policy, the Commission and the Member States should begin preparatory work on the European External Action Service.

3.   NATURE AND FUNCTIONS OF THE MINISTER

The provisions quoted above make it possible to develop a number of reflections on the nature and functions of the Minister. The *functions* are very important and comprehensive, ranging from the preparation – through the right of initiative[18] – management and implementation (including, to some extent, the oversight of Member States' implementation[19]) of the EU's external relations policies to the chairing of the Council of Foreign Affairs and the external representation of the European Union towards third countries, in international organisations and at international conferences.

What is the *nature* of the beast? It has to be said that the 'double-hatted' nature of the Minister makes him or her a rather peculiar animal within the EU's institutional architecture. On the one hand, he or she is fully part of the Commission, one of the Vice-Presidents of this institution and responsible within the latter for external relations and coordination of other aspects of the EU's external action. In addition, the Commission's President can force him or her to resign. On the other hand, the Minister's 'Communitarian' flank is, all in all, described in rather explicit terms: the restrictive wording of Article I-27(4) (see section 2 *supra*) makes very clear that Commission procedures will only be binding for him or her when exercising responsibilities within the Commission, and even then only to the extent that this is compatible with his or her CFSP and Council-related functions.[20] The Minister's institutional position and tasks appear to make him or her much more of a Council person: he or she presides over the Foreign Affairs Council, conducts, prepares and implements the CFSP and the CSDP and receives Council mandates in this respect. All of this raises important questions of institutional loyalty but also of accountability and checks and balances. As far as the loyalty issue is concerned, it is interesting to point to the Minister's important duty of ensuring the consistency of the EU's external action. This does not only apply to his or her position within the

---

[18] Any Member State, the Minister, or the Minister with the Commission's support, may refer to the Council any question relating to the CFSP and may submit to it initiatives or proposals as appropriate. In cases requiring a rapid decision, the Minister, at his or her own initiative or at the request of a Member State, shall convene an extraordinary meeting of the Council within 48 hours or, in an emergency, within a shorter period (Article III-200(1) and (2)). In some cases, the Minister even has an exclusive right of initiative, e.g. the appointment of a special representative (Article III-203 of the Constitution).

[19] See Article III-195(2), third paragraph, of the Constitution, pursuant to which the Council and the Minister shall ensure that the Member States comply with the principles of active and unreserved support for the CFSP in a spirit of loyalty and mutual solidarity, of cooperation to enhance and develop mutual political solidarity between Member States and of refraining from any action which is contrary to the interests of the Union or likely to impair its effectiveness as a cohesive force in international relations.

[20] It is interesting to read this provision together with the rather strict wording of Article III-209 of the Constitution.

Commission (Article I-27(4), see section 2 *supra*): the Minister is more generally required to assist the Council and the Commission to ensure consistency between the different areas of the EU's external action and between these and its other policies (Article III-193(3), second paragraph).

To whom is the Minister accountable? It is interesting to note European Parliament President Cox's statement in his speech to the European Council in Thessaloniki on 19 June 2003. Referring to one of the improvements contained in the Constitution, Mr Cox mentioned the fact that 'it provides for a unified Foreign Affairs structure under a Minister responsible to the European Council, but accountable to Parliament'.[21] However, the Minister's accountability to the European Parliament apparently only applies to one of his or her hats, namely, in his or her capacity as Member/Vice-President of the Commission. This is also clear from Articles I-25 and III-243 of the Constitution, which demonstrate that there is life for the Minister after the Commission: if a motion of censure were to be carried out in the Parliament, 'the Members of the Commission shall resign as a body and the Union Minister for Foreign Affairs shall resign from the Commission.' Despite his or her double-hattedness, the Minister is strongly linked to the Council and the intergovernmental approach therefore seems to prevail: in any event there will be accountability *vis-à-vis* the European Council, which appoints the Minister and may end his or her term.[22] One might therefore imagine that some see in the Minister a Trojan horse for the Commission and, more generally, for the Community method as far as the EU's external relations are concerned. That being said, it could also be argued that the power of the President of the Commission to request the resignation of the Minister is – at least in theory – a powerful weapon to prevent this 'Trojan effect' from happening, or at least from derailing too much. Be that as it may, the ambivalence of the Minister's status appears to find an extension in the status of the planned European External Action Service. If anything, the wording of Article III-197(3) [(see section 2 *supra*) seems to indicate that the Action Service will not be 'a joint administration within the Commission' as the European Parliament had proposed.[23]

---

[21] Quoted in the Opinion of the European Parliament's Committee on Foreign Affairs, Human Rights, Common Security and Defence Policy of 9 July 2003, attached to the Report on the Constitution of the EP's Committee on Constitutional Affairs of 10 September 2003 (A5-0299/2003) p. 24.

[22] Ibid.

[23] European Parliament resolution of 24 September 2003, loc. cit. n. 7 *supra*, para. 23. Note that the opinion of the European Parliament's Committee on Foreign Affairs, Human Rights, Common Security and Defence Policy of 9 July 2003, attached to the Report on the Constitution of the EP's Committee on Constitutional Affairs of 10 September 2003 (A5-0299/2003) p. 24, favoured a '*single* administration within the Commission' [emphasis added] and adds that 'the current wording of the Draft Constitutional Treaty brings a greater risk of confusion'. See also the conclusions of the Committee on Foreign Affairs, Human Rights, Common Security and Defence Policy at p. 26, para. 4.

Finally, what is clear by now is that the appointment of the President of the Commission, the President of the European Council and the Minister will be part of one integrated political exercise and balancing act. The IGC indeed decided to add a declaration to the Final Act regarding Articles I-21, I-26 and I-27 in which it is stated that, '[i]n choosing the persons called upon to hold the offices of President of the European Council, President of the Commission and Union Minister for Foreign Affairs, due account is to be taken of the need to respect the geographical and demographic diversity of the Union and its Member States.'

4.   CONCLUDING REMARKS

The Minister is an interesting innovation of the Constitution. The position may lead to the European Union speaking more with a single voice in the world and, in that sense, to a further strengthening of the European Union as a global actor. However, the present contribution indicates that the new function raises many issues, especially in terms of institutional loyalty, accountability and checks and balances. The Minister is not a panacea for a lack of political will, and the creation of the position does not, of course, as such lead to a more coherent and forceful foreign policy. In that respect, the instruments and decision-making procedures of the CFSP and the CSDP may still need further revision and fine-tuning. A Minister whose hands are tied behind his or her back due to a lack of consensus among Member States does not make for a powerful foreign policy either.

It will be interesting to see how the Minister will prevail through the upcoming ratification and referenda debates. It has already been argued by some that the creation of a Minister of Foreign Affairs is tantamount to a European 'super State'. It will also be interesting to see how the creation of the Minister and of the President of the European Council will contribute to the debate on a 'European government'. It has already been deplored in the European Parliament that the Convention and IGC did not create a Minister for Economic Affairs in order to make the economic dimension of EMU work better and implement the Lisbon strategy.[24] Europe has challenging times ahead, dear Fred.

---

[24] See the Opinion of the EP's Committee on Economic and Monetary Affairs of 2 September 2003, attached to the Report on the Constitution of the EP's Committee on Constitutional Affairs of 10 September 2003 (A5-0299/2003) p. 40, para. 5.

THE MEMBER STATES UNDER THE CONSTITUTION: PRELIMINARY INVESTIGATIONS

W.T. Eijsbouts[*]

1.   THE MESSAGE

The Draft European Constitutional Treaty sends a message loud and clear about the Member States' future in the European Union. It appears in Article IV-7. This key provision, essentially maintaining the mechanism of Article 48 EU, leaves the Member States fully in charge of future amendment or revision. The message is that the Member States are not on the way to being phased out, let alone eclipsed, by the Union's evolution. *The Member States are here to stay and to hold centre stage.*

As disturbing as it is simple, this message will be the subject of the following pages. It raises a number of desperate, seemingly rhetorical questions. Is this the end of supranationalism and the community method? Is it the final blow to the illusion of Europe as a political entity? Finally, is it not blatantly inconsistent with the very idea of an EU *constitution*?

This last incongruity provides the most convenient launching pad for the present discussion. There seems, indeed, to be a sheer contradiction between the title of the document ('Constitution') and its Article IV-7, which leaves amendment in the founders' hands. There is nothing wrong, to be sure, with the instrument itself having the character of a treaty and being called a 'Treaty establishing a Constitution for Europe'. Many national constitutions, notably that of the United States, have been created by means of a treaty and still bear that character (cf., Art. VII of the US Constitution). No, the problem lies with the *continued* predominance of the original contracting parties in its further existence and evolution. According to classical constitutional wisdom, a real constitution, once created, takes further amendment out of the founders' hands, assigning this task to the institutions it has called forth. The *'constituant'* is replaced, in the words of France's revolutionary priest and constitutional authority, Emmanuel Joseph Sieyès, by the *'constitué'* (cf., Art. V of the US Constitution and Art. 79 of the German Basic Law). This is

---

[*] Professor of European Law, Jean Monnet Chair of European Constitutional Law and History, University of Amsterdam.

The European Union: An Ongoing Process of Integration – Liber Amicorum Alfred E. Kellermann
© 2004, T.M.C. Asser Instituut, The Hague, and the authors

what defines the creation of a new State and sets off its constitution from a treaty, which is amended (and can be terminated) by the original constituant(s) – hence the contradiction.

Contradiction is a logical category, however; the life of the law, as life in general, is not a matter of logic (cf., Holmes). In this paper, the paradox will be turned into an urge to rethink some of the European Union's fundamentals. It will send us into uncharted but promising constitutional territory. First, this paper seeks to address the above-mentioned incongruity. Then, it will recast the Member States into a new capacity, namely, that of an EU institution. Finally, it will open up further perspectives on this line of thought. These perspectives are much wider than the present author expected at the outset, and they can therefore only be hinted at. Let it be seen as a tribute to Fred Kellermann's style of life and action that all this should be attempted by using somewhat unorthodox forms of legal and practical thinking.

2.   AUTONOMY

How square and conclusive is the contradiction between the instrument's title of 'Constitution' and its Article IV-7, which leaves amendment in the hands of the founders? A constitution is a document formally expressing political autonomy for a body politic. Its amendment by external powers is a formal denial of such autonomy. Autonomy consequently is the key quality to be discussed. It is the flexible version of that quality of a political community which in legal discourse has settled under the term of sovereignty and has fossilized into conceptual intransigence. This is one good reason, among others, why we prefer using the older concept of autonomy. Like sovereignty, political autonomy is not a strictly legal quality, but it lends itself well to legal expression and discussion

Autonomy for a community is best expressed by a legal rule that simply takes evolutionary powers away from the original creators. But this is by no means the only way of expressing it, let alone a full condition. The European Union itself is a case in point. It has long been established that the European Communities enjoy appreciable autonomy in relation to their Member States. This autonomy was expressed, if not created, by the Court of Justice in its early case law and has been developed by way of further case law and practice. It is embodied in doctrinal chapters that are the stock of every textbook on EU law. In *Costa-ENEL*, the Court stated that the Community's legal order was entitled to its constitutional autonomy. In *Les Verts*, the same Court later ventured into qualifying the EC Treaty as a 'constitutional charter.'

Now one need not rely on such self-enhancing qualifications, even if they come from law courts. Autonomy is not created by its expression in ECJ judgments.

What seems more conclusive is that the Member States themselves have not only acquiesced in this evolution but that they have furthered it. They have gone along with the Court's logic of supremacy, direct effect, and so forth. They have learnt to appreciate these doctrines even more than the celebrated European citizens have (who as yet remain to be enchanted). Even if most of the Member States stick to the formality of their own sovereignties individually, they know that, in the context of the Union, its relevance is mostly negative and consequently limited. They have learnt to appreciate the enhanced (if complicated) capacity for action obtained through the use of sovereign powers pooled and wielded by the EU institutions.

This explains that there is, as a matter of fact, *autonomy of action* for the Union's institutions. What is more important and more difficult to grasp is that there has also proved to be, as a matter of fact, *autonomy of evolution* for the Union. The Member States individually have very often been overruled or outwitted by the circumstances and by each other, not to mention forces such as historical necessity, into accepting a new structure for the Union which, had they been asked individually, they would have rejected out of hand. There is no need to give many examples, as they abound. Most famous is the majority decision forced on the 1985 Milan European Council by Italian Prime-Minister Bettino Craxi to start negotiations leading to the Single Act, in which Margaret Thatcher was simply outvoted. This did not prevent the Single Act from quickly materializing and being a success, and from being exploited mostly by the same Mrs Thatcher and her successors.

The question now is how to reconcile this actual autonomy of evolution with standard constitutional logic, which rules out the former in a situation where the founders have a monopoly on revision. To begin answering this question it helps pointing out that every real constitutional structure has not one but three different sources. Next to constitutional legislation (leading to formal constitutions, basic laws, etc.), there is first constitutional *case law*. Much of present-day constitutional structure in countries is made up of case law. Students of constitutional law in the United States get little but case law to read, and thus it is in many countries. And thus it is in the study of EU law.

Apart from constitutional legislation and case law, the third and least studied source of constitutional structure and, notably, *evolution*, is the category of rules referred to as 'constitutional practice'. This source-category covers rules that arise not out of legally prescribed legislative or judicial procedure but out of the crude settlement of political conflicts or political expediency in practice. In the United Kingdom, such rules are often called 'conventions', in other countries 'unwritten constitutional law'. Their legal character is undecided, however, which is not a problem as they are neither created nor applied by judicial institutions. Not only their creation but also their evolution is attended to by political practice. In the

United Kingdom, as in the Netherlands and other countries, crucial and fundamental parts of the constitutional structure – first of all the 'confidence principle'
premising a cabinet's life on support by a parliamentary majority – are conventional in nature. They have been created and are both tested and enforced not in
court but in day-to-day political life. In fact, they are the best and most subtle
feelers of the constitution into the realities of situation and evolution.

If constitutional structure has three distinct sources, its evolution also proceeds
not through just one but through three different channels. This is the simple and
sufficient reason for arguing that autonomy of constitutional origin and evolution
does not absolutely require formal autonomy of statutory constitutional amendment. True, we like to see a constitution as not only a structure but also as the
moment or rather the *act* of constituting a new political body. Such a 'constitutional moment' is best and most clearly furnished by the formal adoption of a
binding constitutional document transferring power from outside to inside the
system. But autonomy may also come into being and evolve through case law and
practice. In such cases, the temporal element of passage is more difficult to grasp,
and this is what we now need to do. Lacking a clear constitutional moment, or
constitutional turn, ambiguity will persist regarding the status of the political
body in question. In *temporal* terms (ambiguity is a mere *logical* category), we
will find that there is a situation of *suspense*. Suspense (from *sus-pendere*, to hang
up) is literally a situation in which the conditions or elements for a new structure
are being generated and brought into circulation, but are prevented from falling
into place, like solvables in a solvent. This is the present constitutional situation
of the European Union with which scholars are having such a hard time: there has
been constitutional justice for decades; constitutional practice for almost as long
(notably in the form of intergovernmental and interinstitutional political deals);
there are constitutional elements of government and representation; and there is a
constitutional discourse. All these elements are waiting for a snap of the fingers
or a decisive moment to land (crystallize, precipitate) into objective reality.

The Constitutional Treaty's adoption might, but need not, provide this land-
ing. Such has become the European integration's addiction to its state of suspense
that we should not be surprised to find it extended in a significant measure *even
beyond* the eventual formal Constitution's adoption.

This condition of prolonged suspense requires a sophisticated treatment of the
temporal aspects involved in the Union's constitutional turn. What you are now
going to read is not rhetorical alchemy but normal thinking practice applied to a
theoretical problem. First, we need to acknowledge at this moment that it is
possible and increasingly probable that the Union will somehow and sometime
take a constitutional turn and that this will involve many of the above-mentioned
elements which have already been brought into circulation or suspense. These
will then settle into an unambiguous, objective structure. This allows us to qualify

those elements as constitutional from the point in time of their origin (*ex tunc*). Examples of such elements are *statutory*, such as the motion of censure (Art. 201 EC), *judicial*, such as direct effect, and *conventional*, such as the Luxembourg compromise, the Ioannina Compromise and various interinstitutional agreements.

This means that we may *already* adopt a reading of the situation that draws to some extent on this possible or probable reality. In a way, this reality may be considered as already existing, insofar as that, at some later point in time, it may turn out with hindsight already to have existed presently (May 2004) and before.

Insofar as this is so, and always subject to this proviso, we are now in a position to redefine that element in the structure that concerns the Member States and to proceed with the business at hand, which is to recast the Member States, jointly, as an institution of the Union.

3.   THE MEMBER STATES JOINTLY

As has now been demonstrated, the hypothesis of an existing European constitutional situation is *not* affected by the fact that the Member States are still posing as *'Herren der Verträge'*. The opposite then becomes envisageable. If and insofar as there is a Constitution, and the Member States wish to be in charge of its modification, constitutional logic reverses steam, putting these same Member States in charge and allowing them to be recast as an EU institution empowered under the Treaties.

Indeed, the power of treaty making and amendment is the most formidable power in the life and function of European Union. Treaty making and amendment create both the basic substantive norms valid throughout the Union and the legal bases for the latter's further action. This power is being applied with increasing frequency and success. Between 1986 and 2004, there has been a linear acceleration in the rhythm of Treaty creation and modification (1986, 1992, 1997, 2001 and 2004). There is no denying that the institution wielding this power should be paramount over the others on the Union power map. Officially that institution is mentioned nowhere in the present Treaty nor in the Constitutional Treaty. It is not the Council, nor the Commission, nor the Parliament. It is not even the European Council, nor any combination of the former. The agent is, in fact, the Member States acting in concord, under double check of unanimity (Art. 236 EC and later Art. 48 EU).

Under purely institutional logic, this would lead to the same impasse or contradiction as before, only from the other side. The fact that the most important power in a system does not lie with its institutions is, again, a denial of the system's constitutional status. This is no news. The news is that, obversely, constitutional status for the system will tend to draw this powerful agency inside.

In other words, if we adopt the idea, real or hypothetical or somewhere in between, of some constitutional quality for the Union, then the Member States may be *read into* the Union's constitutional structure. Such a reading becomes all the more compelling as these Member States stick to their amendment monopoly with greater determination.

This modest logical realism is confirmed by standard historical constitutionalism. Historically, outside powers have often been key players inside constitutional polities. There have been times when kings considered themselves above their constitutions. By force and by law, however, such kings have gradually been drawn inside and under their own constitutions. This is the force of the great evolution from which the European constitutional tradition was built. To be real and not a mere sham, any constitution must contain the key holders of power. It need not include or control them fully. There will always be residues of power that are uncontained. But the constitution has no business leaving them out altogether, save to lose the right to its very title.

The 'Member States Jointly', as we may call the institution, has become or is becoming an institution through a combined and successive set of circumstances, both legal and political. The principal legal circumstance is the existence and repeated implementation of Articles 236 and 237 EC Treaty and their successor provisions, Articles 48 and 49 EU. These provisions have consolidated the Member States into a compound, forcing them to act as a single body for revision of the EU Treaties and the accession of new Member States. This extremely rigid legal procedure was meant originally as a guard against light-hearted change. It turned into an asset for dynamism when, at the end of the Cold War and the 'return of history', combined with the accession urge of newly independent European States, it actually became imperative to adapt and modify the Treaties with increasing frequency. This is how the *political circumstance*, the second ingredient, arose. Necessity repeatedly drove the Member States together into their compound, consolidating them together into a distinct element of political reality.

The Union has always been a dynamic entity. For a long time, between 1950 and 1990, when treaty amendment was difficult, it was mostly judicial and bureaucratic activism that took care of this potential. In 1974, purely as a result of political practice, the European Council was created. However, these channels became insufficient in 1989 after the fall of the Berlin Wall when, from being a heavy constraint on modification and accession, as they were intended, Articles 48 and 49 turned into a legal power crucial to the Union's subsistence in Europe's demanding and turbulent reality. At this time, it was patently obvious that neither the European Parliament nor the other EC institutions had the capacity to master this situation. In fact, the only institution with such capacity proved to be the European Council, representing the Member States in an existential fashion and as a political compound. This is how the Member States themselves could legitimately begin to understand the need to and possibility of remaining in charge for the time being. And this is why it is essential for the other parties involved to draw these Member States inside the EU structure, like in the case of the European Council.

The first step on the way to submission is definition.

4.   DEFINITION

We are not arguing that the Member States will or need to be swallowed whole, together or apart, into the Union's Constitution. That would obviously be nonsense. The only thing that constitutional logic indicates, in combination with the Member States sticking to their treaty-making power, is that these Member States should not be left wholly outside. Hence it is necessary and realistic to devise some limited capacity and some modest format for them to be understood, apart from their many other capacities, as a Union institution.

Once admitted as an institution, the Member States need to have their nature and action defined. In comparison to other institutions, the Member States are subject to few constraints of a logical or temporal character. When acting to amend the Treaties, they are largely free as regards both the form and the substance of their action. When acting to select justices or other functionaries for the Union, or to adopt the Union's own resources decision, they are under the Treaties' logical and temporal constraints. When acting fully outside the Treaties, the Member States are mostly under mere factual constraints of solidarity.

The first question to be solved is of a formal nature: can there exist any EU institutions other than those expressly defined and empowered in the Treaties (or Constitution)? To answer this question one needs to look into the term 'institution'.

The word 'institution' can be used either in a definite and restrictive sense or in an open and general sense. In the restrictive sense, EU institutions are only those explicitly given that name and status by the Constitutional Treaty. This is presently the case with the original EC institutions as mentioned in Article 7 EC. In a *general* sense, institutions are those bodies or collectivities that are to a relevant extent actually defined by the organization and its life and that wield actual powers under its charter or other basic rules of constitutional practice. In the Union context, bodies like Coreper and the famous regulatory committees serve as examples of institutions that created themselves, so to speak, and only subsequently entered the system's formal set-up.

The most powerful example of such an institution created outside the Treaty is, of course, the European Council, which created itself in 1974. It is useful to consider this example more closely.

To define the European Council's constitutional position on the EU power map, the present Treaties do not suffice. One needs to take the general legal and political life and structure of the organization as a basis of reference and analysis. The European Council is crucially instrumental in the process of EU legislation and even treaty making. This role is absent from the Treaties and all but absent from the Constitutional Treaty. Now one may stick to the fiction that the European Council plays no real role, and indeed its actions are mostly not legally binding. However, it is realistic to consider the European Council an institution of European Union, in a general sense, both in relation to the word 'institution' and in relation to the word 'European Union' (comprising the Communities). In fact, it made sense to consider the European Council an institution of the Community (in the singular, general sense) as of its foundation in 1974, even though it had no formal powers at all under the Community Treaties. Its role in EC treaty making was the same as it became in the European Union.

The European Council's evolution points towards two useful and possible amplifications of the concept of 'institution' beyond the internal legal definition. The first is to stretch the legal definition beyond the institution's internal charter. The second is to stretch the institutional definition beyond legal analysis. It is thus with legal persons in general: part of their functional system is defined outside of their organizational charter, by general contextual legal and other rules and facts.

It remains to take the step from the European Council to the 'Member States Jointly'. A similar exercise that, in the face of rearguard action, has established the former institution legally and doctrinally for the Union is now in order for the Member States. At this point, however, the present author (who went through a similar exercise for the European Council five years ago) must avow that this is beyond the scope of the present contribution. An article on this topic will be published in the first volume of *European Constitutional Law Review* of 2005.

5.   CONCLUSION, RELATIVISM AND PERSPECTIVES

The basic argument made in this paper is that it is feasible and even intelligent to incorporate the Member States into the Union's institutional framework. Far from conflicting with the Union's constitutional status, as it would appear to do at first sight, this inclusion might constitute the Constitution's greatest single novelty. The *possibility* arises from the admission that there are and have been other ways for the Union to acquire essential autonomy and constitutional status than through the express surrender by the founders of their treaty-making power. Once this is admitted, it can be understood how treaty making and other key powers held and exercised by the Member States jointly are part of the Union's autonomous existence, released from the Member States individually. The following step is to define the Member States jointly as a Union institution.

This initial investigation goes no further than this and merely opens up perspectives for inquiry and discovery. To conclude, let us look at some of these promises or perspectives. First, this investigation enables us to escape from the sterile opposition between the mutually exclusive conceptions of the Union as either an intergovernmental or a supranational body, by showing that it is possible to account for the full involvement of the Member States in the Union while allowing for the latter's original and constitutional evolution.

Second, this reading provides the constitutional stamp of approval for the Union's description as a 'federation of States' by Jacques Delors, a term that is often treated as desperately hybrid.

Third, on a practical level, it signals hope for other EU institutions so far blatantly excluded from the key power of amendment, notably the European Parliament. Once the Member States have worked their way into becoming an EU institution, i.e. a *constitué*, wielding the power of constitutional amendment, this power will have become a Union power. The ability to carve out a share of this immense and crucial power has thus moved within the reach of other institutions, notably the European Parliament. It need not be a matter of formal constitutional revision. Practice is preferable.

EUROPEAN UNION EXECUTIVES: OUT OF THE SHADE, INTO THE SUNSHINE?

Deirdre Curtin*

1.   INTRODUCTION

Fred Kellermann has been prominent from the very early days among those Dutch lawyers who welcomed the incoming tide of EEC law (as it then was known) into the estuaries and up the rivers of the Dutch legal landscape. His open mind and commitment to the foundational ideals of legal integration are tangible from his very earliest writings to his more recent activities assisting the latest batch of Member States in joining forces in the wetlands of the European Union. In the time span of Fred Kellermann's activities, the tasks and terrain of EU lawyers has increased considerably in complexity. For many decades, EU lawyers could afford to focus their attention and consequent analysis on the formal components of the institutions and in particular the legal texts governing their activities. Even in the aftermath of the Treaty of Maastricht in 1993 this was the accepted legal perspective. It followed that for EU lawyers who read only the wordings of the respective Treaties, at any rate, the new European Union did not represent an institutional unity with the European Community and, moreover, that only the traditional European Community could be considered an international organisation in legal terms.[1] It has only been in relatively recent years that a more nuanced approach has taken into account more of the informal components of the institutions as well as what has been termed the legal and institutional 'practices'

---

* Professor of International and European Governance, Utrecht School of Governance, University of Utrecht.
[1] See, for example, J.H.H. Weiler, 'Neither Unity Nor Three Pillars, The Trinity Structure of the Treaty on European Union', in J. Monar, et. al., eds., *The Maastricht Treaty on European Union, Legal Complexity and Political Dynamic* (Brussels, European Interuniversity 1993) pp. 49-62. See C. Koenig and M. Pechstein, *Die Europäische Union: der Vertrag von Maastricht* (Tübingen, Mohr 1995) pp. 6 and 20-63. See also R. Dehousse, 'From Community to Union', in R. Dehousse, ed., *Europe After Maastricht* (Munich, Beck 1994) p. 5; H.G. Schermers and N.M. Blokker, *International Institutional Law*, 3rd edn. (The Hague, Martinus Nijhoff 1995) p. 977; and R. Barents and L.J. Brinkhorst, *Grondlijnen van Europees recht*, 7th edn. (Alphen aan den Rijn, Samson H.D. Tjeenk Willink 1996) p. 471.

The European Union: An Ongoing Process of Integration – Liber Amicorum Alfred E. Kellermann
© 2004, T.M.C. Asser Instituut, The Hague, and the authors

that are often neglected when analysing the European Union.[2] This approach revealed that, as a matter of *practice*, various institutions developed their roles in a manner which evolved towards more institutional unity across the spectrum of very different policy areas, and that the rigid distinction between the supranational and intergovernmental 'pillars' was more flexible and even unitary in terms of the approach taken than a reading of the appropriate Treaty texts would indicate.[3] The development of such legal and institutional 'practices' is of course an incremental and cumulative process, often leading to formal changes in the constituent Treaties or acts themselves or as explicit 'interinstitutional agreements'.

In applying this legal-institutional approach, formal and informal activities, rules, processes, declarations and so forth are included in the analysis of the manner in which the role and tasks of an institution have evolved. This is particularly informative with regard to the Council of Ministers, which is traditionally conceptualised as the intergovernmental organ *par excellence* and which was conceived as the pivotal decision-making organ (alongside the European Council) in the context of the two new 'intergovernmental' pillars. What had begun to emerge in the legal practices over the years with regard to the executive functions of the Council has been confirmed in the Treaty establishing a Constitution for Europe (hereinafter, the 'Constitutional Treaty'). It is clear that the Council's executive powers do not only involve the implementation of laws. Indeed, the recent practice of the Council has been to delegate such implementation tasks to the Commission, even in the field of Justice and Home Affairs (JHA). In an increasing number of cases, the Council as an executive power has a function *independent* of the legislature. This is the case with acts in the Common Foreign and Security Policy (CFSP) area, by which the European Union defines its policy towards third countries, some acts in the field of police cooperation, as well as acts concerning the workings of Economic and Monetary Union, which aim at reacting to particular situations that are hardly liable to *ex ante* legislative regulation. This can be termed the 'autonomous' role of the Council acting as an 'executive' power.

The European Council was for many years considered to operate outside the framework of the formal Treaty provisions and to constitute an 'informal' organ with a highly political role. Gradually, though, the European Council was given specific powers and competences in various Treaty amendments. Peter Ludlow

---

[2] M. Jachtenfuchs and B. Kohler-Koch, 'Governance and Institutional Development', in A. Wiener and T. Diez, eds., *European Integration Theory: Past, Present and Future* (Oxford, Oxford University Press 2004) pp. 97-115.

[3] D.M. Curtin and I.F. Dekker, 'The EU as a "Layered" International Organisation: Institutional Unity in Disguise', in P. Craig and G. de Búrca, eds., *The Evolution of EU Law* (Oxford, Oxford University Press 1999) pp. 83-136.

describes the European Council as 'the arbiter of systemic change, the principal agenda setter, the ultimate negotiating body and the core of the EU executive.'[4] According to the European Union's own website 'only the European Council can give the European Union a shot in the arm... It has acquired such importance and legitimacy today that it is difficult to imagine that there was a time when it did not exist.'[5] At the same time, one of the problems is that the European Council does not keep to its broad mandate but increasingly, as noted by Javier Solana, Council Secretary-General and High Representative for the CFSP, 'is ... asked to spend time on laborious low-level drafting work which adversely affects normal Community procedures.'[6] In other words, there is a clear example here of the growing confusion of the roles and responsibilities of the different institutions and associated bodies. This fact exacerbates the difficulties of external political supervision.

At the same time, the Constitutional Treaty attempts to formulate a much more explicit 'separation of powers' than has hitherto been the case, especially with regard to the legislative-executive distinction (legal instruments and their hierarchy). In so doing, some consider that it alters the existing 'institutional balance',[7] considered by many (the Commission and many Community lawyers) as a hitherto sacrosanct part of the EU constitutional and legal system. The most striking change to the 'institutional balance' is the fact that the European Council will now be headed by a (semi-)permanent 'President' who will steer the work in the Council and its committees. In a sense, it makes explicit what has been implicit to insiders for some time and that is the fact that, in practice, the European Union has over the course of the past decade evolved into, *inter alia*, a multiple-headed, centralised 'executive' power[8] composed not only of the Commission, which traditionally occupied the central seat in terms of federal-type executive power, but also of the Council, which has incrementally acquired more executive-type powers and a larger and more influential administration (the Council's 'Secretariat') as well as various other bodies and organs (Europol and Eurojust to mention just two).

The Constitutional Treaty attempts to inculcate a clearer distinction between, in particular, the legislative power and what is in fact the executive power. The

---

[4] P. Ludlow, *The Making of the New Europe: the European Councils in Brussels and Copenhagen 2002* (Brussels, EuroComment 2004) p. 12.

[5] See <http://www.ue.eu.int/en/info/eurocouncil/index.htm>.

[6] Report by J. Solana 'Preparing the Council for the Enlargement', Brussels, 11 March 2002, Council of the European Union, Doc. No. S0044/02, available at: <http://europa.eu.int/futurum/documents/speech/sp070302_2_en.pdf>.

[7] See, for example, B. Smulders, 'Kritische kanttekeningen bij de gevolgen van het "ontwerp-verdrag tot vaststelling van een grondwet voor Europa" voor het institutionele evenwicht', 9 *Nederlands Tijdschrift voor Europees Recht* (2003) pp. 246-252.

[8] See further Curtin and Dekker, loc. cit. n. 3, at pp. 83-136.

executive power is defined more in terms of what it is not, namely, it is not the legislature and does not adopt legislative acts: it adopts *non-legislative acts*. Despite lacking conceptual and terminological precision, the Constitutional Treaty does, for the keen reader, make *visible* that the non-legislative power in the European Union is exercised not only by the Commission but also by the Council (and in a number of cases even by the European Council). This empirical fact is confirmed at several levels in the Constitutional Treaty. Yet the Constitutional Treaty itself also falls short of 'constitutionalising' a framework for the administration of the European Union as a whole, despite the fact that its ambition and purpose is to take a unitary and coherent approach to the Union's institutional and legal framework.

2.   THE EU EXECUTIVES IN THE SHADE?

In modern political systems, executives generally have two types of power: '*political*, the leadership of society through the proposal of policy and legislation' (agenda-setting and initiation of measures) and '*administrative*, the implementation of law, the distribution of public revenues and the passing of secondary and tertiary rules and regulations'.[9] The executive can be defined as 'the part of a governmental system which takes decisions and enforces the states' will, as opposed to making laws, although modern political systems in fact allow their executives to legislate.'[10] I deliberately use the term 'executive' to span the political *and* administrative spheres and to be part of both. In other words, it expresses the idea that the administration is part of the system of government and that administrators complement the political role of those who are either elected (as in principle the Ministers in the Council/European Council) or appointed by those who are elected (in the case of the Commissioners). Moreover, it takes issue with those who try to separate the realm of 'administration' too strictly from that of politics. History teaches us in that regard that the greater the level of separation, the greater the risk that so-called administrators will overrun the realm of policy using the claim of scientific principle to handle an ever-enlarging complex of phenomena.

Traditionally, acquired wisdom would have us believe that the European Community did not have its own executive power, but rather that its decisions were in the vast majority of cases executed (implemented) by the Member States and their national executive authorities on its behalf (subject to the overriding

---

[9] S. Hix, *The Political System of the European Union* (Basingstoke, Macmillan 1999) p. 21.

[10] D. Robertson, *A Dictionary of Modern Politics*, 3rd edn. (London/New York, Europa Publications 2002) p. 178.

duty of loyalty copper-fastened in Article 10 EU). It was only in relatively exceptional cases (competition policy, for example, among a few other policy fields) that the Commission could be regarded as performing functions itself that could be considered as innately executive in nature. Of course, even that residual narrative was a little more dense given the fact that such executive power as it did indeed enjoy had been delegated to it by the Council, which factually had been conferred with the original executive power by the Treaty (Article 206 EC). Furthermore, in formally delegating the power to the Commission, the Council reined it in via an elaborate committee system composed of national experts (comitology).[11] This is a key aspect of the 'Community method'.

As time went by, the Commission as the (residual) executive power was, in a nutshell, unable to cope with the increase in its tasks over a range of policy areas, and outsourcing or contracting out to private third parties became the manner of performing some of its (executive) functions, in common with public administrations around the world.[12] At the same time the Commission set about creating a network of 'independent' Community bodies with (clearly defined) executive-type tasks, such as information collecting and so forth[13] and more recently trumpeted the creation of (a series) of much more far-reaching American-style 'regulatory' agencies.[14] This independent 'fourth branch' of government, as it is often referred to,[15] is justified by its defenders on the grounds of efficiency (technical expertise) and the legitimacy of non-majoritarian institutions.[16]

At the same time, what can be termed a parallel executive power developed in the shadows of the basic constituent texts. This basically stemmed from the fact that, in setting up and giving substance to the European Union as a novel international organisation, the Treaty of Maastricht (and its successors) omitted to provide the possibility that the new executive power acquired by the Council (especially by the Presidency and in practice by the Secretariat-General and its new Secretary-General/High Representative for the CFSP) could be delegated to the Commission and subjected to 'comitology' in due course. As a result, what

---

[11] Council Decision 87/373/EEC of 13 July 1987 (First Decision) and Council Decision 1999/468/EC of 28 June 1999 (Second Decision) laying down the procedure for the exercise of implementing powers in the Commission.

[12] See further Committee of Independent Experts, 'Second Report on Reform of the Commission – Analysis of current practice and proposals for tackling mismanagement, irregularities and fraud', Vol. I (1999) para. 2.3.4, available at: <http://www.europarl.eu.int/experts/pdf/rep2-1en.pdf>.

[13] E. Chiti, 'The Emergence of a Community Administration: The Case of European Agencies', 37 *CMLRev.* (2000) pp. 309-343.

[14] European Commission, *White Paper on European Governance*, COM (2001) 428 final, 25 July 2001, available at: <http://europa.eu.int/comm/governance/white_paper/index_en.htm>.

[15] See, for example, G. Majone, *Regulating Europe* (London/New York, Routledge 1996) p. 17.

[16] See further R. Dehousse, 'Constitutional Reform in the European Community: Are There Alternatives to the Majoritarian Avenue?', *West European Politics* (1995) pp. 118-136.

has happened over the course of the past ten years is that the Council, at precisely the same time as its legislative power developed (both as a result of its interaction with the European Parliament in co-decision and its independent legislative and policy-making power in the new policy areas and in particular with regard to justice and home affairs), developed its own original executive power in quite a substantial manner in the *EU* policy areas. In other words, the Council as an institution of the European Union acquired and exercised a series of (executive) tasks that would normally have been entrusted to the Commission under the Community system. Thus, the Presidency of the Council (aided considerably by the Secretariat-General of the Council) is responsible for representing the Union in CFSP matters, implementing common measures and expressing the Union's position in international organisations and at international conferences. The Treaty of Amsterdam strengthened this role by enabling the Council to instruct the Presidency to negotiate an international agreement on behalf of the Union and by entrusting the Presidency with the same tasks in JHA policy areas as in the CFSP.

The Presidency likes to be perceived as the Council's political 'motor': it drives things forward and has a policy planning role in setting the direction of the Council's work and ensuring that it is completed within reasonable deadlines (often the end of a particular Presidency).[17] On the other hand, what is often underestimated in this explanation is the driving role played by the bureaucracy (permanent officials) and by the national civil servants, who reside permanently in the Council's underbelly of working parties, coordinating committees (Article 36 EU), SCIFA and so on, in driving forward specific measures (within the broad parameters of policy set by the Member State holding the Presidency at a given moment in time). The General Secretariat of the Council has evolved significantly during this timeframe, from having a passive notary/registrar role to a much more active role in assisting the Presidency:

> 'not only in the application of procedures, but also in preparing for substantive negotiations; at the same time, the role of the Legal Service has become established and has developed to encompass intergovernmental conferences; in general, the six-monthly rotating Presidency with its increased role has made it more and more necessary to call upon the General Secretariat's assistance in ensuring continuity and efficiency of work by giving successive Presidencies the benefit of the experience it has accumulated over the years.'[18]

---

[17] See Trumpf-Piris Report, *Operation of the Council with an Enlarged Union in Prospect – Report* by the Working Party set up by the Secretary-General of the Council, CFSP Presidency Statement (Brussels 1999).
[18] Ibid.

Political scientists are beginning to recognise the fact that the General Secretariat of the Council indeed has a very pivotal role to play in behind-the-scenes outcomes and has even shifted outcomes closer to its own vision of the manner in which the European Union has evolved on a number of occasions.[19]

The General Secretariat of the Council has incrementally assumed a role which parallels that played by the Commission administration in other (EC) policy areas. Since the Treaty of Maastricht, it has in practice acquired specific executive tasks that would normally have been delegated to the Commission in the Community system. For example, the development of significant aspects of JHA policy-making has been based on action plans, such as the Action Plan on Organized Crime[20] or the Tampere Action Plan – this is closely linked to the emergence of a more autonomous role for the Council Secretariat. Thus, the Secretariat has been charged with the task of implementing various recommendations contained in the High Level Report. In that context, it has taken initiatives independently of the Member States themselves. More recently, a number of Council instruments have conferred the Council (in practice its General Secretariat) with tasks concerning the evaluation of implementation measures that are very similar to what is carried out by the Commission with regard to the classic EC areas. Moreover, the appointment of a High Representative for the CFSP (who at the same time serves as the Secretary-General of the Council) provided for in the Treaty of Amsterdam made this point particularly clear, as the relevant tasks include the framing, preparation and implementation of the Union's foreign policy decisions.

At the same time, the Council has in recent years set up a number of free-standing, independent organs that have incrementally acquired far-reaching powers. Thus Europol, established by multilateral Convention under the terms of the Maastricht Treaty, is in the process of acquiring operational powers, the very point vigorously denied at the time it was set up and the original Convention was ratified. Eurojust was set up more recently and was established by Council decision, not requiring Member State ratification, precisely so that its powers and tasks could be amended more easily with the passage of time. These 'Union' bodies acquire powers and executive tasks in an incremental fashion that is not very 'visible'. Some discussion has taken place concerning the fact that representatives of the European Parliament should be included, at the very least as

---

[19] See, for example, D. Beach, 'The Unseen Hand in the Treaty Reform Negotiations: The Role and Influence of the Council Secretariat', 11 *Journal of European Public Policy* (2004) pp. 408-439; and T. Christiansen, 'Out of the Shadows: The General Secretariat of the Council of Ministers', in R.M. van Schendelen and R. Scully, eds., *The Unseen Hand: Unelected Legislators in the EU* (London, Frank Cass 2003) pp. 80-97.

[20] Action plan to combat organized crime (adopted by the Council on 28 April 1997), *OJ* 1997 C 251/1-16, 15 August 1997.

observers, in order to strengthen the political supervision of the activities of Europol, but this has not been effectuated in practice. In recent years, Europol has quite extensively exercised its power to negotiate and conclude international agreements with third countries and other international organisations, most recently and controversially with the United States on the exchange of personal information. The 'political control' was provided by the Council of Ministers, which authorised the Director of Europol to conduct secret negotiations with the United States on various issues, including the exchange of personal information. The results of these negotiations were then presented to the Council and the Director of Europol was again 'authorised' to proceed to signing the agreement as negotiated. This illustrates the tip of the iceberg in terms of the external relations activities of such organs, which take place in a type of constitutional no-man's land with no public or parliamentary debate (either European or national) on the issues involved nor any possibility of scrutiny of the measure prior to its formal adoption.

The final report of the European Convention's Working Party on Justice and Home Affairs underscores the need for a clearer distinction between the Council acting in its legislative capacity and the Council exercising specific executive functions, which specifically seems to turn on what is termed 'operational collaboration'. This brought with it the (proposed) creation of a more efficient structure for the coordination of operational cooperation at *high technical level* within the Council, namely the merging of various existing working groups and redefining the mission of the so-called 'Article 36 Committee', so that in the future it can focus on coordinating operational cooperation rather than becoming involved in the Council's legislative work. The idea that this reformed structure would focus on the coordination and oversight of the entire spectrum of operational activity in police and security matters (*inter alia*, police cooperation, fact-finding missions, facilitation of cooperation between Europol and Eurojust, peer review and civil protection) took root in the Draft Constitution as proposed to the IGC. As the Committee of Independent Experts put it in its second report: 'the distinction between formulating and implementing policy, namely between policy and operational matters is a falsely rigid one, difficult to define in principle and even more difficult to apply in practice.'[21]

3.   THE EU EXECUTIVES MOVE INTO THE SUNSHINE?

The classic story with regard to both the Council and the European Council was that the issue of the 'appointment' of its members did not arise, as they were

---

[21] See n. 12 *supra*.

automatically members *ex officio* because of their status in the national domain of politics with a rotating Presidency every six months. This changed in the lead-up to and outcome of the European Convention, as the need to provide the European Union with a more permanent form of leadership became more urgent with the imminent expansion to twenty-five Member States. Some defend the role and position of a strong President of the European Council and/or the Council not only as realistically expressing the balance of power in the European Union, but also as being more democratic than a strong Commission.[22] The reasoning, in a nutshell, is that 'the European Council is composed of elected politicians who can rely on support in their own country. The manner in which the Commission members get their jobs has little to do with democracy.' The focus is thus on the leadership the European Council President can give to the Union as a whole, with the (very) long-term perspective that the European Council President can one day be directly elected by the peoples of the European Union. The implication of such arguments is that the peoples of Europe must in the meantime be happy with a President with far-reaching executive and agenda-setting powers simply on the basis that, meeting behind closed doors, he or she may once have been elected by the people of one Member State. Even that is not certain, as it is no longer provided in the final version of the Draft Constitution of July 2003 that the President must once have been a member of the European Council itself.

With regard to the other members of the European Council (and the Council), the argument is made that the decisions they may take will be indirectly legitimate since, as Article I-45(2) of the Constitutional Treaty reminds us, 'Member States are represented in the European Council and in the Council by their governments, themselves accountable to national parliaments, elected by citizens.' In other words the governments are indirectly accountable, under the system of representative democracy, to the national parliaments and ultimately to the people. However, the legitimacy that national governments can claim via national elections is rather threadbare in practice. It relies on a formalistic conception of democracy, in which a process or system is democratic if somewhere in the line of events someone was elected in free and fair elections. The House of Commons Select Committee describes the fallacy in this argument in clear terms: 'whereas members of the Council of Ministers individually are in theory accountable to their national parliaments and their electors, the role of individual Ministers in collective decisions arrived at secretly cannot be reliably ascertained and Ministers therefore cannot be held to account.'[23] This view that

---

[22] See, in particular, T. Eijsbouts, 'Presidenten, parlementen, fundamenten. Europa's komende constitutie en het Hollands ongemak', 78 *Nederlands Juristenblad* (2003) p. 662.

[23] See House of Lords Select Committee on European Scrutiny, 'The Convention on the Future of Europe and the Role of National Parliaments', Session 2002-2003, 24th Report (5 June 2003) para. 11, available at: <http://www.publications.parliament.uk/pa/cm200203/cmselect/cmeuleg/63-xxiv/63-xxiv.pdf>.

members of the Council and European Council are individually responsible to their respective national parliaments, has in practice always been highly problematic because of the fact that the Council meets in secret. Although the Constitutional Treaty proposes some change in the sense of requiring the Council to meet henceforth in public when it is discussing and adopting *legislative* proposals, many problems remain with regard to its non-legislative activities as well as with regard to all the activities of the European Council.

In conclusion, it can be said that both the Council and the European Council are ensconced very weakly in a surrounding web of politics. Their political and administrative tasks, unlike those of the Commission, are not subject to much (if any) parliamentary scrutiny (either European or national). The newly introduced multi-annual Work Programme of the Council will be presented to the European Parliament, but appears to be perceived as a largely technical exercise and not one that requires the transfer of information to and communication with national political arenas. Government ministers from the Member State holding the Presidency often appear before European Parliament committees and there is also a system whereby the European Parliament can submit oral and written questions to the Presidency of the Council. (Finally, one of the most significant procedures available to the European Parliament to force, *inter alia*, the Council to submit information is laid down in the provisions enabling it to set up a temporary committee of inquiry to investigate alleges contraventions or misadministration. Information leading to the decision to set up such a committee of inquiry may reach the European Parliament by petition or through the Ombudsman.)

In recent years, it has become especially clear that a secret administrative culture is at the heart of many of the European Union's problems and exists right across the spectrum of its institutions and organs. When the Santer Commission felt forced to resign in the aftermath of the publication of the First Report of the Committee of independent Experts in March 1999, the boils of secrecy and lack of (collective) responsibility of the Commission were rather publicly lanced. The gist of the general problem, according to the Committee, was openness and transparency, as linked with responsibility and accountability. In the Committee's view, these fundamental principles urgently needed to permeate the European Union's political and administrative culture *in all areas and at all levels*.

There are a number of very basic problems in analysing the manner in which the Council of Ministers interacts with the nascent (European) public space. The first and still prominent reason relates to the fact that many of its (non-legislative) decisions are taken behind closed doors. Moreover, the actual decisions are taken by a host of working parties and committees and are often merely rubber-stamped at the stage of Council meetings. In recent years, shafts of light have penetrated the previously opaque Council fortress, largely due to the nascent freedom of information policies and the obligations contained in the European Freedom of

Information Act.[24] At the same time, the Council in 2001 pro-actively introduced a digital register of its documents (in advance of its legal obligation to do so), which far exceeds the Commission's equivalent. Even though problems remain, the fact is that it is possible to track down the activities of many of the working parties, committees, agencies and so forth, as well as of the Council itself, by means of a dedicated and professional use of the Council's register.

Yet only those with a relatively professional approach and serious dedication to pursuing lines of inquiry can hope to have any success in reading, analysing and appreciating the significance of Council decisions or requesting access where access is not immediately available in digital form. To my knowledge, only two groups of actors have been active in this regard so far. The first falls within the category of those democratic intermediaries populated by so-called civil-society organisations with a broad public interest mandate. A well-known example of such organisations is *Statewatch*, which describes itself as

> 'a non-profit-making voluntary group founded in 1991 comprised of lawyers, academics, journalists, researchers and community activists. Its European network of contributors is drawn from 12 countries. Statewatch encourages the publication of investigative journalism and critical research in the fields of the state, civil liberties and openness'[25]

and has maintained, already for some years, a very extensive and easily accessible website and special observatories on various issues, such as one on the anti-terrorism measures under discussion post-September 11.[26] Its digital portal covers all the relevant institutions involved in the various stages of decision-making processes in the issue areas of justice and home affairs as broadly defined. The user is thus saved the task of trawling through the separate databases maintained by the different institutions and spared the need to put the different pieces of an often complicated puzzle together. It is all there, readily and easily accessible. In addition, the activities of *Statewatch* include the very pro-active activity of tracking the new documents that are placed on the Council's register on a daily basis (a not inconsiderable task) and requesting – under the rules concerning the access to documents that are now formally in place and legally enforceable via the Ombudsman – the (many) documents mentioned by title and number but not

---

[24] Regulation (EC) No 1049/2001 of the European Parliament and the Council of 30 May 2001 regarding public access to European Parliament, Council and Commission documents, *OJ* 2001 L 145/43. See further M. de Leeuw, 'The Regulation on Public Access to European Parliament, Council and Commission Documents in the European Union: Are citizens better off with their new right of access to documents?', 28 *European Law Review* (2003) pp. 324-348.

[25] See <http://www.statewatch.org/about.htm>.

[26] See <http://www.statewatch.org/observatory2.htm>.

made available to the public via the register. The practice of the Council has developed to the point where, in principle, it now makes those documents accessible to everyone (via PDF file) and not just to *Statewatch*. In other words, the self- appointed task of *Statewatch* has been to force back very actively and incrementally the curtain of secrecy still shrouding the work of the Council, by obtaining public access via the Council's register (as constantly updated) and ultimately in some cases by relaying information obtained via more classic media to the wider public sphere enabling public debate and deliberation.

The second group of actors consists of those national parliaments that have set up their own digital databases to facilitate and inform the public of the activities of their own parliamentarians (and possibly their interaction with certain expert groups on the outside). An example from this group is the First Chamber (*Eerste Kamer*) of the Dutch Parliament, which in 2003 established an elaborate website specifically in the field of justice and home affairs, where the formal role of the European Parliament has to date been small.[27] The fact that, according to the provisions of the Constitutional Treaty, the Council will (if and upon the Treaty's entry into force) be under a formal legal obligation to meet in public when adopting legislation by whatever procedure (general or specific), provides an important opening into the democratic space of the various national parliaments, although without an agreed record of what was said and done at the meetings there will be endless scope for differences of interpretation. In any event, however, the situation remains unchanged with regard to those secret meetings in which the Council adopts policy coordination measures, sets the policy agenda and discusses operational collaboration. The additional step of adopting a general rule to the effect that other non-legislative meetings should in principle also be held in public, with the option of providing for duly reasoned exceptions, was not taken or even considered in the Constitutional Treaty.

What is missing from this analysis is the fact that the Council itself does not consider that it has a role in 'communicating' more widely to the public the nature and focus of its activities in a manner that is 'digestible' for the latter, be it at European or national level. This has everything to do with the fact that the Council still labours under its foundational myth, namely, that it is an intergovernmental body that operates by a process of diplomatic negotiation and compromise and that it is not an autonomous actor in the policy process with a duty to 'communicate' widely about its plans and priorities and draft decisions. This too can explain why, unlike the Commission, the Council has not considered the fact that it too needs to develop a serious communications policy, as well as procedures and processes for consulting with interested actors before it adopts certain decisions, and why it has

---

[27] See <http://www.eerstekamer.nl>.

not seriously begun a process of linking its decision-making operations and the public sphere of communication and deliberation.

4. THE VISTA OF NON-DEMOCRATIC NON-MAJORITARIAN EU INSTITUTIONS AND ORGANS?

Constraints of space have permitted no more that a rather impressionistic sketch of the broader parameters of executive power as it has emerged at the level of the European Union over the course of the past decade in particular. What has emerged in these years is the fact that both the Council and the European Council have developed, very incrementally and not very visibly, an executive capacity and executive functions as well as (semi-)autonomous organs and agencies that carry out discrete (but at times politically and operationally important) functions. As a result of the activity in the two allegedly intergovernmental policy areas of CFSP and JHA, there has been a much wider 'contamination' with regard to other policy areas. The Constitutional Treaty can be regarded in some ways as the apotheosis of the evolution in the shadows, as it were, of institutions across the spectrum of the policy areas covered by the European Union. In a sense, the extent to which the pillar distinction does not hold up in practice underpinned much of the preparatory work of the European Convention, not only in terms of the institutions themselves but also, and importantly, in terms of the various legal instruments. Thus, for example, after the adoption of the Framework Decision on the European Arrest Warrant,[28] who could argue that this instrument was not basically the same as a EC Directive, with all the binding implications this entails, in spite of the fact that it expressly did not enjoy 'direct effect'? In addition, after the Tampere summit and its implementation track, for example, who could argue against the fact that the European Council had gradually built up a pivotal steering role in the field of justice and home affairs? Who could claim that the European Court of Justice had not incrementally acquired a much broader jurisdiction (albeit with differences) across the first and third pillars?

With regard to the Council-centred executive strand, it can only be said that there is less overt recognition of the manner in which the powers and tasks of the Council in certain policy areas are both executive in nature and parallel to those exercised by the Commission in the classic Community fields. In other words, it can be argued that what has been happening in an incremental fashion over the course of the past ten years within the European Union has been the development of two parallel administrations, each with their own (quasi-)independent 'satellites'

---

[28] Council Framework Decision 2002/584/JHA of 13 June 2002 on the European arrest warrant and the surrender procedures between Member States, *OJ* 2002 L 190/1-20, 18 July 2002.

(Community bodies/Union bodies). The difference between the two 'strands' is that the Commission is embedded into an (imperfect) accountability system tailored to the types of decisions it takes and the powers it has and that the Council (and European Council) are not, at any rate not with regard to the decisions it takes as a body.

There has traditionally been surprisingly little focus on the Council's executive tasks as opposed to its legislative role. The fact that the latter has grown quite extensively over the course of the past decade seems not only to have gone largely unnoticed but also not to have forced any serious challenge to the continuing validity of the claim that its indirect legitimacy via the national political process is adequate or tailored to the kinds of activities that take place under its institutional umbrella or the types of decisions it takes, which are far removed from any politicised public sphere. In other words, it seems that the grand architects of broad institutional design and constitutional frameworks are quite happy to continue to construct the political system of the European Union in such a manner that 'the behaviour and preferences of citizens constitute virtually no formal constraint on, or mandate for, the relevant policy-makers. Decisions can be taken by political elites with more or less a free hand.'[29] Despite all the rhetoric of ameliorating the much-vaunted 'democratic deficit' and the inclusion of a new chapter in the Constitutional Treaty on the 'democratic life of the Union', procedures for popular control continue to be avoided by Europe's governing elite. Moreover, the expansion of non-majoritarian EU institutions from which politics and parties are deliberately excluded promotes not only the depoliticisation of important policy issues (including police and judicial functions) but also the further disengagement of the citizens from an apolitical European Union.[30] If the European Union continues to side-step the issue of the growing non-legislative component of European governance, the European Constitution will leave gaping accountability deficits that will further compromise the legitimacy of the European polity. In the long term, this would put at serious risk much of the pioneering work done by EU lawyers, Fred Kellermann among them, in welcoming and accommodating this novel legal and political system.

---

[29] P. Mair, 'Popular Democracy and the Construction of a European Union Political System', Paper presented to the workshop 'Sustainability and the European Union', ECPR Joint Sessions, Uppsala, April 2004.
[30] Ibid.

THE FALL OF COMMITTEES?

Ellen Vos[*]

1.   INTRODUCTION

Does the Treaty establishing a Constitution for Europe (hereinafter, the 'Constitu-tion')[1] threaten the continued existence of comitology? Within the framework of the simplification exercise of 'Union instruments', it appears to strongly limit the role of committees that assist the Commission in the implementation of EU legislation. This seems to be in line with the Commission's vision on the future of comitology. In its White Paper on European Governance of July 2001,[2] the European Commission proposed to abolish the comitology system, or at least to severely reduce its importance. In addition, it proposed to restrict the role of the European Parliament and the Council to defining (wherever possible by qualified majority) the essential elements,[3] leaving the Commission the task of defining the technical details via secondary legislation, and hence the responsibility for executing policy and legislation. With this proposal, the Commission clearly seemed to do away with the control by the Member States' representatives sitting on the committees, arguing that the implementing powers should be vested in the Commission alone.[4] According to this view, the Commission's actions should be controlled by means of a 'simple legal mechanism', which would allow the Council and the European Parliament to control and monitor the actions of the Commission.[5] According to the Commission, this would necessitate a review of the existing committees to assess in what form they should continue to exist.[6] This view seems to have been endorsed by the Constitution, which lays down the

---

[*] Professor of EU Law, Co-Director of Studies, *Magister Iuris Communis* (LL.M.) programme, Law Faculty, University of Maastricht.

[1] Treaty establishing a Constitution for Europe, consolidated version (CIG 87/04).

[2] White Paper on European Governance, COM (2001) 428 final.

[3] This was already established in Case 25/70 *Einfuhr-und Vorratstelle für Getreide und Futter-mittel* v. *Köster, Berodt & Co.* [1970] *ECR* 1161.

[4] In its second contribution to the European Convention, the Commission once again repeated this position. See 'For the European Union: Peace, Freedom, Solidarity – Communication of the Commission on the Institutional Architecture', COM (2002) 728 final/2.

[5] White Paper on European Governance, loc. cit. n. 2 *supra*, at p. 31.

[6] White Paper on European Governance, loc. cit. n. 2 *supra*.

'simple legal mechanism' in relation to delegated regulations.[7] Will this lead to the fall of the committee system? This paper analyses what this mechanism entails and what role the Constitution has assigned to comitology in the future.

2.   THE ONGOING COMITOLOGY DEBATE

The 1999 Comitology Decision[8] certainly simplified the committee procedures, improved their transparency and enhanced the involvement of the European Parliament. Under this new Decision, however, the management and regulatory committee procedures still dictate that, in case of disagreement between the Commission and the committees, the draft decisions proposed by the Commission may or, in the case of the regulatory committees, must be referred to the Council.[9] The Decision therefore by no means extinguished the comitology debate entirely.[10] Committee procedures are still viewed as being too complex and insufficiently transparent,[11] and the rules governing the choice of the procedure too vague[12] and lacking in accountability. As the White Paper on European Governance demonstrates, comitology still touches upon the very heart of the exercise of implementing powers at the Community level and, thereby, the Community's institutional architecture. It is hence not surprising that the questions posed by the Laeken European Council on the future architecture of the European Union, its institutions and their democratic legitimacy (both 'input' and 'output'),[13] as well as the subse-

---

[7] Article I-36 of the Constitution.

[8] Council Decision 99/468/EC of 28 June 1999 laying down the procedures for the exercise of implementing powers conferred on the Commission, *OJ* 1999 L 184/23.

[9] For a discussion of this decision, see K. Lenaerts and A. Verhoeven, 'Towards a Legal Framework for Executive Rule-Making in the EU? The Contribution of the New Comitology Decision', 37 *Common Market Law Review* (2000) pp. 645-686.

[10] For a discussion of comitology before the 1999 Decision, see E. Vos, 'The Rise of Committees', 3(3) *European Law Journal* (1997) pp. 210-229.

[11] Although this has improved. See, for instance, Report from the Commission on the working of Committees during 2001, COM (2002) 733 final. In fact, the agendas of various committees are published on the internet. See, for example, <http://www.europa.eu.int/comm/food/fs/rc/scfcah/ general/index_en.html>. See also EIPA, *Governance by Committee, the Role of Committees in European Policy-Making and Policy Implementation – Draft Final Report* (Maastricht, EIPA 2002) p. xxi.

[12] For reasons of consistency and predictability, the 1999 Decision also specifies criteria that are to be applied to the choice of the committee procedure. These criteria are not binding in nature. However, as the ECJ recently ruled, the Community's legislature is nevertheless required to state its reasons when it departs from these criteria. See Case C-378/00 *Commission* v. *Parliament and Council ('LIFE')* [2003] *ECR* I-00937.

[13] See <http://ue.eu.int/en/Info/eurocouncil/index.htm>. The reform of the Treaty on European Union has been heavily debated for many years. See, *inter alia*, J.A. Winter, D.M. Curtin, A.E. Kellermann and B. de Witte, eds.: *Reforming the Treaty on European Union – The Legal Debate* (The Hague, Kluwer 1996).

quent creation of the European Convention early in 2002, rekindled the comitology debate.[14]

3.   COMITOLOGY AND THE CONSTITUTION

3.1   'Simplification' of EU legislation

Eager to simplify EU legislation and introduce a clearer hierarchy of norms,[15] the Constitution establishes a classification of EU acts. This classification is largely in line with the recommendations made by Working Group IX of the European Convention on Simplification, chaired by Giuliano Amato, in its Final Report.[16] Articles I-33 to I-37 of the Constitution thus distinguish between two types of acts: legislative acts (European laws and European framework laws) that are adopted by the European Parliament and the Council jointly (on the basis of a revised co-decision procedure) and non-legislative acts (delegated regulations, European implementing regulations and European implementing decisions) that are adopted by the Commission. In this context, legislation is to be understood in a formal sense, as referring to a specific level within a hierarchy of acts.[17] It is the category of 'non-legislative' acts, in particular, that is relevant to comitology.

The manner in which the Constitution unravels the dual mechanism embedded within comitology, namely the control mechanisms of both the Community legislature and the Member States, is interesting. First of all, Article I-36 of the Constitution stipulates that both European laws and framework laws 'may

---

[14] See L. Allio, 'The Case for Comitology Reform: Efficiency, Transparency, Accountability', in L. Allio and G. Durand, eds., *From Legislation to Implementation: The Future of EU Decision-making*, European Policy Centre Working Paper No. 02 (Brussels 2003) pp. 32-72.

[15] See, e.g., G. Winter, ed., *Sources and Categories of European Union Law: A Comparative and Reform Perspective* (Baden-Baden, Nomos Verlagsgesellschaft 1996). In addition to the need for simplification, the need to improve the quality of Community legislation has also been stressed by many authors. See, e.g., A.E. Kellermann, S. Jacobs and R. Deighton-Smith, eds., *Improving the Quality of Legislation in Europe* (The Hague/Boston/London, Kluwer 1998). Since 1995, the Commission has therefore included a section on legislation, relating mainly to quality and statistical information, in its annual report. In addition, many activities have been carried out in terms of the consolidation, codification and transparency of legislation. See, recently, the Commission's Report entitled 'Better Lawmaking 2002', COM (2002) 715 final, and its Communication entitled 'Updating and simplifying the Community acquis', COM (2003) 71 final.

[16] Final Report of Working Group IX on Simplification, CONV 424/02 (hereinafter, the 'Amato Report').

[17] As explained by Amato during the debate on 17-18 March 2003. See B.J.J. Crum, *Reports on the plenary sessions of the Convention on the Future of Europe*, 17 and 18 March 2003, p. 3, available at: <http://www.epin.org/pdf/report_17mar03.pdf>.

delegate to the Commission the power to adopt delegated European regulations to supplement or amend certain non-essential elements of the law or framework law'. It adds that a delegation may not cover the essential elements of an area, as this is a matter reserved for the law or framework law. Furthermore, European laws and framework laws shall explicitly lay down the conditions of application to which the delegation is subject, with the possibility of empowering the European Parliament or the Council to revoke the delegation or to stipulate that the delegated regulation may only enter into force if no objection has been expressed by the European Parliament or the Council within a period set by these laws (tacit approval). In this the Council will act by qualified majority and the European Parliament by majority. This means that the legislature can directly intervene, without being dependent on the outcome of discussions within a committee composed of national representatives.

Second, delegated regulations are distinguished from implementing acts. According to Article I-36 of the Constitution, delegated regulations are a new category of acts by means of which the legislature is encouraged 'to look solely to the essential elements of an act and to delegate the more technical aspects to the executive'.[18] In this manner, delegated acts 'are less than laws but still more than mere administrative acts'.[19] Article I-37 of the Constitution determines that the Member States are obliged to ('shall') adopt legal measures necessary to implement binding EU acts. Yet, 'where uniform conditions for implementing binding Union acts are needed', Article I-37(2) states that those acts may confer implementing powers on the Commission, or in specific cases that are 'duly justified' and for CFSP decisions, on the Council. Implementing acts are 'acts implementing legislative acts, delegated acts or acts provided for by the Treaty itself'.[20] Furthermore, it is stipulated that European laws lay down rules and principles for the mechanisms through which the Member States control Union implementing acts in advance. This article thereby refines and revises the wording of Article 202, third indent, EC. The mechanism for control by the Member States evidently refers to the committee procedures.[21] It is noteworthy that, as the Member States are explicitly required to implement Community law, it is implied that committees are a means of control for the Member States, and not for the Council.

---

[18] B.J.J. Crum, loc. cit. n. 17 *supra*, at p. 9.

[19] Ibid., at p. 6.

[20] See the Amato Report, p. 9.

[21] Ibid.

3.2   'If I'd wanted you to understand, I would have explained it better'[22]

However, the simplification project seems to have failed. Instead of simplifying EU legislation, the Constitution seems to have made things more complex and confusing. Both the distinction between legislative and non-legislative acts and the distinction between delegated regulations and implementing acts are not convincing.[23] For example, is it not true that delegated regulations are also acts that implement legislative acts and hence should be regarded as implementing acts?[24]

   In its early case law, the European Court of Justice (ECJ) already distinguished between a 'true' delegation of the powers conferred upon the delegating authority and a situation where the authority grants powers to a delegate, but the use of these powers remains subject to oversight by the authority, which assumes full responsibility for the decisions of the delegate.[25] According to the Court, in the latter situation no 'true' delegation takes place. Delegation of powers may accordingly be defined as the transfer of powers from one organ to another, which the latter exercises under its own responsibility. Moreover, the possibility that powers may be delegated is implicitly alluded to in Article 202, third indent, EC and Article 211, fourth indent, EC.[26] These articles stipulate that the Commission exercises the powers conferred upon it by the Council for the implementation of the rules laid down by the latter.

   A systemic interpretation of Article 211's position within the Treaty (together with certain practical requirements) has consistently led the ECJ to hold that

---

[22] This comment by the famous Dutch football player Johan Cruijff was used by Stephen Weatherill to indicate the confusing text on closer cooperation introduced by the Amsterdam Treaty. See Stephen Weatherill, '"If I'd Wanted You to Understand I Would Have Explained It Better": What is the Purpose of the Provisions on Closer Cooperation Introduced by the Treaty of Amsterdam?', in D. O'Keeffe and P. Twomey, eds., *Legal Issues of the Amsterdam Treaty* (Oxford, Hart Publishing 1999) pp. 21-40.

[23] Neither is the distinction between legislative and non-legislative acts. See the criticism by the House of Lords' Select Committee on the EU, *The Future of Europe: Constitutional Treaty – Draft Articles 24-33*, 12th Report, Session 2002-03, HL Paper 71, pp. 11-12, available at: <http://www.parliament.the-stationery-office.co.uk/pa/ld200203/ldselect/ldeucom/71/71.pdf>.

[24] See Einem (Austria, NMP) during a debate on the draft texts of these articles in March 2003, in B.J.J. Crum, loc. cit. n. 17 *supra*, at p. 3. Moreover, delegated acts would simply not be understandable, but might instead be subsumed under the broader category of implementing acts. See Tunne Kelam, speaking on behalf of the majority of the Estonian Parliament, ibid., at p. 6.

[25] The *Meroni* cases: Case 9/56 *Meroni & Co., Industrie Metallurgiche, SpA* v. *High Authority of the ECSC* [1957] *ECR* 11, at 147-149; and Case 9/56 *Meroni & Co., Industrie Metallurgiche, SpA* v. *High Authority of the ECSC* [1958] *ECR* 53, at 169-171.

[26] See H.H. Maas, 'Delegatie van bevoegdheden in de Europese Gemeenschappen', 15 *SEW* (1967) pp. 2-18; and J.V. Louis, 'Delegatie van bevoegdheden in de Europese Gemeenschappen', 26 *SEW* (1978) pp. 802-814. In this context, see in particular Case 16/88 *Commission* v. *Council* [1989] *ECR* 3457.

'implementation by the Commission' is to be interpreted widely.[27] This means that whilst the legislative organs must regulate all essential elements, the power to adopt all measures necessary for the implementation of the rules established may be left to the Commission.[28] These detailed implementation rules[29] also include the imposition of sanctions.[30] In Case 16/88 *Commission* v. *Council* (*Fisheries*), the ECJ held that the concept of implementation in the sense of Article 202, third indent, encompasses both the drawing up of implementing rules and the application of rules to specific cases by means of acts of individual application.[31] In particular, the ECJ thereby referred to the fact that the Treaty itself did not indicate that acts of individual application were to be excluded.[32] Implementation currently also includes the control of the application of Community law and its enforcement, as may be gathered from the general tenor of Article 10 EC.[33]

The Constitution has now consolidated bits and pieces of the ECJ's case law. It confirms both the ECJ's distinction between essential and non-essential elements[34] and the obligation for Member States to implement Community legislation. Subsequently, however, the Constitution divides the concept of implementation into the drawing up of implementing rules (which it refers to as delegated regulations) and the application of rules to specific cases by means of acts of individual application (which it refers to as implementing acts). Whereas the explicit mention of the concept of delegation in the Treaty may be applauded in terms of clarity, it appears from the ECJ's case law on the concepts of delegation and implementation that the use of the terminology 'delegated and implementing acts' might create rather more confusion than clarification or simplification. The differentiation between delegated and implementing acts should therefore be rejected. Instead the concept of implementation and implementing or executive acts should be adhered to, subdivided into 'delegated legislation' and 'genuine executive acts', as proposed by Koen Lenaerts in his evidence before the Working Group on the Simplification of Union Instruments.[35]

---

[27] See, *inter alia*, Case 23/75 *Rey Soda* v. *Cassa Conguaglio Zucchero* [1975] *ECR* 1279, at 1300; Joined Cases 279, 280, 285 and 286/84 *Rau* v. *Commission* (*'Christmas butter'*) [1987] *ECR* 1069, at 1120; Case 22/88 *Vreugdenhil* [1989] *ECR* 2049, at 2079-2080.

[28] See, *inter alia*, Case 25/70 *Köster* [1970] *ECR* 1161; and Case C-345/88 *Butter-Absatz* v. *Germany* [1990] *ECR* I-159.

[29] It follows from the case law that the notion of detailed rules must likewise be widely interpreted. See Case 57/72 *Westzucker* v. *Einfuhr- und Vorratstelle für Zucker* [1973] *ECR* 321, at 338.

[30] See Case C-240/90 *Germany* v. *Commission* [1992] *ECR* I-5383, paras. 38-40.

[31] Case 16/88 *Commission* v. *Council* [1989] *ECR* 3457, para. 11.

[32] Ibid.

[33] See Case 78/70 *Deutsche Grammophon* v. *Metro* [1971] *ECR* 487.

[34] What is essential is a very subjective and imprecise concept. The same applies to what is technical: see House of Lords' Select Committee on the EU, loc. cit. n. 23 *supra*, at pp. 11-12.

[35] Note summarising the meeting of Working Group IX (Simplification) on 17 October 2002, CONV 363/02, p. 4. See also K. Lenaerts and M. Desomer, 'Simplification of the Union's Instru-

3.3   The exercise of delegated powers without comitology?

More importantly, however, the introduction of the concept of delegated regulations implies a radical reform of the institutional balance of powers between the
legislative and executive powers carried out by the institutions and, more broadly,
between the Commission and the Member States. The recommendations of the
Amato Report, which were closely followed in the Constitution, are therefore not
merely of a technical character, as the name of the Working Group – Simplification of Union Instruments – would suggest, but of high political value. Articles I-
36 and I-37 of the Constitution thus give more power to the Commission to
implement the legislative acts of the European Parliament and the Council and
confirm its role as almost the sole executive. Under the current regime, the
exercise of delegated powers would be carried out under a committee procedure
and hence with the possible influence of the Member States.

   The text of Articles I-36 and I-37 of the Constitution demonstrates that
comitology has largely been disregarded by the Member States and has remained
mainly an interinstitutional issue, emphasising only one of the dual functions of
comitology: control by the Council and/or the Parliament. The elimination of
committees with regard to delegated regulation is replaced by the 'simple control
mechanism', giving Parliament and Council the right to revoke the delegation or
to veto the proposed Commission measures (tacit approval). This may be problematic for a number of reasons.

   First, it should be observed that the distinction between delegated regulations
and implementing acts must be determined on a case-to-case basis, depending on
the degree of political discretion they involve. Apart from the fact that the
terminology used is regrettable, as explained above, it should be recognised that
at times it will be difficult to establish in advance whether a measure is merely of
a technical nature or whether it involves more political issues, as we have learned
from the cases involving comitology.

   Second, one may wonder whether, and if so how, the 'simple' mechanism of
control by the Parliament or the Council will work in practice. How will the
Council be able to identify that a draft delegated act of the Commission exceeds
the delegation provided for or touches upon major political sensitivities? Here it is
useful to recall the function of comitology as a safety net (*'filet'*) or alarm
mechanism signalling that a topic should perhaps be considered politically
sensitive. Since the Plumb-Delors agreement of 1988, which gave Parliament the
right to be informed, Parliament has struggled to set up a coherent system for

ments', in B. de Witte, ed., *Ten Reflections on the Constitutional Treaty for Europe* (Florence,
European University Institute 2003) p. 116 ff, available at: <http://www.iue.it/RSCAS/e-texts/
200304-10RefConsTreaty.pdf>.

controlling committee-based decision making by the Commission. Today, fifteen years later, this system seems to work quite well. Abolishing comitology and conferring a right of recall on the Council would mean that the Council also has to set up an accurate internal system to follow the Commission in the exercise of its delegated powers. Such a mechanism would therefore have to be operated either by the Council's working groups or by COREPER.[36] In view of the fact that members of COREPER are often also involved in comitology,[37] and in view of the fact that these issues will in principle be of a political nature,[38] it is most likely that COREPER will fulfil this role.[39]

More fundamental, however, is the disregard of the valuable input that Member State representatives and/or bureaucrats might have in the implementation of legislative measures at the Community level. The ease with which comitology has been eliminated in the exercise of delegated powers is quite remarkable.[40] Are Member States fully aware of the impact of these proposals? With regard to delegated regulations, certainly, decision making by the Commission alone will in most cases be more efficient, as far as time is concerned, than under comitology. But will it also be more effective? A recent comprehensive study of committees coordinated by the European Institute of Public Administration[41] confirms the many positive elements of comitology.[42] It suggests that comitology is very effective in reaching consensus in difficult questions of implementation and in managing routine applications of EC law. More important is its contribution to the efficient and effective implementation and application of EC policy in and by the Member States. It concludes that eliminating comitology or reducing the frequency of committee meetings would seriously endanger

[36] For an analysis of the operation of the Council working groups, see E. Fouilleux, J. De Maillard and A Smith, 'Council Working Groups: Their Role in the Production of European Problems and Policies', in EIPA, op. cit. n. 11 *supra*, at pp. 58-87.

[37] For example, Member State representatives in the former Standing Committee on Foodstuffs often appeared to have already participated in the preparation of directives under the umbrella of COREPER. See E. Vos, *Institutional Frameworks of Community Health & Safety Regulation* (Oxford, Hart Publishing 1999) pp. 110-189.

[38] Which is the decisive criterion for determining whether matters involve delegated regulations.

[39] See G. Durand, 'Montesquieu Wakes up: Separation of Powers in the Council of Ministers', in L. Allio and G. Durand, op. cit. n. 14 *supra*, at p. 19.

[40] However, some convention members proposed amendments to delete the article on delegated regulations: Amendments 107 Kirkhope, 108 Kelam and others, 109 Stockton and 110 Heathcoat-Amory. See Reactions to draft Articles 24 to 33 of the Constitutional Treaty – Analysis, CONV 609/1/03 REV1, p. 13.

[41] EIPA, op. cit. n. 11 *supra*.

[42] See, *inter alia*, M. van Schendelen, ed., *EU Committees as Influential Policymakers* (Aldershot, Ashgate 1998); C. Joerges and E. Vos, eds., *EU Committees: Social Regulation, Law and Politics* (Oxford, Hart Publishing 1999); and C. Joerges, 'Comitology and the European model? Towards a Recht-Fertigungs-Recht ['a justice-making law'] in the Europeanization Process', available at: <http://www.arena.uio.no/cidel/Workshop_Firenze/contJoerges.pdf>.

efficient policy application and implementation. It furthermore underlines that 'abolishing the management and/or regulatory procedure could negatively affect the delicate balance between Commission and Council in policy execution'.[43] Moreover, practice demonstrates that comitology may be extremely important in the sense that national positions are also taken into account in the implementing phase for reasons of proper enforcement and compliance with Community decisions. Striving for more effective decision making and better policies would thus require that Member States are consulted in the implementing phase, also with regard to 'delegated regulations'. The question remains whether this should occur within the framework of comitology or within another, looser mechanism or network.

4.   ARTICLES I-36 AND I-37 OF THE CONSTITUTION REVISITED

Removing the involvement of comitology in the adoption of delegated regulations would certainly mean that the number of meetings will be reduced, and probably the number of committees too, which would save time and money. Yet, at the same time, more work is likely to be transmitted to the Council and hence to COREPER and/or its working groups that have to monitor the Commission in the exercise of its delegated powers. This, in turn, might trigger negotiations involving several national positions within COREPER and/or its working groups, which might not be very appropriate, in view of the fact that they form part of the legislative function. In addition, in view of the 'thin lines' that connect them with their own governments, to whom they are directly responsible,[44] the accountability of the members of these bodies may even be more problematic than that of comitology members. The proposed distinction between delegated regulation and implementing acts, combined with the introduction of the 'simple' monitoring mechanism, should therefore be rejected.

Yet, in view of the current shortcomings of comitology as regards its transparency and efficiency, the enlargement of the European Union and the resulting increase in the committee members, comitology needs to be reformed. The question remains how this should be achieved. I would like to advance some suggestions in this regard. First, I would like to stress that any reform or simplification of procedures should address the indissoluble intertwining of the delegation of powers and comitology. Therefore, true simplification and rationalisation of Union instruments and functions would, in my opinion, require a revision of Articles I-36 and I-37 of the Constitution on delegated regulations and

---

[43] EIPA, op. cit. n. 11 *supra*, at p. xxiii.
[44] Ibid., at p. xv.

implementing acts. Both articles should be replaced by one article that makes the Commission responsible in the same manner for all executive (or non-legislative) acts, thereby merging delegated (Article I-36 of the Constitution) and implementing acts (Article I-37 of the Constitution) whilst retaining their conceptual difference. In order to encourage the legislature to delegate more powers whilst retaining control, one could simply give both branches of the legislature (the European Parliament and the Council) a right of recall over delegated acts,[45] if one believes that this will really bring about more delegation.[46] For the same reason, instead of giving the legislature an option to delegate, as currently envisaged ('European laws and European framework laws may delegate'), one could think of introducing a quasi-obligation to delegate powers to the Commission ('shall in principle delegate').

Whilst it must be clear that it is the Commission that bears the responsibility for the executive acts, account must also be taken of the successful practice of management and regulatory committees, which force the Commission to consider national situations and problems and take objections advanced by committee members more seriously than would be the case in relation to mere advisory committees. This would therefore enhance the effectiveness of Union measures and could be achieved by giving committees the possibility, as a matter of principle, to request that a topic be referred to the legislature (by qualified majority) in certain cases (to be established in advance by the legislature). Such a mechanism, if laid down in the Treaty, would truly simplify and could even replace the existing management and regulatory committee procedures.

On a more practical level, and in order to enhance transparency and visibility, one could furthermore envisage a reduction in the number of committees by gathering several committees dealing with similar topics under one umbrella committee, as has already been done in the case of the committees operating in the field of food safety, which now make up the Standing Committee on the Food Chain and Animal Health.[47] In order to reduce the costs involved and to counter problems relating to the increasing number of committee members, one could

---

[45] This solution was indeed suggested by some Convention members. See EIPA, op. cit. n. 11 *supra*. Amendment 143 Kelam and others allowed for the possibility of recall by the legislature for implementing acts (in line with Amendment 108 Kelam and others, which proposed to delete delegated acts). See Reactions to draft Articles 24 to 33 of the Constitutional Treaty – Analysis, CONV 609/03, p. 13.

[46] When retaining comitology and introducing the possibility for committees to have the matter sent back to the legislature, there appears to be no need for the Council to set up an internal monitoring system.

[47] Article 58 of Regulation (EC) No. 178/2002 of the European Parliament and of the Council of 28 January 2002 laying down the general principles and requirements of food law, establishing the European Food Safety Authority and laying down procedures in matters of food safety, *OJ* 2002 L 031/1.

think of increased use of innovative communication tools such as intranet and a greater use of working groups, whilst strictly limiting access to committee meetings to the members of the committee in question (one member and one alternate per Member State). Furthermore, in combination with the use of a closed communication circuit, more use could be made of written consultations. One could take the procedure currently followed for the authorisation of high-tech or biotech medicinal products as an example. In the framework of this procedure, the opinion of the Standing Committee on Medicinal Products for Human Use is in principle given in writing. Each Member State is allowed twenty-two days to forward written observations on the draft decision to the Commission (this may be shorter in cases of urgency), whilst each Member State may still request that a draft decision of the Commission is discussed in a plenary meeting of the Standing Committee, giving its reasons in detail. Moreover, where, in the opinion of the Commission, a Member State's written observations raise important new questions of a scientific or technical nature, which have not been addressed in the opinion delivered by the Agency, the chairperson will suspend the procedure and refer the application back to the Agency for further consideration.[48] Such a reform would represent a significant step towards a true simplification and rationalisation of EU instruments and could refocus the Union's institutional balance of powers. In this context, comitology clearly has a bright future ahead of it.

---

[48] See Article 10 of Regulation (EC) No. 726/2004 of the European Parliament and of the Council of 31 March 2004 laying down Community procedures for the authorisation and supervision of medicinal products for human and veterinary use and establishing a European Medicines Agency, *OJ* 2004 L 136/1.

FRAGMENTATION IN THE GOVERNANCE OF EU EXTERNAL RELATIONS: LEGAL INSTITUTIONAL DILEMMAS AND THE NEW CONSTITUTION FOR EUROPE

Ramses A. Wessel*

'The Union's external policy is not easy to define. It goes beyond the traditional diplomatic and military aspects and stretches to areas such as justice and police matters, the environment, trade and customs affairs, development and external representation of the euro zone. Our aim must be to integrate these different areas and make all the resources available work together well.'
- European Commission, *A Project for the European Union*, 22 May 2002[1]

1.   INTRODUCTION

As recently as a few years ago, it could be shown that regarding the existence and nature of a legal system of the European Union there was no clear legal picture at all and certainly no consensus of opinion. To this very day, one can observe the existence of largely isolated EC, CFSP (Common Foreign and Security Policy) and PJCC (Police and Judicial Cooperation in Criminal Matters) research communities, in which research is frequently 'content driven' rather than reflecting a more institutional approach.[2] Over the past years, a separate school of thought has laid emphasis on the unity of the Union's legal order rather than on the differences between the Union's three pillars. One research group in this school, in which the present author participated, concentrated on two main

---

* Associate Professor of International and European Law, Centre for European Studies, University of Twente. The author may be contacted by e-mail at: R.A.Wessel@utwente.nl.

[1] Communication from the Commission, *A Project for the European Union*, COM (2002) 247 final, 22 May 2002, p. 12. The remaining part of the paragraph is also relevant: 'It is not a question of the "communitarisation" of foreign policy, applying the traditional Community procedures, as this would not be compatible with the emergence of a European military dimension, but nor should we make external policy more "intergovernmental" by extending the powers of the Member States or of the High Representative to the detriment of the Commission. Wholesale "communitarisation" would not today make it possible to embrace the full political dimension of external policy, which is not a mere set of powers, instruments and areas of action; nor would it be able to cater fully for the military aspects.'

[2] For a general survey of the CFSP and PJCC, see E. Denza, *The Intergovernmental Pillars of the European Union* (Oxford, Oxford University Press 2002).

The European Union: An Ongoing Process of Integration – Liber Amicorum Alfred E. Kellermann
© 2004, T.M.C. Asser Instituut, The Hague, and the authors

questions: whether the European Union could be qualified as an international organisation in legal terms, and, if so, whether its institutional legal system is developing in practice towards institutional unity, albeit in disguise. We analysed the Union as a legal institution and defended the thesis that the Union is an international organisation with a unitary but complex character. This conclusion was not only based on the analysis of the Union Treaties and other basic instruments, but also on so-called legal practices, i.e. forms of legal action that are – explicitly or implicitly – employed in order to make the legal institution an operational entity.[3]

With regard to the European Union as a whole, one can thus perceive a clear evolution towards more institutional unity across the spectrum of the European Union, which has taken place incrementally over the course of the past ten years. This evolution tends to manifest itself first in so-called legal and institutional practices of the institutions themselves and only later, when the manner of governance is more established, also in the normative provisions of the European Union (treaties and formal laws). Despite the fact that clear elements of such progress towards institutional unity are present, this evolution exists in unresolved tension with the fact that governance by the European Union is still characterised by (considerable) fragmentation in practice. Or, as one observer holds:

'[What] remains is a fragmented and divided structure, which fails to establish in the area of external powers, as for the internal, an organic and comprehensive framework and a clear allocation of competences between the Union and its Member States.'[4]

This has become apparent in the area of the external relations in particular. The provision in Article 2 EU that the Union is 'to assert its identity on the international scene, *in particular* through the implementation of a common foreign and security policy' (emphasis added), leaves open the possibility of the Union acting outside the CFSP framework in its external relations. The objectives of the other

---

[3] D.M. Curtin and I.F. Dekker, 'The EU as a "Layered" International Organisation: Institutional Unity in Disguise', in P. Craig and G. de Búrca, eds., *The Evolution of EU Law* (Oxford, Oxford University Press 1999) pp. 83-136. See further, D.M. Curtin and I.F. Dekker, 'The Constitutional Structure of the European Union: Some Reflections on Vertical Unity-In-Diversity', in N. Walker, et al., eds., *Convergence and Divergence in European Public Law* (Oxford, Hart 2002) pp. 59-78; R.A. Wessel, 'Revisiting the International Legal Status of the EU', *European Foreign Affairs Review* (2000) pp. 507-537; I.F. Dekker and R.A. Wessel, 'The European Union and the Concept of Flexibility. Proliferation of Legal Systems within International Organisations', in N.M. Blokker and H.G. Schermers, eds., *Proliferation of International Organisations* (The Hague, Kluwer Law International 2001) pp. 381-414; and R.A. Wessel, *The European Union's Foreign and Security Policy: A Legal Institutional Perspective* (The Hague, Kluwer Law International 1999).

[4] Cf. A. Tizzano, 'The Foreign Relations Law of the EU', in E. Cannizzaro, *The European Union as an Actor in International Relations* (The Hague, Kluwer Law International 2002) pp. 135-147 at p. 137.

two parts of the Union indeed imply a role for the Union regarding the external dimension of those issue areas as well, and it has proven to be far too simplistic to distinguish between a European Community in charge of external commercial policy, a CFSP dealing with foreign policy and an isolated PJCC policy for police and judicial matters. The overlapping of certain objectives has been unavoidable from the outset, as practice has refused to be forced into the straitjacket of treaty provisions. Third States and international organisations increasingly approach the Union as such, which has resulted in a practice in which the different modes of governance no longer coincide with the three original pillars. The fact that autonomous legal entities *within* the Union may have set their own external relations regime (as is the case, for example, with regard to Europol) adds immensely to this (institutional and substantive) complexity.

The ambition of this paper is to map the terrain of EU governance in the area of external relations by using the previously developed insights from what has been termed the legal institutional perspective. Moreover, the term governance is deliberately used – instead of other terms more familiar to legal researchers – in order to be able to approach the question in a more flexible manner, taking account of the informal context as well as the legal and institutional practice and, moreover, in order to be able to make a link with more normative issues. While the Community method will be used as an implicit benchmark, the focus will be more or less exclusively on the second pillar. The modes of governance in this area seem to have evolved in an *ad hoc* manner, almost from Presidency to Presidency. At the same time, there has been a certain vulnerability to external influences from other international organisations (e.g. NATO in the second pillar) to third States (e.g. the United States with regard to the fight against terrorism and other issues) that sometimes drive the content. I would like to outline the different institutional factors that may be at the origins of the different ways the external relations of the European Union as such have evolved. Moreover, I will examine and put into context the evidence that the European Union is progressing towards (much) more institutional unity as a result of the work of the Convention on the Future of Europe (and the subsequent IGC) and consider the possible solutions of the new Constitution for Europe with regard to the fragmentation of the Union's external relations.

2.   THE DIFFICULT SEPARATION BETWEEN EXTERNAL
        RELATIONS ISSUES: A TALE OF THREE PILLARS

Practice has not followed the neat separating lines foreseen in the Union Treaty between economics and politics. The international agenda – which includes issues such as environmental protection, social standards, development cooperation, international security, conflict management, sanctions policy and human rights protection – simply does not take the sensitivities of all Member States into account. Political choices are often clearly visible when, for instance, economic policies in the field of development cooperation are made public (often with explicit objectives concerning democracy, the rule of law and human rights). At the same time, economic issues can hardly be approached without political choices (e.g. trade conflicts concerning bananas, beef hormones and more recently steel), while occasionally the link between politics and economics is made explicit (through 'human rights' or 'essential element' clauses in agreements with third States). Hence, it has been rightly observed that 'a considerable part of "foreign policy" actually belongs to the EC's day to day business' and 'the attempt to uphold clear dividing lines between economic and political issues is thus artificial and indefensible in practice.'[5]

Indeed, overlapping competences can easily be found in the relationship between the Community and the CFSP. Apart form the fact that the CFSP is to cover 'all areas of foreign and security policy' (Art. 11 EU), other objectives may also raise questions regarding the division of competences. With regard to *all* CFSP objectives, one could argue that the policies in those areas are at the same time part of the day-to-day practice of the European Union on the basis of the Community Treaty.[6] Keeping in mind the *ERTA* doctrine (internal competences result in external ones), the complexity is being increased because of the fact that CFSP competences may not only conflict with explicit external Community competences, but also with implicit ones.[7] This means that it has become increasingly difficult to fix the division of competences between the pillars in a *Kompetenz Katalog* and that it is better to opt for constant mutual tuning.[8] A practical solution was found in references to instruments that were adopted under another pillar regime, but there are examples of CFSP decisions that already regulate what is expected of the Community in a certain case.[9]

---

[5] S. Griller and B. Weidel, 'External Economic Relations and Foreign Policy in the EU', in S. Griller and B. Weidel, eds., *External Economic Relations and Foreign Policy in the European Union* (Vienna/New York, Springer 2002) pp. 5-22 at p. 12.

[6] The CFSP objectives in Article 11 EU include the safeguarding of common values, fundamental interests and integrity of the Union; the strengthening of the security of the Union; the preservation of peace; the promotion of international cooperation and the development and consolidation of democracy and the rule of law; and respect for human rights and fundamental freedoms.

[7] Cf. A. Dashwood, 'The Attribution of External Relations Competence', in A. Dashwood and C. Hillion, eds., *The General Law of EC External Relations* (London, Sweet & Maxwell 2000) pp. 115-138 at p. 116

[8] Cf. one of the very first studies in this area: M. Cremona, 'The Common Foreign and Security Policy of the European Union and the External Relations Powers of the European Community', in D. O'Keeffe and P.M. Twomey, eds., *Legal Issues of the Maastricht Treaty* (London, Wiley Chancery Law 1994) pp. 247-258 at p. 249.

[9] See more extensively B. Weidel, 'The Impact of the Pillar Construction on External Policy', in Griller and Weidel, op. cit. n. 5, at 23-64 at p. 50; and R.A. Wessel, 'The Inside Looking Out:

The difficult separation can also be seen in the relationship between EC and EU cooperation in the area of police and justice. Enhanced cooperation in this field may be based on both Article 29 EU and Article 135 EC. Also, in the area of data protection, measures relating to the collection, storage, processing and exchange of information (Art. 30 EU) may already be covered by Community instruments concerning data protection on the basis of Article 95 EC.[10] In addition, the combating of fraud allows for a choice between Article 280 EC or a measure on the basis of PJCC, in which the prevention of fraud forms part of the general objectives.[11]

An example of 'pillar-overarching' decisions may be the Common Strategies, which according to Article 13 EU are meant to deal with areas in which the Member States have important interests in common.[12] So far, Common Strategies have been adopted by the European Council on the Russian Federation, Ukraine and the Mediterranean.[13] Despite their basis in the second pillar, these Common Strategies address issues covering the entire Union. More generally, however, the intensification of the Union's external relations has lead to a need to take decisions whose scope supersedes mere economic or political foreign policy. The internal diversification of competences has thus resulted in a complex picture whenever the Union engages in relations with third States or other international organisations.

The fragmentation of the mechanisms that govern the exercise of external powers is visible in relation to a number of areas:

1. First of all, the external representation of the Union, including its participation in international organisations, differs between the Community and the other two pillars. In the European Community, the Commission is the most important actor, both in terms of representation and in relation to the negotiation of international agreements (Art. 300 EC). In the area of the CFSP and PJCC, the Presidency and the High Representative take a lead in representing the Union. Agreements are negotiated by the Presidency (Arts. 24 and 38 EU). The complex external representation of the Union may have consequences for its responsibility under international law as well.[14]

Consistency and Delimitation in EU External Relations', *CMLRev.* (2000) pp. 1135-1171 at pp. 1152-1157.

[10] E.g. Directive 95/46/EC, *OJ* 1995 L 281/31, 23 November 1995.

[11] Cf. Weidel, loc. cit. n. 9, at p. 27.

[12] See C. Hillion, 'Common Strategies and the Interface between EC External Relations and the CFSP: Lessons of the Partnership between the EU and Russia', in Dashwood and Hillion, op. cit. n. 7, at pp. 287-301.

[13] Respectively, Decision 1999/414/CFSP, *OJ* 1999 L 157, 24 June 1999; Decision 1999/877/CFSP, *OJ* 1999 L 331, 23 December 1999; and Decision 2000/458/CFSP, *OJ* 2000 L 183, 22 July 2000.

[14] On this subject, see C. Tomuschat, 'The International Responsibility of the European Union', in Cannizzaro, op. cit. n. 4, at pp. 177-191.

2. Decision-making procedures differ substantially, both with regard to voting modalities (qualified majority voting being the default situation in Community matters) and the role of the institutions. While the initiating role in the Community is obviously in the hands of the Commission, the other two regimes are still primarily dependent on initiatives by Member States (in practice often the Presidency) and the special preparatory organs of the Council (such as the Political and Security Committee). In addition, it is well known that the substantial enlargement of the competences the European Parliament enjoys under the Community Treaty have not been followed by a similar boost of powers in the other two pillars.

3. Limited parliamentary control may to some extent be compensated by judicial control. With respect to the CFSP, however, the powers of the Court of Justice are excluded by Article 46 EU.[15] Within the third pillar, the Court's jurisdiction now includes the new preliminary procedure in Article 35 EU. This leads us to conclude that the Court of Justice is left with a limited set of possibilities in the non-Community pillars of the Union. First of all, the Court is allowed to review the required compatibility of CFSP and PJCC measures of the Council with Community law, including the choice of legal basis and the consistency of foreign policy measures ('policing the boundaries'). This includes the Court's use of the non-judiciable CFSP provisions as aids to interpretation.[16] Secondly, it seems clear that the Court has jurisdiction whenever the Council makes use of 'hybrid' acts, covering both matters governed by the CFSP or PJCC as well as matters governed by the Community Treaties. Examples may be found in the area of economic sanctions, development policy, trade policy, anti-terrorism measures or measures related to visa and immigration policy.

4. The available legal instruments differ in all three pillars. This means that in the case of cross-pillar issues, addressees may be confronted with a bundle of decisions that are not always consistent and differ, at least, in their consequences with regard to their legal effects and the possibilities for legal protection.

Nevertheless, EU law generally forces decision-makers to choose a legal basis in one of the pillars. In short, this choice then not only defines the role of the

---

[15] The Court of first instance almost had a chance to settle this question in two cases regarding the validity of Council Decision 1999/612/CFSP concerning additional restrictive measures against the Federal Republic of Yugoslavia. This Decision includes a list of persons subject to an obligation of non-admission in the territories of the Member States. The applicants in the two cases – Miskovic and Karic – challenged the choice of legal basis by the Council and claimed that measures concerning immigration and asylum policy fell within the exclusive competence under Title IV EC and not under Title V EU (CFSP). 'Unfortunately', Case T-349/99 *Miroslav Miskovic* v. *Council of the European Union* and Case T-350/99 *Bogoljub Karic and four others* v. *Council of the European Union* (*OJ* 2000 C 79/35-36) were removed from the register on 6 March 2001.

[16] Cf. Case C-473/93 *Commission* v. *Luxembourg* [1993] *ECR* I-3207, on Article F(1) EU (now Article 6 EU).

institutions (e.g. whether or not there is room for a Commission initiative or co-decision by the European Parliament), but also the road to be followed during the decision-making process (e.g. whether or not there is a role for the Political and Security Committee or other committees), the voting modalities, the type of available instrument, the possibilities for judicial protection and the effect of the measure in the national legal orders. The connected parts of the external policy of the Union may thus result in a varied governance palette.

The treaty-makers were aware of this problem and included a number of principles in the Union Treaty on the basis of which cross-pillar problems are to be solved. Here, consistency and the preservation of the *acquis communautaire* take a lead (Art. 3 EU),[17] while the latter often hinders the former, but also seems to take preference over it. After all, Article 1 EC refers to the Community as the foundation of the European Union, supplemented by the policies and forms of cooperation in the other two areas. Moreover, the *acquis communautaire* is not only to be preserved, but also to be developed. Thus, the CFSP and PJCC appear to be at the service of the development of the Community, as conflicts are to be solved to the benefit of the latter, as implied by Article 47 EU (nothing in the Union Treaty shall affect the Community Treaties). It was clear from the outset that implicit modifications of the Community Treaty are allowed, in the sense that Community law is not completely immune to influences from the other two pillars.[18] The principle of consistency (Art. 3 EU) may serve as a good example in this respect, but one may also point to the single institutional structure (Arts. 3 and 6 EU), the common objectives (Art. 2 EU) or the principles of liberty, democracy, respect for human rights and fundamental freedoms in Article 6 EU. For these provisions to have any effect at all, they will also have to be recognised by the Community (which indeed happens in practice).[19] While the preservation of the *acquis communautaire* thus seems to form the starting point in cases of conflict with the second or third pillar, the functioning of the Community in splendid isolation form these pillars is obviously not in conformity with the unity of the Union's legal order as introduced by the Maastricht Treaty.[20]

This is not to conceal the fact that even within the first pillar we are familiar with fragmented modes of governance. Regarding its external relations, in particular, the Community has not assumed an exclusive competence. Even in

---

[17] On the fuzzy nature of the *acquis*, see further S. Weatherill, 'Safeguarding the Acquis Communautaire', in T. Heukels, N. Blokker and M. Brus, eds., *The European Union after Amsterdam* (The Hague, Kluwer Law International 1998) pp. 153-178. For a recent analysis of the problem of coherence, see P. Gauttier, 'Horizontal Coherence and the External Competences of the European Union', 1 *European Law Journal* (January 2004) pp. 23-41.

[18] See also M. Pechstein, 'Das Kohärenzgebot als entscheidende Integrationsdimension der Europäischen Union', *EuR* (1995) pp. 247-258 at p. 252.

[19] See more extensively Wessel, loc. cit. n. 9.

[20] On this unity, see both publications by Curtin and Dekker cited in n. 3 *supra*.

such a key area as the Common Commercial Policy, Member States still have a role to play in agreements on trade in services and trade-related aspects of intellectual property. The same holds true for many other areas, including the environment or development cooperation. So, even within the Community we come across a mix of exclusive, mixed or even explicitly denied (for instance, regarding defence issues) competences of the Community. As some observers have noted: 'Though not explicitly foreseen by the Community Treaty, "mixity" has thus become a characteristic feature of European foreign policy.'[21] At the same time, however, the exclusivity of Community competences does form a criterion to judge Member States' actions in the other two pillars as well. As the Court held in *ERTA*, in the case of exclusive Community powers, all concurrent powers of the Member States are barred both 'in the Community sphere and in the international sphere', and Member States 'do longer have the right, acting individually or even collectively, to undertake obligations with third countries which affect those [Community] rules.'[22] More recently, in *Centro-Com*, the Court added that where a measure would affect Community competence, Member States are precluded from action on their own, regardless of the possible foreign policy motives of such measures.[23] Thus, we have entered the complexity of the European Union's external relations, in which the fragmentation may not only be explained on the basis of the pillar structure (*horizontal* delimitation), but also on the basis of the relationship of the Union with its Member States (*vertical* delimitation).[24] This is one of the constitutional challenges the Union is facing today.

3.   THE CFSP AND THE OTHER PILLARS: AN INTEGRATED
        APPROACH IN EXTERNAL POLICIES?

In some areas, the Treaties provide solutions for the fact that external policies may have a political as well as an economic or justice and home affairs dimension; in other areas practical solutions have been found. Based on the practice within the European Community, the most obvious solution is the use of a dual legal basis, but this is only possible when the decision-making procedures

---

[21] I. Pernice and D. Thym, 'A New Institutional Balance for European Foreign Policy?', *European Foreign Affairs Review* (2002) pp. 369-400 at p. 372.

[22] Case 22/70 *Commission* v. *Council (ERTA)* [1971] *ECR* 263. See also Tizzano, loc. cit. n. 4, at 139.

[23] Case C-124/95 *The Queen, ex parte Centro-Com Srl* v. *HM Treasury* and *Bank of England* [1997] *ECR* I-81, paras. 26 and 41.

[24] On the last dimension, see more extensively R.A. Wessel, 'The Multi-Level Constitution of European Foreign Relations', in D.M. Curtin, S. Griller, S. Prechal and B. de Witte, eds., *The Emerging Constitution of the European Union* (Oxford, Oxford University Press 2004, forthcoming).

prescribed by the legal bases coincide.[25] An early example is the Joint Action concerning measures protecting against the effects of the extra-territorial application of legislation adopted by a third country (the reaction of the Union to the Cuba and Iran and Libya Sanctions Acts of the United States). This Joint Action was the first one with a dual legal basis, which was located in both the second and the third pillar (former Articles J.3 and K.3(2)(b) EU are mentioned as the legal basis).[26] In addition, it was explicitly connected to an EC Regulation in order to constitute an 'integrated system'. The adoption of the Joint Action was to a large extent superfluous, in view of the scope of the EC Regulation, but the Council obviously intended to create a watertight system to protect the citizens of the Union in all possible issue areas. It was made clear, however, that the Joint Action was to be seen as supplementary to the EC Regulation, since both decisions stipulated that Member States should take the measures they deemed necessary to protect the interests of any person referred to in the EC Regulation 'insofar as these interests are not protected under that Regulation'. A more recent case concerns the Council's Common Positions on combating terrorism and on the application of specific measures to combat terrorism. These decisions clearly combine foreign policy issues with increased cooperation between the operational services responsible for combating terrorism: Europol, Eurojust, the intelligence services, police forces and judicial authorities.[27] The decisions, as well as all subsequent ones related to them, are based on both Article 15 EU (CFSP) and Article 34 EU (PJCC). It is interesting to note that where specific measures are needed to implement these decisions, the Council once again pulls the matter back into one single pillar. Thus, specific measures for police and judicial cooperation to combat terrorism were based on Articles 30, 31 and 34(2)(c) EU only.[28]

This example shows that a combination of legal bases chosen from the second and the third pillar may work because they involve similar decision-making procedures and instruments. At present, this forms the reason why the combination of a Community legal basis with legal bases in the other EU pillars is more difficult. Even if one succeeds in combining the decision-making procedures, there is the problem of finding a legal instrument that may be used across all pillars. An exceptional case concerns the establishment of the new committees in the framework of the European Security and Defence Policy. The decisions to

---

[25] See R.H. van Ooik, *De keuze der rechtsgrondslag voor besluiten van de Europese Unie* (Deventer, Kluwer 1999) Chapter 9.

[26] Council Decision 96/668/CFSP of 22 November 1996.

[27] Council Common Positions 2001/930/CFSP and 2001/931/CFSP of 27 December 2001, *OJ* 2001 L 344, 28 December 2001. For a recent update, see Council Common Position 2003/651/CFSP of 12 September 2003, *OJ* 2003 L 229, 13 September 2003.

[28] See Council Decision 2003/48/JHA of 19 December 2002, *OJ* 2003 L 16, 22 January 2003.

establish the Political and Security Committee, the Military Committee and the Military Staff were all based on Article 28(1) EU and Article 207(2) EC.[29] In this case, the decision-making procedures coincided because Article 28 EU simply refers to Article 207 EC.[30]

The solution is mostly found in a combination of two governance regimes, as in the case of the extra-territorial application of the above-mentioned legislation. The classic example, of course, is the case of economic sanctions, where CFSP and EC measures are presented as complementary. Despite the obvious differences in the separate decision-making procedures needed – the most striking being the need for a Commission proposal under Article 301 EC, the possibility for qualified majority voting under the same provision and the requirement of unanimity under Article 23(1) EU – this combination of legal bases is still the way in which the legal institutional dilemma is approached; apart from the possibility of using either a single CFSP legal basis (arms embargoes)[31] or a single EC legal basis (many sanctions regimes based on UN resolutions). The same complexity occurs with regard to unilateral measures adopted by the Union in cases of the violation of international obligations by a third State (e.g. withdrawal of benefits, suspension of development assistance and/or flight bans) or in cases of the suspension of treaty obligations (e.g. suspending a cooperation agreement because of a fundamental change in circumstance or invoking the human rights clauses in bilateral cooperation or trade agreements).[32] Whereas the suspension of treaty obligations may only be based on the Community Treaty (Art. 300(2), second subparagraph), in the other situations one may come across single CFSP or EC decisions, or combinations thereof, on the basis of Article 301 EC and Articles 14 or 15 EU. Until recently, a similar example could be found in the regime concerning the export of dual-use goods: the economic decision on the export ban was taken on the basis of Article 133 EC, whereas the actual list of goods falling under the regime, as well as their destinations, was established on

---

[29] See Council Decisions 2001/78/CFSP, 2001/79/CFSP and 2001/80/CFSP of 22 January 2001, *OJ* 2001 L 27, 30 January 2001. The same holds true for the subsequent decisions related to the setting up of these committees.

[30] Article 28 EU provides that a listed number of EC provisions shall apply to CFSP as well. Article 207(2) EC regulates the role of the General Secretariat of the Council. While the relevance for the establishment of the Military Staff (as a part of the General Secretariat) is obvious, the article does not seem to relate to the Military Committee or the Political and Security Committee. In that respect, the choice of this legal basis is somewhat surprising.

[31] The rationale for not using Article 301 EC in this situation is to be found in Article 296(1)(b) EC, which permits Member States to take the necessary measures for the protection of their essential security interests connected with the trade in arms.

[32] See more extensively E. Paasivirta and A. Rosas, 'Sanctions, Countermeasures and Related Actions in the External Relations of the EU', in Cannizzaro, op. cit. n. 4, at pp. 207-218.

the basis of Article 14 EU.[33] In 2000, this situation largely came to an end with the introduction of a new Regulation bringing the CFSP parts of the regime within the Community's field of competence.[34] Nevertheless, the tension between common commercial policy (EC) and national security measures (CFSP) continues to exist, as the control of technical assistance related to certain military end-uses continues to be based on the second pillar.[35]

Over the years, this led to situations in which Community competences seemed to be eroded by CFSP measures, while at other times they were actually widened due to the foreign policy activity of the Union as a whole. Examples of CFSP decisions that have seriously thwarted Community policy in a particular area include the monitoring of the elections in Russia and South Africa and the KEDO initiative on nuclear energy in Korea.[36] One could argue that the latter decision in particular clearly concerned a Community matter, but it was nevertheless pulled into the CFSP for political reasons. By using the formula of a Joint Action, the Member States themselves would be more in control and the Commission's influence on external policy would be contained.[37] Other examples include the above-mentioned decisions on the export of dual-use commodities (the CFSP dimension of which could be questionable),[38] the Joint Action on the Middle East peace process (which contained a number of Community issues) and the Common Positions on Rwanda and Ukraine (which were already explicitly criticised by the Commission in 1994 because of the inclusion of Community matters in the operational part of the decisions).[39] In addition, the implementation of the Mostar operation showed that budgetary procedures were also able to create an impression of the 'PESCalisation' of Community principles.[40] The implementation of this operation was in the hands of a special EU Administrator

---

[33] For an overview, see P. Koutrakos, 'Inter-Pillar Approaches to the European Security and Defence Policy: The Economic Aspects of Security', in V. Kronenberger, ed., *The European Union and the International Legal Order: Discord or Harmony?* (The Hague, TMC Asser Press 2001) pp. 435-480.

[34] Regulation (EC) No 1334/2000 of 22 June 2000, *OJ* 2000 L 159, 30 June 2000.

[35] See Council Joint Action 2000/401/CFSP of 22 June 2000, *OJ* 2000 L 159, 30 June 2000.

[36] G. Burghardt and G. Tebbe, 'Die Gemeinsame Außen- und Sicherheitspolitik der Europäischen Union – Rechtliche Struktur und politischer Prozeß', *EuR* (1995) pp. 1-20 at p. 15. H.G. Krenzler and H.C. Schneider, 'Die Gemeinsame Aussen- und Sicherheitspolitiek der Europäischen Union – Zur Frage der Kohärenz', 29 *Europarecht* (1994) pp. 144-161, also point to the danger of Community procedures being affected by CFSP practice. Cf. also S. Keukeleire, *Het buitenlands beleid van de Europese Unie* (Deventer, Kluwer 1998) at pp. 332-337.

[37] Keukeleire, op. cit. n. 36, at p. 333.

[38] See C.W.A. Timmermans, 'The Uneasy Relationship between the Communities and the Second Union Pillar: Back to the "Plan Fouchet"?', 26 *Legal Issues of European Integration* (1997) pp 61-70 at p. 69.

[39] See Common Positions 94/697/CFSP and 94/779/CFSP, also referred to by Gauttier, loc. cit. n. 17, at p. 28.

[40] PESC is the French abbreviation for the CFSP.

who was responsible only to the Presidency and to a permanent advisory group of the Council. The Presidency was responsible for the financial management of the operation, which brought the whole system into conflict with the prerogatives of the Commission in this field.[41] Finally, Common Strategies partly seem to direct Community action as well, irrespective of their CFSP basis. Thus, the 1999 Common Strategy on Ukraine made decisions on the use of Community instruments (para. 38) and even spoke on behalf of the Community in the area of the environment, energy and nuclear safety (para. 56).[42]

Although maybe less frequently, Community competences in the area of external relations have also widened. With the development of the CFSP, the Community has also explored new terrains. A case in point is the Community's contribution to UNMIK, the UN interim administration in Kosovo. On the basis of Regulation (EC) No 1080/2000, the Commission was, *inter alia*, in charge of the division of costs between the European Union and other members of the international community. There was no legal basis for Community action in this area, which left the Council with Article 308 EC (the legal basis of last resort when no explicit legal basis is available).[43] More generally, the Community is often pulled into foreign policy actions that used to be outside its range of activities. Many human rights protection and democracy enhancement operations in third countries do not have an explicit relation to actions in which the Community is competent to engage. However, many of these actions simply require the use of Community funds for actions that have their origin in a CFSP decision.

All in all, this leaves us with a complex picture of the legal institutional dilemmas resulting from the wish to hold on to the different modes of governance chosen for the distinct policy areas of the Union and the need for coherent external action. These dilemmas have also occurred in an institutional sense within both the Commission and the Council. Thus, the attempt to create more coherence by reshuffling the portfolios of the Commissioners does not yet seem to have resulted in improved coordination between the pillars (in fact, this coordination seems to depend mainly on good working relations between the Commissioner for External Relations and the High Representative for the CSFP). The same holds true for the working methods of the Council, where the Political and Security Committee and Coreper both still have different input sources and decision-making tracks. Nevertheless, in some areas (e.g. economic sanctions and suspension of cooperation), the Union seems to have succeeded in assuring more coherence. Thus, for example, Community measures on the promotion (or

---

[41] Keukeleire, op. cit. n. 36, at p. 319.

[42] See Common Strategy 99/877/CFSP of 11 December 1999, *OJ* 1999 L 331, 23 December 1999. On this issue, see more extensively R. Baratta, 'Overlaps Between EC Competence and EU Foreign Policy Activity', in Cannizzaro, op. cit. n. 4, at pp. 51-75.

[43] See Baratta, loc. cit. n. 42, at p. 56.

suspension) of economic and social reconstruction are sometimes combined with CFSP measures on arms trade or travel restrictions for officials.[44] In addition, the recent anti-terrorism measures show that an integrated approach is possible. Because of the fragmentation of the Union's external relations, however, an integrated approach still does not come naturally.

4.   PJCC AND THE OTHER PILLARS: THE DEVELOPMENT OF EXTERNAL RELATIONS IN THE JHA DOMAIN

External relations in the area of Police and Judicial Cooperation in Criminal Matters are booming. An obvious reason is the fast development of the Justice and Home Affairs domain in general. Over the past few years, the Council has adopted almost ten texts per month on JHA issues.[45] Since 2001, external relations in the JHA domain can be found in so-called 'multi-presidency programmes'.[46] As Article 38 EU provides for matters in Title IV EU (PJCC) to be covered by agreements concluded on the basis of Article 24 EU, there is now an explicit competence for the Union to engage in legal relations with third States and other international organisations in this field. So far, two agreements have been signed on this basis: the EU-US Agreement on Extradition and the EU-US Agreement on Mutual Legal Assistance.[47] Although the European Union as such has become a party to the agreements, it is interesting to note that the United States doubted the legal capacity of the Union to conclude agreements and demanded that the individual Member States drew up separate declarations on the applicability of the bilateral assistance and extradition agreements between them and the United States.[48] Apart from these agreements concluded by the Union as such, Article 42(2) of the Europol Convention allows the agency to establish and

---

[44] See, for instance, the Common Positions on Liberia (2001/357/CFSP and 2002/457/CFSP) or the decisions relating to Zimbabwe (Common Position 2002/145/CFSP and Council Regulation (EC) No 310/2002). See more extensively Gauttier, loc. cit. n. 17, at p. 32.

[45] On this issue and on the external relations of the third pillar in general, see J. Monar, 'The EU as an International Actor in the Justice and Home Affairs Domain: Potential and Constraints', unpublished paper presented at the Inaugural Conference of the European Society of International Law, Florence, 13-15 May 2004.

[46] For a recent update, see Council of the European Union, Presidency: JHA External Relations Multi-Presidency Programme, Council Document 5097/04 of 7 January 2004.

[47] *OJ* 2003 L 181, 17 July 2003.

[48] Article 3(2) of the Agreement on Extradition and Article 3(2) and (3) of the Agreement on Mutual Legal Assistance. See S. Marquard, 'La capacité de l'Union européenne de conclure des accords internationaux dans le domaine de la coopération policière et judiciaire en matière pénal', in G. De Kerchove and A. Weyembergh, eds., *Sécurité et justice: enjeu de la politique extérieure de l'Union européenne* (Brussels, Editions de l'Université de Bruxelles 2003) p. 189.

maintain relations with third States and international organisations.[49] The first agreement on this basis was signed between Europol and the United States on the exchange of both strategic and technical information in the fight against a broad range of serious forms of international crime and the exchange of liaison officers. A more comprehensive agreement was signed on 20 December 2002.[50] These agreements, together with the two agreements concluded between the European Union and the United States on extradition and mutual legal assistance, revealed a serious shortcoming in the treaty-making procedure of Articles 24 and 38 EU, as this procedure does not include consultation of the European Parliament, irrespective of the potentially major implications for citizens' rights and freedoms.

It is clear that the fact that different procedures are used in the third pillar, as compared to the Community, adds to the fragmentation of the Union's external relations, as Article 300 EC does call for consultation of the Parliament. But cross-pillar problems are not limited to parliamentary control. The competences of the Community on the basis of Title IV EC (asylum, immigration, border controls and judicial cooperation in civil matters) have a clear relationship with those in Title VI EU. The external competences of the European Community under Title IV have been confirmed by the conclusion of the readmission agreements concerning illegal immigration as well as for the readmission clauses in the Political Dialogue and Cooperation Agreements with Central American countries signed on 15 December 2003.[51] These Community competences on the basis of Title IV EC occasionally overlap with EU competences in the third pillar. Obvious examples may be found in relation to the Schengen *acquis*. Agreements have been concluded or are under negotiation both with Switzerland and with Norway and Iceland regarding the free movement of persons, covering both Community and third pillar issues. Monar points to the fact that this has the effect that, in one and the same article of an international agreement, one aspect falls under Title IV EC and another under Title VI EU, which results in enormous coordination efforts between the Commission, the Presidency and the Member States.[52]

---

[49] See also Council Act of 8 November 1998 providing for an explicit treaty-making power of Europol, *OJ* 1999 C 26/19, 30 January 1999. See also H.G. Nilsson, 'Organs and Bodies of the Third Pillar as Instruments of External Relations of the European Union', in De Kerchove and Weyembergh, op. cit. n. 48, at pp. 205-209.

[50] Respectively, Council Documents Nos. 14586/01 and. 15231/02. See Monar, op. cit. n. 45, at p. 10.

[51] All agreements were based on both Article 300 EC and Article 63(3)(b) EC. See, for example, Council Decision 204/80/EC on the conclusion of the Agreement between the European Community and the Government of the Hong Kong Special Administrative Region of the People's Republic of China on the readmission of persons residing without authorisation, *OJ* 2004 L 17/23, 14 January 2004.

[52] Monar, op. cit. n. 45, at p. 11. See also E. Barbe, 'L'influence de l'Union européenne dans les enceintes internationals', in De Kerchove and Weyembergh, op. cit. n. 48, at p. 213.

In the previous section, I already pointed to the fact that, in particular after the terrorist attacks of 11 September 2001, the relationship between the second and the third pillar has grown closer as well. At present, third pillar anti-terrorism issues are part and parcel of 'political dialogue' meetings, which are generally though to take place on the basis of the CFSP and agreements with third States, combine policies on the basis of both (or even all three) pillars.[53]

5.   DOES THE NEW DRAFT CONSTITUTION OFFER SOLUTIONS FOR THIS FRAGMENTATION?

The draft Treaty establishing a Constitution for Europe (hereinafter, 'the Constitution') – which was finalised by the Convention on the Future of Europe in July 2003 – will be signed in the autumn of 2004, albeit in a somewhat modified version. The question is whether the new provisions will solve the fragmentation of the external relations discussed in this paper.

The most important structural change is that the Constitution puts an end to the pillar structure. We are left with one international organisation – the Union – with competences in the former Community areas as well as in the areas of the CFSP and PJCC. In the area of external relations, moreover, no division is made between economic and political (foreign affairs) issues. Title V of Part III of the Constitution is labelled 'The Union's External Action' and covers all the Union's external policies. In addition, the external objectives of the Union are no longer scattered over different treaties. Instead, Article I-3(4) provides:

'In its relations with the wider world, the Union shall uphold and promote its values and interests. It shall contribute to peace, security, the sustainable development of the earth, solidarity and mutual respect among peoples, free and fair trade, eradication of poverty and protection of human rights and in particular children's rights, as well as to strict observance and development of international law, including respect for the principles of the United Nations Charter.'

Other provisions also add to the idea of the integration of the different external policies. Thus, Article III-194 codifies the existing practice that the former 'Common Strategies' (the term is no longer used) may cover all aspects of the Unions' external action; they are no longer restricted to the CFSP. Secondly, consistency is being sought in the introduction of the Minister for Foreign Affairs, who will not only chair the Foreign Affairs Council, but will also be Vice-President

---

[53] See, for example, the Political Dialogue and Cooperation Agreements, available at: <http://europa.eu.int/comm/external_relations>.

of the Commission. Thirdly, the legal personalities of the Community and the European Union are merged into one legal personality of the new Union. This will certainly simplify matters in relation to the conclusion of treaties and questions of accountability and responsibility. Article III-227 applies to all agreements concluded by the Union and no distinction is made, either in procedure or in legal nature, between the different external policies. Finally, the Constitution puts an end to the different types of instruments that can be used for the CFSP. Common Strategies, Joint Actions and Common Positions make way for the 'European decision', an instrument that may also be used in other (former Community) issue areas.

While these modifications can certainly be regarded as an acknowledgment of the unity of the Union's legal order as it has developed over the years, a number of other provisions indicate that the drafters of the Constitution were not willing to go all the way where the integration of the pillars is concerned. While Community and third pillar issues indeed seem to have been placed on an equal footing (e.g. international representation by the Commission and expansion of qualified majority voting), the CFSP continues to have a distinct nature under the new Treaty.[54] A first element concerns the kind of competences in the CFSP area. Article I-11 lists the competences of the Union in the different areas as exclusive, shared or supporting and supplementary. However, none of these competences relates to the CFSP, as Article I-11 includes a separate paragraph referring to a 'competence to define and implement a common foreign and security policy, including the progressive framing of a common defence policy'. As Cremona has already indicated, it is a little difficult to see what kind of competence it could be, if not one of the other categories.[55] But the simple fact that a special status has been introduced again is striking.

Similar confusion results from the available instruments. Indeed, the CFSP is going to be developed on the basis of one type of instrument, the 'European decision', which is defined in Article I-32(1) as 'a non-legislative act, binding in its entirety. A decision which specifies those to whom it is addressed shall be binding only on them.' Apart from the inherent complexity of this description, the implications are that the choice of this instrument allows for differentiation, as non-legislative acts are not subject to the legislative procedure laid down in the Treaty. The procedure for adopting European decisions in the area of the CFSP indeed still differs from other areas of external relations and comes close to the

---

[54] For an evaluation of the external relations under the new Constitution, see in general M. Cremona, 'The Draft Constitutional Treaty: External Relations and External Action', *CMLRev.* (2003) pp. 1347-1366; and D. Thym, 'Reforming Europe's Common Foreign and Security Policy', *European Law Journal* (2004) pp. 5-22.

[55] Ibid., at p. 1353.

current situation: a limited role for the Commission and the European Parliament and an important (even enhanced) role for the European Council and the Council of Ministers. The Court's jurisdiction continues to be excluded. Despite the overall simplification of the instruments, the Treaty even seems to hold on to the former CFSP instruments, albeit disguised as European decisions. Thus, we can easily find Common Strategies ('European decisions on the strategic interests and objectives of the Union', Arts. I-39 and III-194), Common Positions ('European decisions which shall define the approach of the Union to a particular matter of a geographical or thematic nature', Art. III-199) and Joint Actions ('Where the international situation requires operational action by the Union, the Council of Ministers shall adopt the necessary European decisions', Art. III-198(1)). The chances are high that in practice the current fragmentation of instruments will continue to exist.

This idea is strengthened by the fact that the CFSP still occupies a separate position in the new Constitution. Title V of Part I contains a separate Chapter II entitled 'Specific Provisions', in which the institutional provisions and procedures in the area of the CFSP and the Common Defence and Security Policy are laid down. In addition, Article III-209 underlines this separation by providing that the implementation of the CFSP shall not affect the other competences of the Union, and *vice versa*. Apart from the fact that with this provision the new Treaty purports to prevent not only the 'PESCalisation' of other policies (see section 3 *supra*), but also the 'communitarisation' of the CFSP, this clearly echoes the current text of Article 47 EU. Finally, fragmentation returns in the external representation of the Union. Whereas the general task of the Commission is to 'ensure the Union's external representation' (Art. I-25), this role is excluded in CFSP policies, where the new Minister for Foreign Affairs will take the lead. One could argue that consistency is ensured with the 'double-hatting' construction (the Minister for Foreign Affairs is at the same time a member of the Commission). On the other hand, given the fact that the preparation of CFSP policies will continue to be distinct from other policies, there remains a potential for conflicting policies. Moreover, practice will have to reveal if the Foreign Minister will be able to avoid schizophrenia while serving the Commission and the Council at the same time.

6. CONCLUSION

The current regulation of the European Union's external relations reflects a compromise between the unity of the Union's legal order and the wish to use separate decision-making procedures and instruments in the area of foreign and security policy and police and judicial cooperation. From an institutional perspective, the combination of the modes of governance prescribed in the different pillars in pillar-overarching cases has resulted in a fragmented external policy. To the traditional problems of vertical consistency and delimitation (often resulting in 'mixity'), the pillar structure has added the problem of horizontal consistency and delimitation. Practice shows that although competences are generally strictly divided, both vertically and horizontally, issues cannot always be handled within the safe boundaries of one pillar. Ironically, the legal institutional dilemmas caused by this situation seem to have resulted in a strengthening of the unity of the Union's legal order as practice was forced to shoot holes in the dividing walls between the pillars agreed upon in Maastricht.

The diversity and fragmentation is obstinate because of what economics refers to as 'path dependencies'. Because of the different institutional history of the pillars, which during their development created separate regimes in these areas, it has become difficult to ignore the origins of the cooperation in the three issue areas. With regard to the CFSP, in particular, the new draft Constitution maintains a certain fragmentation, as procedures and instruments continue to be different. At the same time, the unity of the Union's legal order will become more explicit after the dilution of the pillar structure, which may have a converging effect on the variations that still exist.

Finally, when the general EU procedures and instruments become the default choice where decision making with regard to external relations is concerned, the point of gravity within the CFSP may come to rest more on the most sensitive issues (security and defence) and less on foreign relations. This may result in a 'residual character' of the CFSP, because of the inclusion of more and more foreign policy issues in the general external policy of the European Union.[56] At the same time, economic sanctions, dual-use problems and the extra-territorial application of US legislation show that the non-Community pillars have served as an escape when sensitive issues present themselves. The new Constitution continues to offer possibilities in this respect.

---

[56] See also B. Martenczuk, 'Cooperation with Developing and Other Third Countries: Elements of a Community Foreign Policy', in Griller and Weidel, op. cit. n. 5, at pp. 385-418.

FUTURE PATHS OF FLEXIBILITY: ENHANCED COOPERATION, PARTIAL AGREEMENTS AND PIONEER GROUPS

Bruno de Witte*

1.   THE RECENT REVIVAL OF THE PIONEER GROUP IDEA

When the Intergovernmental Conference (IGC) at the Brussels European Council of December 2003 failed to reach agreement on the text of a draft Constitutional Treaty, the President of France immediately recalled the idea of a two-speed Europe, with a pioneer group of countries led by France and Germany. That pioneer group could set out to achieve the ambitious objectives of the draft Constitutional Treaty proposed by the Convention on the Future of the Union, in the absence of an agreement by all twenty-five national governments.[1] This revival of the pioneer group idea did not last for long, though. In the Spring of 2004, the IGC reconvened and there seemed to be a good chance, at the time of writing (May 2004), that the IGC would be able to conclude the work left undone in December 2003 and agree on the text of the draft Constitutional Treaty. Leading politicians from both France (Chirac) and Germany (Fischer) somewhat ruefully indicated that the creation of a pioneer group and the resulting two-speed Europe would not be such good ideas after all.[2]

The pioneer group idea is like some kind of Loch Ness monster of the European integration process, rearing its curiously shaped head at irregular intervals but disappearing again shortly afterwards, leading observers to doubt the reality of what they have seen and to wonder whether the monster will reappear again in the future. In fact, there are likely to be new occasions in the future when the

---

* Professor of European Union Law, European University Institute (on leave from the University of Maastricht).

[1] For references to this aspect of the Brussels summit and some immediate reactions, see 'Support for two-speed Europe gathers momentum', *Financial Times*, 15 December 2003; 'Après le fiasco de Bruxelles, Paris relance l'idée d'une Europe à la carte', *Le Monde*, 16 December 2003; 'Dutch lead criticism of two-speed Europe plan', *Financial Times*, 16 December 2003; H. Grabbe, 'The siren song of a two-speed Europe', *Financial Times*, 16 December 2003; 'Who killed the constitution?, *The Economist*, 20 December 2003; and P. Ponzano, 'Après l'échec du Sommet de Bruxelles: Constitution européenne ou coopérations renforcées?', *Revue du Droit de l'Union Européenne* (2003) p. 549.

[2] See the quotations from their speeches in 'L'Irlande espère débloquer les travaux sur la Constitution', *Le Monde*, 4 March 2004.

The European Union: An Ongoing Process of Integration – Liber Amicorum Alfred E. Kellermann
© 2004, T.M.C. Asser Instituut, The Hague, and the authors

vanguard idea will be canvassed in public speeches by leading European politicians. The first occasion will be the ratification process of the draft Constitutional Treaty. If this Treaty is duly agreed by the governments at the European Council of June 2004, but if one or more States subsequently fail to deliver the necessary ratification of the instrument (because of a failed referendum or some other cause), one may expect that the pioneer group idea will immediately be mentioned again. Even if the draft Constitutional Treaty enters into force in 2006 after having overcome all the national ratification hurdles, the question of its revision will soon arise. It is easy to predict that many of its provisions will soon appear unsatisfactory or unduly constraining, and that some countries will want to see those provisions revised, whereas others will resist further change. Given the rigid insistence of the draft Constitutional Treaty on an overall consensus by all twenty-five Member States on future changes to the Treaty, there may be acrimonious disagreements between the Member States, and plans for pioneer and vanguard groups of States could then be taken off the shelf again. In other words, the creation of a pioneer group of States may be a regular feature of the political and legal discourse about the future of European integration in the years to come.

One could say that the idea of some countries forming the vanguard of the European integration process, and clearing the path for others to follow, is as old as the process itself. The Schuman Plan of 9 May 1950 was specifically addressed only to France and Germany, but other European States were invited to join the proposed Coal and Steel Community, which was designed to be, in Robert Schuman's words, the first basis of a European federation. The Treaty establishing the Coal and Steel Community, signed in 1951 between the original six States, contained an open-ended invitation to all European States to join the Six. The EEC Treaty, signed in Rome in 1957, was similarly designed to set in place a nucleus of economic integration that could be joined by others. This, of course, is also what has happened through the gradual extension of the membership of the European Communities, and later the European Union, from six to twenty-five Member States.

As the membership of the European Union grew, the pioneer idea was gradually presented in the opposite way:[3] it no longer referred to the vanguard role of the EU Member States in relation to the rest of Europe, but rather referred to the core position of a smaller group of countries *among the Member States* that would guide the 'laggard' Member States. In view of the fact that many important policy decisions (including, of course, revisions of the founding Treaties) continued to be subject to the unanimous agreement of all Member State governments, it was felt that those countries that were not willing to envisage a further deepening of European integration were holding the others hostage. The United Kingdom

---

[3] A. Pijpers, 'Editor's Introduction', in A. Pijpers, ed., *On Cores and Coalitions in the European Union* (The Hague, Clingendael Institute 2000) p. 5 at p. 7.

became the archetypical laggard, particularly under its long series of Conservative governments starting in 1979, but other countries soon also appeared to be consistently less keen than others to extend EU powers or to make EU decision-making more supranational.

The vanguard group idea was controversially included in the European Parliament's draft Treaty on European Union in 1984. Its Article 82 provided that the proposed Treaty on European Union would enter into force if ratified by a majority of Member States representing two-thirds of the total population,[4] but it remained silent on what would happen if the non-ratifying Member States would refuse to accept the creation of this new organisation and insist on the preservation of the existing framework of the European Communities. As we know, this question remained entirely hypothetical, because the Member State governments ignored the Parliament's draft Treaty and set out to revise the Treaties by means of a traditional intergovernmental conference, providing for universal ratification of the revision treaty by all Member States. This traditional method was not only successful then in 1986 (with the adoption of the Single European Act), but was equally successful, at least formally, on three successive occasions, with the Treaties of Maastricht, Amsterdam and Nice. The fact that, each time, all the Member States could eventually be kept on board, prevented a full-fledged confrontation with the pioneer group idea.

However, this does not mean that the different degrees of willingness among States to move ahead with cooperation and European integration has not left a strong imprint on the EU legal regime as it developed over the years. There are, in fact, two existing legal mechanisms that provide, in a general way, for the constitution of a separate group of Member States seeking to achieve deeper integration. These two mechanisms have been and can continue to be vehicles for the pioneer group ideology. In the following sections of this paper, I will briefly look at these two mechanisms – enhanced cooperation and partial agreements – in order to assess the extent to which they are also appropriate for the kind of very ambitious vanguard groups that were alluded to by Chirac in December 2003 and earlier on, in 2000, by both Chirac and Fischer.

2.   ENHANCED COOPERATION AS THE 'OFFICIAL' FORM OF FLEXIBILITY

The Treaty of Maastricht introduced major forms of institutional flexibility in the field of Economic and Monetary Union and social policy. These forms of flexibility

---

[4] See R. Corbett, *The European Parliament's Role in Closer EU Integration* (Basingstoke, MacMillan 1998) pp. 170-172.

were presented at the time as (temporary) exceptions and were not advanced as a new, generally applicable mode of addressing the problem of how to deal with the variety of interests and values of the EU Member States. However, not long after the entry into force of the Maastricht reforms, the debate on the constitutional codification of a general regime of 'flexibility' began rather abruptly with a series of speeches and papers presented by leading politicians in the summer of 1994. Right from the start, this debate was linked to enlargement, flexibility being seen in some quarters as a means of sidelining unknown and possibly unpredictable newcomers, but it was also linked, more immediately and pressingly, to the fear of irreconcilable differences of views between the existing Member States. In his William and Mary Lecture given in Leiden in September 1994, John Major, the then British prime minister, welcomed the enlargement of the European Union to the East and stated that the continuing growth in size and diversity of the Union should lead to greater *à la carte* flexibility, whereby overlapping groups of countries would be allowed to cooperate in specific fields of common interest *outside* the main EU institutional framework.[5]

Around the same time, other countries, particularly France and Germany, started canvassing the alternative idea of enabling a stable core group of countries to cooperate across a broad range of policy fields, either *within* or *outside* the institutional framework of the European Union. In particular, while it was never put forward as official German government policy, the so-called Lamers-Schäuble paper presented by the CDU-CSU fraction of the *Bundestag* gave prominent attention to the idea of a core Europe (*Kerneuropa*) of pioneer countries. The paper seemed to envisage a group composed of the original six Member States, minus Italy, that would adopt a common currency and develop other common policies among themselves, and this caused immediate opposition in Italy but also in other Member States.

As a result of the debates in 1994, most governments saw both options (*à la carte* cooperation outside the EU framework and a structured core group either inside or outside the EU framework) as threats to the cohesion of the European Union and to the principle of uniform rights and duties of States that had characterised the European integration process so far. The consensus that emerged during the 1996 Intergovernmental Conference, after long and extensive negotiations, was that some mechanism of institutional flexibility should be put in place, but that it should be contained within the existing EU framework and be made subject to rather strict conditions.[6] Agreement was eventually reached, in the

---

[5] J. Major, 'Europe: A Future That Works', William and Mary Lecture, Leiden Town Hall, 7 September 1994 (Leiden, Leiden University Press 1994); *Agence Europe*, No. 6312, 10 September 1994.

[6] For a political analysis of the negotiation of the Amsterdam flexibility regime, see A. Stubb, *Negotiating Flexibility in the European Union: Amsterdam, Nice and Beyond* (Basingstoke, Palgrave

Treaty of Amsterdam, on a very cautious general mechanism allowing a group of willing States to undertake closer cooperation among themselves while using the institutional mechanisms of the European Union, but, crucially, only if the others would allow them to do so. Thus, the pioneer group idea was emphatically *not* enacted. Indeed, according to one observer, 'much of the debate about flexibility during the IGC focused on a set of regulatory conditions which were designed to prevent the creation of a *directoire* or an *avant garde* group which would forge ahead towards deeper integration, leaving behind those which were either not willing or not able.'[7]

In fact, the conditions for closer cooperation imposed by the Amsterdam Treaty were so rigid that, only one year after the Treaty's entry into force and before the new regime had even been tested in practice, Member State governments started a process of reviewing and, ultimately, redrafting the relevant rules during the IGC that took place in 2000. Closer cooperation had not been on the initial narrow IGC agenda that was agreed by the Cologne European Council in June 1999, but was put there by the Feira European Council in June 2000. The general willingness of Member State governments to consider a reform of the closer cooperation regime may have been inspired by the renewed references, in speeches by the German Foreign Minister, Joschka Fischer, and the French President, Jacques Chirac, delivered shortly before Feira, to the possible need of creating a 'centre of gravitation' or 'vanguard group' *outside* the EU framework if a more flexible system of closer cooperation *inside* the EU were not in place by the time of enlargement.[8] The threat of cooperation outside the Treaty was equally used as an argument to facilitate closer cooperation inside the Treaty in the Commission's contribution to the IGC agenda, in which it stated that 'the need to resort to arrangements for closer cooperation could increase with enlargement. We must ensure that Member States wishing to cooperate more closely together do not do so *outside* the institutional framework laid down by the Treaties, as happened for example with the Schengen Agreement before the [EC and EU] Treaty offered them an alternative.'[9] Similarly, the European Parliament affirmed that 'closer cooperation must be developed within the institutional framework of

---

2002) Ch. 4. For a legal analysis of the Amsterdam rules, see, among others, H. Bribosia, 'Différenciation et avant-gardes au sein de l'Union européenne. Bilan et perspectives du Traité d'Amsterdam', *Cahiers de droit européen* (2000) p. 57; F. Tuytschaever, *Differentiation in European Union Law* (Oxford, Hart 1999) Ch. 3; C.D. Ehlermann, 'Différenciation, flexibilité, coopération renforcée: les nouvelles dispositions du traité d'Amsterdam', *Revue du marché unique européen* (1997) p. 53; Helmut Kortenberg, 'Closer cooperation in the Treaty of Amsterdam', 35 *CMLRev.* (1998) p. 833; and G. Gaja, 'How flexible is flexibility under the Amsterdam Treaty?', 35 *CMLRev.* (1998) p. 855.

[7] Stubb, op. cit. n. 6, at p.49.

[8] See J.V. Louis, 'Post-scriptum: From differentiation to the "avant-garde"', in B. de Witte, D. Hanf and E. Vos, eds., *The Many Faces of Differentiation in EU Law* (Antwerp, Intersentia 2001) p. 379.

[9] *Adapting the institutions to make a success of enlargement*, Commission Opinion on the IGC of 2000, *Bulletin of the European Union*, Supplement 2/2000, at p. 25 [emphasis in the original text].

the Union', and that 'only the Community system offers the necessary guarantees in terms of democratic control, judicial control and solidarity.'[10]

General agreement was eventually reached – surprisingly easily (compared to the difficult negotiations on the same subject during the previous IGC) – on facilitating recourse to closer cooperation.[11] The Treaty of Nice now allows for enhanced cooperation initiatives to be launched by a qualified majority vote in the Council, except in the area of the Common Foreign and Security Policy, where the consensus of all Member States will continue to be required. The substantive conditions for closer cooperation are also somewhat relaxed compared to the Amsterdam regime. Furthermore, the Treaty of Nice sets out to modify the 'critical mass' of Member States required to launch a closer cooperation regime. Whereas, under the former rules established by the Treaty of Amsterdam, cooperation had to involve a majority of Member States, the Treaty of Nice modifies this to 'eight Member States'.[12] Since 1 May 2004, this number corresponds to less than one-third of the total membership of the Union. The reform's half-hidden agenda might well have been to allow the old Member States to cooperate more easily among themselves if and when the enlargement of the European Union appears to dilute the integration ethos.[13] Still, the resulting possibility of establishing systems of enhanced cooperation among a minority of Member States, which are allowed to operate inside the framework of the European Union, has some odd consequences: in a Union of twenty-five Member States, this theoretically allows for the creation of up to three 'vanguard groups' in the same policy field, with all three being allowed to use the organs and mechanisms of the European Union. Even if – as one might ordinarily expect – only one closer cooperation group of eight operates within a specific field of EU policy, it would be odd to see the European Commission and the European Parliament exercising their normal decision-making powers in their normal composition (i.e. with the participation of representatives of *all* the Member States) and spending their limited time and financial resources on policy initiatives benefiting only a minority of eight Member States. These oddities underline the fact that, while it may possibly allow greater flexibility in the development of

---

[10] European Parliament resolution of 25 October 2000 on closer cooperation (2000/2162(INI)).

[11] For a detailed analysis of the flexibility negotiations during the IGC of 2000, see Stubb, op. cit. n. 6, Ch. 5. For a comment on the new rules introduced by the Treaty of Nice, see J. Shaw, 'Enhancing Cooperation After Nice: Will the Treaty Do the Trick?', in M. Andenas and J.A. Usher, eds., *The Treaty of Nice and Beyond: Enlargement and Constitutional Reform* (Oxford, Hart 2003) p. 207; H. Bribosia, 'Les coopérations renforcées au lendemain du Traité de Nice', *Revue du Droit de l'Union Européenne* (2001) p. 111; L.S. Rossi, 'Cooperazione rafforzata e Trattato di Nizza: quali geometrie per l'Europa allargata?', in A. Tizzano, ed., *Il Trattato di Nizza* (2003) p. 41; and F. Tuytschaever, 'Nauwere samenwerking volgens het Verdrag van Nice', 11 *SEW* (2001) p. 375.

[12] Text of Art. 43(g) EU, as amended by the Nice Treaty.

[13] Bribosia, loc. cit. n. 11, at p. 155.

EU policies (and thereby to some extent compensate for the lack of clear-cut reforms on the other matters discussed at the Nice IGC), the decision taken in Nice to facilitate closer cooperation in an enlarged European Union also contains a danger of institutional fragmentation and policy dilution.

Immediately after the signature of the Treaty of Nice, the potential political energy needed to exploit the enhanced cooperation mechanism for forming pioneer groups[14] was diverted into the new constitutional reform process in the framework of the Convention on the Future of the Union. Within that context of across-the-board constitutional reform, flexibility did not emerge as a central issue. None of the Convention's working groups looked specifically at enhanced cooperation and the Praesidium only presented a commented set of draft Articles on this subject in May 2003,[15] that is to say, at such a late stage in the Convention's work that there was little time for a well-considered debate. On the whole, the changes proposed in the draft Treaty once again aim at facilitating closer cooperation compared to the post-Nice situation.[16] The most spectacular element is certainly the emphasis on closer cooperation in the field of defence. Whereas this policy field was previously off-limits for closer cooperation initiatives, it has now been turned into a priority area for experimentation with a range of flexibility regimes. The defence provisions of the draft Treaty, if they enter into force, will provide a legal structure for the creation of a vanguard group, or a series of vanguard groups, in this area. This is an important achievement, especially since some authors have argued that defence is, in reality, the only policy area in which there is a concrete necessity to create a legal basis for a vanguard group.[17] If the draft Treaty will not enter into force, defence cooperation between groups of Member States will have to be organised, as now, on the basis of formal or informal international agreements between the participating States. This leads me

---

[14] For an exploration of possible areas in which Nice-style enhanced cooperation could be used, see F. Dehousse, W. Coussens and G. Grevi, 'Integrating Europe. Multiple Speeds – One Direction?', EPC Working Paper No. 9 (April 2004) pp. 18 ff.

[15] Doc. CONV 723/03.

[16] For a discussion of the flexibility question as the Convention on the Future of the Union went along, see J. Shaw, 'Flexibility in a "Reorganized" and "Simplified" Treaty', *CMLRev.* (2003) p. 279; and E. Philippart and M. Sie Dhian Ho, 'Flexibility and the New Constitutional Treaty of the European Union', in J. Pelkmans, M. Sie Dhian Ho and B. Limonard, eds., *Nederland en de Europese grondwet* (Amsterdam, Amsterdam University Press 2003) p. 109. For initial comments on the final text of the draft Constitutional Treaty, see J.A. Emmanouilidis and C. Giering, 'In Vielfalt geeint – Elemente der Differenzierung im Verfassungsentwurf', *Integration* (2003) p. 454; and, with specific reference to the Common Foreign and Security Policy, D. Kugelmann, 'Kerneuropa und der EU-Aussenminister – die verstärkte Zusammenarbeit in der GASP', *Europarecht* (2004) p. 322.

[17] This is the opinion of François Lamoureux, the principal author of *Penelope*, the draft Constitutional Treaty prepared by a Commission working group and presented in December 2002: F. Lamoureux, 'La Constitution 'Pénélope': une refondation pour en finir avec les replâtrages', in A. Mattera, ed., *Pénélope – Projet de Constitution de l'Union européenne* (Paris, Juglar 2003) p. 7 at p. 30.

to the next section of this paper, in which I will consider the second of the currently available instruments for pioneer initiatives, namely, partial international agreements between a number of EU Member States.

3.   PARTIAL AGREEMENTS: AN OLD-FASHIONED KIND OF
         FLEXIBILITY

When the EEC Treaty was concluded, back in 1957, it was clear to all that the new Community institutions would not provide the exclusive framework for the relations between the six Member States. The EEC Treaty terminated none of the existing bilateral or multilateral treaties between them. During the negotiation of the EEC Treaty, and in the period immediately afterwards, several partial or *inter se* agreements[18] were concluded, also on matters related to those covered by the EEC Treaty. A prominent example of this is the Treaty establishing the Benelux Economic Union, which was concluded on 3 February 1958, that is to say, only one month after the entry into force of the EEC Treaty. In anticipation of this, Article 233 (now Art. 306) EC stated – and still states today – that the EEC Treaty does not preclude 'the existence or completion of regional unions between Belgium and Luxembourg, or between Belgium, Luxembourg and the Netherlands...'.[19]

Benelux cooperation was not the only form of international cooperation between small groups of States. For many years, the hegemonic position of the EC was not well established, and, as Helen Wallace notes, the history of relationships between European countries was also one 'of often vigorous regional groupings and intense special partnerships between neighbours.'[20] She adds that 'it is only quite recently that the argument for conceiving of the EU as all-encompassing in terms of both countries and of functional cooperation has gained momentum.' Ever since the 1950s, there have been numerous examples of international agreements concluded between EU Member States in areas such as tax law, environmental protection, defence, culture and education. Over the years, there have also been numerous forms of structured coordination of views between groups of States. Prominent examples are the Benelux coordination meetings and

---

[18] In this paper, I use the term '*inter se* agreements' as a synonym for partial agreements. It is the term traditionally used in international law for agreements concluded between some, but not all, parties to an earlier agreement.

[19] On the meaning and background of ex Article 233 EC, see particularly J.V. Louis, 'Article 233', in J. Mégret, et al., *Le droit de la Communauté économique européenne*, Vol. 15 (Brussels, Editions de l'Université de Bruxelles 1987) p. 510.

[20] H. Wallace, 'Flexibility: A Tool for Integration or a Restraint on Disintegration?', in K. Neunreither and A. Wiener, eds., *European Integration after Amsterdam: Institutional Dynamics and Prospects for Democracy* (Oxford, Oxford University Press 2000) p. 175 at p. 176.

the meetings and plans prepared by the Franco-German tandem.[21] However, there never was a *directoire*, that is to say, a stable operational alliance composed of only the larger Member States.[22]

The most prominent example of a partial agreement that has the characteristics of a 'pioneer initiative' was the Schengen cooperation regime, composed of an Agreement signed in 1985, an implementing Convention adopted in 1990 and numerous specific decisions subsequently adopted by the Schengen Executive Committee. Schengen cooperation was started at a time when a general consensus on abolishing the controls on persons at the intra-Community borders could not be reached (as it still cannot today, because of the position taken by the United Kingdom). The Schengen instruments were expressly presented as an interim arrangement in preparation of a final regime at EC level, rather than as a separate and rival cooperation regime. The same factors that justified the rule of Article 233 EC whereby the Benelux countries could adopt more advanced measures of integration could be applied to Schengen. Yet, in the course of the years, there grew a concern that Schengen was changing from a laboratory into a stable institutional regime functioning alongside the European Union, and with important deficits in terms of transparency and judicial protection.

So, by the mid-1990s, despite the much broader remit of EU activities since Maastricht, closer cooperation between smaller groups of countries outside the EU framework in matters of migration, border controls and police cooperation became a prominent political reality, and was seen by some observers as a threat to the integrity of the European legal order. Indeed, the wish to avoid *inter se* agreements and to increase the incentives for making the EU framework predominant was one of the strategic objectives pursued by those Member States pushing for a new intra-EU flexibility mechanism during the 1996-1997 IGC.[23] In the words of a close observer of that IGC hiding under the pseudonym Helmut Kortenberg: 'If such a solution [i.e. the general regime of closer cooperation of Art. 43 EU] had not been found, there was a serious risk of further instances of cooperation along the Schengen model, outside the framework of the Community treaties; and, if these examples of cooperation became numerous, there was a risk that a schism would progressively emerge in the Community, with competition from instances of intergovernmental cooperation developing outside the common institutional framework.'[24]

---

[21] For an excellent survey of the operation of those sub-systems up to the late 1980s, see Ph. de Schoutheete, 'The European Community and its Sub-Systems', in W. Wallace, ed., *The Dynamics of European Integration* (London, Pinter 1990) p. 106.

[22] De Schoutheete, loc. cit. n. 21, at p.114.

[23] Wallace, loc. cit. n. 20, at p. 188.

[24] Kortenberg, loc. cit. n. 6, at p. 835.

I have examined the legal issues raised by partial agreements in another publication.[25] *Inter se* international agreements between two or more EU Member States are allowed, but only within the limits set by EU law obligations. Briefly stated, this means that such agreements may not be concluded in areas of exclusive EU competence (e.g. in the field of trade or monetary policy), that they may not affect the normal operation of the EU institutional mechanisms (e.g. the duty of sincere cooperation) and that they may not include any provisions that conflict with EU law or undermine existing EU policies (e.g. by discriminating on grounds of nationality in favour of citizens of some Member States only). If, for instance, Belgium and Germany conclude a cultural cooperation agreement on the basis of which they grant education scholarships to each other's nationals, then the citizens of the thirteen other EU Member States are excluded from the benefit of such scholarships. This is in breach of EC law to the extent that citizens of other Member States residing in Belgium or Germany may not apply for a scholarship.[26]

Intergovernmental cooperation between a limited number of EU Member States is thus perfectly possible, but membership of the European Union imposes certain legal constraints on the scope and content of such cooperation. If they respect the principles of pre-emption, sincere cooperation and primacy of EC law, the Member States may, even after Amsterdam, continue to pursue such closer cooperation through the instruments provided by international law, chiefly through the conclusion of international agreements. If one examines the full picture of the legal relations between the Member States, it appears that flexibility is not new at all, but has always been there. The real innovation, which was tentatively introduced by the Treaty of Maastricht and then amplified by the Treaties of Amsterdam and Nice, is the effort of the Member States to discipline their own behaviour by attempting to bring certain activities that used to take place outside EU law, within the wider framework of public international law, inside the EU structure. This effort has not led to the complete disappearance of partial agreements: these will continue to play a modest but useful role in structuring the intergovernmental cooperation between Member States in fields outside or on the fringes of EU competence (such as culture, taxation and transfrontier cooperation), but will also continue to offer an alternative framework

---

[25] B. de Witte, 'Old-fashioned Flexibility: International Agreements between Member States of the European Union', in G. de Búrca and J. Scott, eds., *Constitutional Change in the EU – From Uniformity to Flexibility?* (Oxford, Hart 2000) p. 31. See also the study by L.S. Rossi, *Le convenzioni fra gli Stati membri dell'Unione europea* (Milano, Giuffrè 2000).

[26] These are the legal facts of the ECJ's judgment in *Matteucci* (Case 235/87 *Annunziata Matteucci* v. *Communauté française of Belgium et al.* [1988] *ECR* 5589). For a more detailed discussion of this and similar situations involving potential discrimination on grounds of nationality, see De Witte, loc. cit. n. 25, at pp. 49-50.

for interstate cooperation in fields of shared EU/Member State competence, particularly where less than eight Member States are willing to cooperate on a given project.

4. CONCLUSION: WHAT KIND OF VANGUARD?

In the light of the foregoing, the reference made by President Chirac to the possible creation of a pioneer group following the December 2003 stalemate on the Constitutional Treaty (and similar statements made by him and by Joschka Fischer in 2000) could be interpreted as follows: in the absence of agreement on the Constitutional Treaty, those countries supporting the draft Treaty could either try to exploit the resources of enhanced cooperation under the Nice Treaty or conclude one or more partial agreements among themselves in order to achieve some of the policy objectives contained in the draft Treaty. However, in using the enhanced cooperation mechanism, they would be constrained by the numerous rules and conditions imposed by the Nice Treaty. First, the Nice Treaty would not allow the 'pioneers' to select the members of the club, since enhanced coopera-tion regimes must be open to all Member States that wish to participate. Secondly, the Nice rules require enhanced cooperation initiatives to be taken by at least eight countries, so that an initiative, for instance, of the six original EC Member States would not qualify. Thirdly, the Nice rules do not allow for enhanced cooperation in areas that fall outside EU competences as defined by the Nice Treaty and also expressly prohibit enhanced cooperation with 'military or defence implications'.[27] This means, for instance, that the Nice mechanism could not be used for the ambitious new defence policy delineated in the draft Constitution.

Hence, in view of the restrictions imposed by the Nice regime for enhanced cooperation, the post-Convention reference to a pioneer group could also be understood as inviting forms of cooperation between smaller groups of Member States *outside the EU institutional framework*. In view of the above-mentioned conditions imposed on such extra-EU cooperation, the conclusion on this point is that specific forms of cooperation outside the core competences of the European Union are perfectly possible, but that the formation of a true core group that adopts binding laws in a large range of crucial policy areas is hardly imaginable because it would unavoidably affect the rights that the other Member States and their citizens enjoy under current EU law.

That being said, many of the statements calling for a pioneer group specify that such an initiative could not be stopped by 'legal technicalities'. In other words, the vanguard States could also deliberately choose to breach existing EU

---

[27] Article 27b EU, as inserted by the Nice Treaty.

rules if this were needed in order to liberate themselves from the strictures of the existing system. These countries would be prepared to break the law and explode the long-established institutional arrangements on the ground that the unreformed European Union no longer allows them to pursue their most cherished political goals and interests. Such a revolutionary move would require strong political resolve and close cohesion among the members of the breakaway group. At the present time, neither the resolve nor the cohesion seem to be there,[28] and it would therefore seem that the strong version of the pioneer group idea will remain on the shelf of Unused Great Ideas for some more time.

Instead, what might happen in the years to come (and the entry into force of the draft Constitutional Treaty would not by itself change this situation) is the confirmation of the existence of three major areas of differentiated integration: the existing areas of Economic and Monetary Union and post-Schengen cooperation in immigration and police cooperation, as well as the new area of defence. Alongside these three major areas, there may be some experimental use of the 'orthodox' enhanced cooperation mechanism to achieve specific goals, but, above all, there will be continued and increasing use of the omnipresent micro-flexibility[29] that has been present in Community law for decades through recourse to minimum harmonisation, soft law and tailor-made opt-outs, which are all already a major characteristic of EC regulatory instruments.[30] In this complex mosaic of differentiation, the soft contours of a vanguard group composed of those countries that participate in all three of the major structural areas of closer cooperation – EMU, post-Schengen cooperation and defence – might arise.[31]

---

[28] See, for instance, the severe assessment by Alexander Stubb, op. cit. n. 6, at p. 167): 'Those promoting an *avant garde* or *pioneer group* of states base their vision on a nostalgic assumption that there is a unitary group, driven by France and Germany, which could drive the integration process forward. Those states usually named in a possible core are precisely the ones that are reluctant to pursue deeper integration.'

[29] I borrow this expression from Dehousse, Coussens and Grevi, loc. cit. n. 14, at p. 54.

[30] For views on this kind of differentiation in secondary EU law, see e.g. G. de Búrca, 'Differentiation within the "core"? The case of the internal market', in G. de Búrca and J. Scott, eds., *Constitutional Change in the EU – From Uniformity to Flexibility?* (Oxford, Hart 2000) p. 133; and E. Vos, 'Differentiation, harmonisation and governance', in B. de Witte, D. Hanf and E. Vos, eds., *The Many Faces of Differentiation in EU Law* (Antwerp, Intersentia 2001) p. 145.

[31] See Emmanouilidis and Giering, loc. cit. n. 16, at p. 466: 'Nach der Differenzierung im Bereich der Schengener Regelungen, in denen drei Mitgliedstaaten weitgehende Ausnahmerechte genießen, sowie der Realisierung der WWU, and der ebenfalls drei Staaten nicht beteiligt sind, wird im Bereich der Verteidigungspolitik der dritte Differenzierungskreis in einem zentralen Politikfeld der Europäischen Union ermöglicht. Die Staaten, die sich letztlich an allen drei Kernen als Vollmitglieder beteiligen, werden de facto das Gravitationszentrum der europäischen Integration bilden.'

PART II

GENERAL PRINCIPLES AND SUBSTANTIVE ASPECTS

USE OF THE INFRINGEMENT PROCEDURE IN CASES OF JUDICIAL ERRORS

Christiaan Timmermans[*]

INTRODUCTORY REMARKS

Most European law specialists, those from outside Europe included, will know the T.M.C. Asser Institute. Its reputation as a centre for European law is well established. That is largely due to the unfailing efforts of Alfred Kellermann, particularly his initiatives over the years to organise international legal conferences in The Hague where, each time, he was successful in bringing together eminent specialists on European law from all over the world. Under his direction, the Institute was able to produce important publications collecting the reports drawn up for those conferences and analysing the results of the discussions. If I am not mistaken, the first conference of this kind was organised in 1985 and addressed as its main theme experiences in Member States with regard to the use (and non-use) of the preliminary procedure of what is now Article 234 EC.[1]

I shall use this occasion to pay tribute to Fred Kellermann by addressing another important branch of the jurisdiction of the Court of Justice of the European Communities, namely, its power under the infringement procedure of Articles 226 to 228 EC to declare on request of the European Commission (Art. 226 EC) or a Member State (Art. 227 EC) that a Member State has failed to fulfil an obligation under the Treaty. The issue I shall address more specifically is the use of the infringement procedure in a situation where a failure to respect Community law is due not to (in)action by a Member State's legislature or executive but to a decision of the judiciary. This is an old question in Community law literature.[2] However, a recent judgment of the ECJ and subsequent developments in the application of the infringement procedure by the European Commission warrant a reopening of the debate.

---

[*] Judge at the Court of Justice of the European Communities.

[1] Henry G. Schermers, et al., eds., *Article 177 EEC: Experiences and Problems*, T.M.C. Asser Institute Colloquium on European Law (Amsterdam, North-Holland 1987).

[2] H.A.H. Audretsch, *Supervision in European Community Law*, 2nd rev. edn. (Amsterdam, North-Holland 1986) pp. 100-105 with further references.

The European Union: An Ongoing Process of Integration – Liber Amicorum Alfred E. Kellermann
© 2004, T.M.C. Asser Instituut, The Hague, and the authors

A POSSIBILITY REMAINING LARGELY THEORETICAL

As early as 1970, the ECJ ruled in the well-known *Belgian Wood* case that 'the liability of a Member State under Article 169 [now Article 226 EC] arises whatever the agency of the State whose action or inaction is the cause of the failure to fulfil its obligations, even in the case of a constitutionally independent institution'.[3] This was the reply the Court gave to an argument of the Belgian Government pleading *force majeure* and arguing on that ground that the action of the Commission had to be dismissed, because of the fact that a bill had already been submitted to Parliament to amend the discriminatory tax treatment in question, that bill however having automatically lapsed owing to the dissolution of the Parliament.

The same idea, namely, that the State must be viewed as a unity whatever the nature of the organ that is actually acting, was expressed again, but in the different context of State liability for damages caused by violation of Community law, in the *Brasserie du Pêcheur and Factortame* cases, where the Court held that the principle of State liability 'holds good for any case in which a Member State breaches Community law, whatever be the organ of the State whose act or omission was responsible for the breach', adding that 'the obligation to make good damages ... cannot depend on domestic rules as to the division of powers between constitutional authorities'.[4] The *Köbler* judgment of 30 September 2003, also in the context of State liability, has clarified that the first quote from the judgment in *Brasserie du Pêcheur and Factortame* must indeed be read as it reads: as also covering the national judiciary, albeit only under particular conditions.[5]

Does the same hold true for the different context of State responsibility for infringements liable to be pursued under the infringement procedure? Before the judgment in the *Belgian Wood* case was rendered, the European Commission had already taken this view in its answers to various parliamentary questions.[6] However, the Commission always advocated a cautious approach in this regard.

An implicit justification for this approach was given in the Commission's answer to question no. 349/69 of Mr Westerterp, when it referred to the opinion of the Legal Affairs Committee of the European Parliament as expressed in the Merchiers Report of 1969, according to which the possible use of the Article 169 procedure would be frustrated by the independence of the judiciary in relation to

---

[3] ECJ, Case 77/69 *Commission* v. *Belgium* [1970] *ECR* 237, para. 15.

[4] ECJ, Joined Cases C-46/93 and C-48/93 *Brasserie du Pêcheur and Factortame* [1996] *ECR* I-1029, paras. 32 and 33.

[5] ECJ, Case C-224/01 *Köbler*, judgment of 30 September 2003, *ECR*, nyr.

[6] Written questions nos. 100/67 by Mr. Westerterp (*OJ* 1967 270/2), 28/68 by Mr. Deringer (*OJ* 1968 C 71) and 349/69 by Mr. Westerterp (*OJ* 1970 C 20).

the executive.[7] Accordingly, the Commission replied to a later parliamentary question urging it to take action under the infringement procedure against Germany, in view of the *Solange-I* judgement of the German *Bundesverfassungsgericht*, that it did not consider such action 'opportune'.[8]

Personally, I have always considered this policy of the Commission, which it has maintained until recently, a wise form of self-restraint. Even if it is legally possible, using the infringement procedure to condemn decisions of what will normally be the highest judicial body of a Member State could indeed create problems of execution because of the independence of the judiciary and the principle of *res judicata*. If a Member State is condemned for the infringement of Community law as a result of a decision of its judiciary, it will normally not be able to undo that decision or force the judiciary to do so. The recent decisions of the ECJ in the *Köbler* and *Kühne & Heitz* cases could not be invoked to argue the contrary. In *Köbler*, the Court was at pains to stress that a successful action for damages because of a violation of Community law attributable to the judiciary would leave the judicial decision in question untouched and would therefore not encroach upon the principle of *res judicata*. The principle of State liability requires reparation of damages but not the revision of the judicial decision that caused the damage.[9] Neither does the decision in the case of *Kühne & Heitz* have any bearing on the principle of *res judicata*. First of all, the issue in that case was not the principle of *res judicata* but the authority of a final administrative decision that can no longer be appealed. Moreover, the exception to this authority that the Court accepted in *Kühne & Heitz* was made subject to special conditions, the first of which being that national law itself allows the administrative organ in question to reconsider its decision.[10]

Apart from the possible problems for a Member State to take the necessary measures to comply with a Court decision condemning it for the violation of Community law by its judiciary, the use of the infringement procedure for this purpose might also unnecessarily burden the cooperative relationship between the highest courts of the member States and the ECJ. Unnecessarily so, because in many cases it is possible to address the problem of the violation of Community law as the result of a national court decision in other ways than by directly attacking the decision by means of an infringement procedure. If the decision of the national court applies national law that is contrary to Community law or interprets that law in a way contrary to Community law, there is no need to take action for infringement against the court decision itself. The Commission would

---

[7] *OJ* 1970 C 20.

[8] Written question no. 414/74 by Mr Cousté, *OJ* 1975 C 54.

[9] ECJ, Case C-224/01 *Köbler*, judgment of 30 September 2003, *ECR*, nyr, paras. 37 to 40.

[10] ECJ, Case C-453/00 *Kühne & Heitz*, judgment of 13 January 2004, *ECR*, nyr.

then be well advised to tackle the problem at its root and pursue the Member State because its national law infringes Community law. Decisions of the national judiciary involving an application or interpretation of national law that is contrary to Community law could be mentioned by the Commission just to illustrate the reality of the infringement. The infringement procedure would thus fully serve its purpose: to secure the amendment of a national law to bring it into conformity with Community law and in doing so solve the problem once and for all. A similar approach could be followed where the judicial decision infringing Community law upholds an administrative practice contrary to Community law. Commission action under the infringement procedure could then focus on that administrative practice and invoke the relevant judicial decision to illustrate the reality of that practice.

What should preferably be addressed through the infringement procedure are not judicial decisions but actions of the legislature or the executive to which these decisions relate. If the infringement could be solved once and for all by an amendment of national law or by changing an administrative practice, using the infringement procedure to this effect would be more effective than using it to attack a national court decision in an individual case. More generally, one might question the wisdom of using the infringement procedure to address individual cases of violation of Community law, not only because of the scarce resources available to the Commission (and the European judiciary) for this purpose, but also because of the limited scope of the infringement procedure as an instrument to provide legal redress to the individual victims of such violations.[11] As far as legal redress for individual persons is concerned, other remedies would seem to be more appropriate, such as a remedy under the State liability doctrine or, possibly, a request to the competent administrative body to reconsider its decision under the conditions of *Kühne & Heitz*.[12]

THE JUDGMENT OF 9 DECEMBER 2003: A WATERSHED?

After these general remarks on the use of the infringement procedure with regard to decisions of national judiciaries that violate Community law, it is time to turn to the judgment of the ECJ of 9 December 2003 in *Commission* v. *Italian Republic* (C-129/00), which has reopened the debate on this issue.[13]

---

[11] Cf. Jean-Pierre Puissochet, 'L'action en manquement peut-elle encore se parer de ses justes vertus?', in Ninon Colneric, et al., eds., *Une communauté de droit, Festschrift für Gil Carlos Rodrígues Iglesias* (Berlin, Berliner Wissenschafts-Verlag 2003) p. 569.

[12] See n. 10 *supra*.

[13] See the annotations by K.J.M. Mortelmans and J.W. van de Gronden, *Ars Aequi* (2004) p. 192, and by R.J.G.M. Widdershoven, *AB* 2004 no. 59.

This judgment is the fourth in a series of cases involving Italian legislation related to the reimbursement of taxes levied contrary to Community law and therefore unduly paid. Community law requires reimbursement, but, in the absence of specific Community rules, the conditions and procedures for obtaining reimbursement are a matter for national law, provided that the well-known principles of equivalence and effectiveness are satisfied. According to the case law, reimbursement can be refused when the amount concerned has been passed on to other traders or the consumer. At issue is the allotment of the burden of proof in this respect. The original legislation explicitly required the taxpayer to deliver the negative proof that he had not passed on those taxes. In *San Giorgio*, this requirement was held to make reimbursement virtually impossible or excessively difficult, and consequently contrary to Community law.[14] The Italian legislation was subsequently amended. The condition that, in order to obtain reimbursement, the taxes that were unduly paid should not have been passed on to others was maintained, but any reference to the distribution of the burden of proof was omitted. In *Dilexport*, the referring Italian court observed that, under the new rule, the Italian courts allowed the administrative authorities to rely on the presumption that taxes are normally passed on to third parties. The Court answered that, if that were the case, such a presumption and the obligation for the plaintiff to rebut that presumption had to be regarded as contrary to Community law. However, it was left to the referring court to establish whether that was in fact the case.[15]

The Commission then lodged an action under the infringement procedure against Italy on the grounds that the provisions of the new legislation, as applied by the Italian administrative authorities and the courts, produced the same results as the previous legislation. The action was successful.

The Court started its reasoning with a reference to the aforementioned *Belgian Wood* case,[16] according to which a Member State's failure may be established under Article 226 EC whatever the agency of the State that is involved, even in the case of a constitutionally independent institution, adding that the scope of national laws must be assessed in the light of the interpretation given to them by national courts (paras. 29 and 30). Given that the rule of Italian law at issue is neutral in relation to the burden of proof and the evidence admissible to prove that the tax charge has been passed on, the effects of this rule must be determined in the light of the construction which the national courts gave it (para. 31). The Court then continued:

---

[14] ECJ, Case 199/82 *San Giorgio* [1983] *ECR* 3595; see also Case 104/86 *Commission* v. *Italy* [1988] *ECR* 1799.

[15] ECJ, Case C-343/96 *Dilexport* [1999] *ECR* I-579.

[16] See n. 3 *supra*.

'32. In that regard, isolated or numerically insignificant judicial decisions in the context of case-law taking a different direction, or still more a construction disowned by the national supreme court, cannot be taken into account. That is not true of a widely-held judicial construction which has not been disowned by the supreme court, but rather confirmed by it.

33. Where national legislation has been the subject of different relevant judicial constructions, some leading to the application of that legislation in compliance with Community law, others leading to the opposite application, it must be held that, at the very least, such legislation is not sufficiently clear to ensure its application in compliance with Community law.'

A subsequent analysis of the judgments of the *Corte suprema di cassazione* cited by the Commission brings the Court to the conclusion that a presumption (of passing on) is being applied, which is contrary to Community law. It then examines the practice of the administrative authorities regarding, in particular, the documentary evidence that must be produced in order to refute that the tax charge has been passed on, and concludes that these practices lead to an unjustified presumption contrary to Community law. The Italian Republic is finally condemned for failing to fulfil its Treaty obligations by 'failing to amend' the Italian rule in question, 'which is construed and applied by the administrative authorities and a substantial proportion of the courts, including the *Corte suprema di cassazione,* in such a way that the exercise of the right to repayment of charges levied in breach of Community rules is made excessively difficult for the taxpayer...' (para. 41 of the judgment).

It is important to point out that this case is not about an infringement by a Member State because of a judicial decision contrary to Community law. Italy has not been condemned because of the fact that the Italian *Corte suprema di cassazione* violated Community law. This was not the object of the proceedings as defined by the European Commission, nor do the terms of the operative part of the ruling warrant such a conclusion. In the conclusions of its application, the Commission asked the Court to declare that 'by maintaining in force' the relevant provision of Italian law 'as construed and applied by the administrative authorities and the courts' Italy had breached Community law. Similarly, albeit slightly differently worded, the Court declared Italy to have breached Community law 'by failing to amend' that provision as it is 'construed and applied by the administrative authorities and a substantial proportion of the courts, including the *Corte suprema di cassazione*'. Both the action of the Commission and the ruling of the Court thus address a failure of the legislature, not of the courts. The difficulties that could arise, particularly with regard to the execution of the judgment, if the judgment were to address a national court decision, as discussed earlier, do not arise at all in this case. The measure necessary to comply with the judgment of the

Court (Art. 228 EC) will have to be taken by the legislature and also partly by the administrative authorities with regard to the rules of evidence they apply.

For these reasons, the judgment does not really break new ground. It does not mark a watershed and should not be read as a general indication of the conditions under which a Member State could be held responsible in an infringement procedure for a decision of its national judiciary that is contrary to Community law. In particular, paragraph 32 of the judgment, which is quoted above, should not be read in this manner. When this paragraph refers to isolated judicial decisions or a construction disowned by the national supreme court that cannot be taken into account, this concerns the question whether the effects of the national legislation as interpreted by the courts are contrary to Community law, not the question whether and under what conditions an individual court decision could be made subject to an infringement procedure. In the end, the infringement with which the Commission reproached Italy and which the Court upheld relates to an infringement by the legislature (and the administrative authorities), not the judiciary.

Indeed, in order to establish whether a rule of national law is compatible with Community law or not, it will sometimes be necessary to take into account the interpretation that is given to this rule by the courts, particularly in those cases where the wording of that rule is not sufficiently clear to establish compatibility. The interpretation given by the courts finally determines what the rule-maker has said. Thus, if a rule of national law is held to be incompatible with Community law in the light of the interpretation of that rule given by the courts, it is the legislature that can be held responsible for the relevant infringement. The Commission could perhaps have directly and exclusively attacked the case law itself as being contrary to the principle of effectiveness. It was wise not to do so.

FINAL REMARKS

More delicate will be those cases where a national court decision directly applies a rule of Community law without any interference of national law. A possible breach of Community law by a court decision in such cases could not be imputed to the legislature. However, where rules of substantive Community law are involved, for instance common agricultural policy or transport policy regulations, these rules will in the first place have been applied by the competent national authorities. Confronted with a national court decision incorrectly applying such rules, the Commission will normally be able to address the practice of application followed by the competent authorities in an infringement procedure, either because this practice is affected by the same breach of Community law or, if it does not, because the Commission wants to ensure that administrative practice remains unaffected by this breach in the future.

In this context, it is interesting to note that, according to a recent press release,[17] the European Commission has started an infringement procedure against the Netherlands because of a judgment of the Dutch *Hoge Raad* (Supreme Court), which in the view of the Commission incorrectly interpreted Regulation 1408/71 on the application of social security schemes to employed persons, self-employed persons and their families moving within the Community.[18] In this case, a worker was transferred by his employer from the Netherlands to Germany. According to Article 14(1)(a) of the Regulation, a worker in principle remains subject to the social security legislation of the transferor State provided his transfer does not exceed a period of one year. For this purpose, the worker receives a certificate confirming that he continues to be covered by the social security regime of the transferor Member State. The worker in question had moved his residence to Germany and considered that from that moment he was no longer liable to pay premiums under the Dutch regime. The *Hoge Raad* confirmed this interpretation and held that, because the worker in question had transferred his residence to Germany, Dutch social security legislation was no longer applicable. A conflict of laws thus being excluded, Regulation 1408/71 did not apply.

In response to parliamentary questions, the Dutch Minister for Social Affairs explicitly stated that the Dutch Government held this interpretation of the *Hoge Raad* to be incompatible with Community legislation.[19] He concluded that the decision of the *Hoge Raad* should remain without any effect in administrative practice in other cases than the case at hand. The position taken by the Dutch Government according to this answer would seem to make it difficult to address an administrative practice contrary to Community law in an infringement procedure. It remains to be seen whether under these circumstances the Commission will continue its infringement procedure.

Of course, there remain cases in which it will not be possible to pursue a breach of Community law attributable to decisions of the national judiciary indirectly, as it were, by focusing on national rules as interpreted by these decisions or administrative practices as confirmed by them. This could occur in cases where a national court does not comply with a Community law obligation directly imposed upon it, such as, for instance, the principle of supremacy of Community law or the obligation under Article 234, third paragraph, EC to refer preliminary questions to the ECJ. If such a breach of Community law is only of an incidental nature, one would be inclined to share the opinion expressed by the

---

[17] IP/04/178 of 9 February 2004.
[18] *Hoge Raad*, Case no. 37.446, judgment of 11 July 2003.
[19] *Aanhangsel Handelingen II* 2003/04, no. 172.

European Commission in 1974 that starting an infringement procedure and, in particular, bringing the case before the Court might not be 'opportune'. However, if such violations were to become intentional and systematic, the infringement procedure might in the end appear to provide little relief. Indeed, were that to happen, the Union would be confronted with an entirely different problem. Systematic infringements of such a nature would seem to outgrow the framework of the infringement procedure. They would develop into a constitutional conflict and call into question the rule of law of the Union and its basic principles. For a constitutional conflict of such magnitude, the final redress under the Treaty might be a procedure under Article 7 of the Treaty on European Union, if the conditions for this procedure are met.

Fortunately, these final remarks are purely of academic interest.

STATE LIABILITY AND INFRINGEMENTS ATTRIBUTABLE TO NATIONAL COURTS: A DUTCH PERSPECTIVE ON THE *KÖBLER* CASE

J.H. Jans*

1.   THE FACTS IN *KÖBLER* [1]

Gerhard Köbler had been employed as an ordinary university professor in Innsbruck (Austria) since 1 March 1986. On his appointment, he was awarded the salary of an ordinary university professor – grade 10 – increased by the normal length-of-service increment. Ten years later, he applied for the special length-of-service increment for university professors under Article 50a of the *Gehaltsgesetz* (Salaries Act) of 1956. He claimed that, although he had not completed fifteen years' service as a professor at an Austrian university, he had completed the requisite length of service if the duration of his service at universities in other Member States of the European Community was taken into account. He claimed that the condition of the completion of fifteen years' service solely in Austrian universities, with no account being taken of periods of service in universities in other Member States, constituted unjustified indirect discrimination under Community law. Köbler then instituted proceedings before the *Verwaltungs-gerichtshof* (administrative court), which referred the matter to the Court of Justice for a preliminary ruling. In the meantime, the Court of Justice had delivered its judgment in *Schöning-Kougebetopoulou*.[2] The Court of Justice asked the *Verwaltungsgerichtshof* whether – in the light of this judgment – it deemed it necessary to maintain its request for a preliminary ruling. On 24 June 1998, the *Verwaltungsgerichtshof* withdrew its request for a preliminary ruling and dismissed Köbler's application, on the grounds that the special length-of-service increment was a loyalty bonus that objectively justified a derogation from the Community law provisions on freedom of movement for workers. Köbler refused to give up and brought an action for damages against the Republic of Austria. In

---

* Prof. Jans (1956) teaches EU law at the University of Amsterdam and public law at the University of Groningen.

[1] Case C-224/01 *Köbler*, judgment of 30 September 2003.

[2] Case C-15/96 *Schöning-Kougebetopoulou* [1998] *ECR* I-47.

The European Union: An Ongoing Process of Integration – Liber Amicorum Alfred E. Kellermann
© 2004, T.M.C. Asser Instituut, The Hague, and the authors

his view, the judgment of the *Verwaltungsgerichtshof* infringed directly applicable provisions of Community law.

2.   THE PRINCIPLE OF STATE LIABILITY FOR JUDICIAL ACTS

The first question the Court had to answer was one of principle. Can the State be held liable for judicial mistakes? The Court observed that it had already held in *Brasserie du Pêcheur and Factortame*[3] that the principle of State liability holds good in any case in which a Member State breaches Community law, whatever the organ of the State whose act or omission was responsible for the breach. It then pointed out the essential role played by the judiciary in protecting the rights individuals derive from Community rules, and that the full effectiveness of those rules would be called into question if individuals were precluded from being able to obtain reparation in the event of errors by the judiciary. The Court particularly stressed the crucial role played by a court adjudicating at last instance, as this is by definition the last judicial body before which individuals may assert the rights conferred on them by Community law. Since an infringement of these rights by the final decision of such a court cannot normally be corrected, individuals cannot be deprived of the possibility of rendering the State liable in order to obtain legal protection of their rights. The Court concluded:

> 'Consequently, it follows from the requirements inherent in the protection of the rights of individuals relying on Community law that they must have the possibility of obtaining redress in the national courts for the damage caused by the infringement of those rights owing to a decision of a court adjudicating at last instance (see in that connection *Brasserie du Pêcheur and Factortame*, cited above, paragraph 35).' (para. 36)

It is striking that the Court went on to consider the main objections Member States had raised against the principle of State liability in respect of these kinds of judicial decisions only after it had stated its position on this matter of principle. In the first place, the arguments put forward were based on the principle of legal certainty and, more specifically, the principle of *res judicata*. While acknowledging the importance of the principle of *res judicata*,[4] the Court dismissed this argument:

---

[3] Joined Cases C-46/93 and C-48/93 *Brasserie du Pêcheur and Factortame* [1996] *ECR* I-1029, para. 32.

[4] See also the judgment in Case C-453/00 *Kühne & Heitz*, 13 January 2004, para. 24.

'[I]t should be borne in mind that recognition of the principle of State liability for a decision of a court adjudicating at last instance does not in itself have the consequence of calling in question that decision as *res judicata*. Proceedings seeking to render the State liable do not have the same purpose and do not necessarily involve the same parties as the proceedings resulting in the decision which has acquired the status of *res judicata*. The applicant in an action to establish the liability of the State will, if successful, secure an order against it for reparation of the damage incurred but not necessarily a declaration invalidating the status of *res judicata* of the judicial decision which was responsible for the damage. In any event, the principle of State liability inherent in the Community legal order requires such reparation, but not revision of the judicial decision which was responsible for the damage.' (para. 39)

Nor did arguments based on the independence and authority of the judiciary fare any better. As regards the independence of the judiciary, the Court observed that the principle of liability in question concerned not the personal liability of the judge but that of the State:

'The possibility that under certain conditions the State may be rendered liable for judicial decisions contrary to Community law does not appear to entail any particular risk that the independence of a court adjudicating at last instance will be called in question.' (para. 42)

And it was clearly little impressed by the argument based on the risk of a diminution of judicial authority: '[T]he existence of a right of action that affords, under certain conditions, reparation of the injurious effects of an erroneous judicial decision could also be regarded as enhancing the quality of a legal system and thus in the long run the authority of the judiciary.' (para. 43)

Finally, the Court considered the argument that it was difficult in many legal systems to designate a court competent to determine such disputes. It observed that application of the principle of State liability could not be compromised by the absence of a competent court. Referring to its well-known judgments in *Rewe* and *Comet*, the Court observed in paragraph 46 that: 'it is for the internal legal order of each Member State to designate the competent courts and lay down the detailed procedural rules for legal proceedings intended fully to safeguard the rights which individuals derive from Community law.' It went on to state:

'Subject to the reservation that it is for the Member States to ensure in each case that those rights are effectively protected, it is not for the Court to become involved in resolving questions of jurisdiction to which the classification of certain legal situations based on Community law may give rise in the national judicial system.' (para. 47)

The Court concluded, in summary,

'that the principle according to which the Member States are liable to afford reparation of damage caused to individuals as a result of infringements of Community
law for which they are responsible is also applicable where the alleged infringement stems from a decision of a court adjudicating at last instance. It is for the
legal system of each Member State to designate the court competent to adjudicate
on disputes relating to such reparation.' (para. 50)

3.   THE CONDITIONS GOVERNING STATE LIABILITY

The Court then discussed the conditions governing State liability. In paragraph
51, it stated the familiar three conditions: 'the rule of law infringed must be
intended to confer rights on individuals; the breach must be sufficiently serious;
and there must be a direct causal link between the breach of the obligation
incumbent on the State and the loss or damage sustained by the injured parties.'
In paragraph 52, it went on to add: 'State liability for loss or damage caused by a
decision of a national court adjudicating at last instance which infringes a rule of
Community law is governed by the same conditions.' However, as regards the
requirement of 'a sufficiently serious breach', it noted that regard must be had to
the specific nature of the judicial function and to the legitimate requirements of
legal certainty: 'State liability for an infringement of Community law by a
decision of a national court adjudicating at last instance can be incurred only in
the exceptional case where the court has *manifestly* infringed the applicable law.'
(para. 53, emphasis added)
   In order to determine whether this condition was satisfied, namely, whether
the infringement was manifest, the national court must take account of various
factors, including:

'the degree of clarity and precision of the rule infringed, whether the infringement
was intentional, whether the error of law was excusable or inexcusable, the position taken, where applicable, by a Community institution and non-compliance by
the court in question with its obligation to make a reference for a preliminary ruling under the third paragraph of Article 234 EC.' (para. 55)

In any event, the protection thus afforded is a minimum protection and this
therefore 'does not mean that the State cannot incur liability under less strict
conditions on the basis of national law.' (para. 57)
   Such claims are governed by the 'ordinary' rules of national law on liability,

'with the proviso that the conditions for reparation of loss and damage laid down by the national legislation must not be less favourable than those relating to similar domestic claims and must not be so framed as to make it in practice impossible or excessively difficult to obtain reparation.' (para. 58)

In paragraph 59, the Court summarised the above one more time:

'In the light of all the foregoing, the reply to the first and second questions must be that the principle that Member States are obliged to make good damage caused to individuals by infringements of Community law for which they are responsible is also applicable where the alleged infringement stems from a decision of a court adjudicating at last instance where the rule of Community law infringed is intended to confer rights on individuals, the breach is sufficiently serious and there is a direct causal link between that breach and the loss or damage sustained by the injured parties. In order to determine whether the infringement is sufficiently serious when the infringement at issue stems from such a decision, the competent national court, taking into account the specific nature of the judicial function, must determine whether that infringement is manifest. It is for the legal system of each Member State to designate the court competent to determine disputes relating to that reparation.'

4.   HOW DID IT END?

Although it is normally for the national courts to apply the conditions for liability (see *Brasserie du Pêcheur and Factortame*, paras. 55-57), in this case the Court felt able to do so itself, as it had all the relevant information at its disposal. As regards the requirement that the rule of law infringed must confer rights on individuals, the Court held that it could not be disputed that Article 39 EC and Article 7(1) of Regulation No 1612/68 were intended to confer such rights. By doing so, the Court also indicated that the primary basis for State liability in respect of judicial errors must be sought in the underlying substantive law rather than in the infringement of the third paragraph of Article 234 EC. This important point will be considered in more detail below.

As regards the requirement that the breach be sufficiently serious, the Court first described the precise course of the proceedings and then, in paragraphs 117 and 118, arrived at the conclusion that – in the light of *CILFIT*[5] – the *Verwaltungsgerichtshof* should have maintained its request for a preliminary ruling. Accordingly, the *Verwaltungsgerichtshof* infringed Community law when it gave

---

[5] Case 283/81 *CILFIT* v. *Ministry of Health* [1982] *ECR* 3415.

its judgment (para. 119). The next step was to examine whether this infringement constituted 'a manifest infringement' of Community law, having regard to the factors indicated in paragraphs 55 and 56. In this case, the Court held that there was no question of a manifest infringement. In the first place, the infringement of substantive law – Article 39 EC and Article 7(1) of Regulation No 1612/68 – could not in itself be so characterised:

'Community law does not expressly cover the point whether a measure for reward-ing an employee's loyalty to his employer, such as a loyalty bonus, which entails an obstacle to freedom of movement for workers, can be justified and thus be in conformity with Community law. No reply was to be found to that question in the Court's case-law. Nor, moreover, was that reply obvious.' (para. 122)

Nor, in the second place, could the infringement of Article 234 EC – the failure to maintain the request for a preliminary ruling – be regarded as 'a sufficiently serious breach':

'the *Verwaltungsgerichtshof* had decided to withdraw the request for a preliminary ruling, on the view that the reply to the question of Community law to be resolved had already been given in the judgment in *Schöning-Kougebetopoulou*, cited above. Thus, it was owing to its incorrect reading of that judgment that the *Verwal-tungsgerichtshof* no longer considered it necessary to refer that question of interpretation to the Court.' (para. 123)

In short, the *Verwaltungsgerichtshof* may have infringed Community law when it gave its decision of 24 June 1998, but 'in the light of the circumstances of the case', there was no reason for the Court to regard this infringement as being manifest in nature and thus as sufficiently serious.

5.   SOME COMMENTS

5.1   The principle of State liability

The matter has finally been resolved. *Francovich*[6] liability does indeed apply to all organs of the State, including a court adjudicating at last instance. In some respects, this decision is not surprising. After *Brasserie du Pêcheur* it was hardly conceivable that the Court would decide that judicial errors could not give rise to liability. In this sense, *Köbler* is fully in line with the Court's judgment in

---

[6] Joined Cases C-6/90 and C-9/90 *Francovich and Bonifaci* [1991] *ECR* I-5357.

Commission v. *Italy*,[7] where Italy was held to have failed to fulfil its obligations under the Treaty because the manner in which Italian courts, 'including the *Corte suprema di cassazione*', applied Italian legislation was incompatible with Community law.

5.2   The conditions

Nor can the conditions for State liability really be considered surprising. The central criterion remains that the breach must be 'sufficiently serious'. The Court does, however, sow some confusion by concluding, after it has pointed out the specific nature of the judicial function, that the State can incur liability only where the national court has 'manifestly' infringed the applicable law. Although the 'judicial function' is not so special that judicial errors should as such be excluded from State liability, regard must be had to the specific nature of this function when determining the conditions. The question is whether the Court here means anything different from what it means when it employs the usual formula for determining whether a breach is sufficiently serious. According to this formula, in the first place, a breach is sufficiently serious where 'a Member State, in the exercise of its legislative powers, has manifestly and gravely disregarded the limits on its powers...', and, secondly, 'where, at the time when it committed the infringement, the Member State in question had only considerably reduced, or even no, discretion, the mere infringement of Community law may be sufficient to establish the existence of a sufficiently serious breach'.[8] The application of the requirement that the breach be 'manifest', particularly in connection with Article 234 EC, is examined in more detail below.

5.3   Primary basis?

In our book on the 'Europeanisation' of Dutch administrative law,[9] we assert that the European dimension of the issue of State liability for wrongful judicial decisions is in fact confined to possible liability for judicial bodies that fail to fulfil their obligations under the third paragraph of Article 234. This view will have to be revised in the next edition. It is clear from the Court's decision in *Köbler* that the *primary* basis for liability is the infringement of the underlying substantive rules. This is because, if the key issue was the infringement of the third paragraph of Article 234 EC, it would have been logical for the Court to concentrate on how the

---

[7] Case C-129/00 *Commission* v. *Italy*, judgment of 9 December 2003.

[8] See, for instance, Case C-118/00 *Larsy* [2001] *ECR* I-5063, para. 38.

[9] J.H. Jans, R. de Lange, S. Prechal and R.J.G.M. Widdershoven, *Inleiding tot het Europees bestuursrecht*, 2nd edn. (Nijmegen, Ars Aequi 2002) p. 402. The authors intend to publish an English version of this book in 2005/2006.

obligation to refer questions to the Court of Justice protects the rights of injured parties when considering whether the rules that had been infringed 'confer rights on individuals'. Instead, in paragraph 103 et seq., the Court discusses whether the provisions of Article 39 EC and Article 7(1) of Regulation 1612/68 confer rights on individuals. Moreover, in paragraph 117, the Court observes that the *Verwaltungs-gerichtshof* ought to have maintained its request for a preliminary ruling. In other words, it infringed the third paragraph of Article 234 by withdrawing its request. To use the terminology of *CILFIT*, the condition that there can be 'no scope for any reasonable doubt as to the manner in which the question raised is to be resolved' was not fulfilled. The infringement of the third paragraph of Article 234 in combination with a wrong application of the underlying substantive law (as was indeed the case in *Köbler*) does not in itself give rise to liability. This is insufficient for the Court to regard it as a 'manifest infringement'. In other words, failure to meet the 'absence of reasonable doubt' criterion in *CILFIT* is insufficient to make the infringement 'manifest'. This seems to imply a double reasonableness test, and this would seem to imply that the Court of Justice allows courts more latitude to make errors than other organs of the State. This is only otherwise in cases where a national court more or less categorically refuses to apply the existing case law of the Court of Justice. In this kind of case, 'strict' liability under *Francovich* applies. As far as case law is concerned, this is unlikely to be the most important category of cases. There are, fortunately, few examples of decisions by the highest national courts where Community law has been ignored.[10]

Wattel has pointed out that the combination of *Köbler* and *CILFIT* could lead to many more references for a preliminary ruling.[11] It is therefore worth quoting again the words the Court used in *CILFIT* to indicate when the highest national court is relieved of its obligation to refer a matter to the Court of Justice on grounds that the matter is obvious:

'Finally, the correct application of Community law may be so obvious as to leave no scope for any reasonable doubt as to the manner in which the question raised is to be resolved. Before it comes to the conclusion that such is the case, the national court or tribunal must be convinced that the matter is equally obvious to the courts of the other Member States and to the Court of Justice. Only if those conditions are satisfied, may the national court or tribunal refrain from submitting the question to the Court of Justice and take upon itself the responsibility for resolving it.' (*CILFIT*, para.16)

---

[10] But see the case of *Dangeville*, European Court of Human Rights, 16 April 2002, and Case C-129/00 *Commission* v. *Italy*.

[11] P.J. Wattel, 'Staatsaansprakelijkheid voor EG-rechtelijk onrechtmatige hoogste rechtspraak', 134 *WPNR* (2003) pp. 840-845.

If this means what it says, this exception does not amount to much. The conditions are so strict that the national court will not readily conclude that it is not required to refer the matter to the Court of Justice. It is therefore quite possible that *Köbler* will lead to considerably more requests for a preliminary ruling 'just to be on the safe side'. This in turn will undoubtedly result in the Court making more active and more frequent use of Article 104(3) of its Rules of Procedure:

'Where a question referred to the Court for a preliminary ruling is identical to a question on which the Court has already ruled, where the answer to such a question may be clearly deduced from existing case-law or where the answer to the question admits of no reasonable doubt, the Court may, after informing the court or tribunal which referred the question to it, hearing any observations submitted by the persons referred to in Article 23 of the Statute and hearing the Advocate General, give its decision by reasoned order in which, if appropriate, reference is made to its previous judgment or to the relevant case-law.'

If the Court were to make more use of this article, this could well adversely affect the already sensitive relationship between the Court of Justice and the highest national courts. It is no secret that national courts are 'not amused' when the Court gives its decision by reasoned order under Article 104(3) of its Rules of Procedure. This is because application of Article 104(3) implies that the court referring the matter is unfamiliar with the case law of the Court of Justice. And courts, especially the highest courts, do not like to be told this. It seems to me that it is high time a national court requested a preliminary ruling on the exact scope of paragraph 3 of Article 234 EC and the *CILFIT* doctrine. In particular, the question should be whether *CILFIT*, in its literal sense, still applies, or whether the criteria need to be revised. As far as the Netherlands is concerned, either the *Afdeling bestuursrecht* (Administrative Law Division of the Netherlands Council of State) or the *belastingkamer van de Hoge Raad* (Tax Division of the Netherlands Supreme Court) – both of which have in the past been confronted with Article 104(3) decisions – might find a cause to refer this matter to the Court of Justice.[12]

In principle, only judgments of courts of last resort can give rise to State liability. And, as is clear from the Court's decision in *Lyckeskog*,[13] in some cases an inferior court may also be a court of last resort. In other words, the court must be one which is obliged to request a preliminary ruling under Article 234 EC. This does indeed seem to me to be the correct principle. A person wishing to appeal against a decision of an inferior court that has applied Community law

---

[12] Joined Cases C-307/00 to C-311/00 *Oliehandel Koeweit and Others* [2003] *ECR* I-1821; Case C-102/00 *Welthgrove* [2001] *ECR* I-5679.
[13] Case C-99/00 *Lyckeskog* [2002] *ECR* I-04839.

'wrongly' must appeal to a higher court, in the same way as where an inferior court has applied national law wrongly. The 'normal' appeal procedure must first be followed, right up to the highest national court, failing which a judicial decision becomes *res judicata* and an administrative decision becomes final.[14]

Nor can I subscribe to the wish to allow liability for the conduct of inferior courts, at least not where it is framed in such general terms. The restriction to courts of last resort implies an 'exhaustion of local remedies rule' before the State can be held liable. The only exceptions I would consider acceptable would be in the cases suggested by Advocate-General Geelhoed.[15] Particularly where inferior courts consistently interpret and apply certain parts of Community law incorrectly, this can discourage litigants from initiating proceedings or going on to appeal. This might justify an exception to the rule, allowing the State to be held liable for the conduct of inferior courts.

5.4   Procedural consequences in Dutch law

It is impossible to tell what the procedural consequences of this decision will be. The Court of Justice disposes of the matter a little too simply in paragraph 58 by referring the matter to rules of national law. Under Dutch law, a *Köbler* action would have to be instituted in a civil action against the State. In other words, in the Dutch legal order, the *Hoge Raad*, the highest ordinary court, would ultimately have to decide on judicial errors of the highest administrative courts: the *Afdeling bestuursrecht*, the *College van Beroep van het Bedrijfsleven* (Trade and Industry Appeals Tribunal) and the *Centrale Raad van Beroep* (Central Appeals Tribunal for the public service and social security matters). However you look at it, this would give the *Hoge Raad* the final word on whether administrative courts have fulfilled their Community law obligations properly. This would mean that *Köbler* had acquired unexpected constitutional implications.

Incidentally, *Köbler* may touch on far greater constitutional sensitivities in other Member States. For example, what if claims for State liability were brought before 'ordinary' courts for errors of constitutional courts such as the *Bundesverfassungsgericht*, the *Corte constitutionale*, the *Arbitragehof*, and so forth?

As regards administrative law mistakes, Steyger[16] and Verhey,[17] among others, note that, in addition to bringing a civil action against the State for a wrongful

---

[14] See further J.H. Jans and K.J. de Graaf, 'Rechtsbescherming - Bevoegdheid = verplichting? Enkele opmerkingen over de uitspraak van het Hof van Justitie in de zaak *Kühne & Heitz*', 10 *NTER* (2004) pp. 98-102.

[15] See his Opinion in Case C-129/00 *Commission* v. *Italy*, para. 63.

[16] E. Steyger, 'Rechtsbescherming – De gevolgen van de aansprakelijkheid van de Staat voor rechterlijke schendingen van EG-recht', 10 *NTER* (2004) pp. 18-22.

[17] In his annotation to Case C-453/00 *Kühne & Heitz* in *JB* 2004/42.

judicial decision or against the public law body responsible for infringing the underlying substantive Community law rule, the injured party can also attempt to obtain an independent decision on reparation from the administrative body concerned. If that body refuses to issue such a decision, he can then take the administrative law route to obtain redress. It can indeed be assumed, on the basis of well-known Dutch case law,[18] that a written decision of an administrative organ on a request for reparation of loss caused within the context of the exercise by that organ of a power based on public law – even if that request does not have a specific statutory basis – is a public law legal act and thus a *besluit* (appealable decision) within the meaning of Section 1:3 of the *Algemene wet bestuursrecht* (General Administrative Law Act). In the light of the decision of the *Hoge Raad* in *Groningen/Raatgever*,[19] it must for the time being be assumed that an injured party can choose which route he takes to obtain reparation.

5.5   *Köbler* combined with *Kühne & Heitz*

Matters become even more complicated if we combine *Köbler* with the Court's judgment in *Kühne & Heitz*. Another avenue open to an injured party is to request the administrative body to 'reconsider' the decision that caused the loss or damage; and under certain circumstances – according to the judgment in *Kühne & Heitz* – it is obliged to reconsider a decision that conflicts with Community law. That being the case, the question arises how this fits in with the obligation under *Brasserie du Pêcheur* to limit the extent of loss or damage? In *Brasserie du Pêcheur*, the Court observed that the injured party must show reasonable diligence in limiting the extent of the loss or damage, or risk having to bear the damage himself. Does this mean that injured parties must now first request the administrative body in question to reconsider its earlier decision before bringing an action against the State for judicial errors? And if this request is rejected, must they then first go through the entire administrative law process before the State can be held liable? In my article on the judgment in *Kühne & Heitz* in *NTER*,[20] I argued that this last question should be answered in the negative, because otherwise matters would drag on forever. It seems to me that requiring this of an injured party goes beyond the bounds of 'reasonable diligence'.

The question that remains unanswered is how we should deal, in procedural terms, with errors of the *Hoge Raad*. It is a moot point whether Articles 6 and 13 ECHR would preclude it from hearing a case in which its own mistake was the subject of the dispute. And Steyger rightly notes in her article in *NTER* that it is

---

[18] *Van Vlodrop, AB* 1997, 229, with note by PvB.
[19] HR 17 December 1999, *AB* 2000, 89, with note by PvB.
[20] See n. 14 *supra*.

not likely that such a procedure – within the same branch of the judiciary – would result in a favourable decision for the injured party.[21]

6.   CONCLUSIONS

The above remarks clarify why I do not feel entirely comfortable with the Court's judgment. Apart from raising many new points of law, it disturbs me because:

- there is no empirical evidence that there really is a problem in the way the highest national courts apply Community law;
- the judgment may well increase the number of unnecessary referrals and thus prolong preliminary ruling proceedings even more;
- this will increase the pressure on the Court of Justice to apply Article 104(3) of its Rules of Procedure, and this in turn is unlikely to improve the relationship with national courts; and
- it may well be necessary to make changes in the national law to channel the consequences of the judgment. Failing this, a hierarchy will be created in the application of Community law where none now exists, and decisions of the specialised administrative courts will become subject to review by the *Hoge Raad*.

It is also debatable whether *Köbler* is consistent with the proportionality principle. Even assuming there is a problem concerning the application of European law by the highest national courts, the solution that has been chosen seems to go further than strictly necessary. It should be remembered that even the *Köbler* doctrine will not be sufficient to prevent national courts from making 'mistakes' when applying Community law. After all, it is the selfsame national court that retains the final word. We all know about Alfred Kellermann's tireless endeavours regarding the training of national judges in European law, but he also understood that European law is firmly rooted in national law. So perhaps there is something to be said for the Dutch system after all, in which liability for judicial acts is only recognised where they infringe fundamental principles of law.[22]

---

[21] See n. 16 *supra*.
[22] HR 29 April 1994, *NJ* 1995, 727, with note by EAA.

RIGHTS v. PRINCIPLES, OR HOW TO REMOVE FUNDAMENTAL RIGHTS FROM THE JURISDICTION OF THE COURTS

Sacha Prechal*

1.   PRINCIPLES AND PRINCIPLES

In the *Second Defrenne* case[1] concerning the direct effect of what was then Article 119 EEC, the United Kingdom argued, *inter alia*, that 'Article 119 does not contain a comprehensive definition of the principle of equal pay for equal work. The very use of the word "principle" indicates that it is concerned with a concept of a very general nature'[2] and that '[t]he need for legislative action on the part of the member States appears from the formulation of the obligation imposed on them by Article 119 in the form of a general statement of principle.'[3] The Irish Government and the Commission seemed to support this point of view, though in less explicit terms. Advocate General Trabucchi disagreed: 'Although the form of words used: "principle that men and women should receive equal pay", may seem too vague and the meaning of the word "principle" itself not be very specific, the purpose of the rule is nevertheless clear: to prohibit any discrimination to the detriment of women with regard to pay.'[4]

The Court dismissed the UK argument in clear terms: '... it is impossible to put forward an argument against its [Article 119 – *SP*] direct effect based on the use in this article of the word "principle", since, in the language of the Treaty, this term is specifically used in order to indicate the fundamental nature of certain provisions, as is shown, for example, by the heading of the first part of the Treaty which is devoted to "Principles" and by Article 113, according to which the commercial policy of the Community is to be based on "uniform principles". If this concept were to be attenuated to the point of reducing it to the level of a vague declaration, the very foundations of the Community and the coherence of its external relations would be indirectly affected.'[5]

---

* Professor of International and European Institutional Law, Europa Instituut, University of Utrecht.

[1] ECJ, Case 43/75 *Defrenne* v. *Sabena* [1976] *ECR* 455.

[2] Ibid., at 459.

[3] Ibid., at 460.

[4] Ibid., at 486.

[5] Paras. 28 and 29 of the judgment.

The European Union: An Ongoing Process of Integration – Liber Amicorum Alfred E. Kellermann
© 2004, T.M.C. Asser Instituut, The Hague, and the authors

Thus while, in the E(E)C Treaty the term 'principle' apparently underlines the fundamental character of the provisions at issue – and to this one may add that ultimately the ECJ found that Article 141 EC constitutes the expression of a fundamental right[6] – the term is used in the opposite sense in the draft Constitution.[7] Article II-52(5), one of the 'general provisions governing the interpretation and application of the Charter' as integrated in the draft Constitution, provides that '[t]he provisions of this Charter which contain principles may be implemented by legislative and executive acts taken by Institutions and bodies of the Union, and by acts of Member States when they are implementing Union law, in the exercise of their respective powers. They shall be judicially cognisable only in the interpretation of such acts and in the ruling on their legality.' One may only wonder what would have happened if a similar provision had been in force at the time when the *Second Defrenne* case was decided! In the present contribution, I will briefly explore the background and the possible effects of this provision.

2.   MERE 'DRAFTING ADJUSTMENT'?

Article II-52(5) was always presented as one of the 'drafting adjustments' that were deemed necessary for the incorporation of the Charter into the draft Constitution. From a (technical) legal point of view, the addition of this new paragraph to Article II-52 was not necessary at all. The distinction between 'rights' and 'principles' already featured in the original Charter, namely in the Preamble – '[t]he Union ... recognises the rights, freedoms and principles set out hereafter' – and in Article II-51(1).[8] The latter provides, *inter alia*, that the institutions and bodies of the Union and the Member States 'shall respect ... rights, observe the principles and promote the application thereof...'. Both passages were, without change, copied into Part II of the draft Constitution. However, for reasons of increasing legal certainty, Working Group II of the European Convention proposed to 'confirm' the distinction between 'rights' and 'principles' and to add the abovementioned paragraph 5 to Article II-52.[9]

Legal certainty was perhaps used as an argument for this 'drafting adjustment', but in that case it was mainly the political certainty for some Member States that feared that a number of rights from the Charter would be 'translated' into legally enforceable claims with financial or other implications at the national

---

[6] Cf., ECJ, Case C-50/96 *Schröder* [2000] *ECR* I-743.
[7] I refer here to the 'Draft Treaty Establishing a Constitution for Europe' (in principle the Thessaloniki version of 20 June 2003).
[8] Cf. Goldsmith, 'A Charter of rights, freedoms and principles', *CMLRev.* (2001) pp. 1201-1216.
[9] Final Report of Working Group II, CONV 354/02, p. 8.

level.[10] From this perspective, it would seem that legal certainty was not one of the key concerns behind paragraph 5. Rather, this paragraph aims to serve as a 'political lubricant' to make two processes run more smoothly: first, the process of incorporating the Charter into the draft Constitution and, second, the adoption of the Constitution in the IGC.

If one considers the effects of Article II-52(5), the price to be paid for the incorporation of the Charter is high. Indeed, the article at issue tallies with the distinction between legal rights (*subjektive Rechte* or *droits subjectifs*) and 'programmatic' or 'aspirational' provisions, which are here somewhat unfortunately referred to as 'principles'.[11] All this is combined with the fear that the Charter may lead to an extension of EU powers. The principle-type provisions do not as such create enforceable rights or positive claims for individuals. They must first be implemented and merely guide the actions of the Member States or the European Union. In the courts, they at most serve as an aid to interpretation or, where appropriate, as a standard to be applied in the context of the review of the legality of the actions of the Member States or the European Union. Yet, exactly in relation to the latter function of these so-called 'principles', there is an additional restriction in Article II-52(5) to the Charter's application. According to this article, the 'principles' shall be judicially cognisable only in the interpretation of and in the ruling on the legality of 'such acts'. The term 'such acts' seems to refer to legislative and executive acts of Union institutions and bodies and the acts of Member States implementing the above-mentioned principles. This implies that an important category of acts, namely those that do *not* implement the principles at issue, cannot be reviewed in the light of the relevant Charter provisions.

If this reading of the article is correct, it amounts to a serious drawback in relation to the current protection of fundamental rights as guaranteed by the ECJ. *All* EC acts, whether they do or do not implement fundamental rights, may be tested against the fundamental rights standard. According to well-established case law, respect for fundamental rights is a condition of the legality of Community acts.[12] In the context of a review of legality, the differentiation between measures that aim at the implementation of a particular obligation and measures that do not is, as far as I am aware, only common in situations where obligations under inter-

---

[10] The government representatives of the United Kingdom and the Netherlands, respectively, were the main champions of this line. Cf., for instance, S. Koukoulis-Spiliotopoulos, 'Incorporating the Charter into the Constitutional Treaty: What future for fundamental rights?', in *Problèmes d'Interprétation, à la mémoire de Constantinos N. Kakouris* (Athens/Brussels 2004), in particular at pp. 243-248; and S. van Bijsterveld and E. Hirsch Ballin, 'De integratie van het Handvest van Grondrechten van de Europese Unie in de constitutie van de Europese Unie', in J. Pelkmans, M. Sie Dhian Ho and B. Limonard, eds., *Nederland en de Europese grondwet* (Amsterdam, Amsterdam University Press 2003) pp. 89-107.

[11] Cf., the quotes from the *Second Defrenne* judgment *supra*.

[12] Cf., for instance, ECJ, C-25/02 *Rinke*, judgment of 9 September 2003, *ECR*, nyr, para. 26.

national law, in particular the WTO, are at stake. Thus, in *Biret*, for instance, the ECJ held that '[i]t is only where the Community has intended to implement a particular obligation assumed in the context of the WTO, or where the Community measure refers expressly to the precise provisions of the WTO agreements, that it is for the Court to review the legality of the Community measure in question in the light of the WTO rules.'[13] However, fundamental rights laid down in a constitutional text are different in nature from WTO rules. Similarly, the considerations behind this WTO case law do not apply to fundamental rights.[14]

As far as the Member States are concerned, *all* Member State measures, whatever EC/EU law provisions they implement, must be compatible with fundamental rights. From a case like *Booker Aquaculture*, for instance, it transpires that when Member States implement and apply a directive they must observe fundamental rights. The directive at issue, namely Directive 93/53 (control of certain fish diseases),[15] by no means intended to give effect to the right of property, the fundamental right relied upon.[16] Nevertheless, national implementing measures were reviewed in the light of the right at issue. Similarly, the Matrimonial Causes Act 1973 and the Births and Deaths Registration Act, at issue in *K.B.*,[17] can hardly be regarded as acts 'which implement Union law'. Yet, the impossibility for a transsexual to marry, which resulted from the combination of these Acts, was in breach of the ECHR and, in the wake thereof, also in breach of Article 141 EC, as far as the entitlement to a survivor's pension was concerned.

Finally – and this is another deficiency of the Charter – Member States are also bound by human rights 'when they act within the field of Union law'.[18] This

---

[13] ECJ, Case C-94/02 P *Biret*, judgment of 30 September 2003, *ECR*, nyr, para. 56.

[14] Cf., the judgment in the *Portuguese Textile* case, where the Court found that the non-application by judicial organs of rules of domestic law that are inconsistent with the WTO agreements 'would have the consequence of depriving the legislative or executive organs of the contracting parties of the possibility … of entering into negotiated arrangements …' and that the review of the legality of measures adopted by the Community in the light of the WTO agreements 'would deprive the legislative or executive organs of the Community of the scope for manoeuvre enjoyed by their counterparts…'. ECJ, Case C-149/96 *Portugal* v. *Council* [1999] *ECR* I-8395, paras. 40 and 46.

[15] *OJ* 1993 L 175/23.

[16] Indeed, things may be different in other cases. See, for instance, ECJ, Joined Cases C-465/00, C-138/01 and C-139/01 *Rechnungshof* [2003] *ECR* I-4989, paras. 68-94.

[17] ECJ, Case C-117/01 *K.B.*, judgment of 7 January 2004, *ECR*, nyr.

[18] Cf., for instance, ECJ, Case C-260/89 *ERT* [1991] *ECR* I-2925 and Case C-60/00 *Carpenter* [2002] *ECR* I-6279. Another relatively recent case makes clear that the broad scope of application of fundamental rights may also work to the advantage of the Member States, namely, as a justification for restrictions of an EC Treaty freedom. Cf., ECJ, Case C-112/00 *Schmidberger* [2003] *ECR* I-5659. On the other hand, it must be admitted that the concrete delimitation of this broad scope is notoriously difficult. In some quarters, moreover, it is argued that cases like *ERT* and *Carpenter* still fall within the scope of the implementation of Union law. For a discussion of these issues, see, for instance, P. Eeckhout, 'The EU Charter of fundamental rights and the federal question', *CMLRev.* (2002) pp. 945-994, in particular at pp. 975-979.

is a wider scope of fundamental rights than the mere reference to the Member States as addressees of the provisions of the Charter '… only when they are implementing Union law' (Art. 51) or '…when they are implementing Union law' (Art. 52(5)). In brief, in the current situation, any act of the EC or of the Member States, acting within the field of EC law, can be reviewed in the light of fundamental rights. The 'reviewable' acts are not limited. Article II-52(5) therefore implies a new restriction and not a 'drafting adjustment'.[19] However, this is not the end of the story. The insertion of paragraph 5 into Article II-52 was accompanied by another 'clarifying exercise' to which I will turn in the next section.

3.   SUPPLEMENTING THE EXPLANATIONS AND THE PREAMBLE

The second line of attempts to restrict the room for manoeuvre of the courts – both European and national – consists in imposing upon them a rule of interpretation. A new sentence was therefore inserted into the Preamble, stating that '… the Charter will be interpreted by the courts of the Union and the Member States with due regard to the explanations prepared at the instigation of the Praesidium of the Convention which drafted the Charter.' This is interesting, in the first place, because these explanations were not endorsed by the Charter Convention. Moreover, according to the Praesidium of that Convention, they were simply intended to clarify the Charter's provisions and have no legal value.[20] As far as the passage in the Preamble is to be understood as a reference to a sort of *travaux préparatoires* or a legislative intent, one can live with it. However, and this is also noteworthy, Working Group II felt obliged to supplement these explanations of the previous 'Charter' Convention, in particular on the issue of 'rights' and 'principles'.[21]

The current text of the Charter as integrated in Part II of the draft Constitution and the above-mentioned supplementing exercise are in many respects remarkable, to say the least.

Neither the text of the various articles nor the (updated) explanations[22] provide reliable guidance. To give just a few examples: Article II-3, the right to the integrity of the person, is referred to in the explanations as 'the principles of Article 3'; Article II-47, the right to an effective remedy and to a fair trial, is

---

[19] Cf., J. Dutheil de la Rochère, 'The EU and the individual: fundamental rights in the draft constitutional treaty', *CMLRev.* (2004) pp. 345-354 at p. 352.
[20] Cf., S. Koukoulis-Spiliotopoulos, loc. cit. n. 10, at p. 246.
[21] Cf., Final Report of Working Group II, CONV 354/02, pp. 8 and 10.
[22] See CONV 828/03 and CONV 828/03 REV 1.

referred to in the explanations as both a right and a principle; and Article II-49 is labelled as 'principles of legality and proportionality of criminal offences and penalties'. In the explanations, the term 'principle' is now replaced by the term 'rule'. Be that as it may, there can be little doubt that the prohibition of the non-retroactivity of criminal laws and sanctions is a matter 'cognisable' by the courts in every relevant respect. According to Article II-26, the Union recognises and respects the right of persons with disabilities to benefit from measures designed to ensure their independence. From the explanations, however, we learn that this is a principle. The area of non-discrimination is also interesting. Article II-20 (Equality before the law) was initially referred to as a 'principle', while the Working Group's explanations change this into 'a general principle of law'. Equality between men and women, provided for in Article II-23, is referred to either as 'equality' or as 'the principle of equality'.

Indeed, one may wonder in how far such a brew, unworthy even of a sorcerer's apprentice, will contribute to legal certainty about the justiciability of the Charter's rights, since this is what everything is about. The underlying concerns are not new but well-known, both in national constitutional law and the international law context, at least insofar as provisions of international human rights treaties can be relied upon in domestic courts.[23] Social, economic and environmental rights are often not justiciable in individual cases in the same way as classic civil and political rights.[24] Yet, any attempt to divide the provisions of the Charter into justiciable 'rights' and 'principles' of very limited justiciability ignores the possible effects of these social, economic and environmental rights, which depend very much on the context in which they are relied upon. A provision such as Article II-15, which guarantees the right to engage in work and to pursue a freely chosen or accepted occupation, can hardly be relied upon as a basis for action for damages against the Union or a Member State because one is unemployed. On the other hand, it may be relied upon against Union or Member States measures that, for example, make the exercise of a certain profession nearly impossible or unreasonably limit the access to certain jobs. To this one may add that even a principle such as the 'precautionary principle' may evolve over time and be used for several purposes. This principle features in the explanations regarding Article II-52(5) to illustrate the fact that 'principles' become

---

[23] In the Netherlands, for instance, it recently came to the fore again in the context of the discussion about abolishing Article 120 of the Constitution, which contains a prohibition for the courts to review legislation in the light of the Constitution. Cf., M. van Houten, 'Rechterlijke toetsing van de wet aan de Grondwet', *NJCM-Bulletin* (2003) pp. 843-859.

[24] For a interesting discussion of the environmental EC law 'principles' and their justiciability, which also illustrates many of the issues raised in this contribution, see N. Dhondt, *Integration of Environmental Protection into other EC Policies; Legal Theory and Practice* (Groningen, Europa Law Publishing 2003), in particular Ch. 3.

relevant for the courts only when the acts implementing them are interpreted and reviewed. Yet, in the light of more recent case law, it would seem that this principle, which has been labelled a general principle of Community law by the Court of First Instance, is becoming more autonomous and may arguably be used as both a sword and a shield, which goes beyond the function ascribed to it in the explanations.[25]

Whether or not a provision containing a fundamental right can be relied upon in concrete cases involves an assessment that is best performed by the courts. In fact, it boils down to a question of direct effect. That is, the courts have to determine whether of not the provisions at issue are 'unconditional and sufficiently precise' to be applied *for the purposes relied upon* by the individual concerned. This requirement is inextricably bound up with justiciability and, therefore, the mandate[26] and expertise of the courts. In this context, the aforementioned *Second Defrenne* case serves as an example of the fact that the ECJ takes mandate and expertise into account when deciding on issues related to social rights.[27] In this case, as is well known, the Court made a distinction between discrimination that can be detected by the courts on the basis of a purely legal analysis, where Article 141 EC has direct effect, on the one hand, and pay discrimination, which exists in entire branches of industry and even the economic system as a whole, on the other. These differences in pay between male and female workers require a much broader analysis than merely a legal one, and thus one in which a court cannot engage. In this respect, Article 141 has no direct effect and this type of discrimination can only be eliminated by additional instruments adopted at Community and national level or by the parties to collective agreements.[28]

4.   AN ASSESSMENT

The concerns voiced above may be summarised as follows: the notorious distinction made in Part II of the draft Constitution between 'rights', on the one hand, and so-called 'principles', on the other, is nothing new and the idea behind this distinction has already been taken into account by the courts. However, any approach that decides *a priori* the degree of justiciability of the provisions concerned is highly unfortunate. It ignores the fact that courts are better placed to

---

[25] Cf., ECJ, Joined Cases T-74/00, T-76/00, T-83/00 to T-85/00, T-132/00, T-137/00 and T-141/00 *Artegodan* [2002] *ECR* II-4945, paras. 182-185.

[26] In particular in terms of the doctrine of separation of powers.

[27] ECJ, Case 43/75 *Defrenne* v. *Sabena* [1976] *ECR* 455.

[28] Confirmed more recently in ECJ, Case C-320/00 *Lawrence* [2002] *ECR* I-7325 and Case C-256/01 *Allonby*, judgment of 13 January 2004, *ECR*, nyr.

do this on a case-by-case basis. Similarly, it ignores the fact that several provisions may have a dual character and cannot simply be assigned to one of the two categories.[29] The coupling of Article II-52(5) with the text of the provisions of the Charter and, in particular, the updated explanations, will lead to many misunderstandings instead of creating clarity. Already, the very notion of a 'principle' is rather misleading. Apparently, it can refer to the core of fundamental values to be upheld in a legal system or to the fundamental nature of certain provisions,[30] as well as to mere aspirations that inform policy-making by the legislator. Somewhat paradoxically, the protection of fundamental rights was introduced into the EC legal system under the label of general principles of (Community) law! Finally, Article II-52(5) introduces a new distinction that was not previously made in the ECJ's fundamental rights case law and amounts to a restriction, namely, between acts that implement the 'principles' of the Charter and those that do not. Only the former may be reviewed in the light of the Charter provision at issue.

If these concerns are considered in the broader context of the draft Constitution, the damage may be limited. In any case, as far as fundamental rights are concerned, which are already protected under EC/EU law – either as fundamental rights *stricto sensu* or by other Community law provisions – one may expect that their interpretation and application will not be affected. In the first place, Article II-53 aims at maintaining the level of protection currently afforded. Second, according to Article IV-3, the case law of the ECJ remains 'the source of interpretation of Union law and in particular of the comparable provisions of the Constitution.'[31]

However, on the other hand, Article II-52(5) is a clear signal to the courts (and any other actors) and may restrain the future evolution of the existing case law. Moreover, it may have an impact on the interpretation of those provisions that do not yet have equivalents in EC/EU law. Finally, one may wonder how such an article will be perceived by judges in the new Member States,[32] who are often used to legal positivism as a main approach and have a less strong tradition of judicial review of government action. Obviously, restraint in the interpretation and application of the Charter's provisions is the main rationale behind Article II-52(5). At the end of the day, this will arguably be to the detriment of individuals who are said to be located at the heart of the activities of the Union.[33]

---

[29] In fact, this was also recognised by Working Group II. Cf., CONV 828/03, p. 51.

[30] Cf., the judgment in the *Second Defrenne* case.

[31] Cf., Article IV-3(4) as laid down in CIG 50/03. In my view, it is not entirely certain whether this provision may be understood as fully maintaining the jurisprudential *acquis communautaire*.

[32] And indeed also *from* the new Member States, that is to say, those who will join the ECJ and CFI and influence interpretation at the European level.

[33] Cf., the Preamble to the Charter.

DECENTRALISATION IN A SYSTEM OF LEGAL EXCEPTION: THE ROLE OF NATIONAL COMPETITION AUTHORITIES UNDER REGULATION 1/2003

Anne-Marie Van den Bossche[*]

INTRODUCTION

The adoption on 16 December 2002 of Council Regulation 1/2003[1] completed the modernisation process launched in 1999 with the publication of the Commission's White Paper.[2] Regulation 1/2003, which entered into force on 1 May 2004, categorically changes the regime that governed the application of Articles 81 and 82 EC since 1962. From the outset, this 1962 regime of shared responsibilities between the Commission, national courts and national competition authorities (NCAs) was sub-optimal, as it was fragmented and incomplete.

Due to their direct effect, Articles 81 and 82 EC could be relied upon in proceedings before national courts.[3] Judges could therefore be called upon, but only to rule on the existence and nullity of a prohibited cartel arrangement (Art. 81(1) and (2)) or on the abuse of a dominant position within the meaning of Article 82. Subject to national enabling legislation,[4] NCAs could – as long as the Commission did not initiate proceedings – apply Articles 81(1) and 82 EC. Cases that *prima facie* qualified for an individual exemption ex Article 81(3), however, could be examined by the European Commission only. This exclusive competence to set aside the prohibition of Article 81(1) is the main reason why the decentralised application of EC competition law remained fairly limited.[5] The fact

---

[*] Professor of European Law, University of Nijmegen; Lecturer on European Competition Law, University of Antwerp.

[1] Council Regulation (EC) 1/2003 of 16 December 2002 on the implementation of the rules on competition laid down in Articles 81 and 82 of the Treaty, *OJ* 2003 L 1/1 (hereinafter: Regulation 1/2003).

[2] White Paper on modernisation of the rules implementing Articles 81 and 82 (formerly Articles 85 and 86) of the Treaty, *OJ* 1999 C 132/1.

[3] Established case law since Case 127/73 *BRT-Sabam* [1974] ECR 313.

[4] Not (always) present in all the Member States.

[5] Notwithstanding the adoption of two notices to this end. The first, adopted in 1993, was on cooperation between national courts and the Commission in applying Articles 81 and 82 of the Treaty, *OJ* 1993 C 39/6. The second, four years later, was on cooperation between national competition authorities and the Commission in handling cases falling within the scope of Articles 81 and 82 of the Treaty, *OJ* 1997 C 313/3. Both notices were replaced on 30 March 2004. See *OJ* 2004 C 101/43 and 54 and *infra*.

The European Union: An Ongoing Process of Integration – Liber Amicorum Alfred E. Kellermann
© 2004, T.M.C. Asser Instituut, The Hague, and the authors

that national courts or NCAs could not decide on the exemption issue made parties rather reluctant to start proceedings before these national actors, and encouraged them to turn to the European Commission instead, as this was the only actor that could apply Article 81 in its entirety.

The main result of Regulation 1/2003 is a major shift in policy with regard to Article 81 EC. Since 1 May 2004, this provision no longer operates within the old system of prohibition, but in one of legal exception: a 'directly applicable system in which the competition authorities and courts of the Member States have the power to apply *not only* Article 81(1) and Article 82 of the Treaty, which have direct applicability by virtue of the case-law of the Court of Justice of the European Communities, *but also* Article 81(3) of the Treaty'.[6] This should not only allow the European Commission to concentrate its efforts on the detection of the most serious infringements, but should also lead to a truly decentralised application of EC competition law. In the case of disputes brought before national courts or NCAs, these actors will be able to apply Article 81 in its entirety. For the assessment, in particular, of compliance with the conditions of Article 81(3), national courts and NCAs will in many cases be able to (continue to) rely on (present and future) group exemptions. In addition, guidance will continue to be provided by guidelines adopted by the Commission.[7] As far as the application of Article 82 EC is concerned, the role of the different actors does not really change. The European Commission, NCAs and national courts will therefore continue to assess whether the conditions for its application are being fulfilled (dominance, abuse of dominance and its effect on trade between Member States).

This contribution will focus on the role of national competition authorities in the system of legal exception. Before doing so, however, some general observations on the relationship between European and national competition law(s) and its implications for the powers of national courts and competition authorities are called for.

NO ONE-STOP SHOP FOR ARTICLES 81 AND 82 EC

Whereas in its proposals the Commission had called for a genuine one-stop shop in the area of Article 81 and 82 EC, and thus for the abolition of the parallel application of national and European competition law with regard to cartels and abuses of dominant positions,[8] the Council of Ministers settled for a considerably

---

[6] Regulation 1/2003, Preamble, Recital 4 [emphasis added].

[7] This practice is not entirely new. See, for instance, the Commission's Guidelines on Vertical Restraints, *OJ* 2000 C 291/1, and the Commission's Guidelines on the applicability of Article 81 of the EC Treaty to horizontal cooperation agreements, *OJ* 2001 C 3/2.

[8] See, in particular, Draft Regulation amending Regulation No. 17/62, COM (2000) 582 final, Article 3: 'Where an agreement, a decision by an association of undertakings or a concerted practice

less far-reaching compromise. According to Article 3(1) of Regulation 1/2003, 'where the competition authorities of the Member States or national courts apply national competition law to agreements, decisions by associations of undertakings or concerted practices within the meaning of Article 81(1) of the Treaty which may affect trade between Member States within the meaning of that provision, they shall *also* apply Article 81 of the Treaty to such agreements, decisions or concerted practices. Where the competition authorities of the Member States or national courts apply national competition law to any abuse prohibited by Article 82 of the Treaty, they shall *also* apply Article 82 of the Treaty.'

The parallel application is, however, not absolute, but confined by a number of conflict rules. First of all, the application of national competition law may not lead to the prohibition of cartel arrangements that are not also prohibited under Community competition law.[9] Secondly, national actors cannot take decisions running counter to an earlier Commission decision.[10] For national courts, however, the application of this second conflict rule is somewhat qualified. Fully in line with established case law, they 'cannot avoid the binding effects of a Commission decision without a ruling to the contrary by the Court of Justice. Consequently, if a national court wants to take a decision that runs counter to that of the Commission, it must refer a question to the Court of Justice for a preliminary ruling (validity review ex Article 234 EC). The latter will then decide on the compatibility of the Commission's decision with Community law. However, if the Commission's decision is challenged before the Community courts pursuant to Article 230 EC and the outcome of the dispute before the national court depends on the validity of the Commission's decision, the national court should, in order to avoid reaching a decision that runs counter to that of the Commission, stay its proceedings until the Community courts have adopted a definitive decision in the action for annulment against the Commission decision.'[11]

A last conflict rule only applies to national courts coming to a decision before the Commission does. Even though (the initiation of) Commission proceedings cannot detract from a court's powers,[12] it 'must avoid adopting a decision that

---

within the meaning of Article 81 of the Treaty or the abuse of a dominant position within the meaning of Article 82 may affect trade between Member States, Community competition law shall apply to the exclusion of national competition laws.'

[9] Regulation 1/2003, Preamble, Recital 8.

[10] Article 16(1) and (2) of Regulation 1/2003.

[11] Commission Notice of 30 March 2004 on the cooperation between the Commission and the courts of EU Member States in the application of Articles 81 and 82 EC, *OJ* 2004 C 101/54 (hereinafter: Court Notice) para. 13. In these cases, interim measures may be ordered to safeguard the parties' interests (para. 14). This notice replaces the above-mentioned notice from 1993 (see n. 5 *supra*).

[12] For the effect of such initiation on NCAs, see Article 11(6) of Regulation 1/2003 and *infra*.

would conflict with a decision contemplated by the Commission'.[13] To that effect, it 'may ask the Commission whether it has initiated proceedings regarding the same agreements, decisions or practices and if so, on the progress of proceedings and on the likelihood of a decision in that case. The national court may, for reasons of legal certainty, also consider staying its proceedings until the Commission has reached a decision.'[14]

THE POWERS OF NATIONAL COMPETITION AUTHORITIES

When turning to the powers of NCAs in the system of legal exception, a number of different issues must be addressed: (1) the origin(s) of the power to apply EC competition law; (2) the procedural rules governing this application; and (3) the actual decisions at the end of the procedure.

A mixed legal basis

One of the novelties of Regulation 1/2003 is that it directly and explicitly empowers NCAs to apply the Treaty competition rules, whereas before it was left entirely to the Member States whether or not to adopt enabling legislation in this regard. All Member States have therefore had to 'designate the competition authority or authorities responsible for the application of Articles 81 and 82 of the Treaty in such a way that the provisions of [Regulation 1/2003] are effectively complied with' and to take all 'measures necessary to empower those authorities to apply those Articles',[15] by either introducing new rules to this end or adapting their national competition legislation accordingly before 1 May 2004.

The procedural rules governing the national application of Articles 81 and 82 EC

Regulation 1/2003 is based 'on the premise that national competition authorities will apply Articles 81 and 82 in accordance with their respective national procedural rules'.[16] The concrete procedural rules and guarantees governing their national application are therefore not (exhaustively) laid down in Regulation 1/2003, but in (amended) national legislation.

---

[13] Article 16(1) of Regulation 1/2003.
[14] Court Notice, para. 12.
[15] Article 35(1) of Regulation 1/2003.
[16] COM (2000) 582 final, p. 12.

The possible outcomes of national proceedings

The actual substantive powers of NCAs follow from Articles 5 and 29 of Regulation 1/2003. According to Article 5, NCAs may require that an infringement be brought to an end; order interim measures; accept commitments; impose fines, periodic penalty payments or any other penalty provided for in their national law; and find that there are no grounds for action on their part when on the basis of the information in their possession the conditions for prohibition are not met. In addition, Article 29 explicitly empowers NCAs to withdraw the benefit of a Commission block exemption in respect of their territory.

THE RULES ON COOPERATION AND CASE ALLOCATION

Somewhat paradoxically, the establishment of a system of legal exception with truly concurrent competences and powers for all competition actors requires the elaboration of clear rules on cooperation between them, in order to ensure consistency in the application of the competition rules. The rules governing case allocation aim at reaching the explicit objective 'that each case should be handled by a single authority'.[17]

The establishment of the European Competition Network(s)

The basic rules for the establishment of the European Competition Network(s) (ECN) are laid down in Regulation 1//2003 and the Joint Statement of the Council and the Commission.[18] More detailed provisions followed with the adoption in March 2004 of a Commission Notice.[19] The use of the singular mode is somewhat misleading, in that the ECN consists of two complementary networks: (1) a vertical network between the European Commission and its national counterparts; and (2) a horizontal network between the latter.

Within the vertical network, the Commission and NCAs operate in close cooperation 'on the basis of equality, respect and solidarity',[20] via an elaborate

---

[17] Regulation 1/2003, Preamble, Recital 18.

[18] Joint Statement of the Council and the Commission on the functioning of the network of competition authorities, Statements to be entered in the Council Minutes, Doc. No. 15435/02 ADD 1 of 10 December 2002, available from the Council Register at <http://register.consilium.eu.int> (hereinafter: Joint Statement).

[19] Commission Notice of 30 March 2004 on cooperation within the Network of Competition Authorities, *OJ* 2004 C 101/43 (hereinafter, NCA Notice). It replaces the above-mentioned notice from 1997 (see n. 5 *supra*).

[20] Joint Statement, para. 7.

system of information and consultation. To 'complete case allocation as quickly as possible',[21] the Commission shall 'transmit to the competition authorities of the Member States copies of the most important documents it has collected with a view to applying Articles 7, 8, 9, 10 and Article 29(1).[22] At the request of the competition authority of a Member State, the Commission shall provide it with a copy of other documents necessary for the assessment of the case.'[23]

Conversely, the competition authorities of the Member States shall, when acting under Article 81 or Article 82 of the Treaty 'inform the Commission in writing before or without delay after commencing the first formal investigative measure'.[24] A similar duty exists with regard to termination decisions. NCAs must indeed inform the Commission 'no later than 30 days before the adoption of a decision requiring that an infringement be brought to an end, accepting commitments or withdrawing the benefit of a group exemption. To that effect, they shall provide the Commission with a summary of the case, the envisaged decision or, in the absence thereof, any other document indicating the proposed course of action. At the request of the Commission, the acting competition authority shall make available to the Commission other documents it holds which are necessary for the assessment of the case.'[25] Where a national competition authority has 'informed the Commission and the 30 days deadline has expired, it can adopt its decision as long as the Commission has not initiated proceedings. The Commission may make written observations on the case before the adoption of the decision by the NCA.'[26] If special circumstances 'require that a national decision is taken in less than 30 days following the transmission of information pursuant to Article 11(4), the NCA concerned may ask the Commission for a swifter reaction. The Commission will endeavour to react as quickly as possible.'[27] In addition to providing the Commission with information, the competition authorities of the Member States may, in any event, 'consult the Commission on any case involving the application of Community law'.[28]

With a view to establishing and strengthening the horizontal network between NCAs, the information and documents provided to the Commission may 'also be made available to the competition authorities of the other Member States'.[29]

---

[21] Joint Statement, para. 12 and *infra*.

[22] Respectively, these articles deal with: Finding and termination of infringement; Interim measures; Commitments; Findings of inapplicability; and Withdrawal of benefit of group exemption in individual cases.

[23] Article 11(2) of Regulation 1/2003.

[24] Article 11(3) of Regulation 1/2003.

[25] Article 11(4) of Regulation 1/2003.

[26] NCA Notice, para. 46.

[27] NCA Notice, para. 47.

[28] Article 11(5) of Regulation 1/2003.

[29] Article 11(3) and (4) of Regulation 1/2003.

Moreover, NCAs 'may exchange between themselves information necessary for the assessment of a case that they are dealing with under Article 81 or Article 82 of the Treaty'.[30]

The successful functioning of both networks depends to a substantial extent on the swiftness of the exchange of information collected for the purpose of applying Articles 81 and 82 EC.[31] Such exchange 'should therefore be allowed between the members of the network, notwithstanding any national provision to the contrary,[32] even where the information is confidential'.[33] Moreover, the information thus exchanged may be used for the application of Articles 81 and 82 of the Treaty *as well as* for the parallel application of national competition law, provided that the latter application relates to the same case and does not lead to a different outcome.[34] The rules are stricter with regard to the use of information to impose sanctions on natural persons. As such sanctions may vary considerably across the various systems, it is 'necessary to ensure that information can only be used if it has been collected in a way which respects the same level of protection and the rights of defence of natural persons as provided for under the national rules of the receiving authority'.[35] The use of information exchanged within the network to impose sanctions on natural persons is therefore confined to cases where the law of the transmitting authority foresees sanctions of a similar kind in relation to an infringement of Article 81 or Article 82 of the Treaty or, in the absence thereof, when the information has been collected in a way that respects the same level of protection of the rights of defence of natural persons as provided for under the national rules of the receiving authority. However, in the latter case, the information exchanged cannot be used by the receiving authority to impose custodial sanctions.[36]

The rules on case allocation within the ECN

As indicated earlier, the rules for allocating cases within the ECN aim at reaching the stated aim of having each case dealt with by the (single) authority best placed to deal with it. This is defined on the basis of three cumulative criteria:[37] (1) the agreement or practice has actual or foreseeable effects on competition within its

---

[30] Article 11(4) *in fine* of Regulation 1/2003.

[31] Such as documents, statements and digital information (NCA Notice, para. 26).

[32] Article 12 of Regulation 1/2003 thus 'takes precedence over any contrary law of a Member State' (NCA Notice, para. 27).

[33] Regulation 1/2003, Preamble, Recital 16. For the corresponding provision, see Article 12(1) and (2) of Regulation 1/2003.

[34] Ibid.

[35] Regulation 1/2003, Preamble, Recital 16.

[36] Article 12(3) of Regulation 1/2003. For an overview of all procedural safeguards for undertakings and individuals, see NCA Notice, para. 28.

[37] NCA Notice, para. 8.

territory that are substantial and direct, is implemented within its territory or originates from its territory (i.e. there is a material link between the infringement and the territory of the Member State); (2) the authority is able to effectively bring an end to the entire infringement (i.e. it can adopt a cease and desist order that is powerful enough to bring an end to the infringement) and can, where appropriate, sanction the infringement adequately; and (3) the authority is able, possibly with the assistance of other authorities, to gather the evidence required to prove the infringement.

Where 'an agreement or practice substantially affects competition in more than one Member State, the Network members will seek to agree between them who is best placed to deal with the case successfully'.[38] In cases 'where single action is not possible (when competition in several Member States is affected and no NCA can deal with the case alone successfully), the Network members should coordinate their action and seek to designate one competition authority as the lead institution'.[39] The Commission for its part 'will be particularly well placed to deal with a case if more than three Member States are substantially affected by an agreement or practice, if it is closely linked to other Community provisions which may be exclusively or more effectively applied by the Commission, if Community interest requires the adoption of a Commission decision to develop Community competition policy particularly when a new competition issue arises or to ensure effective competition'.[40]

In most cases, 'the authority that receives the complaint or starts an ex-officio proceeding will remain in charge of the case. Re-allocation of a case would only be envisaged at the outset of the proceedings where either this authority considers that it was not well placed to act or where other authorities also considered themselves well placed to act.'[41]

Where case re-allocation issues do arise, 'they should be resolved swiftly, normally within a period of two months starting from the date of the first information sent to the network pursuant to Article 11 of the Council Regulation. During this period, competition authorities will endeavour to reach an agreement on a possible re-allocation and, where relevant, on the modalities for parallel action.'[42] Normally, case allocation to either the Commission or the competition authorities 'will remain definitive to the end of the proceedings provided that the facts known about the case remain substantially the same. If so, this implies that the competition authority which has notified the case to the Network will normally

---

[38] Joint Statement, para. 17.
[39] Joint Statement, para. 18.
[40] Joint Statement, para. 19.
[41] NCA Notice, para. 6.
[42] NCA Notice, para. 18.

remain the responsible authority if it is well placed to deal with the case and no other competition authority raises objections during the indicative time period.'[43] Re-allocation of a case 'after the initial allocation period of two months' cannot entirely be ruled out, but should 'only occur where the facts known about the case change materially during the course of the proceedings'.[44]

An important consequence of the foregoing rules is that 'where competition authorities of two or more Member States have received a complaint or are acting on their own initiative under Article 81 or Article 82 of the Treaty against the same agreement, decision of an association or practice, the fact that one authority is dealing with the case shall be sufficient grounds for the others to suspend the proceedings before them or to reject the complaint'.[45] The Commission 'may likewise reject a complaint on the ground that a competition authority of a Member State is dealing with the case'.[46] A similar right of rejection of complaints applies to cases that have already been dealt with by another competition authority.[47]

It should be clear, however, that the Commission cannot be prevented from 'rejecting a complaint for lack of Community interest, as the case-law of the Court of Justice has acknowledged it may do, even if no other competition authority has indicated its intention of dealing with the case'.[48] Inversely, a national competition authority 'may suspend or close its proceedings but is has no obligation to do so. Article 13 of the Council Regulation leaves scope for appreciation of the peculiarities of each individual case. This flexibility is important: if a complaint was rejected by an authority following an investigation of the substance of the case, another authority may not want to re-examine the case. On the other hand, if a complaint was rejected for other reasons (e.g. the authority was unable to collect the evidence necessary to prove the infringement), another authority may wish to carry out its own investigation and deal with the case. This flexibility is also reflected, for pending cases, in the choice open to each NCA as to whether it closes or suspends its proceedings. An authority may be unwilling to close a case before the outcome of another authority's proceedings is clear. The ability to suspend its proceedings allows the authority to retain its ability to decide at a later point whether or not to terminate its proceedings. Such flexibility also facilitates consistent application of the rules.'[49]

---

[43] Joint Statement, para. 12.
[44] NCA Notice, para. 19.
[45] Article 13(1) of Regulation 1/2003.
[46] Article 13(1) of Regulation 1/2003.
[47] Article 13(2) of Regulation 1/2003.
[48] Regulation 1/2003, Preamble, Recital 18.
[49] NCA Notice, para. 22.

Lifting NCAs' competence to continue dealing with a case

Notwithstanding the genuine concurrent competences and powers of NCAs and the Commission, it should be stressed that the Commission is somewhat 'more equal' than NCAs and continues to be able to relieve the NCAs of their competence by initiating its own proceedings,[50] by means of a formal, authoritative act evidencing its intention to take a decision.[51] This can 'occur at any stage of the investigation of the case by the Commission'[52] in two types of situations.

The first situation is where the Commission is the first competition authority to initiate proceedings. Once the Commission has initiated a procedure, 'NCAs can no longer start their own procedure with a view to applying Articles 81 and 82 of the Treaty to the same agreement(s) or practice(s) by the same undertaking(s) on the same relevant geographic and product market'.[53] The second situation is where one or more NCAs have informed the network pursuant to Article 11(3) of the Regulation that they are acting on a given case. During the initial allocation period (the indicative time period of two months described above), the Commission can initiate proceedings with the effects of Article 11(6) of the Regulation after having consulted the authorities concerned. Once the initial allocation period is over, the Commission will only open proceedings with the effects of relieving one or several well-placed competition authorities of their competence pursuant to Article 11(6), in a limited number of situations:[54]

- network members envisage conflicting decisions in the same case;
- network members envisage a decision that is obviously in conflict with consolidated case law; the standards defined in the judgments of the Community courts and in previous decisions and regulations of the Commission should serve as a yardstick; concerning facts, only a significant divergence will trigger an intervention of the Commission;
- network member(s) is (are) unduly drawing out proceedings;
- there is a need to adopt a Commission decision to develop Community competition policy in particular when an similar competition issue arises in several Member States; or
- the national competition authority does not object.

---

[50] Article 11(6) of Regulation 1/2003.

[51] NCA Notice, para. 52. The mere fact that the Commission has received a complaint is therefore not in itself sufficient to relieve NCAs of their competence.

[52] NCA Notice, para. 52.

[53] Article 11(6) of Regulation 1/2003; NCA Notice, para. 53.

[54] Regulation 1/2003, Preamble, Recital 17; Joint Statement, para. 21; NCA Notice, para. 54.

CONCLUDING REMARKS

It was submitted earlier that the establishment of the system of legal exception should not only allow the European Commission to concentrate its efforts on the detection of the most serious infringements, but should also lead to a truly decentralised application of EC competition law. From a European and legal/formal point of view, NCAs have been firmly embedded in the network(s) and hold substantial additional powers. At the national level, preparations to introduce and/or amend national legislation accordingly should have been finished by now. It remains to be seen, however, whether NCAs will actually use their new powers to start proceedings on their own initiative more often and whether individuals will be convinced to 'stay national' when lodging complaints about alleged infringements of Article 81 or 82 EC. Only time will tell to what extent the new law on the books will become the law in action, if at all.

INTERNET: A NEW PARADIGM FOR EU LAW? SOME EXPLORATORY COMMENTS ON A REMARKABLE JUDGMENT

Piet Jan Slot*

1.   INTRODUCTION

According to the front page of *The Economist* of 15 May 2004, e-commerce has taken off. A 14-page special report argues that the Internet offers huge scope for both business and leisure. In 2003, some US$55 billion was spent via the Internet, which amounts to 1.6 per cent of total global retail sales. This may not look very impressive, but the figure was up 26 per cent from the previous year. Furthermore, the impact in specific sectors such as books, travel and auctions is much greater.

Given this hype surrounding the Internet as a means of trading goods and services, there is a lively discussion going on about its impact on law. This is particularly true in the European Union, where the development of e-commerce features high on the agenda. As the preamble of the E-Commerce Directive notes, the development of information society services in the European Union is hampered by a number of obstacles to the proper functioning of the internal market.[1] Of course, aficionados of EU law will immediately point to the case law of the ECJ on the justification of such obstacles. It therefore seems appropriate to devote this contribution in honour of Fred Kellermann to this very topical issue.

In a remarkable judgment involving a German prohibition on internet mail-order services for pharmaceuticals, a full Court of Justice held that the effect of the prohibition had to be looked at on a broader scale than suggested by the interveners, which included the Commission.[2]

---

* Professor of European and Economic Law, Leiden University.
[1] Directive 2000/31/EC of the European Parliament and of the Council of 8 June 2000 on certain aspects of information society services, in particular electronic commerce, in the Internal Market (Directive on electronic commerce), *OJ* 2000 L 178/1. The Directive provides a general framework for the relevant legal aspects of e-commerce. Its preamble provides a useful overview of the relevant legal issues. Of course, in terms of the development of Internet sales, the Directive is relatively old, and new problems requiring fresh solutions keep popping up.
[2] Case C-322/01 *Deutscher Apothekerverband eV* v. *DocMorris and Jacques Waterval* [2003] *ECR* I-0000, judgment of 11 December 2003.

The European Union: An Ongoing Process of Integration – Liber Amicorum Alfred E. Kellermann

This contribution explores some of the questions that come to mind. As the *DocMorris* judgment shows, the first issue relates to the effect of e-commerce on defining obstacles to free movement pursuant to Article 28 EC, including the application of the Keck rule. The same question can, of course, also be raised for the other basic free movement rules: Articles 39, 43, 49 and 56 EC. In this contribution, the questions relating to Article 28 will be used as shorthand for all these basic prohibitions. The second question relates to the effect of e-commerce on the interpretation of the justifications under Article 30 EC or the mandatory requirements. A third question is the effect of e-commerce trading on future internal market directives and the exceptions allowed in such directives. This last part will necessarily have to be limited to some exploratory observations, because an extensive review of relevant areas where fresh directives will be necessary, the way to draft them and the clauses allowing more restrictive national measures therein is well beyond the scope of this contribution.[3]

2.   THE EFFECT OF E-COMMERCE ON FINDING RESTRICTIONS
        PROHIBITED BY ARTICLE 28 EC

In a preliminary ruling at the request of the *Landgericht* of Frankfurt am Main, the *DocMorris* judgment addresses the question whether Section 43 of the German *Arzneimittelgesetz* (Medical Products Act) is compatible with Articles 28 and 30 EC. The German provision prohibits the sale of medicinal products for human use by means of mail order through authorized pharmacies in other Member States on the basis of individual orders placed by consumers over the Internet.

The ECJ first dealt with the compatibility of the litigious provision with Article 28 EC. It made a distinction between pharmaceuticals that are not authorized in Germany and those that are. The Court held that, as to the former category of drugs, the German legislation is not in conflict with Community law, since it implements the obligations of Germany under Directive 65/65.[4] Article 6(1) of this Directive provides that even if pharmaceuticals are authorized in one Member State, they must also, if they are marketed in another Member State, have been authorized by that Member State.

Next, the ECJ turned to the pharmaceuticals authorized in Germany. Legislation prohibiting such sales does not implement Community law and must therefore be assessed under Article 28 EC. The *Apothekerverband* and the Commission,

---

[3] The relevant directives, fourteen in all, are enumerated in the eleventh paragraph of the preamble to the E-Commerce Directive.

[4] *OJ*, English Special Edition 1965-1966, p. 20, repealed and replaced by Directive 2001/83, *OJ* 2001, L 311/67 (the Community Code).

supported by four intervening governments, claimed that the German provision satisfies the Keck test and that it thus falls outside the scope of Article 28. According to them, the German rule applies in the same way, both in law and in fact, to the marketing of domestic products and those from other Member States. The ECJ disagreed with this view. It stated in paragraphs 73 and 74 that:

'73. As regards a prohibition such as that laid down in Paragraph 43(1) of the AMG, it is not disputed that the provision contains both a requirement that certain medicines be sold only in pharmacies and a prohibition on mail-order sales of medicines. It is true that such a prohibition on mail-order sales may be regarded as merely the consequence of the requirement for sales to be made exclusively in pharmacies. However, the emergence of the internet as a method of cross-border sales means that the scope and, by the same token, the effect of the prohibition must be looked at on a broader scale than that suggested by the Apothekerverband, by the German, French and Austrian Governments and by the Commission (see paragraphs 56 to 59 of this judgment).

74. A prohibition such as that at issue in the main proceedings is more of an obstacle to pharmacies outside Germany than to those within it. Although there is little doubt that as a result of the prohibition, pharmacies in Germany cannot use the extra or alternative method of gaining access to the German market consisting of end consumers of medicinal products, they are still able to sell the products in their dispensaries. However, for pharmacies not established in Germany, the internet provides a more significant way to gain direct access to the German market. A prohibition which has a greater impact on pharmacies established outside German territory could impede access to the market for products from other Member States more than it impedes access for domestic products.'

It is the last sentence of paragraph 73 that makes this judgment particularly important for the development of the Internet in the internal market. Surprisingly enough, the Commission took a very cautious approach in this matter.[5] The Commission's approach was also at variance with its stand on the development of new technologies and its earlier Communications concerning the Internet.[6]

---

[5] This is not the first time that the Commission has lacked the courage to champion the principles of the internal market and undistorted competition. Other examples include Case 43&63/82 *VBVB & VBBB* v. *Commission* [1984] *ECR* 19, where the Commission failed to challenge national book cartels, and Case 66/86 *Ahmed Saeed* v. *Zentrale* [1989] *ECR* 803, where the Commission did not argue that Article 82 EC had direct effect in the air transport sector.

[6] See COM (2001) 11 final ('Preventing fraud and counterfeiting of non-cash means of payment'). See also COM (2003) 65 final ('Electronic Communications: the Road to the Knowledge Economy') and SEC (2003) 1342 ('Report on the Implementation of the EU Electronic Communications Regulatory Package').

The view of the ECJ will undoubtedly also be reflected in its future case law. Thus, national bans on Internet sales of other goods and services will not meet the Keck test and hence be incompatible with Article 28 EC.

In this context, it is worth noting that, in the *Gambelli* judgment,[7] the ECJ did not have to address the Italian prohibition on Internet sports bets specifically, neither for its finding of a restriction on free movement nor in its assessment of the justification.

3.   THE EFFECT OF E-COMMERCE ON THE INTERPRETATION OF THE JUSTIFICATIONS UNDER ARTICLE 30 EC OR THE MANDATORY REQUIREMENTS

The use of the Internet as a means of effecting sales of goods and services also has an effect on the possible justifications of the restrictions imposed by Member States, as demonstrated by the *DocMorris* judgment. The key argument made by the *Apothekerverband* and several intervening governments was that the purpose of the prohibition on the sale by mail order for products such as pharmaceuticals is to ensure that the customer receives individual information and advice from the pharmacist. Direct face-to-face contact with the customer is vital to ensure the safety of medicines and pharmacovigilance. The customer's individual physical and psychological state, bearing, life-style and current medication are factors that should be taken into account during the consultation. The Greek Government pointed out that the case law of the ECJ and certain Community law provisions placed importance on the method of distributing medicines in pharmacies and on the role of the pharmacist.

The counterarguments of the defendant stressed that sales via the Internet provide adequate guarantees for the customer. The pharmacies are subjected to the normal supervision of the national authorities, in this case the Dutch authorities, and to the requirement that orders be checked internally. Furthermore, the technical potential of the Internet, in particular the ability to prepare customized interactive pages, can be used to ensure optimal health protection.

The ECJ first turned to the relevant Community legislation and observed that these rules provide for the need to specify the classification of medicines. Member States must indicate whether or not pharmaceuticals are subject to prescription. The Court also noted that Directive 97/77 on distance selling specifically allowed Member States to adopt measures to prohibit the marketing of certain goods, in particular medicinal products.

---

[7] Case C-243/01 *Piergiorgio Gambelli* [2003] *ECR* I-0000, judgment of 6 November 2003.

The Court concluded that its review of the justifications should consider non-prescription medicines, on the one hand, and prescription medicines, on the other.

The ECJ firmly rejected the argument of the *Apothekerverband* in favour of the prohibition of Internet sales of non-prescription medicines for the protection of health:

'113. First, as regards the need to provide the customer with advice and information when a medicinal product is purchased, it is not impossible that adequate advice and information may be provided. Furthermore, as the defendants in the main proceedings point out, internet buying may have certain advantages, such as the ability to place the order from home or the office, without the need to go out, and to have time to think about the questions to ask the pharmacists, and these advantages must be taken into account.'

It also rejected the argument related to the disadvantages of 'virtual pharmacists':

'114. As to the argument that virtual pharmacists are less able to react than pharmacists in dispensaries, the disadvantages which have been mentioned in this regard concern, first, the fact that the medicine concerned may be incorrectly used and, second, the possibility that it may be abused. As regards incorrect use of the medicine, the risk thereof can be reduced through an increase in the number of on-line interactive features, which the customer must use before being able to proceed to a purchase. As regards possible abuse, it is not apparent that for persons who wish to acquire non-prescription medicines unlawfully, purchase in a traditional pharmacy is more difficult than an internet purchase.'

The Court was far more deferential in its treatment of arguments regarding the prohibition of prescription medicines.

'117. The supply to the general public of prescription medicines needs to be more strictly controlled. Such control could be justified in view of, first, the greater risks which those medicines may present (see Article 71(1) of the Community Code) and, second, the system of fixed prices which applies to them and which forms part of the German health system.
118. As regards the first consideration, the fact that there might be differences in the way those medicines are classified by the Member States, so that a particular medicinal product may be subject to prescription in one Member State but not in another, does not mean that the first Member State forfeits the right to take more stringent action with regard to that type of medicinal product.
119. Given that there may be risks attaching to the use of these medicinal products, the need to be able to check effectively and responsibly the authenticity of doctors'

prescriptions and to ensure that the medicine is handed over either to the customer himself, or to a person to whom its collection has been entrusted by the customer, is such as to justify a prohibition on mail-order sales. As the Irish Government has observed, allowing prescription medicines to be supplied on receipt of a prescription and without any other control could increase the risk of prescriptions being abused or inappropriately used. Furthermore, the real possibility of the labelling of a medicinal product bought in a Member State other than the one in which the buyer resides being in a language other than the buyer's may have more harmful consequences in the case of prescription medicines.'

The Court also accepted that sales through the Internet could pose a risk of seriously undermining the financial balance of the social security system, which may constitute an overriding general-interest reason capable of justifying restrictions.[8] However, it found that neither the *Apothekerverband* nor the governments had put forward any arguments for such a justification.

In summary, it may be said that the Court found that the German ban was not justified in relation to non-prescription medicines but justified in relation to prescription medicines.

It is interesting to note that, in the part of the judgment where it deals with the justifications for prescription medicines, the ECJ did not refer to any of the positive features of the Internet as it did in relation to non-prescription medicines. Instead, it focused on the need to limit the risks involved in the use of these pharmaceuticals.

What conclusions can be drawn from this part of the judgment? Does the advent of the Internet change the Court's case law? As the treatment of the arguments related to non-prescription medicines shows, it will firm up the standard for justifications as regards restrictions on free movement. This trend may continue as the technical potential of the Internet increases. It is to be expected that this tenor of the Court's case law will also become more visible in those areas of the economy where public interest issues are not a matter of life and death. Such areas include, for example, travel and leisure, rights to immovable property (time-sharing), misleading and comparative advertising, consumer information, injunctions for the

---

[8] It reiterated its well-known case law on healthcare services:
'122. Although aims of a purely economic nature cannot justify restricting the fundamental freedom to provide services, it is not impossible that the risk of seriously undermining the financial balance of the social security system may constitute an overriding general-interest reason capable of justifying a restriction of that kind (see *Kohll*, paragraph 41; *Vanbraekel*, paragraph 47; *Smits and Peerbooms*, paragraph 72; and Case C-358/99 *Müller-Fauré and Van Riet* [2003] *ECR* I-0000, paragraphs 72 and 73). Moreover, a national market for prescription medicines could be characterised by non-commercial factors, with the result that national legislation fixing the prices at which certain medicinal products are sold should, in so far as it forms an integral part of the national health system, be maintained.'

protection of consumers, product liability, consumer credit, investment services in the securities field, distance marketing of consumer financial services and services that are transmitted point-to-point, such as video on demand.[9] In this context, it is important to be aware of the need to improve the security of the Internet.[10] Another element that may be important is the availability of Internet access and, for extensive services, broadband connections. The more widespread Internet availability becomes, the greater its role in providing the necessary transparency and information for the protection of important societal objectives.

On the other hand, the Court's approach to the justifications for the prohibition on Internet sales of prescription medicines shows that it is not prepared to forego its well-established careful attitude *vis-à-vis* perceived genuine public interest concerns. A different issue is whether this approach can be maintained in areas where such prohibitions no longer serve a useful purpose as a result of increasing Internet sales. Online services may well be such an area. If that is the case, the maintenance of national prohibitions may backfire and be self-defeating to the extent that prohibitions will no longer be proportionate.

It is interesting to note that the German Government abolished the ban on Internet sales, including prescription pharmaceuticals, as of 1 January 2004. An important consideration for the Government seems to have been the effect the ban had on the prices charged by the German pharmacists.[11]

4. THE EFFECT OF E-COMMERCE ON THE DEVELOPMENT OF FUTURE INTERNAL MARKET DIRECTIVES AND EXCEPTIONS ALLOWED IN SPECIFIC INTERNAL MARKET DIRECTIVES

It would seem that the *DocMorris* judgment will necessarily have an effect on the perceived need to adopt further directives for the internal market, as well as the way they will be drafted and their interpretation.

The increased penetration of the Internet in society and its enhanced role in internal market sales will further highlight the necessity to define objectives of general interest at the Community level. This is already spelled out in the preamble of the E-Commerce Directive. The jurisdictional issues raised by commerce through the Internet are multifarious, and the international community is only just beginning to address them. Substantial additional efforts are required.[12] The usual

---

[9] These are the areas mentioned in paragraphs 11 and 18 of the E-Commerce Directive.

[10] 'Special Report', *The Economist* (15 May 2004) p. 14.

[11] This is another example of the ECJ upholding a ban that soon thereafter was lifted by the relevant government. See Case C-157/94 *Commission* v. *Netherlands* [1997] *ECR* I-5699, where the ECJ upheld the Dutch import ban on electricity that was lifted during the proceedings.

[12] Cf. paragraph 21 of the E-Commerce Directive.

workhorse of the internal market, 'home-state control', may be a useful starting point but will require further fine-tuning and alignment with broader efforts at the international level.

The increasing importance of Internet sales will effect the interpretation of existing directives in two ways. On the one hand, it will lead to a more liberal, that is to say pro-market, interpretation of the safeguard and escape clauses contained in the directives. On the other hand, it will induce the courts to restrict the discretionary margin of Member States when it comes to evaluating measures taken by Member States in accordance with the respective directives based on the minimum harmonization principle.

An overview of the impact of the judgment on the interpretation of safeguard and escape clauses necessarily has to proceed on a directive-by-directive basis, carefully analyzing these clauses in the context of the relevant directive and preferably also against the background of the situation in some major Member States. This is a time-consuming study that has to be undertaken separately at a later stage.

As to the interpretation of the discretionary margin attributed to the Member States in the respective directives, it is important to understand the proper legal standard that is to be applied. There has been some debate about the proper standards against which to assess the compatibility of such national measures. This point has now been addressed by the ECJ in paragraphs 63 and 64 of the *DocMorris* judgment, where it explicitly rules that these measures have to be assessed on the basis of Articles 28 and 30 EC. This rule has also been assumed in the literature.[13] As this judgment has highlighted the effect of Internet sales, this effect should henceforth be included in any analysis of free movement restrictions. Further details about the impact of such an analysis must await a full review of such clauses in the specific directives. Once again, future studies will have to shed more light on this issue.

5.   CONCLUSION

The *DocMorris* judgment opens up a wide array of interesting questions for the future study of the internal market and the effects of the Internet. The person to whom this contribution is dedicated will undoubtedly be pleased to observe that his work at the Asser Institute will have to continue at an ambitious pace in order

---

[13] G. Meier, 'Bemerkung zum Urteil "DocMorris"', 15 *EuZW* (2004) p. 225. Meier refers to the Court's judgment in Case C-324/99 *DaimlerChrysler* [2001] *ECR* I-9897, which according to him also reflects this approach. See further M. Dougan, 'Minimum Harmonisation and the Internal Market', 37 *CMLRev.* (2000) p. 853 at p. 866 et seq.; and P.J. Slot, 'Harmonisation', 21 *ELRev.* (1996) p. 378 at p. 385.

to keep track of such trends. The new generation will have the benefit of being able to build on the research of the waning generation and will be equipped with the tools developed by their predecessors such as Fred Kellermann.

'THE ETHOLOGY OF A PAPER TIGER': THE EUROPEAN UNION AND DOPING IN SPORT

Robert Siekmann and Janwillem Soek*

1.   INTRODUCTION

There is no specific reference to sport in the EC Treaty. However, sport has always been one of the Community's concerns. The inclusion of a Declaration on Sport in the 1997 Amsterdam Treaty sent a strong political signal about the new importance accorded to sport and its values by the Heads of State and Government. Moreover, sport is indirectly affected by many Community policies, such as those to do with health (doping), audiovisual policy, education, training and youth and so on. In the draft Treaty establishing a Constitution for Europe, which was approved by the Heads of State and Government at the Intergovernmental Conference in Brussels on 18 June 2004, sport is mentioned in Article III-182 (Part III, Title III, Chapter V, Section 4 on Education, youth, sport and vocational training), which states that the Union shall contribute to the promotion of European sporting issues, while taking account of the specific nature, the structures based on voluntary activity and the social and educational function of sport (Art. III-182(1), final sentence), and that the Union shall aim to develop the European dimension of sport, by promoting fairness and openness in sporting competitions and cooperation between bodies responsible for sports and by protecting the physical and moral integrity of sportsmen and sportswomen, especially young sportsmen and sportswomen (Art. III-182(2)(g)).

Sport, as an economic activity in the sense of Article 2 EC, must comply with Community law, in particular the provisions relating to the free movement of workers. An ECJ judgement from 1974 (*Walrave*) established that sport is subject to Community law to the extent that it constitutes an economic activity. Since then, various cases (*Donà, Bosman, Deliège* and *Lehtonen*) have confirmed this approach. It is significant that the judgement that aroused more media interest

* Dr Robert C.R. Siekmann is Director of the Asser International Sports Law Centre and Janwillem Soek is a senior researcher at the Centre and is specialised in doping and the law and the legal aspects of football hooliganism. Recent articles on doping by Soek include: 'The Legal Nature of Doping Law', 2 *ISLJ* (2002) pp. 2-7; 'The WADA World Anti-Doping Code: The Road to Harmonisation', 2 *ISLJ* (2003) pp. 2-11. The authors would like to thank Hans Mojet, junior research fellow at the Centre during the first half of 2004, for his useful comments.

than any other in the history of Community case law was a sports-related one (the *Bosman* judgement).[1]

This paper devotes particular attention to the subject of doping as dealt with by the European Union so far.[2] Doping and the law is a major theme of the research programme of the Asser International Sports Law Centre, which was established in 2001.[3] Other current EU-related themes of the Centre include social dialogue in European professional football[4] and football hooliganism.[5] The

---

[1] Cf., in particular, R. Parrish, *Sports law and policy in the European Union*, European Policy Research Unit Series (Manchester/New York, Manchester University Press 2003).

[2] Cf., *The European Union and Sport – Legal and Policy Documents* (The Hague, T.M.C. Asser Instituut/T.M.C. Asser Press 2003), which is the first volume in the Asser series of collections of documents on international sports law containing material on the intergovernmental (interstate) aspect of international sports law. The previous collections are: R. Siekmann and J. Soek, eds., *Basic Documents of International Sports Organisations* (The Hague/Boston/London, T.M.C. Asser Instituut/Kluwer Law International 1998); R. Siekmann, J. Soek and A. Bellani, eds., *Doping Rules of International Sports Organisations* (The Hague, T.M.C. Asser Instituut/T.M.C. Asser Press 1999); and R. Siekmann and J. Soek, *Arbitral and Disciplinary Rules of International Sports Organisations* (The Hague, T.M.C. Asser Instituut/T.M.C. Asser Press 2001).

[3] Cf., K. Vieweg and R. Siekmann, eds., 'Legal Comparison and Harmonisation of Doping Rules – Final Report in the framework of the pilot project for campaigns to combat doping in sport in Europe', Project No C 116-15, European Commission, Directorate-General for Education and Culture (CD-ROM).

[4] In September 2003, the *Promoting the Social Dialogue in European Professional Football* project was started. The project is carried out in cooperation with the European Federation of Professional Football Clubs (EFFC) and is co-financed by the European Commission in Brussels (Directorate-General for Employment and Social Affairs). It is a two-tier project, as it addresses both the fifteen 'old' EU Member States and the ten 'new' Member States that acceded in May 2004, plus the candidate countries of Bulgaria and Romania (accession planned for 2007). Both components of the project consist of seminars and workshops that are held in every 'old' and 'new' Member State in the course of one year (until September 2004). In addition, as regards the 'new' Member States, pilot studies are carried out per country giving a detailed overview of its organisation of professional football and the state of affairs as regards industrial relations in this field. The project aims to inform the local football communities and to promote awareness of the possibilities offered by the European Social Dialogue between employers and employees, which is an instrument that has been laid down in the EC Treaty. The basis of all the seminars and workshops is a publication published by the EFFC in cooperation with the Asser International Sport Law Centre in 2003: R. Branco Martins, *European Sport's First Collective Labour Agreement* (EFFC 2003).

[5] December 2003 saw the start of the *Football Hooliganism with an EU Dimension: Towards an International Legal Framework* research project, which is co-financed by the European Commission in Brussels under the AGIS Programme (Directorate-General for Justice and Home Affairs) for the duration of one year (until December 2004).

The background to this study is that, under the provisions of Article 29 EU, the European Union's objective shall be to provide citizens with a high level of safety in its territory by promoting common action by the Member States in this field. The main objective of the project is to collect and analyse relevant international and national 'public' legislation and the applicable 'private' rules of the relevant international football federations (FIFA and UEFA) and the national football associations in the fifteen EU Member States and ten accession countries in order to determine the legal differences and to make recommendations for the possible development of a common and coherent international legal framework.

European Union's involvement in doping in sport might be described as that of a 'paper tiger', in whose ethology three phases of development may be distinguished. This paper looks at the question of the legal basis of EU involvement in doping in sport.

2.　　'A LETHARGIC TIGER': THE CODE OF CONDUCT AGAINST DOPING IN SPORT

In 1988, Stewart-Clark (MEP) asked the Commission whether it was willing to support legislation at European level to ensure that neither promoters nor athletes from any country would be able to gain unfair advantage over those of other Member States.[6] He felt he could ask the question because, in his opinion, sport was so extremely commercialised 'that it can only be regarded as an economic activity, especially when practised at the highest level.'[7] Though sport – generally speaking – did not have a substantial legal foundation in the Treaty, the Commission was obliged to express its opinion regarding doping in elite sport, since 'this represents a distortion of competition in the most literal sense.' The answer given on behalf of the Commission stated that it was 'not planning any legislative action in this area.' In the first place, the Commission was of the opinion that Recommendation R(84)19 of the Council of Europe – on a European charter against drug taking in sport – was a sound basis for any initiatives the Member States might wish to undertake in this area. The Commission also believed that the actions proposed in its Communication to the Council and the European Parliament concerning Community actions to combat the use of illicit drugs[8] should be given absolute priority, as the use of drugs in sport was a relatively minor problem compared to the consumption of illicit drugs generally.

In May 1989, the Council invited the Commission 'to examine the circumstances, purposes and frequency of screening for the use of illicit drugs by means of urine testing.' At the end of the year, the Health Council requested the Commission 'to examine the question of health data on drug addiction, including the addictive abuse of medicines.' On the basis of the request to the Commission, Scott-Hopkins put a question to the Commission in which he asked what new proposals the Commission intended to bring forward to discourage drug taking by

---

[6] Written question no. 1856/87, 18 December 1987, answer on behalf of the Commission, 1 March 1988, *OJ* 1988 C 160/15.

[7] The Court of Justice ruled on several occasions that 'as an economic activity', sport was subject to Community legislation. Cf., Case C-36/74 *Walrave* v. *UCI* [1974] *ECR* I-1405; Case C-13/76 *Donà* v. *Mantero* [1976] *ECR* I-I333; and Case C-222/86 *Heylens* v. *Unctef* [1987] *ECR* I-4097.

[8] COM (86) 601 final.

those involved in competitive sport.[9] The Commission answered that it had been invited by the Council and the Ministers of Health of the Member States meeting within the Council of 16 May 1989[10] to examine the circumstances, purposes and frequency of screening for the use of illicit drugs by means of urine testing. Studies were undertaken with regard to this problem, which according to the Commission would also cover the illicit use of drugs in sport. Moreover, the Commission had been asked by the Health Council of 13 November 1989[11] to examine the question of health data on drug addiction. In the opinion of the Commission, this examination would include the addictive abuse of medicines. At the end of 1990, the Council put more pressure on the Commission by approving a resolution in the field of drug abuse in sport.[12]

Like the Commission, the Council placed the problematic nature of the use of illicit drugs in sport in the framework of public health. In the words of the Council, 'the use of drugs, including the abuse of medicinal products, which is damaging to health, is increasingly prevalent in Europe, particularly in sport.' Furthermore, it declared in the above-mentioned resolution that 'one important objective of the fight against the use of drugs in sport should be the protection of the health of those taking part in sporting activities.' The use of doping was contrary to various directives in the field of public health.[13] The Council invited the Commission, assisted by a Group of Experts appointed by the Member States, to draft and circulate, in close conjunction with the Member States, a code of conduct to combat the use of drugs in sport, based on guidelines set out by the Council, by the end of 1991, with a view to the Olympic Games in 1992. In continuation to the resolution, the Council issued a declaration in mid-1991 in which it requested 'swift implementation of the action called for'.[14] In a written

---

[9] Written question no. 346/90, 26 February 1990, answer on behalf of the Commission, 3 April 1990, *OJ* 1990 C 259/27, 15 October 1990.

[10] *OJ* 1989 C 185/2, 22 July 1989.

[11] *OJ* 1990 C 31/1, 9 February 1990.

[12] Resolution of the Council and of the Representatives of the Governments of the Member States, meeting within the Council of 3 December 1990 on Community action to combat the use of drugs, including the abuse of medicinal products, particularly in sport, *OJ* 1990 C 329/4-5, 31 December 1990.

[13] Directive 65/65/EEC (*OJ* 1965 22/369, 9 February 1965, as last amended by Directive 89/341/EEC (*OJ* 1989 L 142/11, 25 May 1989)); Directive 65/65/EEC; Directive 75/319/EEC (*OJ* 1975 L 147/13, 9 June 1975, as last amended by Directive 89/381/EEC (*OJ* 1989 L 181/44, 28 June 1989)); Directive 75/319/EEC (as amended by Directive 89/341/EEC); and Directive 84/450/EEC (*OJ* 1984 L 250/17, 19 September 1984).

[14] Declaration by the Council and the Ministers for Health of the Member States, meeting within the Council of 4 June 1991 on action to combat the use of drugs, including the abuse of medicinal products, in sport, *OJ* 1991 C 170/1, 29 June 1991. See also Commission Communication to the Council and the European Parliament on the European Community and Sport, 31 July 1991, 4. Action contre le dopage, SEC (91) 1438/F.

question, Vertemati (MEP) pointed out that the approach of the doping problem should not be limited to high-level sport.[15] He noted that a proportional increase could be observed in the number of private gymnasiums in all EU Member States. Moreover, those gymnasiums were frequently administered by unqualified personnel and there was a risk that their activities might escape any kind of control by the health authorities. Investigations had brought to light the use of harmful substances in such gymnasiums in order to stimulate muscular development and improve performance. It had also been established that there was a direct relationship between the use of those substances and the occurrence of pathological symptoms such as tumours and that, in extreme cases, the use of such substances might be a direct cause of death.

Vertemati asked the Commission if it would consider carrying out intensive investigations into the ways in which such substances were distributed and administered and to examine the possibility of regulating the use of such substances and prohibit the marketing of those substances that are proved to have harmful effects. In its answer, the Commission did not enter into the merits of the question and only pointed out that it had already been invited by the Council 'to draft, in close cooperation with the Member States, before the end of 1991, a code of conduct to combat the use of drugs in sport, and to propose to the Council measures of Community interest, taking into account the measures already initiated by government sporting authorities, the Council of Europe and international sporting organizations.' The Code of Conduct was presented in February 1992 and was approved by Council resolution of 8 February 1992[16] 'as an instrument serving to inform and educate the public in general, and, more specifically, young people, as well as the circles concerned.'

'Code of Conduct against Doping in Sport
1. Young people shall be encouraged to play the leading role in advocating that participation in sport should be free from doping and urged to promote this attitude amongst themselves.
2. Parents shall be encouraged to foster in their children a positive attitude to participation in sport, to provide them with moral support in their efforts and to reinforce the basic values of good health, fair play and team spirit.
3. Schools, universities and other training centres shall promote the attainment of success through fair play and advocate that participation in sporting activities shall be free of doping agents and methods.

---

[15] Written question no. 1314/91, 24 June 1991, answer on behalf of the Commission, 5 September 1991, *OJ* 1991 C 323/26, 13 December 1991.

[16] Resolution of the Council and of the Representatives of the Governments of the Member States, meeting within the Council of 8 February 1992 on a code of conduct against doping in sport, *OJ* 1992 C 44/1-2, 19 February 1992.

4. Athletes, as role models, shall help to re-establish confidence in both sport and society being free from doping.

5. Health professionals have an obligation to be fully informed of the effects of doping agents and methods and to provide advice to the individuals who come into professional contact with them.

6. Those forming the entourage of sportsmen and women (managers, trainers, coaches, etc.) must play an active role in preventing doping and encouraging fair play.

7. Organizations involved with sports activities, including those related to the Olympic Movement, shall re-emphasize the spirit of fair competition.

8. Sports organizations at national and international levels shall cooperate on issues related to the status and control of doping.

9. Testing laboratories shall continue to maintain high-quality and reliable drug-testing procedures. They shall also monitor for the presence of new substances having the potential for performance-enhancement and inform the appropriate authorities for action to be taken.

10. The media shall provide the general public with information about athletes' training programmes and not merely the outcome of sporting events, as well as relevant information on the negative consequences of doping for health.'

In a parliamentary question of 23 July 1992,[17] André (MEP) asked the Commission to tell the European Parliament – in connection with the request of the Council to draft a code of conduct – what stage its work in this field had reached and whether it intended to organise a large-scale information campaign aimed at sportsmen, sportswomen and the general public once the code of conduct had been drafted. In fact, as already noted, the code had already been drafted and was even approved at the beginning of that year by the Council. One might have expected questions concerning the adequacy of the code in tackling the doping problem, but this proved not to be the case.

A long period of silence reigned after the paperwork eruptions of 1991. In November 1993, a hearing was held by the Committee on Culture, Youth, Education and the Media on the subject of sport and doping.[18] The hearing has not been documented. In a resolution of the European Parliament,[19] the Commission and the Council were called upon once again to acknowledge expressly the European Union's responsibility in the fight against doping in sport, both from an ethical standpoint and in the interests of public health. Besides these institutions,

---

[17] Written question no. 1446/92, 16 June 1992, answer on behalf of the Commission, 23 July 1992, *OJ* 1992 C 289/58, 5 November 1992.

[18] See European Parliament resolution of 27 April 1994, *OJ* 1994 C 205/484, 6 May 1994.

[19] Ibid.

the European Parliament also called on national and international sports federations, the Member States and the International Olympic Committee to continue their policies to prevent and combat doping in sport in a vigorous manner.

Only in May 1995 was a substantial written question concerning doping put to the Commission.[20] Sindal (MEP) asked the Commission if it had meanwhile undertaken any action in the field of doping. In its answer, the Commission pointed to the same directives that it had pointed to in its resolution of 1990. 'The Commission does not intend to put forward any new legislative proposals specifically directed at the testing of sportsmen for the illegal use of performance enhancing substances.' Replying to a question submitted by Amadeo (MEP) in November 1995,[21] the Commission stated that 'although [it] has no powers to introduce binding legislation on the testing of sportsmen and sportswomen for the illegal use of performance-enhancing substances, it has been able to take some initiatives.' One of those initiatives was the drafting of the Code of Conduct three years earlier in 1992. The Commission also declared that it had submitted a proposal to the Parliament and the Council for a decision adopting a programme of Community action on the prevention of drug dependence and a Communication on the same subject stressing the need for information specially targeted at young people in the right places, such as at sports centres.[22] Outside of taking action in the field of public health and in the field of the manufacture and marketing of pharmacological products, the Commission had no other option than to take action on health promotion, information, education and training within the framework of action in the field of public health.

Nevertheless, in 1996, the Commission was once again confronted with a written question that was similar in nature to previous questions:[23] 'Does the Commission not agree that the use of such substances should be banned by means of a Community law?' Once again, the Commission declared that it had no intention of proposing specific legislation relating to the testing of sportsmen for the illegal use of performance enhancing substances.

More that two years later, Blak (MEP) again called for action on the part of the Commission in the fight against doping.[24] Blak did not pose his question in the context of public health, as his predecessors had done, but in the context of employment. Since athletes were increasingly regarded as employees as a result of the EU Treaties, Blak asked whether the Commission had therefore considered whether this employee status might conflict with current regulations on doping,

---

[20] Question of 22 May 1995, *OJ* 1995 C 213/62, 17 August 1995.

[21] Question of 27 September 1995, *OJ* 1996 C 56/28, 26 February 1996.

[22] COM (94) 223.

[23] Written question no. E-0471/96 by Boniperti, 9 February 1996, answer on behalf of the Commission, 7 May 1996, *OJ* 1996 C 217/50, 26 July 1996.

[24] Written question no. E-1262/96, 24 May 1996, *OJ* 1996 C 305/71, 15 October 1996.

which could prevent athletes from exercising their profession. Initially, the Commission answered that it was conducting a detailed investigation of the problem raised by Blak and would inform him of the outcome as soon as possible. A few months later, after a thorough investigation, the Commission came back to the question.[25] It informed Blak that no questions or complaints had been received by the Commission dealing with the matter he had raised. Also, the Commission claimed to know nothing about the cases to which he referred. Enquiries with some of the sports organisations indicated that no such cases were known at that time. The Commission therefore invited Blak to draw attention to any case in which doping and freedom of movement overlapped, promising that it would be more than willing to make a preliminary assessment of such a case.

In December 1998, Tamino (MEP) picked up the thread of the conversation started by Blak. In his question,[26] he stated that 'in view of the fact that professional sportsmen are in every respect workers and that, pursuant to Directive 89/391/EEC of 12 June 1989,[27] employers are under a duty to evaluate the risks and, on the basis of that assessment, ... all necessary measures for the safety and health protection of workers [had to be taken].' The question that followed this thesis again tended towards the sphere of public health. Specifically, Tamino asked whether the Commission did not believe that the use of pharmaceutical products to improve the physical performance of sportsmen, often with serious side-effects, was incompatible with the Community provisions safeguarding the health of workers. In addition, on the basis of Article 129 EU, which was laid down to protect the health of all citizens, and consequently all sportsmen, he asked the Commission whether it could indicate what measures it intended to take and whether it believed that it should take action on this issue by means of a legislative proposal at European level. In its response, the Commission was of the opinion that sportsmen and sportswomen were only covered by the provisions of the above-mentioned Council Directive concerning measures to encourage improvements in the safety and health of workers at work[28] to the extent that they were regarded as workers within the meaning of Article 3 of the Directive, which defined them as 'any person employed by an employer'. The use by sportsmen and sportswomen of pharmaceutical products in order to improve their physical fitness may represent a risk to the health of workers. Therefore, the employer should, in the light of the first general principle of prevention, take steps to avoid safety and health problems at work. The Commission did not go any further than

---

[25] Answer on behalf of the Commission, 31 October 1996, *OJ* 1996 C 305/71, 15 October 1996.

[26] Written question no. E-2906/98, 2 October 1998, answer on behalf of the Commission, 9 December 1998, *OJ* 1999 C 142/55, 21 May 1999.

[27] Council Directive 89/391/EEC of 12 June 1989 on the introduction of measures to encourage improvements in the safety and health of workers at work, *OJ* 1989 L 183/1, 29 June 1989.

[28] Ibid.

to say 'that the consumption of drugs for the purpose of enhancing physical performance should be regarded as harmful and therefore be strongly discouraged.'

The Commission also responded in this well-known fashion to the question of Lienemann (MEP) as to whether the Commission was inclined 'to pursue a more active Community policy to combat the use of drugs in major European sports events in order to promote healthy sporting activity',[29] by stating that 'The EC Treaty confers no powers on the Community to develop a common policy to combat the use of drugs.' The Commission, aware of the problem, was disposed to seek to mobilise the instruments available to it in the context of various Community policies and JHA cooperation. The Council was prepared to carry the matter a step further than the Commission. During a meeting of the Council on 14 and 15 May 1998 in Nicosia, the need for 'new laws to be adopted and for ethical solutions to be found to the specific problems of modern sport, in particular ... doping' was expressed. On 11 and 12 December 1998, the Council advocated a mobilisation of all forces available in the fight against the use of illicit drugs in sport.[30] The European Parliament was also prepared to carry the matter a step further than the Commission. In a resolution of 17 December 1998,[31] it emphasised the role of sport as a means of social and cultural integration and noted that this role should be taken into consideration in the drawing up of Community education, youth and public health policies. There was, so declared the Parliament, a need for better coordination and complementarity, with a view to standardisation, between the measures and initiatives adopted within national law and by the European institutions, the Council of Europe and European and international sporting organisations. The Parliament called on the Commission 'to put forward proposals with a view to implementing a harmonised public health policy to combat doping and establishing cooperation in research, prevention, information provision, medical cheeks on sportsmen and women, controls on the distribution and movement of doping substances and a crackdown on the networks which product and distribute banned doping substances.' A member of the Committee on Culture, Youth, Education, the Media and Sport remarked in December 1998:

---

[29] Written question no. E-3183/98, 27 October 1998, answer on behalf of the Commission, 11 December 1998, *OJ* 1999 C 182/49, 28 June 1999.

[30] Presidency Conclusions of the Vienna European Council: '96. The European Council underlines its concern at the extent and seriousness of in sports, which undermines the sporting ethic and endangers public health. It emphasises the need for mobilisation at European Union level and invites the Member States to examine jointly with the Commission and international sports bodies possible measures to intensify the fight against this danger, in particular through better coordination of existing national measures.'

[31] European Parliament resolution on urgent measures to be taken against doping in sport; *OJ* 1999 C 98/291, 9 April 1999.

'Sportsmen and women set examples to Europe's young people. They pay far more attention to what sportsmen and women are doing than to what politicians are doing. This is an issue that crosses national frontiers. It cannot be dealt with by nation states acting alone. It requires cooperation at international level. The Commission has a responsibility. Europe has a responsibility.'[32]

3.   'THE TIGER BECOMES AWARE OF ITS ROLE': PARTICIPATION IN WADA

In March 1999, in a written question,[33] Amadeo (MEP) argued that the existing national measures aimed at combating the practice of drug use in sport were no longer sufficient, let alone effective. The issue of doping had become an alarming phenomenon that went beyond the frontiers of individual States. Like Vertemati in 1991, Amadeo took a broader approach to the doping problem in his question than just the realm of high-level sport: 'What does the Commission think about issuing, as a matter of urgency, a directive aimed at harmonising the existing national measures?' Unlike in its responses to foregoing written questions, the Commission did not refrain from adopting an active attitude on this occasion.[34] 'In view of the various stances taken, the Commission has set up a working party with the Member States and with the Council of Europe as an observer, in order to study possible Community action on such issues as those raised by the Honourable Member.'[35] The findings of the working party were discussed during an informal meeting of the Sport Ministers of the EU Member States in Paderborn

---

[32] Debate in report of proceedings of 17 December 1998, p. 38. See Report of the Committee on Culture, Youth, Education, the Media and Sport on the Commission Communication to the Council, the European Parliament, the Economic and Social Committee and the Committee of the Regions on a Community support plan to combat doping in sport, 17 July 2000, COM (1999) 643.

[33] Written question no. E-0175/99, 11 February 1999, answer on behalf of the Commission, 15 March 1999, *OJ* 1999 C 325/80, 12 November 1999.

[34] Shortly before that date, at the beginning of February 1999, the Commission had taken part in the World Conference on Doping organised by the IOC.

[35] Cf., although getting ahead of the chronology of the occurrences, written question no. P-2818/99 by Mennea, 10 January 2000, answer on behalf of the Council, 10/11 April 2000, *OJ* 2000 C 303 E/116, 24 October 2000. It appears that the initiatives the Commission and the Council were about to take did not go far enough for Mennea. He pointed out that 'cases of sports doping are regularly brought before the national courts in several Member States and the problem is causing increasing concern in the sports world.' Mennea felt it was essential that there would be common legislation that would be applicable to all Member States. He asked the Council '[to] use its powers to promote the introduction of Community criminal legislation, whose general principles would be adopted by, and binding on, all Member States.' Although the Council was aware of the problem posed by doping in the world of sport and although it attached great importance to it, it declared – shortly and sweetly – that no initiative has been submitted to the Council.

between 31 May and 2 June 1999. The Ministers came up with a list of opinions. The most striking opinions were that, in order to combat doping efficiently, a coordination of doping legislation was vital, a uniform list of prohibited substances and methods was needed, the sanctions on the use of doping had to be deterrent and, above all, that an international independent and transparent anti-doping agency had to be created to implement an efficient fight against doping.[36]

During the World Conference on Doping, which took place on the initiative of the International Olympic Committee (IOC) at the beginning of 1999 and in which the European Union participated, the IOC's proposal to establish a World Anti-Doping Agency (WADA) was approved. With regard to the creation of WADA, the European Union was invited by the IOC to play an important role. The Ministers in Paderborn were disposed to accept this role. In a Communication to the Commission,[37] Commissioner Reding threw light on the position that the European Union should adopt: 'Either the Commission rejects the IOC's invitation outright ... or the Commission considers the possibility of participating in the Agency.' Shortly before, the Commission was of the opinion that the European Union was not suited to playing a role in the fight against doping. However, we have seen above that in the last years of the 20th century that stance had shifted somewhat.

In October 1999, that shift reached a point that Reding could say objectively 'would seem to be in contradiction with the tasks entrusted to the Commission under the responsibilities invested in us.' 'It would also be a rebuff to the Heads of State and Government, who, at the Vienna European Council, expressed the wish to *"intensify the fight against this scourge"* and emphasised *"the need for mobilisation at European Union level"*, as well as to the European Parliament, which, in a resolution adopted on 17.12.1998, supported the proposal concerning the creation of this Agency and expressed the hope that the Commission would take part therein.' Reding supported the involvement of the European Union in the creation of WADA, but on the condition that 'the Agency should be genuinely transparent and independent; that its Board should be composed equally of representatives of the sports movement and representatives of the public authorities; that its aim should be to establish common procedures and criteria for the fight against doping; and that the participating parties, notably the sports organisations concerned, should undertake to respect the established standards, criteria and procedures.'

---

[36] Conclusions of the Council Presidency on the occasion of the informal meeting of the Sports Ministers of the European Union, Paderborn, 31 May to 2 June 1999.

[37] Communication to the Commission – The fight against doping in sport: Proposal by the International Olympic Committee for a World Anti-Doping Agency, 13 October 1999.

4.   'THE TIGER BECOMES ACTIVE AND GROWLS': COMMUNITY
          SUPPORT PLAN TO COMBAT DOPING IN SPORT

In the Community Support Plan to Combat Doping in Sport of 1 December
1999,[38] the Commission gave itself a not entirely justifiable compliment by
asserting that 'it should be recalled that Europe has traditionally played a flagship
role in combating doping, notably since the adoption on 16 November 1989 of the
European Anti-Doping Convention[39] by the Council of Europe.' In fact, it was not
the European Union that had played the pioneer role in combating the use of
doping in sport, but the Council of Europe. However, the tables were turned after
this Communication.[40] No longer would the Commission stand behind the
touchline with good intentions and recommendations. With this Communication,
it wanted to present measures 'to accommodate the demands made by the other
Community institutions and bodies in the field of combating doping.' In the
Communication, the reader is informed that doping has increasingly taken on the
shape of a systematic and organised misuse of medicines.[41] Because sport had
increasingly developed itself in an international direction, the fight against doping
should also have a supranational dimension.

      While the subsidiarity and the autonomy of sporting organisations had to be
respected, the Commission suggested that the European Union could contribute to
the international fight against doping by encouraging different countries to adopt
a similar approach and by making use of existing Community policies and
resources. The Commission presented a 'three-pronged approach' comprising
expert opinion on doping, participation in the creation of WADA and mobilisation of the resources at the disposal of the Community.

---

[38] Communication from the Commission to the Council, the European Parliament, the Economic
and Social Committee and the Committee of the Regions on a Community support plan to combat
doping in sport, 1 December 1999, COM (1999) 643 final.
[39] Council of Europe, European Treaties, ETS No. 135.
[40] In fact, the Commission followed a tendency that was accelerated in 1997 by the Declaration on
Sport, attached to the Treaty of Amsterdam, amending the Treaty on European Union, of 2 October
1997: 'The Conference emphasises the social significance of sport, in particular its role in forging
identity and bringing people together. The Conference therefore calls on the bodies of the European
Union to listen to sports associations when important questions affecting sport are at issue. In this
connection, special consideration should be given to the particular characteristics of amateur sport.'
[41] Cf., Resolution of the European Parliament on the Commission Report to the European Council with a view to safeguarding current sports structures and maintaining the social function of sport
within the community framework – The Helsinki Report on Sport, 7 September 2000, *OJ* 2001 C
135/274, 7 May 2001, A5-208/2000: 'D. having regard to the increase in doping and the alarming
infiltration of this sector by organised crime, with serious consequences as a result of the ongoing
legislative vacuum; having regard to the increasing abuse of pharmaceutical products which is
seriously damaging the health of sportspersons; having regard to the need for European sporting
authorities to draw up a common set of rules to be applied to the issue of doping.'

One of the most important points of departure in the Communication is support for the creation of WADA, which was meant to pave the way for cooperation between the Olympic Movement and the various public authorities. 'Nobody disputes that the sports organisations have neither the resources nor the powers to check the spread of doping. Hence, government action is indispensable. One of the major merits of this future Agency will be to enable the two major players in the war on doping to work hand in hand.' In the discussions that were aimed to lead to the creation of WADA, common understanding was reached on the point that both sport and public authorities should be equally represented on the governing board of WADA, as well as on the point that important decisions should be taken on a consensual basis. In October 1999, the IOC invited the Council Presidency and the President of the Commission to finalise the statute of, and participate in, WADA. The Member States and the Commission decided to honour this invitation and to start negotiations with the IOC. The positions defended by the Member States in agreement with the Commission notably concerned WADA's independence and transparency, as well as its precise remit. At a meeting on 2 November 1999, the IOC and the European Union reached agreement on the draft statute of WADA. WADA was founded on 10 November 1999.

On the strength of the agreement reached with the European Union and the Council of Europe, the IOC formally deposited the Agency's statutes with a view to establishing the Foundation Board. During an initial period ending on 1 January 2002, the European Union would have two representatives on the Foundation Board, appointed *ad personam*, and the Commission would have the status of an observer. For the first two years of its life, the Agency would be funded by the IOC. The European Union would thus be in a position to decide formally, acting on a proposal from the Commission, on whether to play a full part in the Agency's work, including the financial aspects. With this in mind, the Commission was in a position to start preparing a proposal to the European Parliament and the Council with a view to formalising the Community's participation in the work of WADA. The proposal would include the requisite budget forecasts to comply with the financial commitments of the public authorities with representatives on the Management Board. These commitments would begin to apply as of 1 January 2002.

On 7 December 1999, the Council decided to consult the Economic and Social Committee (ESC) on the Community Support Plan to Combat Doping in Sport. According to the ESC, 'the Communication draws attention to a problem that has become very serious in the public's mind following the discovery that doping is almost general practice in certain sporting events.'[42]

---

[42] Opinion of the Economic and Social Committee on the Communication from the Commission to the Council, the European Parliament, the Economic and Social Committee and the Committee of the Regions: Community support plan to combat doping in sport, Rapporteur: Mr Bedossa, 24 May 2000, *OJ* 2000 C 204/45-50, 18 July 2000.

The ESC positioned itself completely behind the initiatives mentioned in the Communication of the Commission. It was especially pleased with the implication of the European Union in the founding of WADA: 'The EU has to make its presence felt, join in the action and share its knowledge in order for this international authority to succeed, while at the same time guaranteeing that the principles of independence and operational transparency are respected.' However, the ESC has some reservations regarding the Community Support Plan. To its regret, the ESC did not find any ideas in the plan regarding the construction of a basic Community system that could form the framework for a structured fight against doping and protection of sportspersons' health by the public authorities of the Member States. In the opinion of the ESC, such an approach would have made it possible to set out guidelines for a European body of measures aimed at preventing and fighting against doping on the basis of three pillars: the creation of a genuine, active Community policy of prevention; the development and harmonisation of repressive measures covering both disciplinary action against sportspersons convicted of doping offences and penal measures against those involved in doping networks; and a continuation and stepping-up of medical and pharmacological research, both at theoretical and clinical level.

The Committee of the Regions (COR) was also asked for a commentary on the Community Support Plan. In its opinion,[43] the COR identified, *inter alia*, the weak spot in the position of the European Union in the fight against doping: the lack of a legal basis in Community law: 'The Committee is of the opinion that in the absence of any reference to sport in the Treaty there is a need for a new partnership between the European Institutions, the Member States, sports organisations and other public bodies to promote the development of sport founded on an agreed code of ethics, equity and fair play, while preserving its integrity and independence.' A method to sidestep the lack of a legal basis can be found in the opinion of the Committee on the Environment, Public Health and Consumer Policy,[44] namely, the drawing up of a directive on combating doping in sport on the basis of Article 152 EC (now Article 129 EC) on public health.

The Report of the Committee on Culture, Youth, Education, the Media and Sport concerning the Support Plan, which is also referred to as the Zabell Report after its rapporteur, recalled that the Commission had planned to put forward a

---

[43] Opinion of the Committee of the Regions on a Communication from the Commission to the Council, the European Parliament, the Economic and Social Committee and the Committee of the Regions on a Community support plan to combat doping in sport, Rapporteur: Mr Murray, 15 June 2000, *OJ* 2000 C 317/63, 6 November 2000.

[44] Opinion of the Committee on the Environment, Public Health and Consumer Policy for the Committee on Culture, Youth, Education, the Media and Sport on the Communication from the Commission to the Council, the European Parliament, the Economic and Social Committee and the Committee of the Regions on a Community support plan to combat doping in sport, Draftsman: Mihail Papayannakis, 21 June 2000, COM (1999) 643.

proposal for a Council recommendation under Article 152 EC on the prevention of drug-taking in sport (especially in amateur sport).[45] 'Moreover, the new framework Public Health Action Plan, to be proposed shortly, will provide another opportunity to focus on anti-doping measures.' In her conclusion, Zabell writes: 'As colleagues will recall, the Committee called in its opinion for the Committee on Constitutional Affairs on the forthcoming Intergovernmental Conference for the creation of a separate legal basis for Community action in the field of sport.' For the time being, and in the absence of such a legal base, the Commission had done a good job in identifying the action it could take under existing Treaty provisions. As pleased as she was with the activities undertaken by the Commission, Zabell still called on that institution 'to act more boldly'. The Community could, for instance, accede to the European Anti-Doping Convention adopted by the Council of Europe.

In the resolution drawn up by the European Parliament on the basis of the Support Plan,[46] one again finds a call for the inclusion in the Treaty of a legal basis for Community action in the field of sport. The resolution calls to mind 'that recent rulings by the European Court of Justice have confirmed that sport does have specific characteristics which allow special treatment in the application of EU law, making obvious the need for a legal basis for sport in the Treaty.' However, if one reads the resolution closely, one concludes that the Parliament also comes to the conclusion that the Commission cannot go any further than 'to include in its information campaigns about the dangers of doping products information about the possible harmful effects of "nearly-doping products", as well as discouraging department stores, sports shops, gymnasia, etc. from selling these products.' In imitation of what Zabell had proposed, the Parliament called on the Commission to present a recommendation to the Council under Article 300 of the Treaty as soon as possible, with a view to the accession of the European Community to the European Anti-Doping Convention.

Finally, mention should be made of the meeting of the Council and Representatives of the Governments of the Member States at the end of 2000.[47] During this meeting it was agreed, *inter alia*, that the European Union and its Member States

---

[45] Report of the Committee on Culture, Youth, Education, the Media and Sport on the Commission Communication to the Council, the European Parliament, the Economic and Social Committee and the Committee of the Regions on a Community support plan to combat doping in sport, Rapporteur: Teresa Zabell, 17 July 2000, COM (1999) 643.

[46] Resolution of the European Parliament on the Commission Communication to the Council, the European Parliament, the Economic and Social Committee and the Committee of the Regions on a Community support plan to combat doping in sport, 7 September 2000; *OJ* 2000 C 135/270, 7 September 2000, A5-203/2000.

[47] Conclusions of the Council and the Representatives of the Governments of the Member States, meeting within the Council of 4 December 2000 on combating doping, *OJ* 2000 C 356/1, 12 December 2000.

'will be represented [in WADA] by the President-in-Office of the Council and a member of the Commission'. That member would be able to speak on matters within the Community's sphere of competence in accordance with the Treaty and the case law of the Court of Justice, given that there is no direct Community competence in the area of sport. In recent years, there have been no new substantial developments in the European Union in the field of doping in sport.

5.   CONCLUSION

As to the legal basis of the European Union's involvement in doping in sport, it may be observed that the European Union's anti-doping policies were not devoid of a specific legal basis. As doping is not just a matter of sport, but indeed a general societal problem and more particularly a public health problem, the legal basis for Community action to combat doping in sport was usually Article 152 EC (public health).

The evolution of the activities of the European Union in the field of doping in sport can be divided in three phases. Characteristic of the first phase is the lethargic attitude of the Commission with regard to sport in general and doping in sport in particular. At that time, the Commission considered the use of drugs in sport a relatively minor problem. If the Member States wished to take initiatives in the field of doping, they were obliged to turn to the Council of Europe. The Commission did not see any possibility to take the initiative. Under heavy pressure from the Parliament and the Council, the Commission reluctantly drafted a Code of Conduct: a kind of ten commandments regarding doping. During the second phase, the Community displayed a more enterprising spirit. The European Union was invited by the Olympic Movement to participate in the founding of a world-wide anti-doping agency (WADA). The third phase can be characterised by a change in attitude. The European Union positioned itself wholeheartedly on the side of the Olympic Movement and drafted the Community Support Plan to Combat Doping in Sport. The European Union saw an opportunity to join in the war against doping, albeit that it fought this war by proxy. Of course, the new article on sport in the draft Treaty establishing a Constitution for Europe will strengthen the European Union's position in the field of sport in general and in the fight against doping in particular, as it directly allows the Union to take coordinating, complementary or supporting action in the field of sport.

Our dear friend and colleague, Alfred Kellermann, can certainly not be considered a 'paper tiger', let alone a 'lethargic' one! He always was and continues to be very active as an organiser of academic communities and a networker *pur sang* in the field of European law and international relations. He is also a sportsman, still playing his beloved lawn tennis and, in the past, participating enthusiastically in the Asser Institute's football team.

THE EUROPEANISATION OF THE INTERNATIONAL MARITIME SAFETY AGENDA: ARE WE BETTER OFF LEAVING IT TO THE IMO?

Frans A. Nelissen*

When one is requested to contribute to a book paying tribute to Dr Alfred E. Kellermann h.c., the obvious thought is that this contribution has to contain elements of EU law, since Fred has devoted a major part of his working career to this particular field of international law.

In fact, he deserves a lot of credit for being one of the initiators and organisers – the engine one might say – of what after thirty-five years has become a something of a tradition, namely, the annual seminar on EU law for academics and specialists in the field, known as the 'Asser Colloquium on the Law of the European Communities/Union', which takes place in The Hague every year in September. In addition, he deserves a lot of credit for his other accomplishments in this field, especially those in relation to the 'new' Member States and the EU applicant countries.

As I am not a specialist in the law of the European Union, however, this contribution examines some developments in a related field of law, that of environmental protection, a topic to which Fred devoted quite some attention during his recent 'Russian period'. More specifically, this paper deals with the topic of safety of navigation from an environmental protection perspective,[1] at the intersection of the law of the sea, international environmental law and EU law.

This contribution focuses specifically on EU action, and occasionally on the actions of some of its Member States, in relation to the safety of navigation at sea, as compared to international global action and with reference to several serious accidents in European waters with severe environmental consequences involving oil tankers, such as the 'Erika' off the coast of France in December 1999 and the 'Prestige' off the west coast of Galicia, Spain, in November 2002.

Over 90 per cent of the external trade of the European Union is transported by sea. In terms of volume, shipping is the most important mode of transport.

---

* General Director of the T.M.C. Asser Institute; Professor of International Environmental Law, University of Groningen.

[1] Limited to the protection of the marine environment in relation to the transport of – mainly – oil.

The European Union: An Ongoing Process of Integration – Liber Amicorum Alfred E. Kellermann
© 2004, T.M.C. Asser Instituut, The Hague, and the authors

'By virtue of its geography, its history and the effects of globalization, maritime transport is, and will continue to be, vital for European Union economies. However, European citizens also expect shipping to be safe and clean so, as a result of recent accidents, there is understandable public concern about lack of safety at sea and about the pollution caused by the maritime sector.'[2]

At Community level, the issue of safety of navigation can be said to have really started playing a role in 1993, with the adoption by the Commission of its first Communication dealing with maritime safety, entitled 'A Common Policy on Safe Seas'.[3] Earlier attempts for a Community shipping policy can be said to date back to 1985, but these focused on free and fair competition rather than on safety of navigation. In the period before 1993, an EU action programme on the control and reduction of pollution caused by hydrocarbons discharged at sea was set up by the Council.[4] Although the need for action to improve maritime safety was implicit in the resolution in question – as so often, legislative action was taken as a response, in this case to a grave accident involving the oil tanker 'Amoco Cadiz' that took place off the coast of Brittany, France, in March 1978 causing enormous pollution – real legal action was left to be taken at the international global level. The European Union was not performing the role of an important player in this respect.[5]

The idea was to leave international legislative action in this field to the international global institution for maritime shipping, the International Maritime Organisation (IMO), which was originally founded as the Inter-Governmental Maritime Consultative Organisation at the United Nations Maritime Conference in Geneva in 1948.[6] The IMO is a so-called specialised agency of the United Nations. Its main mandate concerns international shipping – overseas international transport – and specifically the safety aspects of international shipping. After the accident involving the oil tanker 'Torrey-Canyon' in 1967, which caused an environmental disaster by spilling more than 100,000 tons of crude oil, the IMO also started to concentrate on the environmental aspects of shipping. This combination resulted in the IMO's work programme for 'cleaner seas and

---

[2] See the European Maritime Safety Agency website, welcome page, at: <http://emsa.eu.int>.

[3] See 'Accidents an impetus for maritime safety for a better protection of the maritime environment', at: <http://europa.eu.int/comm/transport/maritime/safety/index_en.htm>.

[4] Council Resolution of 26 June 1978.

[5] A few other legislative measures of the European Union are worth mentioning in this context, such as the Council Directive 79/115/EEC of 21 December 1978 on the compulsory pilotage of vessels by deep-sea pilots in heavily sailed, high-density maritime areas such as the North Sea and the English Channel (both of which are also designated as so-called 'special areas', as part of the 'North West European Waters', under Annex I of the MARPOL Convention) and Council Resolution of 19 June 1990 on the prevention of accidents causing marine pollution.

[6] The IMCO Convention entered into force in March 1958.

safer ships'.[7] Its most important organs, insofar as relevant here, are the Legal Committee, created in 1967, the Marine Safety Committee (MSC) and the Marine Environment Protection Committee (MEPC), created in 1973, which was eventually granted formal institutional equality with the Member States.[8]

Coming back to 1993, the Commission issued a Communication analysing the maritime safety situation in Europe, entitled 'A Common Policy on Safe Seas'. The catalysts[9] for the start of a Community policy in this field were the grave accidents, again causing enormous pollution in European waters, involving the oil tanker 'Aegean Sea', off the coast of La Coruña, Spain, in December 1992, and only a month later the oil tanker 'Brear', which ran aground off the Shetland Islands, United Kingdom, in January 1993. In addition, it is claimed that the abandoning of the unanimity rule for maritime decision-making process as of 1 January 1993 also played a role here.[10]

The Common Policy outlined a framework for a common maritime safety policy based on four pillars, three of which are directly relevant here. The first two encompass:

- the convergent implementation of existing global international (read: IMO) rules; and
- the uniform enforcement of global international (again read: IMO) rules by EU port States.

The third pillar is even more interesting in that it marks the European Union's first step in the direction of becoming a more important international player in the field, although it is not as far-reaching as having unilateral plans, that is to say, for the entire EU region. This pillar encompasses:

- 'reinforcement of the EU's role as the driving force for global international rule-making'.[11]

The Commission included an action programme in the Communication, highlighting the main decisions to be taken to improve maritime safety in Europe and to better protect European coasts.[12]

---

[7] See F.A. Nelissen, *Scheepswrakken en wrakke schepen – Een volkenrechtelijke beschouwing vanuit milieu-perspectief* (The Hague, T.M.C. Asser Institute for International Law 1997) pp. 11 and 26.

[8] Ibid., p. 237.

[9] See the section on maritime safety on the European Commission's transport website, at: <http://europa.eu.int/comm/transport/maritime/safety/index_en.htm>.

[10] Ibid., at p. 2.

[11] See n. 9 *supra*.

[12] Ibid.

Between 1993 and 2002, on the basis of this action programme, the Commission presented more than ten different legislative proposals that have all been adopted by the Council, ranging from, for example, a Directive on the implementation of international safety regulations by all ships visiting European ports and a notification system for ships carrying inherently dangerous or noxious substances and bound for or leaving EU ports to a Directive on mutual recognition of so-called 'classification societies' within the European Union. According to the latter, only highly reliable and professionally competent bodies will be recognised by the European Union and will be allowed to carry out the mandatory surveys and certification on behalf of the EU Member States.

In 1997, the European Commission began a campaign for 'quality shipping'. Up to that point, the EU approach had been that generally accepted international rules and standards[13] should be rigorously upheld, implemented and enforced. The European Union did not have unilateral legislative aspirations in the field of maritime safety. This can also be deduced from the Opinion of the Economic and Social Committee on the 'Communication from the Commission to the Council, The European Parliament, the Economic and Social Committee and the Committee of the Regions "Towards a new maritime strategy"',[14] although the document had more to do with competition – whether the EU was doing enough to promote EC fleets and to halt the decline in the Community's shipping industry – and only dealt indirectly with marine safety, in combination with the topic of substandard (non-EU) shipping:

> 'Member States should pursue common objectives in this respect within the international bodies and ... there is scope for the Commission to play a coordinating role. In particular, as stated in the Opinion on Safe Seas in November 1993, the policy of converting appropriate non-binding IMO Resolutions into binding international instruments is preferable to enforcing these resolutions only at EC level although the latter course of action may be contemplated in particular cases if the general policy has proved unsuccessful. There is, however, a risk that this could lead to regionalization.'[15]

This brings us at the issue of the importance of implementation and enforcement. In general, it is claimed by many that nowadays that implementation matters much more than the need for new legislation. According to De La Fayette, '[w]ith the adoption of a large number of instruments in the past quarter

---

[13] For this formula, see Art. 211 of the LOS Convention.
[14] *OJ* 1997 C 56/9.
[15] Ibid, at para. 6.1.2.

of a century, the focus of international environmental law has turned towards their effective implementation and to compliance both by state parties and by private entities whose behaviour they regulate'.[16] It is not a coincidence that the IMO itself, when announcing its new objectives in 2000, identified implementation and compliance as the main challenges for the future.[17]

When dealing with the implementation and enforcement of international rules and standards with respect to shipping, the phenomenon of 'port State control' comes to the fore. According to this phenomenon, ships that are voluntarily present in the port of a State that is not the flag State of the ship are inspected in these ports to determine their conformity to international standards. The relevant international instrument in this respect, the 1982 UN Convention on the Law of the Sea (hereinafter, the 'LOS Convention'), also known as Montego Bay Convention, which has been in force since 1994, deals with port State control in Part XII ('Protection and Preservation of the Marine Environment'):

'When a vessel is voluntarily within a port or at an off-shore terminal of a State, that State may undertake investigations and, where the evidence so warrants, institute proceedings in respect of any discharge from that vessel outside the internal waters, territorial sea or exclusive economic zone of that State in violation of applicable international rules and standards established through the competent international organization...'.[18]

It is uncontested that the phrase 'the competent international organization' refers to the IMO.[19] In the authoritative commentary on the LOS Convention the authors state as follows:

'The focal point of the compromise regarding the protection and preservation of the marine environment is found in recognition of a single international organization which is competent to establish the international rules and standards for the prevention, reduction and control of pollution of the marine environment, namely, in principle, the International Maritime Organization.'[20]

---

[16] Louise de la Fayette (Director of the Centre for Environmental Law, University of Southampton), 'The Marine Environment Protection Committee: The Conjunction of the Law of the Sea and International Environmental Law', 16 *The International Journal of Marine and Coastal Law* (2001) pp. 155-238.

[17] See 3 *IMO News* (2000). See also De La Fayette, loc. cit. n. 16, at p. 221.

[18] Art. 218(1) of the LOS Convention ('Enforcement by Port States').

[19] See, e.g., R.J. Dupuy and D. Vignes, eds., *A Handbook on the Law of the Sea*, Volumes I & II (Dordrecht, Martinus Nijhoff Publishers 1991) p. 1200. See also Nelissen, op. cit. n. 7, at p. 238.

[20] M.H. Nordquist, S. Rosenne and A. Yankov, eds., *United Nations Convention on the Law of the Sea 1982 – A Commentary*, Vol. IV (Dordrecht, Martinus Nijhoff Publishers 1991) p. 22.

Let us return to the issue of port State control. Under international law in general and the law of the sea in particular, States have the right to apply conditions to ships seeking access to their ports. Once in their ports, the States are entitled, under the port State control regime, to inspect these foreign ships. The LOS Convention even contains an obligation to detain these ships should they not meet the conditions for safety and environmental protection:

> '... States which, upon request or on their own initiative, have ascertained that a vessel within one of their ports or at one of their off-shore terminals is in violation of applicable international rules and standards relating to seaworthiness of vessels and thereby threatens damage to the marine environment shall, as far as practicable, take administrative measures to prevent the vessel from sailing.'[21]

Port State control constitutes one of the major innovations in the law of the sea of the last decades. The safety of international shipping is enormously enhanced by its application and this has everything to do with the implementation and enforcement of existing international legislation or, in the words of the Convention, 'applicable international rules and standards'.[22] Before these articles were accepted as law, no State other than the flag State of the ship was allowed to exercise jurisdiction with respect to the pollution of areas of the oceans outside its territorial waters. Port State control is one of the mechanisms for effectively tackling flag States that are lax in applying international standards for the safety of navigation and for marine environmental protection.

Because a significant number of flag States, especially those acting as so-called 'flags of convenience', were not complying with internationally accepted rules and standards as incorporated, for example, in such IMO Conventions as MARPOL, on marine environmental protection in relation to shipping, and SOLAS, on the safety of shipping,[23] and because inspections by individual States alone would not be sufficient to enforce the regulations contained in these Conventions on an international scale, port State control *cooperation* between States is considered by many as the most effective tool to reduce unsafe and substandard shipping. After all, ships could simply avoid ports in which they are subjected to inspections, but this would not be possible if inspections were coordinated at regional level.

It is in this area that Europe can truly be called a world leader. Following the 'Amoco Cadiz' accident, European States started to work on a unique regional

---

[21] Art. 219 of the LOS Convention.

[22] In other words, rules that are binding on the flag State as well as on the port State.

[23] The International Convention for the Prevention of Pollution from Ships (MARPOL) of 1973/1978 and the International Convention for the Safety of Life at Sea (SOLAS) of 1974.

agreement on coordinated port State control to facilitate cooperation in inspecting ships that are present in ports in the European region. This resulted in a regional legal instrument known as the Paris Memorandum of Understanding on Port State Control of 1982, which sets an example for agreements of this kind.

Since then, the IMO has been very active in encouraging the strengthening of the port State control system and promoting its extension to other regions around the world. With a view to ultimately achieving worldwide coverage, so that substandard ships would have nowhere to go, the IMO actively supported and encouraged the development of further regional agreements, as a result of which eight regional agreements on port State control are currently in operation. In addition to Europe, agreements have been adopted for the following regions: Latin America (1992), Asia-Pacific (1993), the Caribbean (1996), the Mediterranean (1997), the Indian Ocean (1998), West and Central Africa (1999) and the Black Sea (2000).[24] All that remains is the conclusion of a regional agreement for the Gulf region in the Middle East.[25]

However, it is Europe that sets the example, not the European Communities or the Union. The European port State control regime does not concern an orchestrated action on the part of the Union.[26] In fact, it is questionable whether the European Union needs to be a decisive player in respect of the safety of navigation to begin with.

Port State control is also 'not a panacea for all problems'.[27] It cannot be regarded as the sole tool for rectifying irresponsible flag State behaviour. This is one of the reasons why in 1992 the IMO established a new Subcommittee on Flag State Implementation, which has to report to the MSC and the MEPC to encourage and assist flag States in the implementation of their international legal obligations concerning ship safety and environmental protection,[28] obligations that are clearly incorporated in treaty law:

'States shall adopt laws and regulations for the prevention, reduction and control of pollution of the marine environment from vessels flying their flag or of their registry. Such laws and regulations *shall at least have the same effect as* that of generally accepted international rules and standards established through [the IMO] …'.[29]

---

[24] See, among others, De La Fayette, loc. cit. n. 16, at p. 223.

[25] Ibid., at p. 222.

[26] However, the Community did follow Europe's example and incorporated it in its own legislation by enacting Council Directive 95/21/EC, later amended by Directive 2001/106/EC of the European Parliament and of the Council of 19 December 2001.

[27] See K. Mitroussi, 'Quality in Shipping: IMO's role and problems of Implementation', 13 *Disaster Prevention and Management* (2004) p. 57.

[28] See also De La Fayette, loc. cit. n. 16, at p. 222.

[29] Art. 211(2) of the LOS Convention [emphasis added].

In this context, it is worth mentioning that all major flag States are party to the LOS Convention and therefore bound by this obligation. Furthermore, due to the phrase 'generally accepted international rules and standards', the main IMO shipping conventions (i.e. SOLAS and MARPOL) are, to use EU terminology, 'directly applicable'. The scope of this paper does not allow for further explanation, but this system of generally accepted rules and standards also constitutes one of the major innovations in the law of the sea since the entry into force of the LOS Convention.[30]

Nevertheless, tightening flag State obligations and increased port State control were not able to prevent new accidents from happening. Within a relatively short period after the adoption of the above-mentioned measures, the accidents involving the 'Erika' and the 'Prestige' occurred. Both accidents caused the European Union to reconsider its strategy with regard to international shipping. Public outcry, especially in France and Spain, certainly provided the impetus for this. This phenomenon was also observed in the context of earlier maritime accidents.

With regard to the latest EU actions taken to avoid oil tanker accidents, two sets of measures can be discerned: those taken after the 'Erika' accident, known as the Erika I and Erika II packages, and those taken after the 'Prestige' accident.

The Erika I package encompasses the strengthening of the existing Directive on EU port State control[31] and the existing Directive governing the activities of classification societies and also put forward an EU initiative to accelerate the worldwide phasing-out of single hull oil tankers that was accepted by the IMO and led to a tightened timetable (completion by 2015 at the latest). All three measures were adopted by the European Parliament and Council in December 2001 and the Member States were required to implement them by mid-2003 at the latest. At the Nice European Council in December 2000, the Member States were even called upon to implement these measures earlier.

The Erika II measures included the creation of the European Agency of Maritime Safety (EMSA) – in order to have an independent, technical body at the European level to ensure the effective application of all the regulations on safety and protection of the marine environment that have been adopted and to facilitate cooperation between Member States to enhance maritime safety and the prevention of pollution by ships[32] – a Directive on the establishment of a notification system for improved monitoring of maritime traffic in European waters and the raising of the limits on the amount of compensation for the victims of oil pollution.

---

[30] For further information, see, among others, Nelissen, op. cit. n. 7.

[31] Directive 2001/106/EC. See also n. 23 *supra*.

[32] See the EMSA website, at: <http://emsa.eu.int>. EMSA was established by Regulation (EC) No. 1406/2002 of the European Parliament and of the Council of 27 June 2002.

The EU Directive on the monitoring of maritime traffic also included provisions on an obligatory 'black box' (voice data recorder) on ships, automatic identification systems and the important issue of 'refuge' for ships in danger or distress. It required each Member State bordering the sea to establish places of refuge for ships in distress.[33] It was due to be implemented by February 2004 at the latest, but it was recently announced that the Commission will start procedures against twelve Member States, including the Netherlands, for not having implemented the Directive.[34] After the 'Prestige' accident, the European Union went even further in this area, with European Transport Commissioner Loyola de Palacio launching 'a major maritime safety crackdown in a bid to prevent further disasters'.[35]

In its 'Prestige' Communication, the Commission formally requested the Member States to speed up the implementation of the maritime safety measures adopted following the 'Erika' disaster – or even to implement them ahead of schedule – in accordance with the commitment given earlier at the Nice European Council. In addition, for the first time, the Commission published a 'blacklist' of ships refused access to EU ports between July and November 2003 in the *Official Journal*[36] and published on its website a list of substandard ships that could have been banned if the new European maritime safety rules had already entered into force. This is a list of vessels that may be banned from EU ports if they are detained one more time (detentions from January to November 2003).[37] What is not very encouraging is the number of EU Member States, especially the group of ten that recently joined, and applicant countries that appear as *flag* States on this list. Fro example, ships from Cyprus (7) and Malta (4) are categorised as 'medium risk' and ships from Turkey (40+) and Romania (6) even as 'very high risk'.[38]

Furthermore, Regulation (EC) No. 1726/2003 of the European Parliament and the Council was adopted to establish 'an accelerated phasing-in scheme for the

---

[33] Although a discussion of the behaviour of Spain with regard to the 'Prestige' when it was in distress and a more general discussion on the existence of a right of refuge for ships would be interesting, especially in light of recent developments in relation to possible as well as perceived (environmental) threats posed to States that could potentially offer refuge, the scope of this contribution does not allow for a proper handling of these issues.

[34] See *NRC Handelsblad*, 27 February 2004.

[35] See Environment Watch Online, 'Water Management', December 2002, p. 9.

[36] A requirement of the latest port State control directive, Directive 2001/106/EC, in force since July 2003.

[37] Doc. IP/03/1547, Brussels, 14 November 2003, Annex II, containing some 150 ships.

[38] According to 'Desperately Seeking Erika', *Fairplay*, 5 February 2004, 'of the 10 countries joining, the two largest registers, Cyprus and Malta, both remain on the Paris MOU black list [...]. Estonia, Latvia and Poland all reside on the grey list and [...] Romania and Turkey are categorised as "very high risk" flag states'.

application of the double-hull or equivalent design requirements of the MARPOL 73/78 Convention to single-hull oil tankers, and to ban the transport to or from ports of the Member States of heavy grades of oil in single-hull oil tankers'.[39] In its Preamble, the Regulation states:

> 'The Commission and the Member States should make every effort to ensure that rules similar to those contained in this Regulation amending Regulation (EC) No. 417/ 2002 can be established in 2003 at a worldwide level, through an amendment of the MARPOL Convention. Both the Council and the Commission welcome the willingness of the International Maritime Organisation (IMO) to hold an additional meeting of the Marine Environment Protection Committee (MEPC) in December 2003 to facilitate an international solution regarding the accelerated phasing-out of single-hull oil tankers and the introduction, in the short term, of a ban on single-hull oil tankers carrying heavy grades of oil'.[40]

> 'The Community is seriously concerned that the age limits for the operation of single-hull oil tankers in Regulation (EC) No. 417/2002 are not sufficiently stringent. Particularly in the wake of the shipwreck of the category I single-hull oil tanker 'Prestige' of the same age as 'Erika' (26 years) those age limits should be further lowered.'[41]

In accordance with the Commission's proposal that the fifteen nations 'work as a single bloc within the IMO, with the EU executive as its representative', arguing that 'only by speaking with one voice within the International Maritime Organization can we have a bigger say',[42] the Preamble states that '[t]he Commission should be given a mandate by the Council and the Member States to enable it to negotiate the adoption of the provisions of this Regulation in the IMO'.[43]

The Commission also envisaged 'possibly limiting transport of dangerous goods by sea in the Exclusive Economic Zone' and proposing to the IMO and the EU Member States '[a] requirement to carry heavy fuel in modern double hull tankers ... as a crisis measure, until the double hull regulation has reached its full implementation. It is important to have such rules covering not only ships coming to EU ports, but also ships that pass in transit close to Member States' coasts'.[44]

The 'Prestige' accident also caused French and Spanish officials to repeatedly declare their waters – meaning the adjacent seas in a broad sense, including the

---

[39] Art. 1 ('Purpose') of the Regulation. The Regulation has been in force since October 2003.
[40] Para. 2 of the Preamble.
[41] Para. 3 of the Preamble
[42] See Environment Watch Online, loc. cit. n. 35, at p. 11.
[43] Para. 10 of the Preamble.
[44] See *Newsletter of the Directorate-General for Energy and Transport* (May 2004) p. 8.

EEZ – closed to this type of oil tanker. Unfortunately, such declarations, though understandable in relation to national populations, are legally unfounded. In fact, States – and more specifically coastal States – have to grant such ships – including the very old ones that can hardly be regarded as seaworthy in comparison to, for example, ships carrying nuclear materials – admittance to their territorial waters, even so close to their shores.[45] This is due to the LOS Convention, which needs to be amended before such declarations – of the Commission, France and Spain – can become a legal reality.

With regard to the EU's reconsideration of its strategy with regard to international shipping since the 'Erika' and 'Prestige' accidents and the question whether it would be wise for the European Union to have its own regulations in the field of safety of navigation – meaning that it would not have to wait for others to be able to act – the following may be said. To begin with, it is understandable that such thoughts come up in the first place. Shortly after the 'Erika' accident, for example, France was scheduled to assume the EU Presidency in June 2000. This accident was only one in a long series of pollution disasters involving ships off the coast of France, which obviously concluded that this was one too many[46] and that drastic action had to be taken. It therefore put heavy pressure on the Commission, which also felt obliged to act due to the many accidents that had threatened European coasts in recent years.

Moreover, reaching agreement within the European Union in this respect is possibly easier than at the global level within the IMO, as the latter is faced with clashes between those Member States that strive for higher standards of safety of navigation – presumably coastal States – and those that are more reluctant – often maritime powers with major interests in shipping. Nevertheless, reaching agreement within the IMO is preferable when it comes to the safety of navigation, as demonstrated, for example, by the issue of classification societies and substandard ships. Some of these societies are known for their laxity in applying international safety standards. They carry out unscrupulous investigations and therefore do not reveal and identify substandard ships. These ships can thus continue sailing, including in EU waters. This phenomenon cannot be stopped through EU action in respect of classification societies alone, however good its record with respect to EU registered ships. These substandard and possibly even unseaworthy ships can be in transit through EU waters without actually visiting EU ports. Without giving effect to generally accepted international (IMO) rules and standards, the European Union and its Member States are not even allowed,

---

[45] For an extensive analysis of the legal implications of the LOS Convention with respect to navigational rights of these types of ships, see Nelissen, op. cit. n. 7.

[46] The 'Prestige' accident also severely polluted the French coast.

legally, to enact laws and regulations that apply to the design, construction, manning or equipment of foreign ships in EU waters.[47]

However, this is not to say that EU action is worthless in this respect. In fact, it has proven to be very helpful. The threat by the European Union to take regional action if the IMO did not act quickly to change the regulations with regard to single-hull oil tankers at the international level resulted in unprecedentedly swift action within the IMO towards an extremely rapid phase-out scheme for these tankers on a worldwide scale. This shows the value of EU action in respect of shipping and at the same time reveals what the European Union can do best: not the enactment of regional standards but putting pressure and baring its teeth at the international (IMO) level to speed up measures that are needed globally, since the seas and the transport business are global.

In conclusion, in the words of EU spokesman Gilles Gantelet, '[t]here is no miracle measure that will prevent another Prestige or Erika. It is the conjunction of all measures being implemented properly that will work'.[48] In this respect, it is contended that unilateral and regional action is not the solution. Although (morally) understandable as a reaction to outraged public opinion, it could threaten global solutions, while the global scale of marine safety and environmental protection problems calls for global regulatory measures. A perfect example of this is the requirement for double-hulled tankers, introduced unilaterally by the Oil Pollution Act (OPA) in the United States in 1990 as a result of the 'Exxon Valdez' accident off the coast of Alaska in 1989. A side effect of this unilateral requirement was that single-hulled tankers began to shift to Asian and European routes.[49]

Thanks to the prompt and successful response of the IMO, the threat of conflicting regional regulations has more or less been kept under control, the European Union having concluded that it is sufficiently satisfied with the progress made. However, 'the uncomfortable message will not be lost on the IMO that Brussels is ready and willing to fill any vacuum which it perceives to exist in the global standard-setting process'.[50] This is a message that has proved to work. At the same time, it is to be hoped that the IMO can continue to follow the pace of EU initiatives in the field of maritime safety, so that the necessary measures continue to be taken at the appropriate level.

---

[47] See Art. 21 of the LOS Convention.

[48] See 'Desperately Seeking Erika', *Fairplay*, 5 February 2004, p. 18.

[49] See T. Höfer and L. Mez, 'Effectiveness of International Environmental Protection Treaties on the Sea Transport of Mineral Oil and Proposals for Policy Revision', in A. Kirchner, ed., *International Marine Environmental Law: Institutions, Implementation and Innovations* (The Hague, Kluwer Law International 2003) p. 112.

[50] See International Chamber of Shipping website, Key Issues 2002, at: <http://www.marisec.org/isf/isfkey2002/index.htm>.

'On the international scene, Europe's presence is being felt more and more, as it uses its political clout and expanded tonnage to ensure that where it goes the rest of the world will follow'.[51] We can only hope that the European Union will keep this pioneering approach 'on board' for the foreseeable future.

---

[51] See 'Desperately Seeking Erika', *Fairplay*, 5 February 2004, p. 19.

THE TEACHING OF EUROPEAN AND INTERNATIONAL LAW: THE NEED FOR CURRICULUM CHANGE

Gerard J. Tanja*

1.   INTRODUCTION

Most parts of Fred Kellermann's academic life have been devoted to the teaching of European law in its broadest sense. Together with Bert Voskuil, the founder of the T.M.C. Asser Institute and a leading force behind its expansion, he was one of the instigators of the famous Asser College Europe post-graduate programmes, which allowed Eastern European students to study European law in The Hague, which at the time was quite revolutionary. Asser College Europe became an instant success and is at present generally regarded as one of the most successful European academic partnerships. Fred played a crucial role in the realisation and expansion of this project.

The programme also resulted in various academic spin-offs for the Asser Institute, including EU-funded research projects, legal harmonisation projects, projects devoted to the development and design of European legal curricula in the new Member States and international conferences.

In addition, in his capacity as General Secretary of the Asser Institute, Fred took it upon himself to organise biannual international conferences on topical issues and developments in European law and European integration. In his own creative and innovative way of putting the programmes (and budgets) together, Fred always managed to deliver high quality, prestigious and intellectually stimulating meetings with top speakers and with a solid conference publication as a result. Again, as with his contribution to Asser College Europe, Fred played a crucial role in the further development of the teaching of European law at the Asser Institute by organising these events.

During the past five years of his academic career, Fred has increasingly focused his attention on European legal curriculum design, legal approximation and harmonisation research and legal topics relating to the accession of new Member States. I had the privilege of working with Fred on some of these projects during the last years of my directorship at the Asser Institute. We worked on projects in

* Dr Gerard J. Tanja, World Firm Management, Clifford Chance LLP, Amsterdam-London.

The European Union: An Ongoing Process of Integration – Liber Amicorum Alfred E. Kellermann
© *2004, T.M.C. Asser Instituut, The Hague, and the authors*

Bulgaria, Slovenia and the Czech Republic. It turned out to be great learning experience for me regarding influence, diplomacy, pragmatism and how to circumvent procedures and formalities and gain direct access to high-placed persons like ministers, secretaries of state and even presidents during the rather short period of time that we were implementing such projects in the above-mentioned countries. But we also had long discussions about the teaching of European and international law, what the 'ideal' future European law curriculum should look like in the Member States and what kind of knowledge and skills young professionals, whether academics or practitioners, should (or need to) possess in order to pursue a successful European and international career.

It is for this reason that I have decided to focus in my contribution to this *Liber Amicorum* in honour of Fred Kellermann on the teaching of European and international law and the changes in the curriculum and approach that, in my opinion, are necessary. In doing so, I will restrict myself to an analysis of the challenges facing large international law firms when trying to recruit young graduates in continental Europe and the United Kingdom for their tax, mergers and acquisitions/corporate and international finance and banking practices. As the research indicates, some 30 per cent of our future lawyers and practitioners in continental Europe will probably work in such an environment or be heavily affected by developments in these legal areas. Those who are involved in and responsible for curriculum design and delivery (i.e. the law faculties) should therefore take the needs and requirements of such a large group of their current 'clients' into account.

2.   SCOPE AND BACKGROUND

Despite fundamental and historical changes in Europe and new developments at the European business and legal practitioners level, the teaching of European and international law and the approach to such teaching in continental Europe is still based on a rather static educational model that was introduced some forty years ago. The question is whether the contents of those curricula in Europe and this traditional approach to the teaching of European and international law meet the (educational and practical) requirements posed by current international relations, legal practice and the demands of an increasingly complex and integrated globalised political, cultural, business and financial system. Especially integrated, international and globally operating law firms that specialise in corporate practice and financial transactions are confronted with this question. Businesses and law firms operating in these areas are confronted by a growing gap between market (and personal) requirements and what universities and law schools deliver.

It is recognised that curriculum design and development and the delivery of educational products for legal practitioners is not just the responsibility of law schools and universities. Increasingly, local bar associations and the ultimate consumers of such services, i.e. law firms, financial services companies, governments, industry and so forth also have a responsibility to identify and indicate their needs and requirements clearly. Only in this way can market expectations be met.

This paper focuses on some of the more pertinent developments in the European geography and is limited to the identification of the most pressing issues, questions and problems with which legal practitioners in internationally active continental law firms are confronted and what they need when recruiting graduates.

Some initial conclusions and recommendations are formulated in section 5. It is not my intention to (attempt to) formulate definitive and final answers, but to stimulate innovative, creative and out-of-the-box educational thinking and discussion on how we can address the future challenges – both at the operational level and at a more conceptual level – on the European continent.

Section 3 addresses the main issues regarding educational and career development facing law firms that are active at global level and law firms operating in predominantly local markets but with (some) international practice and clients. Although these two types of law firm are confronted with fundamentally different recruiting problems and the knowledge and skills they are looking for in their graduate recruits differs, there are also some interesting similarities in terms of needs and requirements Career development issues relating to lateral and more senior hiring is excluded from the scope of this paper.

Whereas section 3 focuses on educational problems encountered by private and commercial practice, section 4 addresses some of the consequences of such problems for the design and development of (new) European and international legal curricula. Section 4 also contains suggestions and ideas to overcome some of the major stumbling blocks in order to arrive at a more efficient, effective and 'tailored' academic educational system delivering 'products and services' that are aligned to the needs and requirements of the main target groups or 'clients' of such services.

3.   GLOBAL AND LOCAL LAW FIRMS

3.1   Global law firms: needs and requirements

The major challenge for European law firms operating at global level and servicing clients that operate in multiple jurisdictions is to attract (and retain) top talent: young recruits that possess the right 'mix' of legal and non-legal competences and skills necessary to advise demanding international clients in and across the different jurisdictions of the world. Whereas the 'war for talent' may no longer be as prominent as it was a few years ago in some business sectors (primarily IT, strategic consulting, financial services and investment banking), due to the economic slowdown, the continental European legal sector is still confronted with a limited pool of graduate recruits that have the required skills and abilities. A sound knowledge of European and international law is one of those required technical skills!

At the same time, client satisfaction research undertaken by major law firms indicates that Fortune 500 companies and other international clients expect and request the delivery of legal services that:

a. are of a consistently high *legal* quality;
b. can, at the levels of service and quality, be compared to what they expect (and generally receive) from strategic management consultants, IT consultants and accountancy firms;
c. go beyond the delivery of *mere* legal knowledge in a *technical* sense: increasingly, clients require the ability to deliver integrated legal 'services' and 'products' that can be used as a basis for sound *business* decision making (e.g. *'Don't tell me what the legal problems are and why I cannot do something – tell me how we can pragmatically circumvent and address the problems and make it happen!'*); and
d. are well 'managed' at the *operational* level and consist of 'integrated' pieces of advise in case of complex multi-jurisdictional and multifaceted projects.

In other words, international clients do not only expect correct technical legal advice capabilities (at national and multi-jurisdictional level), but also want a lawyer who can operate as a sound *legal business consultant/adviser*. This is one of the crucial elements that current European and international legal curricula completely lack or do not address. It requires the incorporation of elements into the legal curriculum that go beyond mere legal aspects/knowledge.

Despite the enormous growth in all kinds of LL.M. programmes focusing on European and international law (which show a spirit of local academic *intra*-preneurship but in essence are 'more of the same') and the recognition that on-the-job learning is far more important and efficient than traditional classroom teaching, none of the continental European law faculties appear to provide programmes that meet the above-mentioned requirements. An exception to this rule is perhaps the recent (private) Bucerius initiative in Germany. The increasing complexity resulting from the Bologna process also affects bar associations and law firms. Unfortunately – and actually quite astonishingly – most (international) law firms and local bar associations in Europe barely showed any interest in such developments until quite recently. The only notable exception has been the United

Kingdom, where large law firms and the Law Society have been able to develop, through coordination and consultations, a comprehensive traineeship programme for international law firms that is conducted in close cooperation with the academic world. In all other continental European jurisdictions, most law firms and bar associations have continued their policy of pretending that European harmonisation in the area of the regulation of the legal profession is just another trend that might go away, so that they can continue their policy of 'splendid isolation'.

So what do law faculties need to do in order to address a problem that is affecting the (potential) labour market for some 25-30 per cent of our current European law graduates and has forced (international) law firms and national bar associations to invest millions of euros in the professional and career development of young lawyers? In this context, it is worth mentioning that international financial institutions, the investment banking sector and other professional services firms active in mergers and acquisitions and the financial services industry are facing similar problems.

3.2   Global law firms and challenges for academic institutions

Academic institutions involved in the teaching of European and international law face some interesting challenges. Fundamental is the recognition of the need to change current patterns and approaches to the *teaching* of law. In addition, certain academic and institutional 'barriers' that impede the delivery of more suitable programmes for the above-mentioned target groups also need to be addressed. The introduction of the bachelor-masters structure and the Bologna process, in combination with a more outward-looking approach, may provide the necessary incentive to overcome the institutional lethargy that is present in so many universities and law faculties.

To service globally operating law firms, continental law faculties may wish to consider some of the more important recommendations for change at the legal and technical level:

a. Recognition, at graduate level, of the need to introduce a further specialisation in 'European and international legal practice', with an emphasis on European/international business and trade law, European/international company law, competition law, international finance and project finance law (including capital markets) and conflict of laws.
b. The introduction of a strong and mandatory *comparative* legal component covering the major continental European legal systems (and not just the basics!).
c. A *mandatory* introduction to Anglo-American law and common law (this last recommendation can perhaps be combined with the one under point b.

d. A strong focus on legal issues and processes arising in multi-jurisdictional transactions, mergers and acquisitions, international finance practice, etc. (This also includes legal issues relating to corporate governance, the Alien Torts Statute and ethical entrepreneurship, etc.) Preferably this should be done in a highly interactive environment, making use of real-life case studies, simulations, web-based learning tools and know-how management systems.

A more fundamental change is, perhaps, the recognition that (re)focusing on such technical/legal issues at graduate level is not sufficient. Practitioners and graduates pursuing a career in an international or global law firm need this type of additional extra-legal skills and knowledge. Examples of this include effective business communication and presentation skills and other MBA-style programme components like project (case and transactional) management skills. At this level, law faculties need to include programmes that also focus on the basics of legal *consulting* skills. This could be done in a second masters year as part of a new curriculum in European and international practice, which should be developed in close coordination and consultation with international law firms and national bar associations. Such firms should then also be involved in the organisation of internships that should be a mandatory part of the curriculum.

Apart from the legal curriculum implications and general business skills that need to be addressed, there is one other major component that should receive appropriate and prominent attention. A new specialised curriculum for European and international practitioners should also address international accounting principles and standards, business valuation techniques and a good general understanding of the major international financial and economic markets.

It is shocking to see that, unless they have decided to pursue an MBA in combination with their law studies, most graduates from continental European law faculties who decide to pursue a career in European and international legal practice can barely read or understand the profit and loss account of a multinational company. Most of them have no understanding of the international business environment in which their future clients (let alone their employer) operate. Awareness of the economic and business environment is virtually non-existent. This is a sad but inescapable fact.

Some familiarity of graduates with the underlying economic motives of or rationale for companies to merge with or acquire other companies or to postpone or speed-up an IPO is essential in order to be able to provide value-added legal advice at European and international level. Law faculties barely stimulate and in the current climate have little opportunity to offer 'out-of-the-*legal*-box' thinking, which is essential for their graduates in their new roles as European and international lawyers.

I am fully aware of the fact that a large part of this awareness can only be developed via *on-the-job* learning. Hence my plea for another – if necessary privately or company-financed – curriculum element: a mandatory internship of at least six to nine months after graduation (or combined with the final law school examination). It is here that international and national law firms with a large international client base are becoming involved and committing themselves to actively participate in a new masters programme. There is therefore yet another fundamental change to be considered: academic and practice *partnering* models need to be developed and *dual*-learning systems need to be introduced. In other words, law faculties and bar associations need to rethink the way in which they deliver the 'learning' of European law.

Unfortunately, even at graduate level, the learning *delivery vehicle* of the majority of continental European law faculties is still the traditional (and rather ineffective) classroom system, with a primary focus on the delivery of theoretical and technical legal knowledge. While this may have been the only valid model in the past due to the sheer size of the numbers involved and the overriding focus on finances and shrinking budgets, this approach is not sustainable in the future and appears to be an outdated learning delivery model at graduate and post-graduate level, as it is not aligned to what the graduates will experience in real life. It has downgraded most law faculty curricula in relation to what a professional school is supposed to deliver and has, in spite of what most faculty and university staff will claim, lost most of its *academic* appeal and character, especially in the field of law. Adding the above-mentioned elements can bring back some of those elements that should be inherent in every academic curriculum.

Furthermore, if combined with some sort of managed internship of a certain duration, the introduction of a mandatory *dual*-learning delivery component will probably have a higher return on investment and effectiveness compared to 'just' classroom teaching, as (post-)graduate students will personally *experience* what it takes to put together a European or international deal or transaction (and not just in a technical legal sense) and why project management and cultural awareness are so important and why they should read the Harvard Business Review or the Economist!

Partnering between international law firms and academic institutions (and between academic institutions with different specialisations), especially in this area of the law, can offer various advantages and opportunities and is beneficial for all stakeholders: students, law firms and law faculties. It ensures that theoretical and practical experience is supplemented and that the knowledge and know-how of both the academic and the legal practitioner are combined, so that added value is created for everybody.

3.3   Local law firms with international/regional services

In the near future, the position and business requirements of locally operating law firms in continental Europe will change (and to a certain extent already have changed). As a consequence, the educational requirements for and skills of their graduate recruits need to change. Such changes will also demand a reorientation and/or adjustment of the European and international law curriculum offered by law schools on the continent.

Developments within the continental legal sector mean that, within the *national* legal sector, five basic 'types' of local law firms will emerge (are already emerging) in the major European jurisdictions:

- small law firms focusing solely on national and/or local clients (either specialised or general practice);
- small law firms focusing on niche markets basically serving national clients (national 'boutiques');
- mid-sized law firms (niche and/or general practice) serving mainly national clients, some of which have international/regional interests;
- mid-sized law firms (niche and/or general practice) serving national and international clients that belong to an international network of law firms (employing a referral system but not providing integrated and seamless legal services); and
- mid-sized law firms working closely with one of the big accountancy firms and concentrating mainly on national and international in-house legal advice, tax advice and legal advice that is related to finance and capital markets, mergers and acquisitions and the corporate affairs of the clients of their 'accountancy/consultancy mother firms'.

Recent market research and estimates of professional recruitment agencies indicate that of the approximately 50 per cent of law graduates that opt for a career in a law firm, some 50 per cent will be employed in one of the categories of law firms mentioned above. Hence, it is obvious that this is an important target group for law schools as well. Given the different market requirements of the various national market segments in which these firms operate, the European and international legal curriculum that is offered must be tailored to these requirements as much as possible. Law faculties and national bar associations have to recognise these developments, and some generic recommendations will be formulated for local firms that service European and international clients, which can primarily be found in the mid-sized category. This will be done in the next section, where some of the major consequences of the above-mentioned developments (at national and international level) are analysed for their effects on European and international law curricula design.

4.   CONSEQUENCES FOR EUROPEAN AND INTERNATIONAL
         LAW CURRICULA

4.1   **How should law schools 'service' the future international lawyer?**

For graduates aiming to work in this type of law firm or business sector, including those who opt for consultancy, international financial institutions or investment banking, a basic knowledge of the main concepts of public international law at undergraduate and graduate level is sufficient. In their future careers, public international law plays virtually no role. However, students who want to special-ise in European business law and want to advise on multi-jurisdictional transactions need to be familiar with the underlying concepts of the Alien Torts Statute, US and UN sanctions regimes, immunities, and so forth.

At the same time, it is necessary to pay much more attention at undergraduate level to private international law (but not the family law as this is totally irrele-vant in this sector) and conflict of laws issues. Basic courses must become mandatory, with further voluntary courses at graduate level.

As already mentioned above, European and international business law (includ-ing the main aspects of ethical entrepreneurship, risk management and corporate governance in Europe, the United States and the United Kingdom) should be the main focus. Other mandatory curriculum modules are European and international finance law and practice, capital markets, European and international banking law. These modules and courses are extremely important and must be mandatory at both undergraduate and graduate level. Voluntary courses on international commercial arbitration (UNCITRAL, ICSID, various ICC procedures and national arbitration law) need to be introduced at undergraduate level, with further (voluntary) specialised programmes at graduate level (e.g. courses for litigators on the investigation of witnesses, experts, etc., like those offered by the Law Society in the United Kingdom).

Knowledge of WTO law, international trade dispute settlement procedures and investment protection would also be valuable assets and can be offered (voluntarily) at graduate level. Such programmes lend themselves extremely well to the imple-mentation of 'partnering' and dual-learning recommendation mentioned earlier. These can then be combined with practice-oriented programmes at (post-)graduate level focusing on the preparation and implementation of international transactions, multi-jurisdictional deals, deal management and/or legal project management (including courses on legal writing in English for non-native speakers and cultural awareness). Partnering – in whatever format suits the partners best – probably offers the preferred 'learning' approach, as most academic lecturers at law schools lack the practical experience and qualifications to adequately explain the relevant processes, procedures and flows of documentation involved.

At undergraduate level, basic courses in comparative law need to be introduced. These courses should be mandatory and should set out the basic concepts of the major jurisdictions in continental Europe in a comparative framework. For various reasons, a mandatory programme on Anglo-American and/or common law at undergraduate level is also recommended (see also above), which could serve as a basis for (post-)graduate programmes that could build on it. The growing importance of these disciplines for internationally oriented legal practice in continental Europe is underestimated in academic circles. Without a sound knowledge of the basics of common law concepts and Anglo-American law, it is extremely difficult for graduates and young practitioners to service national as well as global clients, communicate professionally with their future American and British colleagues and *really* understand legal issues within the common law system and how they can be solved within European civil law systems, and *vice versa* of course.

It has become apparent that most graduates from continental European law schools coming to international law firms generally lack so-called professional consulting skills and the ability to think 'out-of-the-legal-box', while such client-focused skills are in fact extremely important for being successful and credible as an all-round European legal business adviser. The introduction at graduate level of voluntary, multidisciplinary, MBA-style programmes, where the focus is on issues like (legal) project management, cultural awareness, general consulting skills (communication, presentation, teamwork, etc.) and client relationship management skills. is therefore recommended. Such a programme should also include some modules on international business organisation and governance, finance and accounting (which is obviously a core module that should be taught at both undergraduate and graduate level), business awareness (including how the *legal* business is organised and fits together), international economics, economic drivers that determine the valuation of companies and the functioning of capital markets, derivatives, and so forth. This, or a similar set of modules, could be part of a graduate programme in European and international practice, together with the above-mentioned elements. An internship, organised in close consultation with national bar associations and law firms, would be a mandatory part of the programme. Such internships would need to be financed by law firms and the legal sector. Supervision could be institutionalised via a mentoring system operated by universities or law schools.

At graduate level, we need to ensure that there is sufficient space for truly academic 'learning' achievements and projects. If this means that future graduates who want to work in international legal practice have to work long(er) hours, so be it. Law schools should not be too afraid to challenge and innovate. As currently perceived by law firms throughout Europe, the gap between what the international practitioners market needs and what law faculties actually deliver is widening and deepening. A more outward focus on the part of university staff and a greater knowledge and experience of this legal market would immediately reveal that, once outside the protective walls of their universities and law schools, graduates are expected to invest (much) more than the average 25-30 weekly hours they currently invest in their legal studies. Lawyers and international practitioners with large (investment) banks participating in such a mandatory internship programme also need to take responsibility in this regard.

The above-mentioned suggestions regarding 'partnering' and 'dual-learning systems' could alleviate some of the worries concerning the consequences of the development and introduction of such programmes.

5. CONCLUDING OBSERVATIONS

This contribution has focused on some of the required changes in the current European and international legal curricula of European law schools, in so far as they relate to those who envisage a career in (integrated) international law firms with global clients or national mid-size firms with an international practice. Several shortcomings in existing curricula have been identified and some recommendations have been made at the substantive, procedural and conceptual level. A plea has been made for the introduction of a revised European and international curriculum and an innovative approach to its introduction and implementation. At the conceptual, delivery and didactic level, it was argued that current classroom-based programmes, in particular, are unsuitable for implementing the new curriculum in relation to the above-mentioned graduate target groups. Dual-learning systems and partnering arrangements need to be worked out, while the introduction of certain MBA-style modules is also considered essential.

Unfortunately, the academic community is a rather self-contained regime. Discussions on the design, introduction and implementation of major innovations and/or necessary adjustments to existing curricula will therefore quite often be dominated by more inward-oriented, institutional interests. Hence, it is normal that such discussions quite often focus more on *intra*-preneurial considerations and procedures than academic *entre*-preneurial considerations that aim to optimise a law school's services to its 'clients' and the legal recruitment market. Vested interests, time-consuming decision-making procedures and the absence of practical experience and knowledge of the international legal labour market make it extremely difficult to realise a new curriculum for legal practitioners favouring a European and international working environment. Partnering and dual-learning arrangements, in whatever format or framework, may be a way to get around such barriers. Unfortunately, local bar associations and law firms have not always taken responsibility in this regard. Until recently, for example, bar associations and law firms have not shown much interest in discussing the consequences of the Morgenbesser Decision, the implementation of the Bologna process or the fundamental changes in the European legal marketplace with law schools and universities. Hopefully, it is not too late to start this discussion and reconsider some of the newly developed masters programmes.

Perhaps there is a future role here for Fred Kellermann: he would undoubtedly be able to develop an innovative European curriculum along the above-mentioned lines that contains modules and courses that address the gaps that have been identified. He would undoubtedly also be able to short-circuit complex and time-consuming *intra-* and *inter*-university debating societies and design a challenging European curriculum that goes beyond addressing its legal components in a technical sense. With the diplomatic skills and extensive network he possesses, he would be able to forge partnerships between theory and practice, between and within academic institutions and with prestigious lecturers.

It is impossible to deal with all the consequences of the changes in the European legal world and to focus on all 'graduate target groups' that need to be serviced by law schools within the confines of this paper. For this reason, I have not focused on the role and place of European and international law in relation to those who opt for an international academic or political-diplomatic career or those who prefer to work for a European or international organisation. For the same reason, the role of technology, e-learning instruments, *blended* learning methods and so on have not been discussed, although such methods can easily be introduced within the context of partnering and dual-learning systems and certainly require further investigation by qualified university staff involved in the development and introduction of new curricula. In international practice, such methods and concepts have already been used and are widely applied, quite often in combination with advanced know-how management, IT tools and learning management systems. For 'learning' purposes, it is essential and indispensable to familiarise students with such tools.

The main intention of this paper was to provide some ideas and food-for-thought for the discussion on the future of European and international legal studies and international legal curricula design in continental Europe, while at the same time acknowledging that further and more in-depth analysis is required. Hopefully, it will help to stimulate European thinking on curriculum design.

PART III

THE NEW MEMBER STATES AND EASTERN EUROPE

SUPREMACY OF CONSTITUTIONS IN THE CONTEXT OF CONSTITUTIONAL PLURALISM

Evgeni Tanchev[*]

1.   SUPREMACY AND HIERARCHY OF THE NATION STATE CONSTITUTION

The significance of the constitution as a fundamental law and a supreme judicial act has been established in continental Europe ever since the time of Ferdinand Lassalle, as well as in view of the Magna Carta – albeit with some degree of inconsistency – since the reign of King Edward III of England. The founding character and supremacy of written constitutions have acquired axiomatic validity and prevail in the definition of what constitutes a constitution.[1]

The constitution of a Nation State is the supreme act within the hierarchy of regulatory instruments. Adopted by the constituent authority as the holder of popular sovereignty, the constitution is at the top of the pyramid of legal sources. In the national legal system, the hierarchy of the sources of law is predetermined by the hierarchy of institutions that have adopted them.

Inherent supremacy stems out of the generic character of the constitution. The content of the constitution is not determined by compliance with any national legal requirements or preceded by other binding national legal instruments. The constitution is the primary regulator of basic social relations.[2] Constitutional

---

[*] Prof. Evgeni Tanchev, Judge at the Constitutional Court of the Republic of Bulgaria.

[1] Contemporary Bulgarian constitutionalists, substantiate – albeit in a different manner – the supremacy and the founding character of the Constitution. The clarification of these issues in this paper is therefore limited to the most schematic approach and to highlighting new trends that have an impact on the supremacy and the founding character of the Constitution. See B. Leoni, *Freedom and the Law* (1962) pp. 77-78; M. Cappelletti and W. Cohen, *Comparative Constitutional Law* (Charlottesville 1977) pp. 5-6; S. Stoichev, *Constitutional Law of the Republic of Bulgaria*, Part 1 (Sofia 1998) pp. 71-78; E. Drumeva, *Constitutional Law* (Sofia 1998) pp. 110-112; B. Spassov, *A Teaching on the Constitution* (Sofia 1997) pp. 25-34; and G. Bliznashki, *The Form of the State* (Sofia 1999) pp. 25-26.

[2] Constitutionalists sometimes go to extremes by claiming that the constituent power creates the political and legal order *ex nihilo*. See U. Preuss, 'Constitutional Power-Making for the New Polity: Some Deliberations on the Relations between Constituent Power and the Constitution', in M. Rosenfeld, ed., *Constitutionalism, Identity, Difference and Legitimacy* (Durham, Duke University Press 1994) pp. 143-164.

The European Union: An Ongoing Process of Integration – Liber Amicorum Alfred E. Kellermann
© 2004, T.M.C. Asser Instituut, The Hague, and the authors

norms have a generic character and are derived from the consensus achieved by the constituent power during the drafting of the constitution. The supremacy of the constitution in contemporary Nation States has been recognised as a constituent component of the constitutional State founded on the rule of law.

Being the ultimate expression of popular sovereignty, constitutional supremacy has a universal effect covering all physical and legal persons within the territory of the Nation State. This constitutional supremacy is also founded on the stipulation that the fundamental constitutional values, principles and norms define the basic legal arrangement and are 'decomposed' into laws and bylaws. According to the doctrine of the autopoiesis of the legal system,[3] constitutional supremacy maintains the hierarchy and eliminates contradictions blocking the effect of legal acts. The supremacy of the constitution has a formal aspect, i.e. maintaining hierarchy in the system of sources of the law, but also defines the material content of laws and regulatory instruments of lower legally binding force. The compliance of legislation with the constitution is an immediate effect of constitutional supremacy.

The practical implications of the constitution's direct effect on legislation and law enforcement require clarification of the issues related to the inherent hierarchy of the constitution itself, based on the different legally binding force of constitutional norms. In constitutional theory, attempts have been made to establish a grading system applicable to the provisions of the constitution. Hierarchical schemes have also been devised for the purposes of interpreting fundamental laws.[4]

Under the inherent logic of constitutions, the more specific provisions must express the reasons for the constitution and must be interpreted in compliance with the norms that are of a more abstract nature and proclaim goals, values and principles. However, the provisions on principles are more abstract and more difficult to specify by the authorities in charge of administering the law.[5] There

---

[3] N. Luhman, 'Autopoiesis, Handlung und Kommunikation', 11 *Zeitschrift für Soziologie* (1982) pp. 366-379; G. Teubner, ed., *Autopoietic Law: A New Approach to Law and Society* (Berlin/New York, Walter de Gruyter 1988); and G. Teubner, ed., *Dilemmas of Law in the Welfare State* (Berlin/New York, Walter de Gruyter 1986).

[4] Some may be founded on the differentiation between constitutional provisions. See B. Schloer, 'Categories of Constitutional Norms', at <http://www.uepala.kiev.ua/eng/law/99.pdf>; N. Nenovski, 'Is the act on the revision of the Constitution subject to constitutional court supervision?', 1 *Juridical World* (2000) pp. 32-52 at pp. 46-47.

[5] It should be noted in this respect that the hierarchy of values in constitutional philosophy, which to a major extent defines the limits of constitutional regulation, as well as the logical sequence and subordination in the arrangement of the basic primary and derivative social relations, should not be interpreted as an effort to introduce a hierarchy in the regulatory contents of the fundamental law. The opposite assumption would imply that more abstract provisions, which define the contents of the specific provisions, should be allocated a higher priority within the framework of the direct application of the constitution. In this case, the formulations contained in the preamble to the

can be no doubt that all the norms set out in a constitution are supreme in relation to all other legislative acts, have one and the same priority and have to be observed all legal subjects. Still, the direct and immediate effect of the constitution requires the identification of some distinctions between the legal power of constitutional provisions, according to their objective, contents and location in the constitution.[6] It is especially important to take account of the considerations behind the logical structure of the constitution when establishing a legal hierarchy of the norms.

The non-amendment clauses in some constitutional systems pose restrictions on the legislative, executive and judicial branches of power and the constituent authority.[7] A rigid constitution founded on the separation between the constituent and the constituted authorities implicitly introduces a restrictive regime and procedure for constitutional amendment.

The norms stipulating prohibitions, especially in relation to negative fundamental human rights, have priority in the direct effect of the constitution. The self-executing constitutional norms and provisions of international agreements also have a higher legally binding force due to the primacy of the international law and hence must be treated in preference to constitutional provisions, leaving legal interpretation to the legislator.

Constitution should have a priority for the institutions administering the law. The experience of Western democracies indicates that the institutions, and most of the judiciary, refer to the preamble only in the absence of more specific constitutional provisions. The same applies to the most specific constitutional norms. Because of their technical and provisional character, the transitional and final provisions of the Constitution should not be automatically allocated a higher priority than the rest of the constitutional norms.

[6] In this respect, the Constitutional Court maintains that the direct effect of the Constitution will be manifested in a different manner, depending on the specific content of each constitutional provision, and makes a distinction between provisions referring to the form of government, and to the functions and the structure of the institutions of the State that are charged with the application of the principle of the separation of powers, and the fundamental rights and freedoms of the citizens. See the motivation of Decision No. 10 of 6 October 1994, Constitutional Court Case No. 4/94, *Official Gazette* No. 87 of 25 October 1994.

[7] A typical example would be the ban on revising the form of government, which dates back to the Constitution of the Third French Republic and has been included in Article 89 of the current French Constitution of 1958, Article 139 of the Italian Constitution of 1947 and Article 110 of the Greek Constitution of 1975. The Fundamental Law of the Federal Republic of Germany of 1949 stipulates that federalism; the democratic and social character of the Republic; the main principles of the nation's sovereignty; the supremacy of the Constitution above legislative, executive and judicial power; the right of resistance against any attempts to destroy the established constitutional order; the sanctity of human dignity; the inalienability and inviolability of constitutional rights; and the immediate effect of fundamental rights are not subject to amendments. The Romanian Constitution of 1991 seems to have introduced the longest list of bans on amendments in the provisions of Article 148. The national, independent unitary character of the State; the republican form of government; territorial integrity; the independence of the judiciary; political pluralism; the official language; human rights; and the guarantees for the execution of these rights are not subject to amendments.

Procedural constitutional norms, which have a formal and secondary character compared to substantive norms,[8] and substantive provisions are equally binding.

The preamble proclaiming the objectives and goals of the constitutional government, as well as the transitional and final provisions designed to 'implant' the constitution in the legal order at the time of its adoption, are exceptionally important, but their effect is strongly limited within the impact of the constitution on the administration of the law.

Constitutional supremacy is evolving in the context of the transformation of the contemporary Nation State.[9]

First of all, constitutional supremacy has to be based on the imperative of legitimacy. With the progress of modern civil society, constitutions have emerged as the basis of the law and legality of the State if the constitution matches the democratic criteria for legitimacy.[10] From a constitutional point of view, legitimacy has substantive and formal dimensions. In terms of contents, constitutional democracy is bound to reflect a specific system of values that provide moral and philosophical foundations, while supporting the public conviction that the existing institutions match the interests of the legal subjects.[11] The high level of correlation between the legal and the living constitution raises its substantive legitimacy, which by means of constitutional supremacy assures the practical aspects of legality in the political and legal system.[12] The formal dimensions of legitimacy are related to compliance with rational, legally institutionalised procedures that channel the constitutional consensus generated in a free public discourse when devising abstract impartial constitutional provisions.[13]

The legitimacy of democratic institutions is a precondition for their supremacy and legality that is safeguarded in constitutional States.[14]

The classical principle of constitutional supremacy is assuming new dimensions with the development of relations between national legal systems and the international legal order.

---

[8] For more details on the specific characteristics of the procedural norms on constitutional law, see S. Nacheva, *Procedural Norms in Public Law* (Sofia 1983) pp. 16-27; V.O. Luchin, *Constitutional Norms and Legal Relations* (Moscow 1997) pp. 83-86.

[9] Venice Commission, 'The Transformation of the Nation State in Europe at the Dawn of the 21 Century', Science and Technique of Democracy Report No. 22 (Strasbourg, Council of Europe 1998).

[10] The distinction between the traditional, charismatic legitimacy and the judicial legitimacy of political behaviour dominates the content of political social sciences. M. Weber, *Economy and Society*, Vol. I (New York, Bedminster Press 1968) p. 215.

[11] C. Schmitt, 'The Legal World Revolution', in 72 *Telos* (1987) [special issue on C. Schmitt]; S.M. Lipset, *Political Man, The Social Bases of Politics* (Garden City, N.Y., Doubleday 1960) p. 77.

[12] For more details, see E. Tanchev, 'Constitutional Safeguards of Legality and Legitimacy', Report to the 1999 Civil Service Forum, European Institute of Public Administration, Maastricht.

[13] J. Habermass, *Morals, Law and Democracy* (Sofia 1999) pp. 279-308.

[14] The illegality of a constitution or of rulers that derogate from a constitution by their actions are a basis for resistance against despotic regimes or civil disobedience.

Contemporary constitutional States recognise the primacy of international law. However, the systems for the implementation of treaty obligations are different, due to the choice between monism and dualism in national constitutions.[15] The incorporation of treaty provisions follows two types of procedures.[16] According to the monistic system, which is dominant in Europe, international treaties become an integral part of national law after having been ratified. Under dualism, the implementation of treaties does not take place by ratification but by drafting a special law or by amending existing national legislation.

A comparative analysis of European systems demonstrates another type of difference, which is related to the position of international treaties in the national legal order. In some countries, like Belgium, Luxembourg and the Netherlands, international treaty provisions have supranational effect and stand above the legal system, superseding the authority of constitutional norms. According to the constitutional practice of other countries, like Austria, Italy and Finland, treaties that have been ratified by a special parliamentary majority have the same legally binding effect as constitutional provisions.

A third approach to treaty obligations under the monistic system in Europe places them above ordinary parliamentary legislation but under national constitutions, in accordance with their legally binding effect. This is the current practice in Bulgaria, Germany, France, Greece, Cypress, Portugal, Spain and other countries. In the Czech Republic, Lichtenstein, Romania, Russia and Slovakia, only treaties relating to human rights stand above the ordinary legislation.[17]

Bulgaria's Constitution of 1991 proclaims the primacy of international treaties that have legally binding force and supersede contradictory provisions of national legislation. Under the monistic approach, international treaties that have been constitutionally ratified and promulgated and have come into force in Bulgaria are

---

[15] On different legal orders in the dualistic system and integrating both legal orders in monism, see M. Kumm, 'Towards a Constitutional Theory of the Relationship between National and International Law (Part I): International Law, National Courts and the Arguments from Democracy', Colloquium in Legal, Political and Social Philosophy, NYU School of Law, 30 October 2003, pp. 1-2, available at <http://www.law.nyu.edu/clppt/program2003/readings/kumm1and2.pdf>; L. Wildhaber, *Treaty-Making Power and the Constitution* (Basel, Helbing & Lichtenhahn 1971) pp. 152-153.

[16] P. van Dijk and G.J.H. van Hoof, *Theory and Practice of the European Convention on Human Rights* (Boston 1990) pp. 11-12; A. Drzemczewski, *European Human Rights Convention in Domestic Law* (Oxford, Clarendon Press 1985) pp. 33-35.

[17] See A.E. Kellermann, J.W. de Zwaan and J. Czuczai, *EU Enlargement: The Constitutional Impact at EU and National Level* (The Hague, T.M.C. Asser Press 2001) pp. 525-557; C. Economides, *The Elaboration of Model Clauses on the Relationship between International and Domestic Law* (Strasbourg, Council of Europe Press 1994) pp. 91-113 at pp. 101-102; L. Erades, *Interactions between International and Municipal Law* (The Hague, T.M.C. Asser Institute 1993); A. West, et al., eds., *The French Legal System: An Introduction* (London, Fourmat Publishing 1992) p. 45. See Й.Фровайн, Европейската конвенция за правата на човека като обществен ред в Европа (София 1994) 32; Вж също така Л.Кулишев, Прилагането на Европейската конвенция за правата на човека в българския правен ред, сп.Закон, бр. 2, 1994, pp. 3-25.

considered part of the domestic law of the country. They take precedence over any conflicting rules of domestic legislation. In an interpretative ruling, the Constitutional Court of Bulgaria has extended the validity of this constitutional provision to include all treaties signed before the entry into force of the Constitution, provided they comply with the requirements of Article 5(4) of the Constitution.[18]

An examination of Articles 85(3) and 149(1) and (4) of the Bulgarian Constitution, in conjunction with Article 5(4) of the Constitution, indicates that the Constitution has ranked international treaties second to the Constitution itself, but above all national legislation.[19] In this way, the primacy of international law complies with the requirements of Article 2 of the UN Charter regarding Nation State sovereignty.[20]

The process for implementing international treaties is different from the interaction between the EU legal order and the legal systems of the Member State. Due to the transfer of sovereignty, provisions of EU law prevail over national constitutional norms and have a legally binding effect after the Member States have been notified. That is why the implementation of international treaties bears no similarity to the obligation to comply with the *acquis communautaire* when adapting national constitutions and approximating national legislation in order to give supranational, direct, immediate and horizontal effect to primary and secondary EU law.[21]

---

[18] The Constitutional Court ruled that the legal effect of treaties signed and ratified before the 1991 Constitution entered in force is determined by the regime that was in effect at that time and, in particular, according to the requirements for their publication. The treaties are part of the Bulgarian legal system if they are published or if there was no requirement to publish them. If they are not published they do not have primacy over contravening provisions of national legislation. They may acquire superseding effect over the contravening norms of Bulgarian legislation from the moment of their official publication. See Мотиви на Решение N 7 от 1992 г. по к.д. N 6 1992, ДВ, N 56, от 1992 г.

[19] Article 85(3) stipulates that the signing of international treaties that require constitutional amendments must be preceded by the passage of such amendments. Under Article 149(1)(4), the Constitutional Court rules on the consistency between the international treaties signed by the Republic of Bulgaria and the Constitution prior to their ratification, as well as on the consistency between laws and universally accepted standards of international law and the international treaties to which Bulgaria is a signatory. See E. Konstantinov, ed., *The Constitution and the Participation of Bulgaria in International Agreements* (Sofia 1993); G. Tisheva and I. Muleshkova, 'Relations between the domestic legislation of the Republic of Bulgaria and the international human rights standards', 1 *Human Rights Journal* (1997) pp. 4-9.

[20] The supranational, direct, immediate and horizontal effect of EU law is established by the proposed EU clause in the Constitution providing for the transfer of sovereign powers to the European Union and its institutions.

[21] These undisputed characteristics of European law were formulated by the Court as early as the beginning of the 1960s: Case 26/62 *N.V. Algemene Transport- en Expeditie Onderneming van Gend & Loos* v. *Netherlands Inland Revenue Administration* [1963] *ECR* 1; Case 6/64 *Costa* v. *ENEL* [1964] *ECR* 614. See in detail E. Stein, 'Lawyers, Judges and the Making of a Transnational

Bulgaria's Constitution of 1991 incorporates both functional and institutional guarantees to maintain its supremacy. The democratic principles of popular sovereignty, separation of powers, political pluralism and the rule of law are designed to assure constitutional supremacy in the functioning of constitutional government. The specialised, concentrated, abstract and posterior review of the Constitutional Court is a further constitutional guarantee of the supremacy of the Constitution.

2.   SOVEREIGNTY AND THE DISTRIBUTION OF AUTHORITY
       IN FEDERATIONS AND IN THE CONSTITUTION OF THE
       EUROPEAN UNION

The new EU Constitution has provided not for supremacy but for primacy in relation to the exercise of the competencies conferred upon the Union.[22] The primacy of the new EU Constitution is influenced by the issues of sovereignty and the division of competences between the Union and the Member States.

2.1   Sovereignty in federations and in the EU Constitution

State sovereignty has been defined as the ability of the Nation State to determine its domestic and foreign policy alone and independently from the other subjects of international law.[23] Although the Nation State sovereignty proclaimed in the UN Charter[24] has been the benchmark of the post-World War II international legal

---

Constitution', 75 *American Journal of International Law* (1981) pp. 1-27; P. Pescatore, 'The Doctrine of "Direct Effect"', 8 *European Law Review* (1983) pp. 155-157; J. Weiler, 'The Community System: The Dual Character of Supranationalism', 1 *Yearbook of European Law* (1981); A. Easson, 'Legal Approaches to European Integration in the Constitutional Law of the European Union', in F. Snyder, *Collected Courses of the Academy of European Law*, Vol. VI, Book I (Kluwer Law International 1998) pp. 41-155.

[22] See the comment of J. Dutheil De La Rochère and I. Pernice, in J. Dutheil De La Rochère and I. Pernice, 'European Union Law and National Constitutions', WHI-Paper 18/02 (2002) p. 3.

[23] Some authors analyse the contents of State sovereignty in several different ways. Krasner maintains that, in international relations, State sovereignty is exercised in the first place as West-phalian sovereignty, which excludes the intervention of external legal and political subjects in defining the internal organisation of the national State; legal sovereignty is manifested in the requirement for international recognition of States; and interdependent sovereignty covers the methods employed by States to control transborder migration. See S. Krasner, *Sovereignty* (Princeton, Princeton University Press 1999) p. 9.

[24] According to Article 2(1), the organisation is based on the principle of the sovereign equality of all its members. Article 2(4) states that all members shall refrain in their international relations from the threat or use of force against the territorial integrity or political independence of any State, and Article 2(7) proclaims a ban on the intervention in matters that are essentially within the domestic jurisdiction of any State.

order, the principle is not an absolute one, as it is balanced with other principles and values regarding democratic governance. Ever since the time of Emmerich de Vattel, the protection of basic human rights has been a frequent argument in favour of limiting State sovereignty to guarantee freedom.[25]

Globalisation, on the one hand, and the economic and political power of States as subjects of international relations, on the other, are preconditions for the erosion of the sovereignty of countries that are smaller in terms of territory, economic potential and population. This trend again reveals the superiority of political sovereignty over legal sovereignty, manifested both internally and in the area of international relations. After the end of World War II, the scope of State sovereignty was also narrowed by the principle concerning the primacy of international law over national law in all democratic States governed by the rule of law.

The European integration process makes the State sovereignty issue particularly acute.[26] The European integration architecture has evolved from a regional organisation, via a special *sui generis* international union, to reach a unique non-statal political system of European States[27] and – in the more distant future – a federal union, though one unknown to classical federalism and confederalism. The multi-level government in the European Union is a triad of Community, intergovernmental and federal methods that ensures the successful development of the Member States and the supranational formations of the European integration architecture.

The basic trend in terms of State sovereignty is not its elimination but parallel coexistence, so-called 'open statehood', with Member States delegating political powers to the European Union and its institutions. The movement towards a federal union does not automatically imply the loss, abdication or full transfer of sovereignty to the European Union. In the classical federations, Member States do not lose their sovereignty and do not assume the status of territorial entities typical to the unitarian State. In fact, in all forms of classical federalism, the success of the political union depends first of all on the advance consensus concerning sovereignty and the division (vertical separation) of powers between the institutions of the union and those of the Member States.

---

[25] E. de Vattel, *The Law of Nations* (Philadelphia 1835) pp. 94-96.

[26] This aspect of sovereignty was been discussed in the Bulgarian legal literature before the European Union was established, see Д. Георгиев, Суверенитетът в съвременното международно право и сътрудничеството между държавите, София, 1990, pp. 70-81.

[27] De Vattel is the first to write about Europe as a political system, meaning that the national States on the old continent are linked as a single body in the sense that they are united by a common interest to maintain order and protect freedom. Of course, the European Union today is not a political system within the meaning attributed to this notion by De Vattel. See E. de Vattel, op. cit. n. 25, Book 3, Chapter 3, section 47.

The history of federalism is full of solutions on sovereignty in complex State formations. The different sovereignty doctrines in federalism distinguish between different holders of sovereignty and identify several holders of sovereignty within one people and one territory. One group of constitutionalists accepts the concept of the divisibility of sovereignty between the federation and the Member States. Both actors are thus holders of sovereignty,[28] and there are two sovereignties in the federation: that of the Union and that of the Member States. Member State sovereignty is natural and primary and the sovereignty of the Union is a derivative one, formed by the delegation of rights by the Member States establishing the federation.

According to another school of constitutionalists, sovereignty is indivisible and the Member States or alternatively the federation are the holders of sovereignty. Whenever constitutionalists maintain that sovereignty belongs to the Member States, they essentially identify the federation as a confederation. Thus, immediately before the US civil war, the representatives of the southern States justified their sovereignty on the basis that it preceded the formation of the federation.[29] Federal bodies are only agents of the subjects of the federation and have strictly limited powers.[30] The organisation and functioning of federal institutions comes closer to the intergovernmental method established after World War II in the field of Community law.

Other constitutionalists maintain that sovereignty is indivisible but that it belongs to the union only.[31] The States forming the federation are not sovereign. At the same time, however, the members of the federation preserve a degree of autonomy from the central government, including their own constitution and citizenship, which makes them significantly different from the territorially differentiated administrative subdivisions of a decentralised unitary State. Today, though they lack their own sovereignty, German *Länder* are considered constitutionable formations.[32] The cooperative federalism doctrine, which was developed in the United States as early as the 1930s and in Germany during the second half

---

[28] This view is expressed by J. Madison, *A. De Tocqueville about the USA*, L. Duguit, Конституционное право, С.Пб., 1907, pp. 189-194, and G. Waitz, *Grundzüge der Politik* (Breslaw 1862) pp. 161-176. In modern times, this school is represented by L. Siedentop, Демокрация в Европа, София, 2003, pp. 132-133.

[29] Sovereignty forms a single whole; to divide it is to destruct it. See J. Calhoun, *A Disquisition on Government*, Vol. I (Boston 1881) p. 118.

[30] M. von Seydel in Germany also maintains that sovereignty is indivisible and belongs to the States forming the federation. See M. von Seydel, *Staatsrechtliche und politische Abhandlungen* (Freiburg 1893) p. 15.

[31] P. Laband, *Das Staatsrecht des Deutschen Reiches*, Vol. I (Tubingen 1911) p. 91.

[32] E. Stein, *Staatsrecht* (Tubingen, Mohr Siebeck 1998) p. 103; The same view is maintained by O. Kiminih in a seven-volume commentary of the Fundamental Law of the Federal Republic of Germany, Государственное право Германии (Москва 1994) т 1, 77.

of the 20th century, grants flexibility to the federal State. According to the representatives of this school, constitutional regulation is directed, on the one hand, towards cooperation and overcoming the conflicts between central government and the *Länder* and, on the other, towards coordination of the relationship between the *Länder*.

In his day, Carl Schmitt noticed defects of sovereignty in federalism. He identified the antinomy that theoreticians come to in their attempts to build a sovereignty framework for federal States. If sovereignty is single and indivisible, then the existence of the federation is practically impossible. If it belongs to the federation and the subjects of the federation are non-sovereign formations, the federation itself becomes a unitary State. In the opposite hypothesis, where the Member States are the holders of sovereignty, it turns out that there is a confederacy or an international union.[33]

Pragmatically, the European constitutional discourse has avoided contradictions and antinomies of sovereignty in federations. The gradual success in uniting Europe is definitely a result of functional cooperation and the evolution of Community methods. The incomplete political union has been compensated for by economic cooperation and Community law-based integration as a new transnational order having direct, immediate and universal effect with respect to all legal subjects in the Member States. The Maastricht Treaty has placed on the agenda the issue of the partial transfer of sovereignty, which was provided for even earlier in the constitutions of some Member States. The Constitutional Treaty goes beyond 'open statehood', as it replaces multi-level government with the distribution of competences between the European Union and the Member States.

Champions of integration try to tone down Eurosceptics' criticism of the radical federalisation of the European Union by referring to the EU Constitution as a constitutional treaty, on the one hand, and by refusing to solve the problem of State sovereignty in a federal system of government, on the other. But it is well known from the history of federations that it is the content of the legal act and not its title that shapes the union.[34]

Instead of following the beaten track of division or unity of sovereignty, the thinkers of European integration have coined the 'pooling of sovereignties' formula. The idea of pooling and sharing sovereignty itself was substantiated by

---

[33] C. Schmitt, *Théorie de la constitution* (Paris 1993) pp. 517-522.

[34] In his federation doctrine, C. Schmitt notes that 'the federal treaty is a constitutional treaty' and its content immediately forms the federal constitution and becomes part of the constitution of each Member State. See C. Schmitt, op. cit. n. 33, at p. 518. The work of the European Convention appears to paraphrase his thesis, reformulating it to mean that the development of a constitutional treaty establishes a federal union.

Harold Macmillan as early as 1962.[35] Instead of going into meaningless scholastic disputes, politicians and theoreticians offer a practical solution that combines the supremacy of the union with the supremacy of the Member States by fixing their areas.[36] Thus, in a globalised environment, the protection of national interests requires States to pool their sovereignties and not to oppose this development.[37]

The distribution of competences between the Member States and the EU institutions is the practical solution that avoids the antinomies of sovereignty in federalism and acts as a precondition for the introduction of a horizontal and vertical division of powers in the European Union. However, even the most precise and comprehensive separation of powers in federal constitutions has not always ruled out conflicts. The setting of constitutional jurisdictions in Europe after 1920 was the basic method of dispute resolution between union governments and Member State institutions overstepping their powers.

2.2   Division of competences in federations and in the EU Constitution

The distribution of authority between the Member States and the European Union is an important *accomplishment* of the EU Constitution. It is related to the issue of the holders and the transfer of sovereignty, as well as to the evolution of the very nature of the European Union from functional integration to multi-level constitutionalism and integrative federalism.

The European Union is currently a *supranational entity*, and certain decisions of the European Court of Justice provide grounds for characterising EU law as a specific supranational legal system based on equality and the rule of law. It is founded by limiting the sovereign authority of the Member States in favour of the Communities, which are delegated, both express and implied competence. *Supranational, direct, immediate and universal effect* is the basic principle defining the operation of Community law in the internal legal order. The European Union

---

[35] 'Accession to the Treaty of Rome does not imply a unilateral waiver of sovereignty on our part, but a pooling of the sovereignties of all parties concerned, mainly in the economic and the social area. Delegating some of our sovereignty, we will get in turn part of the sovereignty delegated by the other members.' See H. Macmillan, 'Britain, the Commonwealth and Europe' (Conservative Policy Committee 1962).

[36] N. MacCormick, 'Beyond the Sovereign State', 56 *Modern Law Review* (1993) p. 16.

[37] On the European Union's Internet site, the introduction to the EUs institutions is preceded by the common understanding on pooling of sovereignty. 'The European Union is not a federation like the United States. Nor is it simply an organisation for co-operation between governments, like the United Nations. It is, in fact, unique. The countries that make up the EU (its 'member states') pool their sovereignty in order to gain strength and world influence none of them could have on its own. Pooling sovereignty means, in practice, that the member states delegate some of their decision-making powers to shared institutions they have created, so that decisions on specific matters of joint interest can be made democratically at European level.' See <http://europa.eu.int/institutions/index_en.htm>.

has no equivalent in the history of federations and confederations, but the distribution of authority between the centre and the Member States might be compared to various federal models.

The political consensus surrounding the creation of federation is shaped by a federal constitution that distributes competences. The evolution of federalism creates a diversity of authority resulting from the distribution of competences between the institutions of central government and the Member States.[38] Authority is attributed by the primary and secondary vertical division of powers in federalism. Federal constitutions explicitly establish exclusive competences of the union and the Member States, which cannot be overstepped, and joint (concurrent) authority exercised under specific conditions by both levels of the multilevel government. The primary distribution of authority is followed by a secondary differentiation, where the vertical dimension of the principle of separation of powers is specified. The powers outlined as a result of the secondary distribution of competence can be:

- implied;
- inherent;
- reserved; or
- denied to the central government and the subjects of the federation, either separately or jointly.

The history of federalism indicates that preserving the constitutional regulation for tens or hundreds of years has generated tension due to the changing social context. The constitutional framework of the vertical division of powers in federations takes shape through the arbitration of constitutional jurisdictions or constitutional review by the judiciary.[39]

---

[38] The literature outlines many models of federalism, which reveals the diversity in the regulation of the distribution of competences between central government and the subjects of the federation. The distribution of competences constitutes the vertical dimension of the division of powers first outlined by J. Madison in the United States. On the US, German and Swiss models of distributing authority in federations, see W. Lehmann, 'Attribution of Powers and Dispute Resolution in Selected Federal Systems', WP European Parliament, AFCO 103, Luxembourg, 2002. See also Ж. Петева, Европейският конституционен проект – от функционализъм към федерализъм в сп. Международни отношения кн. 3, 2003, pp. 43-56.

[39] In fact, the intervention of bodies charged with constitutional control has not only settled factual disputes between bodies on the basis of the constitution, but has also ensured through interpretation, while preserving the constitutional text, the dynamics of the distribution of authority, where the constituent power has been inactive. Constitutional courts have thus guaranteed the smooth functioning of federal government by settling disputes or brought constitutional provisions on the distribution of authority in line with new realities by compensating for the inactivity of the constituent power.

Compared to the models of federalism, the European Union is unique entity where political integration is rather underdeveloped, but widespread economic cooperation together with the necessary legal regulation is in place, which in turn creates a need to expand supranational competences.

Multi-level government and constitutionalism are major features of the European Union. Like federal law, Community law has *primacy*. The exclusive nature of some aspects of Community authority is not explicitly provided for in the founding Treaties and has been justified by the case law of the European Court of Justice.[40] A presumption of competence on the part of the Member States involved in the decision-making process on Community authority is applied.

The Court does not use the terminology of the distribution of powers. Instead, it has established the term 'exclusive competence of the Communities', as well as two types of Community authority, *specific powers*, which are related to implied authority, and *non-specific powers*, which are exercised if there is no legal basis to apply specific authority.[41]

Subsidiarity[42] and *proportionality* are the fundamental principles regulating the distribution of authority in the areas of shared competence of the Community and the Member States. The objective of the subsidiarity principle is to guarantee efficient distribution of authority and decision making that is close to citizens. As stated in the Amsterdam Treaty's protocol on subsidiarity and proportionality, subsidiarity is a *dynamic* concept. In Articles 94, 95 and 308 EU, the Communities' authority is expanded to cover issues on the building and functioning of the common market and on the achievement of other objectives of European integration that are not regulated in the Treaties as spheres of supranational competence.

The issue of the explicit differentiation of powers of the European Union and the Member States is not new to the European integration process. It was outlined in the two federal drafts of a constitutional treaty prepared by Altiero Spinelli in 1984 and by Fernand Herman in 1994.

In the EU Constitution, the distribution of competences is regulated in Part I, Title III: Competences of the Union. The provisions on the distribution of competences reflect the continuity of the principles established in the previous development of the European integration process and bring functionalism and the Community method closer to the federal method.

Article I-11 of the Constitution states that the fundamental principle of express conferral of powers acts as a guarantee against power concentration in the EU

---

[40] The Court usually applies 'selective exclusiveness' to some issues that fall within Community competence. Other issues are subject to joint competence.

[41] See K. Lenaerts, 'Constitutionalism and the Many Faces of Federalism', 38 *The American Journal of Comparative Law* (1990) pp. 213-218.

[42] The subsidiarity principle was first introduced in the Single European Act (1987), but only in the area of environmental protection. Since its recognition as a general principle of Community law in the Treaty on European Union (1993), it has been applied in all areas of joint competence.

institutions and that the principles of subsidiarity and proportionality govern the exercise of Union competences. The Union acts within the authority delegated by the Member States, which preserve the other competences that are not expressly delegated to the EU institutions. At the same time, based on the subsidiarity principle, the European Union can act beyond its express competences only and insofar as the objectives in question cannot be attained by the Member States and would be better performed at EU level. The subsidiarity principle is applied in accordance with the special protocol attached to the Constitution and is subject to control by the Member States' Parliaments. The EU institutions should exercise authority according to the proportionality principle, which provides that the content and form of EU action should not exceed the level necessary to attain the objectives of the Constitution.

The division of authority follows a simultaneous implementation of the functional and sectoral approaches. *The exclusive competence of the European Union* implies that only the Union can legislate and approve legal acts in a specific area, whereas the Member States can act in the area of this authority only when they are authorised by the European Union to implement these acts. The European Union has exclusive competence to establish the necessary competition rules for the functioning of the internal market and in the areas of:

- monetary policy in the Euro-zone;
- the Common Commercial Policy;
- the customs union; and
- conservation of marine biological resources.

The European Union enters into international treaties where that is laid down in a legislative act of the European Union or where that is necessary to exercise its competence or relates to an internal act of the European Union. It is competent to promote and coordinate Member States' economic and employment policies, as well as to define and implement the Common Foreign and Security Policy and gradually define EU defence policy.

The concurrent (shared) authority of the EU and the Member States are realised through their authority to legislate and adopt legally binding acts in corresponding areas. The Member States exercise this competence where the European Union has not exercised it in advance or has ceased to exercise it. Joint competences are applied in:

- the internal market;
- the area of freedom, security and justice;
- agriculture and fishery;
- transport and Trans-European networks;
- energy;

- social policy;
- economic, social and territorial unity (cohesion);
- environment;
- consumer protection; and
- general public health safety problems.

In the area of research, technological development and space, development cooperation and humanitarian aid, the European Union is competent to approve and implement programmes, however without preventing Member States from exercising their competences. The European Union's *implied competences* originate from the expressly regulated powers as a necessary tool for their implementation. The Member States' *exclusive competences* are all other competences not delegated to the European Union in the Constitution. Finally, it may be assumed that a more detailed definition of competences would meet serious political resistance in European Union's institutions and Member States, because of the need to adopt amendments to the Constitution. The transfer of sovereignty formula would prove insufficient for formulating the precise power distribution. The waiver of this line of constitutional development will in turn generate conflicts that the European Court of Justice or a future EU Constitutional Court would be able to solve effectively.

The brief survey indicates that the ratification of the EU Constitution will bring clarity and comprehensiveness to the institutional and legal structures, but a single hierarchy of methods, institutions and legal acts like in national constitutions will not be established. The inverse hierarchy[43] of EU governance by means of the intergovernmental and Community methods will be preserved, though it will function in more effective manner by improving the interrelationships between EU and Member State institutions. The primacy of the EU Constitution reflects legal supremacy within the divided competences and inverse hierarchies where the different holders, acting in the sphere of the exclusive competences of the EU and Member State institutions, have priority.

3.   THE EU CONSTITUTION AND GLOBAL CONSTITUTIONALISM IN THE COMING CONSTITUTIONAL PLURALISM

The term 'global constitutionalism' has a wide range of connotations. It has been approached from a comparativist prospective as an instrument of analysis of national models of constitutional government around the world, but not within the symbiosis of the constitutionalisation of power relationships in the contemporary

---

[43] V. Roeben, 'Constitutionalism of Inverse Hierarchy: The Case of the European Union', Jean Monnet Working Paper No. 8/03, Jean Monnet Center, NYU School of Law, 2003.

globalisation process.[44] The globalisation of constitutionalism and the adoption of constitutions for non-statal entities has been treated in the context of an unwritten constitution within the founding Treaties and in the context of the written Constitution drafted by the EU Convention.

During the last decade, scholars have made attempts to describe a new phenomenon or a new stage in the development of constitutionalism emerging at the global level.[45] They have treated the global as yet another form of governance where power has to be framed within constitutional restraints in order to meet benchmarks of democracy.[46] The primacy of international law, the increasing role of many international organisations (like the WTO) and the development of instruments of human rights law at supranational level have all been regarded as different threads forming the fabric of an emerging global constitutionalism that imposes limitations on the actors involved in the emerging patterns of global governance. Although these phenomena resemble the guarantor function of constitutions, however, it would be an exaggeration and a simplification to look for supremacy of the global rule of law, let alone an emerging unwritten constitution. At present, proposing a draft world constitution is an utopian illusion bordering on science fiction, like the Constitution of Mars.[47] Within the context of global democratic governance, international legal standards have been instrumental in building a bridge between national and global constitutionalism. They provide compliance of different legal orders of contemporary constitutional pluralism. Nowadays, the intensity of legally binding and hierarchical structures are strongest within national constitutionalism; they are present in federalism and are in the process of being affirmed in the relationship between the EU Constitution and the constitutions of the Member States. In global constitutionalism, there is some compatibility of democratic standards but not a full-fledged hierarchy of constitutional orders. Globalisation is still looking for its own constitutional order, and the rule of law and the interaction of global standards with national constitutional orders still has to rely on the principle of *pacta sunt servanda*. Due

---

[44] For the best papers in this field with an analysis of post-World War II trends, see T. Fleiner, ed., 'Five Decades of Constitutionalism', *AIDC/IACL*, Vol. 5 (University of Fribourg, Institute of Federalism 1999) pp. 315-344; T. Fleiner, 'Ageing Constitution', paper presented at the Conference of the Australian Association of Constitutional Law: 'A Celebration of a Federation – The Australian Constitution in Retrospect and Prospect', Perth, 21-23 September 2001; and B. Ackerman's seminal article: 'The Rise of World Constitutionalism', 83 *Virginia Law Review* (1977) pp. 771-798.

[45] Л. Ферайоли, 'Отвъд суверенитета и гражданството. За един световен конституционализъм', Съвременно право (1995) кн. 4, 70-78.

[46] One of the best liberal definitions of constitutionalism emphasising the constitution's role as a frame of government was offered in the second half of the 19th century in the United States by John Potter Stockton: 'The constitutions are chains with which men bind themselves in their sane moments that they may not die by a suicidal hand in the day of their frenzy.' See J.E. Finn, *Constitutions in Crisis* (1991) p. 5.

[47] See K.S. Robinson, 'The Constitution of Mars', in *The Martians* (Harper Collins 1999).

to this fact, the significance of international legal standards increases, since they compensate for the weaker legally binding force of the emerging supranational global constitutionalism.

In a recent paper, Maduro presents a three pillar construct of constitutions in a national and global context.[48] National constitutions are affected by the emerging global constitutionalism, as the latter challenges the role of Nation State constitutions as the utmost expression of sovereignty and as the criterion of the ultimate validity of the legal system. Global constitutionalism influences the status of national constitutional self-determination in the idea of self-government, the form of participation, power distribution and representation. The legal standards established by international treaties and soft law might be interpreted as a fourth pillar through which the emerging global restraints on governance are transposed to national constitutionalism as universal criteria of constitutional governance.

In the past, any attempt to propose international standards would have met the counter-argument of being an intrusion on national and State sovereignty, which was considered to be the heart of State power and citizen's rights, entrenched in national constitutions and legislation.

Expanding constitutional governance at the global level is related to the concept of societal constitutionalism. There are at least two dominant approaches to societal constitutionalism. One of them relates societal constitutionalism to broadening the scope of regulation, which has been one of the main trends of the fourth constitutional generation. However, societal constitutionalism concerns the increasing number of actors participating in the political decision-making process and poses limitations on their actions.[49]

In the context of global constitutionalism, the EU Constitution represents a remarkable event. It surpasses the proposition that the constitution is an attribute reserved for the Nation States. For the first time in history, a non-statal entity has adopted a written constitution.[50] With the EU Constitution mankind has entered the third stage of constitutional civilisation, where constitutional governance has

---

[48] M. Maduro, 'From Constitutions to Constitutionalism: A Constitutional Approach for Global Governance', Lead Paper at the Workshop 'Changing Patterns of Rights Politics: A Challenge to Stateness?', Hanse Institute for Advanced Studies, Delmenhorst, Germany, June 2003, pp. 9-12.

[49] See G. Teubner, 'Societal Constitutionalism: Alternatives to State-Centered Constitutional Theory,' Stores Lectures 2003-2004, available at: <http://www.jura.uni-frankfurt.de/teubner/pdf>.

[50] For a brilliant critique of the 'no demos' thesis as reflected in the German Maastricht decision, see J. Weiler, 'The State "über alles": Demos, Telos and the German Maastricht Decision', EUI WP RSC N95/19. The classical Ellinek trinity of territory, nation and sovereignty as a prerequisite for constitution drafting has been overcome. Some definitions extend the benchmarks of the State by adding independence, effective government, recognition by other States, capacity to enter into agreements with other States, a State apparatus, an organised economy and fictional parts of States as official residences of foreign diplomatic envoys. See LTA Seet Uei Lim, 'Geopolitics: The Need to Reconceptualise State Sovereignty and Security', 25(2) *Journal of Singapore Armed Forces* (1999), available at: <http://www.mindef.gov.sg/safti/pointer/back/journals/1999/Vol25_2/7.htm>.

expanded beyond the Nation State. If we look back in history, three distinct stages in the evolution of governance and constitutionalism can be identified. Mankind lived for millennia in a state without a constitution limiting government power. After the Treaty of Westphalia, and especially after the last decades of the 18th century when the first written constitutions were adopted, constitutions for centuries became the monopoly of the Nation States. The rule of law has been entrenched in a written constitution as the legal form of a State legitimately structuring power, built on the supremacy of constitutional limitations, supporting a hierarchy within the legal and political system to ensure democratic government and protect human rights at the national level.

Non-statal entities like the European Union and perhaps, in the foreseeable future, international organisations like the WTO or the United Nations founded on an agreement between the participating sovereign Nation States with 'open statehood', will entrench the rule of law in a written constitution co-existing and interacting with national constitutions.

Despite the success of EU constitutionalism, however, two primitive conclusions can be ruled out. The adoption of the Constitution does not mean that the European Union has been transformed into a State or a full-fledged federation. In addition, it does not mean that the EU Constitution and the emergence of a global constitutionalism mark the beginning of the withering of the Nation State. Instead, the European Union and global constitutionalism will exist hand in hand with the constitutions of the Nation States and will be made possible through national constitutional and legal systems rather than replacing them. Moreover, Nation States will be the main actors in the evolving constitutional pluralism and will work together with other non-statal actors. In the context of global constitutionalism, like the EU Member States, Nation States will come to an agreement to continue their united action bound not only by international and Community law obligations but by entrenching the rule of law in a written constitution.

Mankind should be proud of the progress of the rule of law, human rights and democratic constitutionalism. However, present achievements only mark the beginning of the fascinating constitutional developments that will take place at global level in the coming decades.

CONSTITUTIONAL PREPARATION FOR EU ACCESSION IN THE NEW CENTRAL AND EASTERN EUROPEAN MEMBER STATES: IS THE RULE OF LAW BETTER THAN THE RULE OF POLITICS?

Jenő Czuczai*

I.   INTRODUCTION

The 1st of May 2004 brought a new, historic impetus to the European integration process, due to the fact that ten new Member States joined the European Union. This eastward enlargement process is unprecedented and unique for at least two reasons. First, in the previous enlargements of the European Union (and before that the European Communities), the maximum number of new Member States admitted at one time was only three. Now, in the course of the so-called first wave of the EU eastward enlargement process, ten new Member States have joined the European Union. Moreover, one should not forget that eight of the ten new Member States are so-called Central and Eastern European countries in transition, which means that, during the last fifteen years, these countries have already gone through a very demanding, difficult and complex process of systemic transformation. These Central and Eastern European countries have therefore had to combine their economic and to some extent political transition processes with all the challenges of the artificially accelerated preparatory tasks for EU accession. These parallel processes represent a tremendous burden and undertaking, which has been shouldered primarily by the people living in this part of Europe. And we should not forget about this if we really want to understand the new members in the 'club'. The second reason that this eastward enlargement process is unique is that, while preparing for the accession of the new Member States, the European Union itself has in the meantime been going through many unprecedented reforms, especially in terms of its constitutional refounding (or

* Dr Jenő Czuczai is a Barrister at Law; Vice-President of the European Law Academy, Budapest; Visiting Professor of Law at the College of Europe, Bruges-Natolin; and President of the Hungarian FIDE Association. This paper is based to a large extent on presentations that I have delivered for the last two years in Slovenia, Croatia, Turkey, Bulgaria, Romania and Serbia and Montenegro on this subject in the framework of the MATRA multi-country project on the impact of accession on the national legal orders of the candidate countries and new Member States, which was developed at policy level and later managed in an excellent manner from the very beginning by Alfred Kellermann. Many thanks are due to him for this important initiative. The usual disclaimers apply.

The European Union: An Ongoing Process of Integration – Liber Amicorum Alfred E. Kellermann
© 2004, T.M.C. Asser Instituut, The Hague, and the authors

redesign). The ever-developing and changing EU *acquis* (in particular the constitutional *acquis*) has made the task of the new Member States to prepare for accession even more burdensome, difficult and demanding.

This goes some way towards explaining why, for instance, the adaptation process to the EU constitutional *acquis* caused so many new challenges for the new Member States, in particular those in Central and Eastern Europe, in terms of the novelties, complexity, sensitivity and difficulty, even in codificatory technical terms, of this last stage of membership preparation. One of the very few experts on EU law who already in the mid-1990s recognised the important fact that, in constitutional terms, the preparation for accession in the new Member States should be clearly differentiated from previous relevant experiences, because of its obvious connection to the post-Soviet political, legal, psychological and socio-logical environment in Central and Eastern Europe, was Alfred Kellermann from the famous T.M.C. Asser Institute in The Hague.

I remember well that when I first met him in Budapest in 1997, as well as many times thereafter, he was arguing – like a honorary ambassador – that a much better-organised constitutional preparation would be needed for the candidate countries in Central and Eastern Europe (including the reform of the judiciary) in order that the rule of law (and the effectiveness of EC law) could already be maintained in an enlarged European Union immediately after their accession. During the last five or six years, Alfred Kellermann has really done a lot to achieve this goal. He organised the Hague Colloquium on European Law in 2000, which was devoted to the topic of EU enlargement: constitutional challenges at EU and national level, and resulted in a very successful publication, which is now a reference book all over Europe. Following this, he did his best to launch the MATRA project on the impact of accession on the national legal order in the (pre-)candidate countries. This pro-gramme, which started in 2002 and will be finished this year, has been greatly appreciated by the participating countries, namely, Turkey, Bulgaria, Romania, Serbia and Montenegro, Croatia and Slovenia. Last year, finally, he served as a consultant on EU law in the Russian Federation for almost a year.

All these facts are strong evidence of the fact that Alfred Kellermann has a strong commitment to Europe and the European integration process, as well as great sympathy towards the new democracies in Central and Eastern Europe. That is why this article is dedicated to him as an expression of my appreciation for all his efforts on behalf of Europe and of our shared belief in the importance of the rule of law.

II.   DEFINITIONS

In order to properly address the main topic of this paper, namely, a comparative analysis of the EU accession-related constitutional adaptation process in the new Member States, it is important, first of all, to clarify the meaning of the EU constitutional *acquis*. Why? Because when talking about the constitutional impact of the European Union's eastward enlargement process on the individual candidate countries in Central and Eastern Europe, I believe that this *terminus technicus* is the most important point of reference, which must be defined before addressing any kind of pre-accession-driven constitutional adaptation process and the maturity thereof. How to define, therefore, what the EU constitutional *acquis* is about? What we can say is that there is neither a clear-cut definition in the current secondary literature on EU law of the fifteen 'old' Member States nor in that of the new Member States. We can also submit as a legally relevant fact that in the course of the so-called '*acquis* screening process' under the accession negotiations, there was no special screening chapter on the EU constitutional *acquis*.

Nevertheless, I think that we can identify some possible main elements of the EU constitutional *acquis*, such as: (1) in Treaty-based EU primary law, there are some provisions in the founding Treaties that, in my view, are undoubtedly of a constitutional nature, for example: Article 6(1) and (2) EU, Article 7 EU, and Articles 5, 10, 12-13, 220, 226-227, 230-232 and 295 EC, etc. (in this respect, see also ECJ, Opinions 1/91 *EFTA* and Opinions 1/94 and 2/94, etc.); (2) the common constitutional traditions of the Member States; (3) the European Convention on Human Rights and the case law of the European Court of Human Rights; (4) there are also examples of EC secondary legislation that have constitutional significance, for example: Regulation (EC) No 1049/2001 of the European Parliament and of the Council regarding public access to the European Parliament, Council and Commission documents, etc.; (5) there are also some EC 'soft-law' measures that are important in this regard, such as the European Commission's White Paper on Good Governance, etc.; and (6) there is also a remarkably large judicial *acquis* (consisting of about 200 preliminary rulings and other judgements) created by the ECJ in order to define the constitutionally relevant cornerstones and/or fundamental public law pillars of the EU legal order (just think of the historical developments from the *Van Gend en Loos* case to the *Köbler* case in this regard!).[1]

---

[1] An interesting question in this context is whether the so-called four freedoms in the context of the EC single market are part of the EU constitutional *acquis*? In my opinion, the answer is 'no' for at least two reasons. First of all, because the EU constitutional *acquis* is not negotiable, whereas the EC single market *acquis*, including the four freedoms, is negotiable, as we have seen in the accession negotiations under the EU eastward enlargement framework. There were negotiating chapters for all the four freedoms, plus separate chapters on competition and State aid. Moreover, some (although not all that many) transitional arrangements have been agreed for the four freedoms by the parties. Secondly, my way of thinking follows the classic division of the legal order into areas of public law and private law, even at EU level. This means that even if one could argue that the four freedoms should be regarded as falling under the European Union's constitutional framework, I could only support such an approach by separately addressing 'EC economic constitutionalism', which however (and obviously) has completely different scientific and philosophical characteristics, primarily because of its private (or economic) law footing.

We should also consider the main features of the so-called EU constitutional *acquis*, in order to better understand its merit, qualitative and quantitative nature. I think that there are two main characteristics regarding this part of the accession *acquis*, namely, that it is 'constantly evolving, developing' (see, for example, the recently finished constitutionalisation process at EU level and its main product, the Treaty establishing a Constitution for Europe,[2] or the EU Charter, etc.) and secondly that *it is not negotiable*! This means that, if a candidate country wants to join the European Union, this part of the accession *acquis* must in any case be fully taken on and properly implemented from the very moment of the accession.

Moreover, what we can also see regarding the EU constitutional *acquis* is that this term is of a dialectic nature, because it is also intended to describe the recent (newly emerged or currently emerging) challenges of the constitutional developments at both levels, namely, at EU level and at the level of the old and new Member States. Consider, for example, the constitutional traditions of the new Member States: how will they influence the functioning of the European Union's constitutional order after enlargement? Other open issues include the post-Brunner effect in Germany (the key question being whether the national constitution of an EU Member State is subject to EU law and, if so, to which area of EU law); the recent Irish Referendum (the key question being how to approach the function of national referenda in a future enlarged European Union, considering that the new Constitutional Treaty of the European Union will have to be ratified by twenty-five Member States); or how to look at the Cyprus issue from the point of view of the EU constitutional *acquis* (the key question being how to carry out the constitutional adaptation process of a divided island); and so forth. All these issues show that the term 'EU constitutional *acquis*' is really a dynamic and complex one.

In conclusion, when speaking about the constitutional adaptation process to the EU constitutional *acquis* as developing over time, I think that the most important task for the new Member States is to create an adaptive constitutional regulatory framework or, if you like, a kind of codificatory (bridging) solution at the level of the national constitution (or of national constitutionalism!), in order to allow the penetration of the main general principles (doctrines) of EC law into the national legal (constitutional) order (most importantly, the doctrines of 'the supremacy of EC law', 'direct effect' and 'direct applicability'). This task forms the primary constitutional impact of the accession process of any candidate country before its actual admission to the European Union! Nonetheless, based on the experiences of the present fifteen Member States in this area, it can be stated that there is no *à la carte solution* for this task at all. Another important question is whether there is really any need to amend the national constitution before

---

[2] See the provisional consolidated version of the draft Treaty establishing a Constitution for Europe, Brussels, 25 June 2004, CIG 86/04 (hereinafter, the 'EU Constitution').

accession.[3] Can a candidate country join the European Union without an 'EU clause' or without building a 'constitutional bridge' between the EU legal order and the national legal order? This paper will try to address all these issues.

III. COMPARATIVE ANALYSIS OF HOW THE NEW MEMBER STATES HAVE SOLVED THE NECESSARY CONSTITUTIONAL ALIGNMENT TASKS, WITH SPECIAL ATTENTION FOR THE HUNGARIAN EXPERIENCE

Constitutional adaptation to the European Union was not really addressed until 2000, except in the case of Poland and Slovakia. Poland (Arts. 89-91 of the 1997 Constitution)[4] and Slovakia (Arts. 7, 93, 120(2), 125a and 144 of the 2001

---

[3] Many scholars believe, for example, that there is no need for any *a priori* constitutional amendment in order for European candidate countries to join the European Union. These scholars believe that the general principles of the EC legal order will apply automatically after accession, by virtue of the fact that the new Member States will have become signatories to the European Union's founding Treaties. On the other hand, this approach still makes reference to the experience of the founding Member States, especially to the famous German approach (the Solange-doctrine) and the dubious Italian experience (in particular, the fate of Articles 10 and 11 of the Italian Constitution), where without any real so-called constitutional bridges these Member States were able to live with the constantly evolving EC (or today EU) constitutional *acquis*. See in more detail E. Stein, 'Towards Supremacy of Treaty-Constitution by Judicial Fiat: On the margin of the *Costa* case', 63 *Michigan Law Review* (1965) pp. 491-518; and A.E. Kellermann, 'Constitutional Impact of Eastward Enlargement', 2 *Romanian Journal of European Affairs* (2002) pp. 74-81. I think that these comparisons with the founding Member States are misleading and wrong. The ongoing eastward enlargement process is unprecedented and we should not forget that the new Member States are all so-called post-Communist Central and Eastern Europe countries as well as countries in transition. Finally, the EC (EU) accession *acquis* has tripled in comparison to the quantity and quality of the *acquis* that existed at the time when Portugal and Spain joined the European Community.

[4] In the 1997 Polish Constitution, the relevant constitutional texts read as follows. Art. 90(1): 'The Republic of Poland may, by virtue of international agreements, *delegate to an international organisation* or international institution *the competence of organs of State authority* in relation to *certain matters*.' Art. 90(2): 'A statute, granting consent for ratification of an international agreement referred to in para. 1, shall be passed by the Sejm by a two-thirds majority vote in the presence of at least half of the statutory number of the Deputies and by the Senate by a two-thirds majority vote in the presence of at least half of the statutory number of Senators.' Art. 90(3): 'Granting of consent for ratification of such agreement may also be passed by a nation-wide referendum in accordance with the provisions of Art. 125.' Art. 90(4): 'Any resolution in respect of the choice of procedure for granting consent to ratification shall be taken by the Sejm by an absolute majority vote taken in the presence of at least half of the statutory number of Deputies.' Art. 91(1): 'After promulgation thereof in the Journal of Laws of the Republic of Poland (*Dziennik Ustaw*), a ratified international agreement shall constitute part of the domestic legal order and shall be applied directly, unless its application depends on the enactment of a statute.' Art. 91(2): 'An international agreement ratified upon prior consent granted by statute *shall have precedence over statutes* if such an agreement cannot be reconciled with the provisions of such statutes.' Art. 91(3): 'If an agreement, ratified by the Republic of Poland, establishing an international organisation so provides, *the laws established by it shall be applied directly and have precedence in the event of a conflict of laws.*'

Constitutional Amendment)[5] were ready for accession earlier, at least from a constitutional point of view, than the other candidate countries in Central and Eastern Europe.[6] From a Hungarian point of view, I think, that a special feature of Slovakia's constitutional adaptation process is that the new Article 7 declares, *inter alia*, that Slovakia not only has the right to enter the European Union (as 'a union of States') but also to leave it (pending the result of a compulsory referendum)![7]

A special case in terms of its constitutional preparation for EU accession is the Czech Republic (see Arts. 1(2) and 2, new Art. 10a-b and Art. 87(1) and (2) of the 2001 Constitutional Amendment Act).[8] From Hungary's point of view, the most remarkable feature of the Czech approach is that there will be no specific integration clause in the amended Czech Constitution after accession, meaning that in the future the Czech Republic will follow the so-called monist system in full (see amended Art. 1(2) and new Art. 10).[9] This decision was reasoned by stating that there was no need for a special integration clause to be

---

[5] The relevant constitutional texts read as follows. Art. 7(1): 'The Slovak Republic may, by its own discretion, enter into a State union with other States. A constitutional law, which shall be confirmed by a referendum, shall decide on the entry into a State union, or on the secession from such union.' Art 7(2): 'The Slovak Republic may, by an international treaty, which was ratified and promulgated in the way laid down by a law, or on the basis of such treaty, transfer *the exercise of a part of its powers to the European Communities and the European Union*. Legally binding acts of the European Communities and of the European Union *shall have precedence over laws* of the Slovak Republic. The transposition of legally binding acts which require implementation shall be realised through a law or a regulation of the Government according to Art. 120(2).' Art. 7(5): 'International treaties on human rights and fundamental freedoms and international treaties for whose exercise a law is necessary, and international treaties which directly confer rights or impose duties on natural persons or legal persons and which were ratified and promulgated in the way laid down by a law *shall have precedence over laws*.' Art. 144(2): 'Judges in the performance of their function shall be independent and *in decision making shall be bound by the Constitution, by constitutional laws, by international treaty pursuant to Art. 7(2)* and (5), and by laws.'

[6] In terms of EU accession, the National Council of the Slovak Republic on 23 February 2001 passed Constitutional Act No. 460/1992, which amended the Slovakian Constitution in order to establish the necessary constitutional adaptations to the EU legal order. See A.E. Kellermann, J.W. de Zwaan and J. Czuczai, eds., *EU Enlargement: The Constitutional Impact at EU and National Level* (The Hague, T.M.C. Asser Press 2001) pp. 334-335.

[7] See Art. 93(1) of the Slovakian Constitution.

[8] The Czech Parliament adopted the amending Constitutional Act 395/2001 on 18 October 2001 in preparation for the forthcoming EU accession. It entered into force on 1 June 2002.

[9] The relevant constitutional texts read as follows. Art. 1(2): 'The Czech Republic respects international law.' Art. 10: 'The promulgated international treaties, approved by the Parliament before their ratification and binding for the Czech Republic, are the part of the legal order. If the international treaty stipulates something else than the statute, the *international treaty is to be applied*.' Art. 10a(1): 'By means of an international treaty some powers of the organs of the Czech Republic *can be transferred* to an international organisation or institution.' Please note that new Art. 10b(1)-(3) of the Czech Constitution, as amended, deals with the future relationship between Parliament and Government in EU matters, which should be regulated in detail in a statute.

built into the 1992 Czech Constitution, since the main doctrines of EC law would in any case be directly applicable in the territory of the Czech Republic after accession, as required under the ECJ's case law and because of the self-executing nature of the European Union's founding Treaties. In the Czech model, the future relations between Parliament and Government on EU matters should be regulated in a separate constitutional law (which to my knowledge has not yet been adopted). The Czech Republic has not addressed the issue of leaving the European Union.[10]

Other new Member States in Central and Eastern Europe only seriously addressed the issues in question during the last stage of the accession negotiations, for example Hungary, while some of them only amended their constitutions in light of the forthcoming EU accession after the conclusion of the accession negotiations, for example Slovenia. Articles 3, 47 and 68 of the 1991 Slovenian Constitution were only amended in February 2003. Under the Slovenian solution, the European Union will not be mentioned in the amended Constitution. Instead, the 'international organisation-based formula' will be used when a 'possible conflict between international law and domestic law' arises, but the conflict of laws issue (i.e. domestic law *vis-à-vis* EU law) is not settled *strictu sensu*. The issue of exiting the European Union is also not addressed, while relations between Parliament and Government on EU matters will be regulated separately (the relevant law has not yet been adopted).[11]

---

[10] Information on the Czech experiences is based on the manuscript of a forthcoming article on the topic, written by Prof. J. Zemanek, Faculty of Law, Carol University, Prague. See further I. Slosarcik, 'Constitutional changes in the Czech Republic and the case law of the Constitutional Court in 2002-2003', 10 *European Public Law* (2004) pp. 3-18.

[11] The relevant constitutional texts read as follows: Art. 3a(1): 'Pursuant to a treaty ratified by the National Assembly by a two-thirds majority vote of all deputies, Slovenia *may transfer the exercise of part of its sovereign rights to international organisations* which are based on respect for human rights and fundamental freedoms, democracy and the principles of the rule of law and may enter into a defensive alliance with States which are based on respect for these values.' Art. 3a(2): 'Before ratifying an international treaty referred to in the preceding paragraph, the National Assembly may call a referendum. A proposal shall pass at the referendum if a majority of voters who have cast valid votes vote in favour of such. If such referendum has been held, a referendum regarding the law on the ratification of the treaty concerned may not be called.' Art. 3a(3): '*Legal acts and decisions adopted within international organisations to which Slovenia has transferred the exercise of part of its sovereign rights shall be applied in Slovenia* in accordance with the legal regulations of these organisations.' Art. 3a(4): 'In procedures for the adoption of legal acts and decisions in international organisations to which Slovenia has transferred the exercise of part of its sovereign rights, the Government shall promptly inform the National Assembly of proposals for such acts and decisions as well as of its own activities. *The National Assembly may adopt provisions thereon, which the Government shall take into consideration in its activities.* The relationship between the National Assembly and the Government arising from this paragraph shall be regulated in detail by a law adopted by a two-thirds majority vote of deputies present.'

Another example is provided by Estonia and Latvia. In Estonia, for instance, there was a hot debate on the relevant legal text,[12] which was adopted on 18 December 2002 but finally entered into force after the positive referendum on EU accession in September 2003, especially because of the rigid sovereignty principle laid down in Article 1 of the 1991 Estonian Constitution.[13] Events unfolded similarly in Latvia.[14]

---

[12] The relevant constitutional text reads as follows: 'The Estonian people adopted by referendum the following Act to complement the Constitution under Article 162.' Art 1: 'Estonia may belong to the European Union, proceeding from the founding principles of the Constitution of the Republic of Estonia.' Art. 2: 'In case Estonia *belongs to the European Union, the Constitution of the Republic of Estonia will be applied, taking into consideration the rights and obligations deriving from the Accession Treaty.*' Art. 3: 'This Act may only be amended by referendum.' Law 1067 SE II of 12 November 2002 on Complementing the Constitution of the Republic of Estonia, which entered into force on 1 May 2004. The big problem with this solution is that the most relevant general principles of Community law, in terms of the constitutional adaptation of the new Member States, like the doctrines of the supremacy of EC law, direct effect and direct applicability cannot be derived from the founding Treaties of the European Union that are currently in force nor from the Accession Treaty *per se*. This is because these doctrinal principles were actually laid down by the case law of the ECJ or, in other words, by the EC judicial *acquis* as constantly developing.

[13] See: in more detail A. Albi, 'The Central and Eastern European Constitutional Amendment Process in light of the Post-Maastricht Conceptual Discourse: Estonia and the Baltic States', 7 *European Public Law* (2001) pp. 433-454.

[14] In the 1991 Latvian Constitution, the relevant article is Article 68, which reads as follows: 'Upon entering into international agreements, Latvia, for the purpose of strengthening democracy, may delegate a part of its State institutions' competences to international institutions. International agreements, in which *a part of State institutions' competences are delegated to international institutions* may be ratified by the Saeima in sittings in which at least two-thirds of the Members of the Saeima participate, and a two-thirds majority vote of the members present is required for the ratification of such an international agreement. Membership of Latvia in the European Union shall be decided by a national referendum, which is proposed by the Saeima.' (Translation by author.) In this regard, see also Art. 79, as amended.

In this context, I think that it is worth mentioning that the only Baltic State where the necessary constitutional changes in terms of EU accession have – to my knowledge – not yet been enacted is Lithuania. However, the most recent draft of new Chapter 14 ('The State of Lithuania and the European Union'), dated 7 July 2003, reads as follows: Art. 146(1): 'Seeking to participate in the European integration and attain common European objectives, as well as to ensure the security of the Republic of Lithuania and the well-being of its citizens, *the Republic of Lithuania shall participate in the EU and confer on it the competences of State institutions in the areas and to the extent which are defined in the founding Treaties of the EU, so that it along with other Member States of the EU would jointly exercise the competences in such areas.*' This is very similar to the Hungarian solution. Art. 146(2): 'The Semais shall consider and resolve the matters of the EU which are within the limits of its competence. The Government shall implement the Union membership rights and duties. The Government shall forthwith inform the Semais and the President of the Republic about proposals to adopt Acts of the EU. Either the Government shall consult the Semais with respect to the issues which are attributed to the competence of the Semais under the Constitution of the Republic of Lithuania, and which are proposed for consideration in proposals to adopt Acts of the EU. Either the Semais or, in accordance with the procedure established in the Semais Statute, the Committee on European Affairs or the Committee on Foreign Affairs may recommend to the Government a position of the Republic of Lithuania as regards the said proposals. The President of the Republic may submit to the Government recommendations with regard to the issues which are attributed to the

IV. PRELIMINARY QUESTIONS CONCERNING CONSTITUTIONAL ADAPTATION FOR EU ACCESSION

Before turning to the analysis on the Hungarian model, it is important to identify *ex ante* the main preliminary questions about EU accession-related 'constitutional bridging' in more general terms.[15] I think that they are as follows:

- Should we really transfer any part of our sovereignty to the European Union? Should we really have a so-called 'integration clause' in our constitutions (which literally means opening the constitution to the three main doctrines of EC law)?[16]
- When to amend the national constitution in order to comply with the EU constitutional *acquis*?
- Should the European Union be mentioned specifically in the modified national constitutions?
- What is the impact of the constitutional adaptation process on national Constitutional Courts and Parliaments and on their workings?
- What about the role of the national central banks (in relation to EMU adaptation) and the reform of electoral rules?
- What are the main challenges from the point of view of implementation (e.g. training of judges)?

---

competence of the President of the Republic under the Constitution of the Republic of Lithuania. *The Government shall take the submitted recommendations into account.*' Art. 146(3): '*Legal norms of the EU* shall be a constituent part of the legal system of the Republic of Lithuania and in the event of the conflict of laws shall have supremacy with respect to the norms laid down by laws and other legal acts of the Republic of Lithuania.'

Finally, some words about Malta and Cyprus. Malta followed the British model of 1972 and on 14 July 2003 adopted the European Union Act, Act V of 2003, Chapter 460 of the Laws of Malta, which is in fact an implementing Act regarding the Treaty of Accession, signed by Malta on 16 April 2003. This Act, which entered into force on 1 May 2004, contains several provisions, the most important being Article 7, which modifies Section 65 of the Maltese Constitution. Section 65 now reads as follows: 'Subject to the provisions of this Constitution, Parliament may make laws for the peace, order and good government of Malta in conformity with full respect of human rights, generally accepted principles of international law and Malta's international and regional obligations, in particular those *assumed by the Treaty of Accession to the EU* signed in Athens on the 16th of April 2003.' This is an interesting solution, which does not address *expressis verbis* the possible future conflict between Maltese law and EU law, especially as regards the Maltese Constitution itself. Concerning Cyprus, it is understood that there was no need for any constitutional adaptation since it employs a purely monist constitutional model.

[15] See in more detail the chapter by J. Czuczai on constitutional challenges in the candidate countries, in Kellermann, De Zwaan and Czuczai, op. cit. n. 6, pp. 411-422 at pp. 419-420.

[16] In this context, I would like to mention that, in case of Serbia and Montenegro, it will be a special issue, to be addressed at constitutional level before EU accession, that it is a 'union of States' as stipulated in the Constitutional Charter.

- What to do about the land issue (which is a sensitive issue in Bulgaria, Latvia, Lithuania, Slovenia, etc.)?
- How should the relations between Parliaments and Governments on EU-related policy making be regulated after accession?
- Regarding human rights, is it necessary, *inter alia*, to amend those constitutional provisions that currently grant (fundamental) human rights only to the nationals (!) of the candidate country?
- Can the national constitution remain 'the supreme law' at national level after accession to the European Union?

V.   THE HUNGARIAN APPROACH

I believe that the Hungarian model on constitutional adaptation to the EU constitutional *acquis* – with special regard to the so-called 'integration (or Europe) clause' – can be summarised as follows.

The Hungarian Parliament amended the Hungarian Constitution (Act No. XX of 1949, as amended several times) on 17 December 2002 (Act No. LXI of 2002,[17] published in *Magyar Közlöny* on 23 December 2002) in light of the forthcoming EU accession. New Article 2A addresses the so-called 'integration clause'. Many experts believe, however, that there is still a constitutional gap in the Hungarian Constitution, namely, that it does not address what happens if national law is in conflict with international law (Art. 7(1) of the Constitution),[18] or in our case in the case of possible future conflicts between Hungarian law and EU laws with direct effect and direct applicability. That is why it is highly likely that the Constitution still needs to be amended after accession, maybe sometime in 2005.

---

[17] Act No. LXI of 2002 was adopted by the Hungarian Parliament on 17 December 2002 and entered into force – with some exceptions – on 23 December 2002. For background literature, see for example (in Hungarian) N. Chronowski and J. Petrétei, 'EU Csatlakozás és alkotmánymódosítás: minimális konszenzus helyett politikai kompromisszum' (EU accession and modifying the Constitution: A political compromise instead of a minimum consent) 8 *Magyar Jog* (2003) pp. 449-466; A. Sajó, 'Az EU csatlakozás alkotmányosságra gyakorolt hatása az új tagállamokban' (The constitutional impact of EU accession on the new Member States) 2 *Fundamentum* (2003) pp. 14-26, and J. Czuczai, 'Kritikai elemzés az EU csatlakozást érintő magyar Alkotmánymódosításról' (A critical assessment on the EU-accession related amendments to the Hungarian Constitution) in J. Czuczai, ed., *Jogalkotás, jogalkalmazás hazánk EU csatlakozása küszöbén* (Law-making and law-enforcement in the light of Hungary's forthcoming accession to the EU) (Budapest, KJK-Kerszöv 2003) pp. 129-151.

[18] Art. 7(1) reads: 'The legal system of the Republic of Hungary accepts the generally recognised rules of international law, and shall further ensure harmony between domestic law and the obligations assumed under international law.'

The Hungarian Government submitted the bill on amending the Constitution in light of EU accession only on 15 October 2002.[19] It should be mentioned that in Hungary the Constitution can be amended only with the support of two-thirds of all members of the Parliament. The Hungarian Parliament, which is unicameral, has 386 members, which means that for the adoption of an amendment to the Constitution at least 255 votes in favour are required. However, an affirmative referendum is not required to amend the constitution in Hungary. This means that today the Constitution can only be amended with the support of the biggest opposition party (Alliance of Young Free Democrats). This is because the Government's coalition partners (Hungarian Socialist Party and Hungarian Liberal Party) have only 198 seats in total, whereas the opposition parties have 188 seats (of which the Alliance of Young Free Democrats holds 165). Act No. LXI of 2002 was adopted by a majority of almost 100 per cent on 17 December 2002, but that was not the end of the matter.

Hungary follows the so-called *dualist constitutional system* at the moment, and wishes to keep this approach in the future too. This means that a special so-called 'integration clause' had to be incorporated into the Constitution. The provision that was finally adopted, new Article 2A(1), reads as follows:[20] 'The Republic of Hungary, for the purpose of becoming a Member State of the European Union through the conclusion of an international agreement, can exercise certain constitu-

---

[19] See Parliamentary Bill No. 1114/2002. Later on, however, the Government withdrew its previous Bill and resubmitted it on 5 November 2002. The new number of the second Bill was No. 1270/2002, which is the one that was finally passed by the Parliament (with several amendments).

[20] It should be mentioned that the recently adopted constitutional amendment to the Romanian Constitution of 1991 contains a solution that is similar to the above-mentioned Hungarian one. The relevant text reads as follows. Art. 145(1): 'Romania's accession to the constituent treaties of the European Union, with a view to transferring certain powers to Community institutions, as well as to *exercising the abilities in common with other Member States stipulated in such Treaties*, shall be carried out by means of a law adopted in the joint session of the Chamber of Deputies and the Senate, with a majority of two thirds of the number of deputies and senators.' Art. 145(2): 'As a result of the accession, the provisions of the constituent Treaties of the EU, as well as the other mandatory Community regulations *shall take precedence over the opposite provisions of the national laws*, in compliance with the provisions of the accession Acts.' Art. 145(3): 'The provisions of paragraphs (1) and (2) shall also apply accordingly for the accession to the Acts revising the constituent Treaties of the EU.' Art. 145(4): 'The Parliament, the President of Romania, the Government, and the judicial authority shall guarantee that the obligations resulting from the accession Acts and the provisions of paragraph (2) are implemented.' (Art. 77 of the amending Constitutional Law, which was approved by a nationwide referendum in Romania on 19 October 2003). It should be added, however, that even after these amendments it remains an unanswered question in Romania whether or not the Constitution of Romania has been made subject to the directly applicable EU *acquis*. This question is even more challenging if we take into account the following provisions of the Romanian Constitution. Art. 11(3): 'If a Treaty Romania is to become a party to comprises provisions contrary to the Constitution, *its ratification shall only take place after the revision of the Constitution*.' This is fine in theory, but what will happen if this obligatory constitutional revision fails in Romania for whatever reason? See also new Art. 1(5): 'In Romania, the observance of the Constitution, its supremacy and the laws *shall be mandatory*.' A similar solution can be found in the previously explored draft Lithuanian 'Europe clause' formula.

tional powers jointly[21] with other Member States to the extent necessary in order to fulfil the obligations and exercise the rights conferred by the founding Treaties of the European Union and the European Communities... This joint exercise can also be conducted independently through the institutions of the European Union.'[22] According to new Art. 2A(2): 'The ratification and promulgation of the agreement referred to in sub-section (1) shall be subject to a two-thirds majority vote of the Parliament.' It should be also mentioned as a special feature of the Hungarian experience that – to my knowledge – Hungary is so far the sixth new Member State (along with Slovakia, Estonia, Malta, Lithuania and Latvia) where the European Union has been specifically referred to in the so-called 'integration clause', and not just by the more general term 'international organisation (or institution)'. I personally think that the specific mention of the European Union in Article 2A should be welcomed.

It was generally believed in Hungary in 2002 that there was no model provision on how to build a bridge between the national legal order of an accession country and the developing legal order of the European Union. That is why Hungary followed its own path and why it is also believed that the 'integration clause' should be drawn up as flexibly and open-mindedly as possible. In many cases, as proved by the history of approach of the old Member States, legal accuracy (dogma) is not really helpful in this exercise.

Hungary still has to amend its Constitution at least once in the framework of a wider package of amending bills,[23] as there are other laws of constitutional significance currently in force that needed to be amended before accession (or now after accession), as well as new questions that need to be addressed in the context of Hungary's accession to the European Union (e.g. the implications of joining EMU, reform of the Act on law-making, etc.). In Hungary, the Parliament will be given very strong powers in the future formulation of EU-related integration policies at national level,[24] following the example of Austria, Denmark and Finland.

---

[21] The draft Bill (No. 1270/2002) still used still the term 'delegate' in relation to powers stemming from the Constitution, instead of the 'transfer' of certain State powers, because the drafters thought that using the term 'delegate' in the amended Constitution might suggest that the 'transfer of certain State powers' by Hungary was deemed to be made possible *temporarily* or, in other words, not with the ultimate purpose of making such constitutional action irreversible. The text that was finally adopted became 'jointly exercise certain constitutional powers with other Member States'.

[22] This solution is very close to the current French model. Art. 88(1): 'La République participe aux Communautés européennes et a l'Union européenne, constituées d'Etats qui ont choisi librement, en vertu des traités qui les ont instituées, d'exercer en commun certaines de leurs compétences.' Art. 88(2): 'Sous réserve de réciprocité et selon les modalités prévues par le Traité sur l'Union européenne signe le 7 février 1992, la France consent aux transferts de compétences nécessaires à l'établissement de l'Union économique et monétaire européenne.'

[23] The package of necessary amending bills has already been submitted to the Parliament. See Bill No. 4486 and the attached draft Bills currently under discussion in the Parliament.

[24] See Parliamentary Act No. LIII of 2004, which entered into force on 24 June 2004.

As mentioned earlier, an important issue in the constitutional adaptation process in Central and Eastern Europe is whether or not the constitution itself should be made subject to EU law. In Hungary, the biggest opposition party believes – and always stresses in Parliament – that EU accession-related constitutional amendments should exclude the supremacy of EU law over the Hungarian Constitution. This means that the Constitution itself should be literally interpreted this way.[25] Personally, I do not entirely share this approach from a scientific point of view.

In Hungary, many scholars believe that the EU accession process will not touch upon our sovereignty. This is because it is now generally believed in Hungary that sovereignty is indivisible – part of the statehood of Hungary and the independence of the country under public international law. It is also widely believed among experts that sovereignty is not transferable, neither partially nor in full. Hungarians therefore believe that after accession Hungary will remain a sovereign (independent) Member State of the European Union. This does not mean that, from an internal point of view, the exercise of certain constitutional powers arising from the Hungarian Constitution should (or will) not be restricted in such a way that, following accession, those powers can only be exercised jointly with other Member States with respect to Hungary within the framework of the EU institutions.

A special dimension of the constitutional adaptation process in Hungary is clearly related to the ongoing constitutionalisation process in the European Union, embodied in the new EU Constitution. In this context, an important issue will be how the European Charter of Fundamental Rights, which will become compulsory, should be approached by the new Member States and thus by Hungary. The 2002 constitutional amendment did not address this matter at all, not even in the context of Chapter XII on fundamental rights.

As is well known, a successful referendum on EU accession was held in Hungary on 12 April 2003. The participation rate was 46 per cent. The 'yes' vote attracted approximately 84 per cent of the vote, while the 'no' vote attracted approximately 16 per cent. Following the referendum, Parliament authorised the Government to sign the Acts of Accession in Athens on 16 April 2003 (see Parliamentary Resolution No. 37/2003 (IV.15)). The Act of Accession was recently ratified unanimously by the Hungarian Parliament (see Parliamentary Resolution No. 133/2003 (XII.17), published in Hungarian Official Gazette No. 143/2003).

Many experts in Hungary believe that, in the coming years, more emphasis should be placed on training judges (including the members of the Constitutional Court) in EU law, since – in my view also – their approach towards the EU

---

[25] Those who are in favour of this proposal argue that only two constitutions of the old Member States explicitly allow that the supremacy of EC law doctrine could also apply to the Constitution itself (Greece and Portugal). I do not believe that this would actually occur in practice.

constitutional *acquis* will really be the 'proof of the pudding' in terms of how the EU *acquis* and the general principles of EC law will be implemented in practice in Hungary after accession. It is beyond doubt that a lot remains to be done in this respect. In order for judges to be able to apply and interpret the EU *acquis* more smoothly and efficiently in practice, I think that a clear-cut and well-formulated 'Europe clause' at national constitutional level (as well as clear guidance for judges and civil servants for cases where national law will conflict with directly applicable EC legal norms) is essential and crucial if not for any other reason than for educational purposes and so that that the attitudes and habits of the sometimes old-fashioned and conservative judges[26] in Central and Eastern European countries in transition can become more accustomed to the living practice of the constantly evolving EU *acquis* in the years and decades to come. In my view, this requirement is more of a social, socio-political and psychological guarantee for the success of the eastward enlargement process than a legal or constitutional one.

Finally, with regard to the title of this paper, I believe that Hungary, by virtue of the 'Europe clause' that was finally adopted, can best pursue its national preferences in three key ways. First of all, it can rely on the clever phrase 'to the extent necessary' in Article 2A of the Constitution, which can only be interpreted (and thus imbued with practical meaning) by the Constitutional Court. This also means that the role of the Hungarian Constitutional Court will be extremely crucial after accession as far as the proper application and implementation of the EU *acquis* in Hungary is concerned.

The second technique for pursuing national preferences and defending the sovereignty of Hungary (as an EU Member State) if necessary and possible is that Hungary has chosen the so-called minimum approach to EU constitutional adaptation. This means that the 'Europe clause' is very short and flexible, as well as very 'selfish', meaning that it provides different means of possible interpretation after accession. One could even say that, although the adopted text is quite close to the French 'Europe clause', since in many aspects the Hungarian clause remains silent on important EU-related topics (e.g. with regard to the supremacy of EC law, etc.), it to a large extent resembles the former Italian experience regarding how to build a bridge between the national legal order and the EU legal order. This means that the role of the Hungarian Supreme Court (and all the ordinary courts) will also be very important after accession, especially in terms of how to fill the obvious constitutional gaps referred to above.

---

[26] Today, it goes without saying that during the Socialist/Communist period the judges had become accustomed to interpreting law according to the principle of *interpretatio legis grammatica*. In my view, the efficient application of the EU *acquis* requires the use of the principles of *interpretatio legis systematica* and *interpretatio legis teleologica*. We should bear in mind, however, that a majority of the judges in the new Member States in Central and Eastern Europe received their legal education under the old system.

The last way to defend national interests is related to the fact that the constitutional amendments of December 2002 in Hungary did not address the outstanding problem of Article 7(1) of the Hungarian Constitution, namely, concerning what action should be taken if there is a conflict between Hungarian law (including the Constitution) and any EC legal norm that has direct effect and direct applicability after accession. This question is really topical, since, according to the current Hungarian Constitution, all judges and courts are subject to the Hungarian Constitution and Hungarian law, and the courts and other State organs must respect the Constitution, which is binding on them (Arts. 50(3) and 77). In this respect, the constructive role and approach of the Hungarian judiciary will be highly significant after accession.

VI. CONCLUSIONS

With regard to the question posed in the title of this paper, namely, whether the rule of law is better than the rule of politics, I think that, in terms of the preceding comparative analysis of the constitutional preparation for EU accession, it is beyond doubt that the only possible legitimate answer is 'yes'. As I emphasised in the presentation of the Hungarian experience, even in more advanced new Member States, as for example in Hungary, it was necessary and unavoidable to address the so-called 'Europe clause' at constitutional level instead of simply leaving matters to the courts after accession, particularly in terms of building the required bridges between the two legal orders, namely, the legal order of the new Member States and the legal order of the European Union.

Finally, I would like to emphasise again that the European Union's eastward enlargement process goes on. This means that Alfred Kellermann should continue his work and continue to provide more and more insights into the joint (re)constitutionalisation process of the ever-enlarging European Union, both at EU level and at the level of the Member States – not only new ones! – and based on the successes we have achieved so far and the mistakes we have committed in the past in this great and challenging project. In one thing, however, I believe that Fred is not right, namely, concerning whether the Constitution for Europe, once ratified, could and/or would ever replace our national constitutions! If this ever happens, the rule of law could only prevail at EU level, and at national level the rule of politics would be the only rule, at least in the new Member States in Central and Eastern Europe, but maybe in some of the old ones as well!

IMPACT OF EU ACCESSION ON THE NATIONAL LEGAL ORDERS OF NEW MEMBER STATES: THE CASE OF CYPRUS

Nicholas Emiliou*

It is a distinct honour for the current author to have been invited to contribute to this *Liber Amicorum* for Fred Kellermann. Indeed, very few European lawyers may claim to have made such a significant contribution to European Union law as our dear friend Fred has done.

1.   NATIONAL CONSTITUTION

The foundation for the constitutional structure of the Republic of Cyprus,[1] which comprises the Constitution together with two Annexes (containing the Treaty of Guarantee and the Treaty of Alliance), was laid by the Zurich and London Agreements,[2] which were thought to provide the final settlement of the Cyprus problem. The Treaty of Guarantee[3] and the Treaty of Alliance[4] have been given

---

* Dr Nicholas Emiliou, Ambassador of the Republic of Cyprus, Permanent Representative of Cyprus to the European Union. The views expressed in this paper are personal and do not necessarily reflect the views of the Government of the Republic of Cyprus.

[1] The Republic of Cyprus was set up by means of the Treaty of Establishment between Cyprus, Britain, Greece and Turkey. The Treaty provides that the Republic 'shall comprise the island of Cyprus … with the exception of two areas defined in Annex A of this Treaty, which areas shall remain under the sovereignty of the United Kingdom.' This secured British military bases on the island.

[2] The Zurich and London Agreements of 11 and 19 February 1959, respectively, declared Cyprus an independent republic, whose independence, constitutional order and territorial integrity were guaranteed by the United Kingdom, Greece and Turkey.

[3] The Treaty of Guarantee between Cyprus, on the one hand, and Britain, Greece and Turkey, on the other, aimed at the protection of the constitutional order created by the Zurich and London Agreements and the exclusion of political or economic union of the island with any State. The three guarantor powers guaranteed the continued existence and maintenance of the constitutional order as well as the independence and territorial integrity of Cyprus. By means of Article IV, each of the three guarantor powers reserved 'the right to take any action with the sole aim of re-establishing the state of affairs established by the present Treaty', provided that 'common or concerted action may not prove possible'.

[4] The Treaty of Alliance was concluded between Cyprus, Greece and Turkey and provided that military contingents of each State should be stationed in the territory of the Republic. This had the purpose of securing the parties' responsibility to resist any attack or act of aggression directed against the independence or territorial integrity of Cyprus.

The European Union: An Ongoing Process of Integration – Liber Amicorum Alfred E. Kellermann
© 2004, T.M.C. Asser Instituut, The Hague, and the authors

constitutional force.[5] The Constitution of the Republic of Cyprus of 1960 is rigid, detailed and complex. The 1960 Constitution 'stands out as the centrepiece of an intricate network of international agreements and undertakings, delicately but inextricably interwoven with one another and with the Constitution itself...'.[6]

According to paragraph 21 of the Zurich Agreement, several of its provisions had to be included in the Constitution of the Republic of Cyprus as fundamental – basic articles, not subject to any revision or amendment. These basic articles, stipulated by the Constitution itself to be unalterable,[7] include all or parts of forty-eight separate articles out of a total of 199. On the other hand, according to Article 182(2) and (3) of the 1960 Constitution, any other provision of the Constitution (i.e. non-basic provisions) 'may be amended, whether by way of variation, addition or repeal' by a law passed by a majority vote comprising at least two-thirds of the total number of the Representatives belonging to the Greek community and at least two-thirds of the total number of the Representatives belonging to the Turkish community.

As a result of the deliberate withdrawal of the Turkish Cypriots and their refusal to participate in the state organs of the Republic since 1964, the Supreme Court of Cyprus, in its landmark judgment in *Attorney General of the Republic* v. *Ibrahim*,[8] adopted the doctrine of necessity. This doctrine has been further elaborated by case law as an integral part of the legal and constitutional order of the Republic, so much so, that it is possible to deviate temporarily from strict compliance with constitutional provisions. In other words, the doctrine has been applied in Cyprus to validate public acts facing procedural difficulties which it is impossible to remedy because of the political boycott by the Turkish Cypriot leadership and, later, foreign invasion. Thus, pending the solution of the political problem, any necessary constitutional amendments of non-basic constitutional provisions may be adopted by a law passed by a majority of at least two-thirds of Greek Cypriot members of the House of Representatives.[9]

Article 169 of the 1960 Constitution deals with the means of ratification of treaties, conventions and international agreements as well as their effect on internal law. The Constitution of Cyprus vests the power to ratify in different authorities of the Republic, depending on the subject matter of the treaty, convention or international agreement. Cyprus is a monist country. In the Republic of Cyprus, a treaty negotiated or signed under a decision of the Council

---

[5] Art. 181 of the 1960 Constitution.

[6] S.A. de Smith, *The New Commonwealth and its Constitutions* (London, Stevens 1964) p. 285.

[7] Art. 182(1) of the 1960 Constitution. A list of these basic articles of the Constitution is to be found in Annex III thereto.

[8] (1964) *CLR* 195.

[9] On this basis, there have been, since 1985, a number of amendments to non-basic provisions of the 1960 Constitution, such as Art. 111.

of Ministers and ratified by a law passed by the House of Representatives and published in the official Gazette of the Republic acquires superior force to any municipal law.[10] A ratifying law comes into operation on the date of its publication in the Gazette unless provided otherwise.[11] According to Article 169 of the Constitution, subject to the provisions of Article 50 and Article 57(3) of the Constitution,[12]

-   all international treaties and agreements relating to commercial matters, economic co-operation (including payments and credit) and *modus vivendi* are concluded under a decision of the Council of Ministers;
-   every other international treaty, convention or agreement, negotiated and signed under a decision of the Council of Ministers, is concluded and becomes operative when approved by a law made by the House of Representatives; and
-   every treaty, convention and agreement (concluded in accordance with the above provisions) is published in the Official Gazette of the Republic and on its application has superior force to any municipal law, on condition that such treaty, convention or agreement is applied by the other party thereto.[13]

The 1960 Constitution contains no provisions providing for the transfer of competences to international organisations nor does it allude to any similar concepts.

The Constitution, under the terms of Article 179(1), is the supreme law of the Republic and is therefore not within the ambit of the definition of 'municipal law' within the meaning of Article 169(3), which covers any ordinary law prior or consequent to an international treaty.[14] Thus, the hierarchy of norms in the Cypriot legal order is (a) the Constitution, (b) international treaties and (c) ordinary laws.[15] A treaty is therefore inferior to the Constitution and the latter prevails in case of any inconsistency between constitutional provisions and the provisions of the treaty.[16]

On the other hand, it is clear that Community law – which is based on treaties between the EC Member States – forms a distinct legal system which is capable

---

[10] See Art. 169(2) and (3) of the 1960 Constitution.

[11] See Art. 82 of the 1960 Constitution.

[12] Arts. 50 and 57(3) of the 1960 Constitution concern the right of veto of, respectively, the President and the Vice-President of the Republic.

[13] For a clear statement by the Supreme Court as to when such reciprocity is excluded, see the Supreme Court's judgment in *Malachtou* v. *Armefti* (1987) 1 *CLR* 207.

[14] For the definition of the term 'law', see Art. 186(1) of the 1960 Constitution. See also the Supreme Court's judgment in *Malachtou* v. *Armefti.*

[15] See, for example, *Eracleous* v. *The Municipality of Limassol* (Appeal No. 5793), judgment of the Supreme Court of 14 December 1993, which recalled the above hierarchy.

[16] See *Malachtou* v. *Armefti.*

of creating directly effective rights for those subject to it. These Community rights are not only independent of national laws but are also to be regarded as superior to them. The acceptance by national courts of the supremacy of Community law is a prerequisite for its full reception into national law.

In the Cypriot constitutional order, executive power is ensured by the President (and the Vice-President) of the Republic (Art. 46(1) of the 1960 Constitution) and it is exercised by the Council of Ministers (Art. 54(1) of the 1960 Constitution). The legislative power of the Republic is exercised by the House of Representatives 'in all matters' except those expressly reserved to the Communal Chambers under the Constitution (Art. 61 of the 1960 Constitution).[17] The Supreme Court exercises all the judicial power of the Republic, including constitutional matters, such as the constitutionality of laws, conflicts of competence between the organs of the Republic and electoral petitions.[18]

Under Article 179(1), the Constitution is the supreme law of the Republic. On the other hand, Community law by its own terms is supreme and takes precedence over all national law, including national constitutions. It should be noted, however, that Article 179 is not a basic provision of the Constitution and can therefore be amended under the procedure provided for by Article 182.

Moreover, membership of the European Union involves a partial loss or transfer of the exercise of sovereign powers in favour of the Union. This, *prima facie*, appears to sit uneasily with Article 61 of the 1960 Constitution, which provides that the House of Representatives exercises the legislative power of the Republic 'in all matters'. Article 61 is a basic article and is therefore unamendable.

A way of overcoming the above-mentioned difficulties would be to amend Article 169 of the 1960 Constitution (a non-basic provision), in accordance with the procedure prescribed in Article 182, by adding specific paragraphs reflecting, *mutatis mutandis*, the contents of Articles 29(4)(3), 29(4)(4), 29(4)(5) and 29(7) of the Irish Constitution.[19] The adoption of such an amendment would cover the

---

[17] The Communal Chambers were designed to serve as legislative, executive and economic authorities in religious, educational, teaching and cultural affairs of the two Cypriot communities, as well as issues of personal status. See Arts. 86-111 of the 1960 Constitution.

[18] See Arts. 133-164 of the 1960 Constitution. The jurisdiction of the Supreme Court is derived from Arts. 136 and 152 of the Constitution. See also Law 33/64.

[19] Art. 29 of the Irish Constitution provides, *inter alia*, as follows. Art. 29(4)(3): 'The State may become a member of the European Coal and Steel Community (established by Treaty signed at Paris on the 18th day of April, 1951), the European Economic Community (established by Treaty signed at Rome on the 25th day of March, 1957) and the European Atomic Energy Community (established by Treaty signed at Rome on the 25th day of March, 1957). The State may ratify the Single European Act (signed on behalf of the Member States of the Communities at Luxembourg on the 17th day of February 1986 and at The Hague on the 28th day of February 1986).' Art. 29(4)(4): 'The State may ratify the Treaty on European Union signed at Maastricht on the 7th day of February 1992 and may become a member of that Union.' Art. 29(4)(5): 'The State may ratify the Treaty of Amsterdam amending the Treaty on European Union, the Treaties establishing the European Communities and

actual accession of the Republic to the Union as well as the transfer of the exercise of national executive, legislative, judicial and treaty-making powers to the EU institutions, thus pre-empting the potential problems posed by Articles 54(1), 61(1), 136, 152 and 169 of the 1960 Constitution.

Moreover, for reasons of clarity and legal certainty, Article 179(1) of the Constitution (also a non-basic provision) could be amended as follows: '*Subject to the provisions of Article 169* [t]his Constitution shall be the supreme law of the Republic.' Such an amendment would ensure that constitutional provisions do not affect the Treaty of Accession and Community law in any way and would safeguard their supremacy over the Constitution.

Any amendments to the 1960 Constitution necessitated by the accession of the Republic to the European Union will be enacted by the House of Representatives under Article 182(2) and (3) of the Constitution. The 1960 Constitution contains no provision concerning the possibility of holding a referendum, even though there is nothing in the Constitution precluding this possibility.

The House of Representatives ratified the Treaty of Accession on 14 July 2003,[20] on the basis of Article 169 of the Constitution, following an opinion by the Attorney General to the effect that no amendment of the Constitution was necessary prior to the ratification of the Treaty.

2.   ROLE OF THE JUDICIARY

According to the Supreme Court's case law,[21] an international treaty, being inferior to the Constitution by virtue of Article 179(1), is subject to judicial review in the sense that the constitutional provisions prevail in case of any inconsistency between them and the provisions of the treaty. A treaty does not, *stricto sensu*, repeal municipal law but only has superior force to it, taking precedence in its application. Such a treaty retains its nature as part of international law. However, having regard to its nature and its connection with the international obligations of the Republic, it cannot be amended or repealed by any posterior law contrary to its provisions or the provisions of the Vienna Convention on the Law of Treaties.[22] According to the

---

certain related Acts signed at Amsterdam on the 2nd day of October, 1997.' Art. 29(7): 'No provision of this Constitution invalidates laws enacted, acts done or measures adopted by the State which are necessitated by the obligations of membership of the European Union or of the Communities, or prevents laws enacted, acts done, or measures adopted by the European Union or by the Communities or by institutions thereof, or by bodies competent under the Treaties establishing the Communities, from having the force of law in the State.'

[20] See Ratifying Law N35(III)2003, published in the *Official Gazette* No. 3740 of 25 July 2003.

[21] See *Malachtou* v. *Armefti*.

[22] The Vienna Convention on the Law of Treaties was ratified under Art. 169 of the 1960 Constitution by Law 62/76.

Supreme Court, a ratified treaty delineates not only the international obligations of the State, as defined therein, but also the internal law until the day that, under its own provisions or in accordance with the Vienna Convention on Treaties, it ceases to be operative.

Article 169 of the 1960 Constitution does not apply only to treaties affecting rights and obligations of the State but also covers all treaties, conventions and agreements ratified and concluded in conformity with paragraph 2 thereof, provided that all other requirements are satisfied.[23]

According to the Supreme Court case law, the requirement of reciprocity under Article 169(3) is waived in the case of:

> 'treaties whose nature, objective and function in the international relations and the international legal order exclude the condition of reciprocity. Such are multilateral conventions the object of which is not to create any subjective or reciprocal rights for the contracting parties themselves but their objective and their intent is to promote certain principles of law, moral and legal values and which a contracting party signs and ratifies only for the realisation of this objective. Examples are: Conventions for the protection of human rights and the improvements and formulation of common rules and the achievement of social justice.
>
> ...
>
> Where there is any international mechanism of control or supervision, the condition of reciprocity again cannot validly be raised.'[24]

Self-executing treaties are directly applicable:

> 'We agree ... that for a treaty to be applicable it must be self-executing... We need not in this case attempt to give a general definition of the term "self-executing treaty". Pious declarations and provisions relating to political and international relations in a convention are not self-executing provisions. Only such provisions of a Convention are self-executing which may be applied by the organs of the State and which can be enforced by the Courts and which create rights for the individuals; they govern or affect directly relations of the internal life between the individuals, and the individuals and the State or the public authorities. Provisions which do not create by themselves rights or obligations of persons or interests and which cannot be justiciable or do not refer to acts or omissions of State organs are not self-executing. International law is primarily a law between States and

---

[23] See *Malachtou* v. *Armefti*.

[24] Ibid. See also *Shipowners Union* v. *The Registrar of Trademarks & Others* (1988) 3 *CLR* 457.

normally treaties have effect upon States only. As it has been pointed out by the Permanent Court of International Justice (Series B. No. 15), this rule can be altered by the express or implied terms of the treaty, in which case its provisions become self-executing. If treaties contain provisions with regard to rights and duties of the subjects or the contracting States, their courts, officials, and the like, these States must take such steps as are necessary, according to their Municipal Law, to make these provisions binding upon their subjects, courts, officials and the like (Oppenheim's *International Law*).[25]

The question whether or not treaties are self-executing is influenced by the wording of the convention, its provisions and the relevant constitutional law in a given country ...'.[26]

In the same case, Pikis, J. observed:

'Ratification by the legislature incorporates the treaty or convention, as the case may be, into domestic law by virtue of the legislative power vested in the House of Representatives (Article 61 of the Constitution); and if its provisions are self-executing they acquire the force of law quite independently of paragraph 3 of Article 169 (of the Constitution) or its impact on domestic legislation. The point is exemplified by the decisions of the Supreme Court in *Mizrahi* v. *The Republic*[27] and *Kannas* v. *The Police*[28] in which the Court referred to the European Convention on Human Rights ratified by Law 39/62 as an integral part of our domestic legislation without at all inquiring into the question of reciprocity. A provision of a treaty or convention is self-executing if the rights vested or the obligations imposed thereby are comprehensively defined to the extent of making them, without further addition or modification, enforceable before a court of law...'.[29]

In respect of the question whether the courts in Cyprus recognise a rule of interpretation whereby national law must be interpreted in conformity with international obligations, there are indications, in the case law of the Supreme Court, that such a rule has been adopted, at least as far as treaties whose 'intent is the promotion of values and the protection of human rights' are concerned.

In its judgment in the *Shipowners Union* v. *The Registrar of Trademarks & Others* case,[30] the Supreme Court stated (per Stylianides J.):

[25] L. Oppenheim, *International Law*, Vol. 1: Peace, 8th edn. (London, Longmans 1955) p. 924.
[26] Per Stylianides J. in *Malachtou* v. *Armefti*.
[27] (1968) 3 *CLR* 404.
[28] (1968) 2 *CLR* 35.
[29] See *Malachtou* v. *Armefti* at 234-236.
[30] (1988) 3 *CLR* 457.

'The aforesaid international instruments[31] are not only relevant, but should serve as a guide to the interpretation of our constitutional provisions...

Before concluding I would like to stress that it is the duty, not only of the Courts, but all authorities of the Republic, including executive, administrative and legislative, to secure within the limits of their respective competence the efficient application, both of the Part II of the Constitution – Fundamental Rights and Liberties – and the ratified International Conventions for the enjoyment of the rights and freedoms declared and safeguarded thereby...'.

Accession to the European Union is not expected to have a significant impact on the structure, rules of procedure, practice and workload of the courts of the Republic, at least in the short or medium term.

3.   ROLE OF THE NATIONAL PARLIAMENT

The task of harmonising national legislation with the *acquis communautaire* has been successfully completed by the House of Representatives. This task was facilitated by the setting up of a special parliamentary fast-track system together with the establishment of a special Committee for European Affairs. This Committee examines all legislative instruments that are required for the approximation of national legislation to the *acquis*. All bills that were submitted to the House of Representatives in the context of the harmonisation process were examined directly by this Parliamentary Committee, irrespective of the specific topic they sought to regulate. Following the examination of those bills by the Committee, they were submitted to the plenary for adoption. The House made extensive use of this procedure and adopted the majority of *acquis*-related legislation in this way.

The possibility to approve framework laws by the House and allow for technical dispositions to be adopted through administrative regulations by Ministries (notably in the field of internal market legislation) also contributed positively to the harmonisation process.

The House of Representatives supervises the executive's ability to implement the various harmonisation bills once they have been enacted.

The extent to which the House will be able to exercise control over decisions taken by Ministers in the Council of the European Union is rather limited. This is

---

[31] Author's note: For example, the European Convention on Human Rights, ILO Convention No. 87 concerning Freedom of Association and Protection of the Right to Organise, and the UN Covenant on Civil and Political Rights.

due to the fact that the Republic Cyprus is organised on the basis of a presidential system of government[32] based on the doctrine of the separation of powers, which is applied in a rather more vigorous manner than elsewhere in the European Union, where the majority of Member States are parliamentary democracies. Thus, in Cyprus, the Government is independent of the confidence of the House of Representatives.

4.   TREATY ESTABLISHING A CONSTITUTION FOR EUROPE

The adoption of the Treaty Establishing a Constitution for Europe by the Heads of State and Government last June forms a landmark in the process of advancing European integration. The eventual enactment of this constitutional text will strengthen the Community legal order, *inter alia*, in the following ways:

a. the Constitution as currently envisaged will substitute the multitude of existing constitutional texts for a single text thus promoting clarity and legal certainty;
b. the existing complicated pillar structure will disappear, but intergovernmentalism will be preserved where this is deemed necessary;
c. the European Union will acquire legal personality, while the European Community will cease to exist as a separate legal entity and will be totally absorbed into the European Union;
d. the Charter of Fundamental Rights will be integrated into the Constitution and will acquire legal value and status;
e. there will be a clear legal basis for the accession of the European Union to the European Convention on Human Rights;
f. there will be a clearer division of Union and national competences;
g. the Union's instruments of action will be simplified;
h. the decision-making procedures will also be simplified;
i. qualified majority voting, as modified, will be extended; and
j. a right of legislative initiative by citizens will be introduced.

There are no obstacles in the Cypriot legal order to the ratification of the European Constitution. Most probably, the European Constitution will be ratified by the Republic of Cyprus through action by the House of Representatives.

---

[32] Art. 1 of the 1960 Constitution.

THE CZECH HUMAN RIGHTS DOCTRINE AS CHALLENGED BY THE EU CHARTER OF FUNDAMENTAL RIGHTS

Jiri Zemanek[*]

1.   SCOPE OF APPLICATION OF THE EU CHARTER

The European Union is founded on the value of respect for human rights,[1] as guaranteed by the European Convention for the Protection of Human Rights and Fundamental Freedoms and as they result from the constitutional traditions common to the Member States and constitute general principles of the Union's law.[2] The Union shall contribute to protection of human rights in its relations with the wider world.[3] The meaning and scope of the rights contained in the Charter of Fundamental Rights of the Union (hereinafter, 'the Charter') as part of the European Constitution shall be the same as those laid down by the European Convention and shall be interpreted in harmony with those traditions.[4] A number of the Charter's rights are recognised in accordance with the national laws and practices governing their exercise, which shall be taken full account of.[5] The interpretation of the Charter cannot restrict or adversely affect the level of protection of human rights.[6] In addition, these rights are to be ensured – with due regard for the principle of subsidiarity – not only by the institutions, bodies and agencies of the Union, but also by the Member States when they are implementing Union law.[7]

The Charter is based on mutual tolerance rather than on a rivalry between the levels of protection. The definition of the scope of application of the Charter reflects complementarity of European, international and national standards of protection. The presumed priority of the European standard would be superseded

---

[*] Jean Monnet Professor of European law at the Charles University in Prague; Member of the European Constitutional Law Network; President of the Czech Branch of the ILA; Member of the Council for Legislation of the Czech Government.

[1] Draft Treaty establishing a Constitution for Europe, CONV 850/03, Art. I-2.

[2] Ibid., Art. I-7(3).

[3] Ibid., Art. I-3 (4).

[4] Ibid., Art. II-52(3) and (4).

[5] Ibid., Art. II-52(6).

[6] Ibid., Art. II-53.

[7] Ibid., Art. II-51(1).

The European Union: An Ongoing Process of Integration – Liber Amicorum Alfred E. Kellermann
© 2004, T.M.C. Asser Instituut, The Hague, and the authors

if – in a concrete case – the international or national standard is more favourable for the individual than the European one. The Charter will be applied only in a subsidiary way, as the European Convention or the national constitutional charter will be recognised as a standard allowing better protection. It is a demanding task, which will challenge the current practice of national authorities, in particular, taking into account the direct effect of the Union's fundamental rights. Can national courts in the new Member States be expected to manage this task? Will they follow the Union's human rights doctrine or tend to be overruled by the Court of Justice's case law?

Fred Kellermann was always worried about these questions and devoted much of his efforts to enhancing awareness of European constitutional issues among judges, practicing lawyers and academics in the new (or at that time future) Member States through workshops, seminars and personal meetings.[8] His contributions in this regard are greatly appreciated in these countries.

2.   THE CZECH JUDICIARY AND FUNDAMENTAL RIGHTS

The direct effect of constitutional rights is a recent phenomenon in the history of the Czech Republic. The modern catalogue of fundamental rights was incorporated into the Czech constitutional order in 1991.[9] It was initially implemented by the Czech Constitutional Court and has only been implemented by the ordinary courts – under the influence of the former's case law – since 1993. Czech practice concerning the direct effect of human rights has lacked experience and doctrinal support for many reasons.

There was no a workable cultural tradition of direct effect in the Constitution, not even in the times of pre-World War II, democratic Czechoslovakia. Instead, the dominant doctrinal opinion shared the established German approach, advocating the position of citizen's rights as a mere 'monologue of the constitution-maker', i.e. without any binding force for courts and public administration.[10] The subsequent Nazi and Communist regimes totally destroyed any sense of relevance regarding the codification of human rights. As a result, generations of lawyers missed out on contemporary developments in the field of democratic human rights thinking. For decades, a gap existed in the approach to modern legal reasoning by means of basic principles and analogy and to the role of judges in

---

[8] For example, the seminars organised by the Czech Supreme Court in Brno in 2001 and by the National Council of Slovakia in Casta-Papiernicka in 2002.

[9] The Charter of Fundamental Rights and Freedoms, Act No. 23/1991 Coll., reinforced – under the terms of succession after the dissolution of Czechoslovakia – by Act No. 2/1993 Coll. (hereinafter, the 'Czech Charter').

[10] F. Weyr, *Ceskoslovenske ustavni pravo* [Czechoslovak Constitutional Law] (Prague 1937) p. 248.

lawmaking, the principal essays of Karl Larenz and Ronald Dworkin were not debated in universities and academic fora, and so forth.

In practice, the heritage of those deficits has resulted in the assimilation of the Czech Charter into statutes. The early traditional *Begriffsjurisprudenz* – expressed as the identification of law with justice and judicial decisions with a simple 'reproduction' of the law, accompanied by the transfer of judge's responsibility for those decisions to the law-maker (legislature) – still has its followers. This reliance on the *a priori* rationalism of legislative measures ensues, rather than from a mistrust of judges associated with the 'old regime' that remain in office, from the momentum ('path dependency') of a certain 'alibistic' behaviour that was used in the past and still feels comfortable at present. First of all, such a simplified *cognitive* approach narrows the scope of fundamental rights to the extent that they are 'covered' by statutory provisions. Second, it establishes a parallelism between the two, limiting the consequences of breaches of law, which in turn degrades the protection of fundamental rights as guaranteed by the Czech Charter and causes the Constitutional Court to become overloaded.[11]

The existing conflict between the prohibition of *denegatio justitiae* and the fragmented law's lack of wholeness is not regularly settled by means of a *decision-centred* approach (*Interessenjurisprudenz*), which emphasises creative judicial activity. The Czech Constitutional Court has fluctuated between both approaches. When engaged in constitutional review, the Constitutional Court has often limited itself to an examination of constitutional procedural rights (fair trial) and avoided the substantive law test, on the basis that it does not wish to interfere, by means of cassation decisions, with the competences of other State authorities beyond the scope of necessity (principle of subsidiarity).[12] The Court has tended to pronounce the infringement of fundamental rights by wilful violation of the law or in the case of an extreme breach of the principles of justice ('affected formalistic approach').[13] On the other hand, when the case at issue largely exceeds the scope of plaintiff's own interests, the Court has considered the general impact of the judgement on fundamental rights.[14]

The answer to the dilemma between the cognitive and decision-centred approaches of the Constitutional Court to the protection of fundamental rights as granted by the Czech Charter may be derived from the following points of departure:[15] (a) this protection cannot be ensured only by the Constitutional Court, but must be guaranteed, first, by ordinary courts of law and public administration

---

[11] P. Holländer, *Ústavněprávní argumentace. Ohlédnutí po deseti letech Ústavního soudu* [Constitutional Law Argumentation. Review of Ten Years of the Constitutional Court] (Prague 2003) p. 64.

[12] No. III. ÚS 148/97 Coll. CC.

[13] No. III. ÚS 224/98 Coll. CC.

[14] No. Pl. ÚS 15/96 Coll. CC.

[15] P. Holländer, op. cit. n. 11, at pp. 71-72.

bodies; (b) the system of legal remedies should be adjusted to the minimalisation rather than the total elimination of wrongful or mistaken decisions, which seems to be impossible – it should result from a balancing of efforts focusing on the rule of law and effective decision making, respecting the principle of legal certainty;[16] (c) the constitutional judiciary can correct only the most grave, extreme violations; (d) a specialised review, concentrated exclusively at the Constitutional Court, is only justified – as the post-World War II and recent Central European experiences show – under specific historical circumstances, when unprepared ordinary courts were suddenly challenged by new tasks connected with the transition from an authoritative regime to a democratic one (e.g. Germany in 1949, Spain in 1976 and the post-Communist countries after 1989); and (e) the automatic conclusion of the violation of a constitutional right due to a violation of statutory law is not acceptable, although it may result – as an exception – from a massive erroneous practice on the part of ordinary courts (like the case law on restitution of property in the 1990s) or when the practice is in need of a new (consistent) approach to the interpretation of law.

In the ten years of its existence, the Czech Constitutional Court has not developed an unambiguous doctrine of human rights, simply because the demands of transition have determined its activities. Nevertheless, some time after the accession of the Czech Republic to the European Union, more transparency and reliability of its case law would be desirable.

3.   THE RESTRAINED APPROACH OF ORDINARY COURTS TO JUDGEMENTS OF THE CONSTITUTIONAL COURT

Another phenomenon, distinctive of the 'new democracies' of the late 1990s, is the striking difference between the mostly positive reception of the Constitutional Court's judgements on human rights by the public and the aversion against their binding force displayed by ordinary courts (for example, the Czech Supreme Court). This criticism was formulated in statements according to which the Constitutional Court, which was allegedly located outside the judicial system, has no jurisdiction to interfere directly in the adjudicative domain reserved for ordinary courts, which cannot – for purposes of constitutional complaints[17] – be counted among 'public authorities'. However, the Constitutional Court has rejected such

---

[16] No. Pl. ÚS 15/01 Coll. CC.

[17] Article 87(1)(d) of the Czech Constitution (Act No. 1/1993 Coll.): '[The Constitutional Court has jurisdiction] over constitutional complaints against final decisions or other actions by public authorities infringing constitutionally guaranteed fundamental rights and basic freedoms', to be read in conjunction with section 72(1) of the Act on the Constitutional Court (Act No. 182/1993 Coll.).

objections, finding them to be motivated by reasons of prestige rather than by sound constitutional arguments.[18]

'Enforceable decisions of the Constitutional Court are binding on all authorities and persons.'[19] Interpretations of this provision differ. The judgements of the Constitutional Court on the *annulment* of laws incompatible with the constitutional order[20] are regarded by ordinary courts, partly supported by legal doctrine, as not binding in their entirety, but only in their sentences, whereas the justification (legal reasoning of the Constitutional Court) could be convincing only on the basis of the actual opinion and its intellectual merits. If the compatibility of a legal provision with the Constitution can be proved by means of a consistent (Constitution-friendly) interpretation, there will be no grounds for its annulment.[21] Relying on such an interpretation tempts the ordinary courts to ignore the Constitutional Court's conclusions as a relevant source of law.[22] In order to assert its opinion, the Constitutional Court might have to resign itself to the self-restraint approach (constitutionality through interpretation) and annul the incompatible law. It seems that the relationship between the Czech Constitutional Court and the ordinary courts needs to be cultivated through correct mutual communication.[23]

The judgements of the Constitutional Court on constitutional complaints against the final decisions of ordinary courts that infringe constitutionally guaranteed fundamental rights and basic freedoms have a *cassation* nature (annulment of the final decision).[24] As the binding force of the reasoning of these judgements is not expressly declared, the ordinary courts sometimes[25] feel free to reopen the proceedings. If this could lead to a breach of the Czech Charter (Article 36: *denegatio justitiae*), the ordinary court should be bound by the legal opinion of the Constitutional Court, at least on a subsidiary basis, in accordance with the Code on Civil Procedure.[26] Stimulated by some scholars, the ordinary courts also reject the *precedential* nature of the Constitutional Court's judgements.[27] They argue that only the sentence (not the justification) of the judgement is enforceable and that its relevance is therefore limited to the individual case, that the Constitutional Court lacks any control (i.e. is not responsible to anyone) and

---

[18] No. I. ÚS 131/93 Coll. CC.

[19] Article 89(2) of the Czech Constitution.

[20] Article 87(1)(a) of the Czech Constitution.

[21] No. Pl. ÚS 48/95 Coll. CC.

[22] For example, the judgement of the High Court in Prague, No. 2 To 77/97.

[23] P. Holländer, op. cit. n. 11, at p. 77.

[24] Section 82(3) of the Act on the Constitutional Court.

[25] For example, the judgement of the Regional Court in Brno, No. 16 Co 160/95.

[26] Section 226 of Act No. 99/1963 Coll., via the reference in section 63 of the Act on the Constitutional Court.

[27] For example, the judgement of the Regional Court in Ostrava, No. 22 Ca 262/97.

that case law of the Constitutional Court could jeopardise the independence of the ordinary courts, 'bound only by laws and international treaties, being a part of the legal order'.[28]

Such a restrictive approach to the binding force of the judgements of the Czech Constitutional Court is the expression of an affected formalism on the part of the ordinary courts. It compels the Constitutional Court to repeated justification in similar cases (causing it to become overloaded). Otherwise, the lack of a basis for the unification of the case law of the ordinary courts would threaten the constitutional principle of equality – the right of all persons to be treated the same way under the same circumstances, i.e. without any casual arbitrariness. The law and its authoritative interpretation should be accepted in all its complexity and should be binding on the ordinary courts as a whole. The case law of the Constitutional Court, which is able to reflect the dynamism of social developments in a far more flexible and adequate way than the time-consuming ordinary courts, should therefore be an additional (material) source of law. The process of appointment of the judges of the Constitutional Court – which requires the prior consent of the Senate of the Czech Parliament – and the possible controlling power of the European Court of Human Rights should be sufficient guarantees of the legality of the case law of the Constitutional Court.

4. ANY REASONS FOR DOUBTS?

Since 1 May 2004, Czech judges have started to become familiar with the protection of human rights under EU law. They still have to familiarise themselves with the preliminary ruling system under Article 234 EC and Article 35 EU, in order to clarify the compatibility of national law provisions with provisions of EU law. After the eventual entry into force of the Treaty establishing a Constitution for Europe, they will have to be experienced in the consistent interpretation and application of EU law. The interpretation and application of the EU Charter of Fundamental Rights in the Czech Republic, which is limited to cases concerning the implementation of EU law,[29] should therefore not present a dramatic problem. However, the Czech courts must also accept and practice the direct effect of the Czech Charter and the relevant case law of the Constitutional Court within the Czech Republic's domestic legal order.

---

[28] Article 95(1) of the Czech Constitution.
[29] Article II-51(1) of the draft Treaty establishing a Constitution for Europe.

EUROPEAN INTEGRATION AND RUSSIA

Yury Matveevsky*

The history of Western Europe after World War II is inextricably related to, and in many respects can be explained by, the development of integration processes in this region. Despite the fact that integration has proved to have a global character – integration processes also take place on other continents – it is Western Europe (where the necessary preconditions were most ripe) that has succeeded in achieving significant results in integration building, embodied in such a 'unique, multilevel, multinational political system' as the European Union.[1]

The European Union is a quasi-governmental structure that represents a complex synergy of the elements of a State and the elements of an international intergovernmental organisation.

The people of Western Europe have followed a hard path on their way to integration – from the creation of regional specialised organisations of a mainly economic character, which gradually expanded their fields of activity, to the establishment of a state-like Union with very wide competences in different areas of public activity. This Union is constantly changing and looking for new institutional mechanisms. Due to integration and unification, Western European countries have succeeded in making an impressive transition from a period of decline, with the two World Wars as its most important landmarks, to a period of gradual rebirth. All this allows us to describe Western European integration as 'the greatest achievement' of the countries of the region in the second half of the twentieth century.[2]

In any case, it is largely due to integration processes that Western Europe managed to turn gradually into a stable zone of peace and prosperity. It achieved a certain dynamic in its internal development and, moreover, became a centre of gravity – 'an attractive integrator' – for neighbouring countries. Though Western European States could not regain the positions of global dominance that they had been loosing during the first half of the twentieth century, the members of the

---

* Professor, Institute of European Law, Moscow State Institute of International Relations (MGIMO University).
[1] A. Moravscik, *The Choice for Europe: Social Purpose and State Power from Messina to Maastricht* (Ithaca, N.Y., Cornell University Press 1998) p. 1.
[2] Y.A. Borko, *From European Idea – to United Europe* (Moscow, Delovaya Literatura 2003) p. 14.

The European Union: An Ongoing Process of Integration – Liber Amicorum Alfred E. Kellermann
© *2004, T.M.C. Asser Instituut, The Hague, and the authors*

European Union have a good chance of turning their organisation into a global centre of economic as well as political influence. Due to the principles and methods that laid the ground for the European Communities and the European Union, this influence can be quite constructive and beneficial for the whole international community.

A large number of material and ideological factors explain the fact that Western Europe launched an integration process. Among others things, mention should be made of the creation of a new system, or even a new model, for governing social relations in most countries in the region. This model is charac- terised by pluralistic democracy, the supremacy of law and a well-developed, socially-oriented market economy.

The new political culture of social relations inside Nation States, formed on the basis of the development of a European civilisation, has helped to lower tensions between different classes in society and to realise social closeness and partnership in order to achieve national goals.

Step by step, this approach was also implemented in international relations, as different States were opting for solidarity for the purpose of achieving common goals by means of dialogue, the creation of institutional mechanisms to overcome conflicts and the rapprochement of positions. All these activities were carried out in full compliance with the law. This model for governing social relations was also implemented in the European Communities and later in the European Union.

The principles and methods associated with the model are highly desirable and should enjoy wider usage in modern international relations now that the interna- tional community has entered a phase of fundamental change. The development of globalisation and integration processes has not only led to a new political and economic configuration of the world economy, but at the same time has resulted in changes in the very basis of the global political structure.

In this situation, when it is absolutely necessary to rally and unify the efforts of the whole international community, the one-sided, arbitrary actions of the one remaining superpower – the United States, which in following its national goals quite often ignores the interests of other countries, including its allies – are particularly dangerous.

In its turn, in order not to stay behind in relation to global developments, Russia should become more actively and purposefully involved in the processes of globalisation and integration. However, in its current condition, the country is experiencing certain difficulties in this regard.

After the collapse of the former Soviet Union, Russia has experienced rampant capitalism of a criminal and oligarchic nature. Despite the goals it has set itself, Russia has not managed to establish a civil society and has not yet consolidated itself as a firm democratic, legal and social State.

The current nature of Russia's participation in the international division of labour and international commercial and economic relations obviously does not fit in with the modern character of these activities. Russia's share in the global turnover of goods is disproportionately low, and the country serves mainly as an exporter of raw materials. Its status as a large international debtor, which for many years could not control the outflow of its national capital, seriously undermines Russia's position. Moreover, Russia cannot make use of the advantages of participation in regional integration.

Taking all these factors into consideration, it may be said that Russia should first of all put its internal affairs in order. The reasons for most of its problems in relation to the global economy lie within its own borders and should be solved by means of internal economic policy. This policy should be clearly targeted at the structural reorganisation of Russia's economy, in order to increase the competitiveness and diversity of its products and reduce the share of raw materials in total exports. Naturally, the process of 'establishing order' in all fields of Russian life should proceed within the framework of the establishment of a democratic, legal State with a socially-oriented economy, that is to say, the socio-political system that exists in a majority of European countries and has been adopted as an example, at least at a declarative level, by Russia's leaders.

All these complicated yet vital tasks can only be carried out by Russia in the context of close and efficient international cooperation. This should take place first of all on the European continent, because Russia has profound historical, spiritual and cultural ties with the countries in question, not to mention the fact that the members of the European Union are Russia's main trade and economic partners (now that the European Union has ten new members, over 50 per cent of Russia's external commercial turnover is connected to the countries of the Union). As for the direct connection of Russia to the European integration process, which is inseparably linked to pan-European cooperation, one should probably distinguish – but not sharply – between two directions: the European Union and the CIS.

The Russian Government justly declares that both directions are a priority in its external policy. However, a considered and consistent line of conduct towards the members of both the European Union and the CIS should constantly support these declarations. Unfortunately, this is not always the case.

There are many reasons why Russia is not in a position to join the European Union, at least for foreseeable future. Russia is too large and problematic. Joining the European Union would also limit Russia's own freedom of action. Apart from that, the European Union is currently at a crossroads. It not only faces the challenge of a significant expansion, but also the adaptation of the new members to the Community's way of doing things. In fact, there are no guarantees that the current expansion will not hamper further integration and weaken the combined power of the Union for some time.

For the next couple of years, the European Union will focus above all on internal problems and will not be able to devote enough attention to its neighbours. An internal document prepared by the European Commission in March 2003 confirms this position to a certain extent.[3] In the current situation, it would therefore be more reasonable for Russia to be more active and consistent in its policy towards achieving a strategic partnership with the European Union, to develop and strengthen contacts with the European Union in those fields where it has real competence and to take concrete, practical steps on the way to a purposeful but careful approximation of Russian law to EU law. Joining the common European economic and social spaces – probably together with other CIS countries but not necessarily with all of them – should be a strategic but nevertheless distant goal for Russia.

At the 12th Russia-EU Summit, which took place on 6 November 2003 in Rome, the parties agreed to consolidate a strategic partnership based on common values, in order to increase stability, security and prosperity on the European continent. At the same time, they reaffirmed their 'shared vision of a united European continent'. The Joint Statement of the Summit once again speaks about the mutual obligation of the parties to contribute to further rapprochement and the gradual integration of the social and economic structures of Russia and the enlarging European Union. In this regard, the parties agreed to intensify and focus their efforts to fulfil the decision to create various common spaces between the European Union and Russia, building on the Partnership and Cooperation Agreement between the Russian Federation and the European Union and the Joint Statement of the St. Petersburg Summit.

Four common spaces between Russia and the European Union are planned:

- a Common European Economic Space;
- a Common Space of Freedom, Security and Justice;
- a Common Space of External Security; and
- a Common Space of Research and Education, including Cultural Aspects.

Common spaces may thus be regarded as important instruments for involving Russia in European integration and, in the long term, even as the building blocks for creating a 'Big Europe' in the future.

To a certain extent, these interconnected common spaces are comparable to the three pillars of the European Union. A special document dedicated to each common space – an agreement or a declaration – was signed in Rome. At the same time, the

---

[3] Communication from the Commission to the Council and the European Parliament, 'Wider Europe – Neighbourhood: A New Framework for Relations with our Eastern and Southern Neighbours', COM (2003) 104 final, 11 March 2003.

agreements adopted in Rome show that the parties are at the very beginning of the path to create common spaces.

So far, a joint concept paper has been worked out only for the first space, that is, the Common European Economic Space (CEES). Even then, if we look at it more thoroughly, this concept paper only covers the first stage of creating the CEES. The CEES itself is described as 'an open and integrated market between the EU and Russia, based on the implementation of common or compatible rules and regulations, including compatible administrative practices, as a basis for synergies and economies of scale associated with a higher degree of competition in bigger markets. It shall ultimately cover in a substantial way all sectors of the economy'.[4] The joint concept paper lists approximately ten priority fields of economic activity for practical cooperation within the CEES framework.

The other three common spaces are defined in a more general way. For instance, the Joint Declaration between the European Union and the Russian Federation on strengthening dialogue and cooperation on political and security matters underlines that the parties agree to reinforce their cooperation in political and security matters with a view to creating a space of cooperation in the field of external security. The fight against terrorism and a joint commitment to prevent the proliferation of weapons of mass destruction were indicated as the cornerstones of this cooperation.

Directions and an approximate framework for partnership and cooperation have thus been defined in a very general way. Now is time to work out the details and, most importantly, to fill with practical content and to develop the existing legal basis for relations between the two parties. A lot will depend on how the parties proceed with practical cooperation in a number of fields that are of a huge mutual interest, including energy, trans-European transportation, communications, space, innovation and high-tech, and environmental protection. It is very important for both parties to understand the significance of the problems they face, and also the fact that the majority of these problems can only be solved through joint efforts. There is no doubt that the effectiveness of partnership and cooperation is closely linked to the improvement of mutual understanding, the ability to see and consider mutual interests and, above all, the growth of mutual trust between both partners.

The prospects for the development of integration within the CIS are generally regarded as uncertain or even very weak. Nevertheless, based on the experience of the past years, a number of economists from Russia and neighbouring countries have recently come to the conclusion that the majority of CIS countries, including Russia, will be able to rebuild and restructure (i.e. modernise) their economies only if they follow the path of a real economic integration with their neighbours,

---

[4] *European Union: Facts and Comments*, Issue 34 (Moscow 2003) p. 36.

or if they launch a gradual and focused preparation for such integration. In this context, Russia should act as the nucleus of integration ('the main integrator'). A number of preconditions for the development of integration in the post-Soviet space are already in place. These include:

- huge deposits of various natural resources in a number of CIS countries, first of all in Russia;
- a large internal market;
- an existing common transportation infrastructure, albeit an outdated one;
- a high level of economic interconnection between the former republics, with fairly good scientific and technical potential in a number of fields of industry; and
- tight cultural links and a common language.

At the same time, it should be recognised that in the years since the collapse of the former Soviet Union, centrifugal forces in the CIS space have increased rapidly. This has caused a lasting recession in industry and an increase in poverty within the population, which have had a very negative effect on the economy. In general, the countries in question have also not profited a lot from shifting the vectors of their development and attempting to orientate themselves towards certain other States.

The CIS, which was created early on in order to facilitate a 'civilised divorce', is very weak in solving tasks of a creative, unifying nature. It is therefore hard to say whether it will be able to act efficiently to facilitate integration in the post-Soviet space today. For the moment, many integration processes here exist only on paper. In this situation, while rebuilding and modernising its economy, which will allow it to become an 'attractive integrator' for other CIS countries, Russia should start by developing integration in various fields with individual countries or groups of countries that show practical readiness for such cooperation. There are a number of fields in which such integration might be developed: energy, transportation systems, the conversion of military-industrial complexes using existing qualified personnel, and so forth.

Now is probably not yet the time for the implementation of large integration schemes covering all or most of the CIS countries. It seems reasonable to pay more attention to market integration at the micro level, that is to say, the development of horizontal links by creating joint ventures and multinational commercial and financial structures. In the future, this would make it possible to approach the restoration of a single economic space based on new principles and create a solid basis for a larger integration project.

While proceeding with integration in the CIS space and the establishment of the appropriate legal basis, it is also useful to consider the experience of legal regulation in the European Union. This would also facilitate the interaction of the new association (or associations) with the Western European integration structure, and maybe even their merger in the distant future. For the moment, the principles and methods associated with the establishment of the European Community, their implementation in legal norms and institutional structures and the taking into consideration of local particularities provide a very important example for the CIS countries.

It is obvious that integration at all levels should be executed in strict compliance with the principles of free will, equality, mutual benefit and independence of all the countries that are parties to this process. The successful development of integration in the post-Soviet space will also increase the role and prestige of CIS countries at the global level and create a decent, reliable and predictable partner for the European Union.

In general, we believe that Russia's integration policy within the CIS should be developed in close harmony with its policies regarding the European Union. In the more distant future, as already noted, the efforts of the parties can be directed towards creating a pan-European economic space – a larger zone of economic integration based on the principles and goals laid down in the Partnership and Cooperation Agreements (PCAs) between the European Union and the CIS countries. Integration steps within the CIS could be duly coordinated within the implementation mechanism of the PCAs, especially as long as the EU common strategy on Russia, the EU common strategy on Ukraine and the Russian strategy for the development of relations between the Russian Federation and the European Union (all adopted in 1999) continue to form the basis for these processes, despite all their shortcomings.

As long as the future of Europe continues to depend on the further development of integration – not only in Western and Central Europe but also in Eastern Europe – it is very important to give practical answers to the following questions: Has real integration started in the CIS? What forms will it take? And how will integration models in Western Europe (the European Union) and Eastern Europe (the CIS) correlate? Finally, it is also important to determine whether, in the future, these parts of Europe will be able to build a common system of integration, which would serve as the most reliable basis for European security, stability and prosperity and would also be a solid guarantor of successful development of the whole of Europe in the current era of globalisation.

THE IMPACT OF EUROPEAN INTEGRATION ON THE DEVELOPMENT OF LAW IN RUSSIA

Gennadi P. Tolstopyatenko[*]

1.   INTRODUCTION

European integration is a versatile process of economic, legal and political unification of the European nations and countries. The European Convention for the Protection of Human Rights and Fundamental Freedoms (ECHR), dated 4 November 1950, serves as a basis for this unification. It is this Convention that served as a basis for future integration (ECSC, EEC and Euratom) as it established those legal values without which economic and political integration is impossible. Even though the ECHR is not an EC Treaty, compliance with its provisions is an integral condition for participation in the European Union. Moreover, Article 6(2) of the Treaty on European Union points out that the ECHR provisions establishing human rights and fundamental freedoms are common principles of EU law. In the EU legal system, common principles serve as guidelines and limits for law making and law enforcement and secure a possibility for justice, even if there is no legal provision to regulate a particular dispute. The ECHR and the establishing Treaties thus comprise a legal basis for forming a Europe-wide system of law.

Russia is not a member of the European Union, but its legal development is strongly influenced by European integration. This shows itself in the following ways. First, Russia has joined the ECHR and is bringing its legislation into conformity with its legal requirements. Second, Russia concluded a Partnership and Cooperation Agreement (PCA) with the European Union in 1994 and 'aims at gradually reaching compatibility of its legislation with the Community legislation' (Article 55 PCA). Third, trends in the development of European law, in

---

[*] Doctor of Law, Professor, Dean of the Law Faculty at MGIMO University, Moscow. Fred Kellermann and I became acquainted and developed a professional relationship while realising a TACIS project to create a European Law Institute in Moscow at MGIMO University. The project goals were reached, and Fred Kellermann, a person of amazing charm and the highest professional standards, played a significant role in this regard. He was very influential in developing interest for European law among the lecturers, students and post-graduates of MGIMO University. Fred Kellermann has helped to create the conditions for continuous cooperation between MGIMO University and the TMC Asser Instituut. Personal contact with Fred has led me and my students to a better understanding of the meaning of the *acquis communautaire* for a pan-European legal culture.

The European Union: An Ongoing Process of Integration – Liber Amicorum Alfred E. Kellermann
© 2004, T.M.C. Asser Instituut, The Hague, and the authors

particular the growth of the role of court practice in the legal system of the European Union and European States, are reflected in the law enforcement and law-making activities of Russian state bodies. Fourth, the development of economic and political cooperation with the European Union promotes the extension and intensification of humanitarian interaction, particularly in the sphere of legal science and education, which potentially strengthens the influence of European legal culture on the formation and development of Russian legal traditions, especially as, historically, Russia has created its law within the framework of the principles of the continental legal family. This paper considers only two aspects of this vast topic: (1) international liabilities and legal order in Russia and (2) possible changes to Russian legal traditions due to the influence of European doctrine and court practice.

2.   INTERNATIONAL LIABILITIES AND LEGAL ORDER IN RUSSIA

Russia's signature and ratification of the ECHR in 1988 means that Russia has chosen the system of European legal values, which is based on the priority of human rights and freedoms. In accordance with Russian Constitution of 1993, the ECHR has become part of the legal order of the Russian Federation (Article 15(4) of the Constitution) and shall be followed by all the state bodies. In case of a conflict between national legislation and the Convention, the latter shall prevail (Article 15(4) of the Constitution) and shall be applied by the Russian courts 'accounting for the European Court of Human Rights' practice'.[1] It is particularly important that, in accordance with Article 46(3) of the Russian Constitution, citizens have a right to apply to the European Court of Human Rights if all available federal means of legal protection have been exhausted. In practice, such applications not only mean additional means of legal protection for a person's rights, but also seriously influence the sense of justice of Russian judges and other representatives of law enforcement. It should be noted that, even before Russia signed the ECHR, all the latter's main provisions were reflected in Title 2 of the Russian Constitution. At the same time, many laws adopted back during the Soviet era of Russian history, which, relatively speaking, do not fully reflect the provisions of the ECHR, have remained in effect. That is why all Russia's law-making activities are aimed at bringing national legislation (particularly in the field of criminal law) into conformity with the provisions of the Constitution and Russia's international legal liabilities.

---

[1] Ruling by the Supreme Court of the Russian Federation of 10 October 2003, 'On general jurisdiction courts applying commonly accepted principles and norms of international law and international treaties of the Russian Federation', 12 *Bulletin of the Supreme Court of the Russian Federation* (2003).

Cooperation with European Union, on the legal basis of the PCA, is an important source of European influence on the development of Russian law. The PCA is an international legal act of a framework nature, whose parties accept that the approximation of legislation is an important condition for strengthening economic relations between them. The framework nature of the PCA decreases the efficiency of its provisions, which stipulate a traditional international legal mechanism (instruments) to achieve the proposed objectives. EU experience demonstrates that using only international legal methods to regulate relations is insufficient for an efficient approximation of legislation between different countries. Harmonisation of EU and Russian legislation on the basis of the *acquis communautaire* would represent a real step towards reaching the objectives formulated in the PCA. Such a legal attitude towards harmonising legislation is not only the most efficient method for resolving specific issues of legal support for economic cooperation between Russia and the European Union, but also for gradually forming a common legal space – especially since some trends in the development of integration law, in particular the growth the role of court practice in the legal system, are noticeable not only in the EU Member States but also in Russia.

3.   COURT PRACTICE IN THE WESTERN EUROPEAN LEGAL TRADITION

Historically, legal practice has not been a source of law in the States of the continental (Roman-German) legal tradition. *Non exemplis, sed legibus, judicatum est* was the principle serving as the basis for the behaviour of lawyers in the continental legal system. At the same time, the modern law of some States establishes a possibility for law-making activities on the part of judges. In France, for instance, Article 4 of the Civil Code imposes a liability on judges to issue a decision following legal tradition and court practice in the absence of a relevant law. A similar provision may be found in the Swiss Civil Code, where Article 1(2) and (3) provides that, in the absence of a relevant law, a judge shall take a decision on the grounds of ordinary legal provisions and, if the latter is impossible, in accordance with his or her understanding of the legal norms that should be adopted if he was a lawmaker. In doing so, the judge shall be guided by his knowledge of doctrine and court practice. It is interesting that the rule established by the Swiss Civil Code, which follows the continental legal tradition, practically replicates one of the principles of the old Anglo-Saxon legal system: the common law presumption regarding the lawmaker's intention.

Even though precedent as a source of law has not been accepted in the States of the continental legal family, the *stare decisis* principle, which is a distinctive feature of the Anglo-Saxon legal tradition, definitely impresses the sense of justice of European judges, irrespective of the fact that they are brought up on a different legal ideology. That is why it is no surprise that, in the absence of precedent as a form and source of law, the decisions of higher judicial bodies on certain questions have the force of precedent in a number of European States. In Germany, for example, the decisions of the Federal Constitutional Court are mandatory when considering similar issues. In Portugal this applies to decisions by the Board of the Supreme Court and in Spain to decisions of the Supreme Court featuring the term *doctrina legal*.[2] In Sweden, the Supreme Court has the right to establish certain directions for law enforcement activities. In Italy, the Court of Cassation formulates 'maxims' that are published in its official reports. These 'maxims' not only detail the provisions of current legislation, but also provide judicial interpretations of norms that fill up gaps in the law and may also differ from the precise meaning of a specific legal act.[3]

Loopholes in legislation, the latter's contradictory character, the wide practice of delegated legislation and the simultaneous need for efficient legal regulation create a need for discretion on the part of judges. In this context, the point of view of C. Pratiç, an Italian judge, is very illustrative: 'A law-maker's claim to settle all possible social situations without any activity to interpret the norms is nothing more than a utopia... A judge shall not limit himself only to the search and application of a norm to a particular case... Having determined the applicable norm, the judge shall interpret it in accordance with the spirit of the entire legal system.'[4]

The aspiration to formally secure a law-making function for judges is strengthened by the example of the European Court of Human Rights and the European Court of Justice, whose decisions regarding the interpretation of ECHR provisions and European law serve as precedents that national judicial bodies are expected to follow in practice.

Relying on support from the constitutional courts of various European countries, the European Court of Human Rights has obtained pan-European recognition of human rights protection as the main priority of national legal orders. Thus, one of the most important areas of constitutional law has become a pan-European system of legal norms determining the development of criminal, civil, administrative and family law of the European countries. The decisions of the European Court of Human Rights serve as a basis for such changes. The European Court of Justice is equally active in influencing the development of law enforcement practice and legislation in the European countries. Relying on the

---

[2] R. David, *Key Current Legal Systems* (Moscow 1988) pp. 130-142.

[3] C.M. Bianca, *Dirrito Civile*, Vol. 1 (Milan, Giuffre 1981) p. 84.

[4] C. Pratiç, 'Le rôle du juge de première instance en Italie', 1-2 *Revue internationale de droit pénal* (1975) pp. 151-152.

principle of subsidiarity, it consistently realises a policy of extensive interpretation of the EC and EU Treaties, establishing prohibitions and limits for the Member States' authorities regarding specific types of activities that in the Court's opinion contradict EU law. European lawyers do not have a single point of view regarding this practice of the Court. Some of them assume that it may lead to the violation of key democratic principles: legal power would loose its position and decisions of general interest would be passed by a 'government of judges'.[5] There is some exaggeration in this, however. Looking at the extension of the EU court system provided for by the Constitutional Treaty from this point of view, one may notice a trend towards the further strengthening of judicial power and an increase in the number of issues to be regulated on the basis of the principle of subsidiarity.

4.   COURT PRACTICE IN THE RUSSIAN LEGAL TRADITION

The strengthening of the role of court practice within the legal system can also be observed in the Russian Federation.

Being a country of the continental legal tradition, Russia did not know a *stare decisis* principle and did not count judicial precedent among its sources of law. However, in emulation of the European countries and under the influence of the European Court of Human Rights and the European Court of Justice, modern Russia views judicial practice not only as law enforcement but also as a source of law. This is apparent from the activities of its judicial bodies and leads to contradictory evaluations of doctrine.

If we analyse the various points of view of lawyers regarding court practice as a source of law, we can identify four main positions:

1. recognition of the normative character[6] of court practice;
2. recognition of the law-making function only for the higher judicial bodies of Russia: the Federal Constitutional Court, the Supreme Court and Supreme Arbitration Court;
3. recognition of the normative character only for the final decisions of the Federal Constitutional Court; and
4. non-recognition of any law-making function for the judicial bodies and relative non-recognition of court decisions as a source of law.

---

[5] René Barents, 'The principle of subsidiarity and the Court of Justice', in Stephen Smith and René Barents, *Neutrality and Subsidiarity in Taxation* (London/The Hague, Kluwer Law International 1996) p. 41.

[6] Containing a legal norm under Russian legal doctrine.

The first point of view is supported by lawyers assuming that the principle of separation of powers not only secures the democratic character of the State, but also the possibility for each branch of government to influence the regulation of public life with the legal means at its disposal. For example, Livshits notes: 'By recognising the judicial system as an independent branch of state power, we recognise a possibility for the courts to adopt legal norms. The resolution of a particular dispute is delivered by the courts in the form of a court decision, which is a binding rule of behaviour. In this sense a court decision is the same as a legal norm.'[7]

The second point of view is that the practice of higher judicial bodies may be a source of law, but this does not apply to the lower courts, whose decisions do not have universal legal importance and may differ with regard to similar cases. At the same time, the final rulings of the higher courts that are of a normative character retain their quality as a source of law only until the lawmaker confirms or cancels them by adopting a relevant legal norm.[8]

Recognition of the normative character of the decisions of higher judicial bodies, in particular those of Russia's Supreme Court, has specific historical roots. During the Soviet era of the State's development, the Supreme Court of the USSR had the right to adopt resolutions containing guiding explanations on the issue of applying legislation that were binding on the lower standing courts (Section 3 of the USSR Supreme Court Act). The Russian Constitution grants the Supreme Court and the Supreme Arbitration Court the right to give 'explanations on the issue of court practice' (Arts. 126 and 127). At the same time, some lawyers assume that '… final rulings by federal courts are undoubtedly the source of law … for example, the Supreme Court of the Russian Federation and the Supreme Arbitration Court of the Russian Federation applying the law in specific cases do the law-making…'.[9] Others think that '… the Russian Constitution (Articles 126 and 127) does not lend the explanations by the Supreme Court of the Russian Federation and the Supreme Arbitration Court a mandatory character…'.[10] However, both groups recognise that the lower courts follow these explanations in their practice. In this context, the point of view of V.F. Yakovlev, President of the Supreme Arbitration Court, is interesting: 'Though Russian legislation does not directly provide for an institute of judicial precedent, the practice of applying legislation as developed by the courts undoubtedly influences

[7] R.Z. Livshits, 'Court Practice as a Source of Law', 6 *Journal of Russian Law* (1997) p. 49.
[8] S.A. Ivanov, 'Court Rulings as a Source of Labour Law', in *Court Practice as a Source of Law* (Moscow 1997) pp. 26-27.
[9] M.S. Salikov, ed., *Constitutional Litigation* (University textbook) (Moscow 2003) p. 170.
[10] B. Strashun, 'Decisions by the Constitutional Court of the Russian Federation as a Source of Law', in *Constitutional Justice at the Dawn of the Millennium. Materials for an International Conference Dedicated to the 10th Anniversary of the Constitutional Court of the Russian Federation* (Moscow 2002) p. 162.

the formation of a court's conclusions when considering a dispute that has arisen in respect of similar problem.'[11] It might be added that the legal opinions of courts developed while applying legislation not only influence further court practice, but also the parliamentary law-making process.

Lawyers recognising the possibility of judicial law-making in principle have different points of view on the issue of the law-making function of Russia's Supreme Court and Supreme Arbitration Court, but all of them regard the Federal Constitutional Court's rulings as a source of law.

Article 125 of the Russian Constitution, which grants the Federal Constitutional Court (FCC) the right to issue interpretations of the Constitution of the Russian Federation that are generally binding, final and relatively normative by nature, serves as the basis for this approach. These are the final decisions of the FCC that are regarded as a source of law. These decisions are issued by the Court in the form of *rulings* and *conclusions* (Section 71 of the Constitutional Court of the Russian Federation Act).

The normative provisions in the rulings of the FCC are usually in the form of *legal opinions* formulated on the grounds of an analysis of the norms of the Constitution. Legal opinions of the FCC are generally binding orders that cannot be contradicted by any other legal act. According to some experts, 'the legal force of the final decisions of the Constitutional Court exceeds the legal force of any legislation (subject, naturally, to acts amending the Constitution...) and is practically equal to the legal force of the Constitution itself... Exceptions may be represented ... by cases in which the Constitutional Court formulates a temporary rule ... [where] the wording of the relevant norms may be changed by the law-maker afterwards, while taking into account the legal opinions of the Constitutional Court.'[12]

Constitutional courts thus significantly influence the development of national legislation, due to their authority to interpret constitutional provisions. However, the claim that the decisions of constitutional courts and constitutional norms have equal legal force requires additional arguments. When evaluating the practice of constitutional courts, some experts characterise their decisions as judicial precedents. For example, when determining the ideas that serve as a basis for constitutional jurisprudence, M. Safyan, President of the Polish Constitutional Tribunal, talks about the creation by the European constitutional courts of a common 'field of precedent law'.[13] R.Z. Livshits, justifying the statement that

---

[11] *Taxes: Application of Tax Legislation by Arbitration Courts*, Book 1 (Moscow 2002) p. 8.

[12] B. Strashun, loc. cit. n. 10, at pp. 170-171. See also N.V. Vitruk, *Constitutional Justice in Russia (1991-2002). Essays of Theory and Practice* (Moscow 2001) p. 116.

[13] M. Safyan, 'The Role of Constitutional Courts in the Process of Creating Constitutional Law', in *Constitutional Justice at the Dawn of the Millennium* (Moscow 2002) p. 128.

court practice is a source of law, highlights the following: 'Past court decisions serve as an example for further court decisions, that is to say, a mechanism of judicial precedent is being established.'[14] It should be noted that the term 'precedent' is used rather frequently in the legal literature concerning the practice of higher judicial bodies. Thus, for example, when characterising some of the decisions by Supreme Court of the Russian Federation, M.V. Baglai, President of the Constitutional Court of the Russian Federation (1997-2003), notes: 'The Supreme Court ... gives explanations on court practice which often have normative meaning by their essence. And though the *precedent* generally binding power of these decisions is still not recognised in the country and a unified practice has not been established, they shall in their totality be considered as a source of ... law.'[15] In fact, we can only talk here about *precedents of interpretation*, as the classic form of precedent is practically impossible in the modern States of the continental legal system, due to the prevalence of parliamentary and delegated legislation.

However, even such a cautious approach to the decisions of higher judicial bodies in Russia gives rise to severe criticism from lawyers who believe that courts by their nature cannot perform a law-making function. 'A court does not create law,' writes V.S. Nersesyants, 'it renders justice, that is to say, it judges and decides in accordance with the law, and then applies it.'[16] Considering the issue of referring court decisions to the sources of constitutional law, O.E. Kutafin notes: 'In our country, judicial bodies are not referred to the law-making bodies. When resolving particular cases, they render justice as one of the forms of applying the law. That is why the Russian Federation does not know such a source of law as judicial precedent... As regards the acts by the Constitutional Court of the Russian Federation, it must be stated that, from the point of view of the Constitution of the Russian Federation and other legislation regulating its activities, the Court cannot create legal norms in the process of carrying out its activities.'[17] Specific examples of FCC rulings that contain normative provisions formulated on the basis of the interpretation of sections of the Constitution are considered by O.E. Kutafin as having been passed in violation of the formal status of the Constitutional Court and beyond its authority. 'Law-making and interpreting are different processes. Law is not created while interpreting, but is only discovered. The State's will is established in the form of a legal act. It is important

---

[14] R.Z. Livshits, 'Court Practice as a Source of Law', in *Court Practice as a Source of Law* (Moscow 1997) p. 11.

[15] M.V. Baglai, *Constitutional Law of the Russian Federation* (Moscow 1999) pp. 27-28 [emphasis added].

[16] V.S. Nersesyants, 'Court Does Not Make Law and Does Not Manage, But Applies the Law', in *Court Practice as a Source of Law* (Moscow 1997) pp. 38-39.

[17] O.E. Kutafin, *Subjects of Constitutional Law* (Moscow 2001) pp. 220-222.

to draw a clear line between explaining already existing norms and creating new legal provisions.'[18]

It is in determining the boundary between the *explanation* and *creation* of legal provisions where the main contradiction between the positions of the supporters and opponents of judicial law making lies. It appears that the practice of the European Court of Human Rights and the European Court of Justice provides numerous examples of the resolution of this contradiction. An extensive interpretation of the provisions of the ECHR and the EC and EU Treaties serves as a basis for such practices: if the lawmaker's will is expressed in the form of a general provision that cannot be directly applied by the court, then the latter shall interpret this provision on the basis of general principles of law and the purposes of the ECHR or EC and EU Treaties. Performing such a task implies an extensive interpretation of the norms of conventions and the formation of judicial opinions, which in fact are the precedents of interpretation. It looks like the point of view of the supporters of law-making by Russia's higher judicial bodies is based to a large extent on the experience of the European Court of Human Rights and the European Court of Justice. The extent to which this position can be developed will depend on whether Russia integrates into the European legal space. Development of cooperation with the European Union would assist in achieving this task. Different forms of interaction, particularly in the sphere of legal science and education, increase the influence of the European legal culture on Russian legal doctrine and the development of a State governed by the rule of law.

5.   CONCLUSION

The formation of a Europe-wide sense of justice is a complicated process that will evolve over the course of many years, gradually changing the established national legal traditions and court practice of the European countries. So far, even in the EU Member States, the judges of the national courts, having been educated in the national legal doctrine, by nature tend to welcome the argumentation of their colleagues in the higher judicial bodies of the State rather than the argumentation of the European Court of Justice.

National court practice contains many examples of critical attitudes towards the decisions of the European Court of Justice, especially if those decisions were passed on the basis of the principle of subsidiarity. Also, irrespective of the issue in question, national judges apply European law in accordance with the constitutional principles and legal and linguistic traditions of their country. Stuck as they are to national legal tradition, these judges do not rush to be guided by the monistic

---

[18] Ibid., at p. 223.

Community doctrine, rightly assuming that *qui nimium properat, serius absolvit*. At the same time, they understand that the unifying activity of the European Court of Justice is required to establish a pan-European law enforcement practice for a united Europe, but any simplification of this complicated process cause them protest. It is natural that, as the integration of economic, political and social life of Europe develops, the national sense of justice will to a large extent become more European. Getting Russian lawyers used to the *acquis communautaire* is even more difficult. Having been brought up in the traditions of the positivist legal school, they have a great deal of difficulty overcoming the absolute prohibition in their minds on courts engaging in law making and the possibility of limiting State sovereignty. However, understanding the fact that it is impossible to develop efficient cooperation with Europe while remaining outside the European legal space raises the hope that the *acquis communautaire* will form the foundation of the legal approximation between Russia and the European Union.

RUSSIA AND THE ENLARGED EUROPEAN UNION: MENDING FENCES WHILE SHAPING A WIDER EUROPE'S ENVIRONMENT

Wybe Th. Douma*

1.   INTRODUCTION

The integration of ten Central and Eastern European States into the European Union on 1 May 2004 forms an unprecedented step in the history of Europe. At the same time, this step forces the European Union to reconsider its relationship with third countries in Europe, notably with its largest neighbour, the Russian Federation. There are numerous reasons for this. Five of the ten new Member States share borders with this country. This raises the need for intensified cooperation on transboundary threats ranging from terrorism to environmental pollution. Furthermore, half of Russia's foreign trade is transacted with the enlarged European Union. Another example of the need for securing a good relationship between the two sides lies in the fact that the European Union imports 20 per cent of its oil and gas from Russia.

The relationship between the European Union, its Member States and Russia is formalised in a Partnership and Cooperation Agreement (PCA) from 1994.[1] Among the objectives described in this document are 'a gradual rapprochement between Russia and a wider area of cooperation in Europe and neighbouring regions'[2] and 'the gradual integration between Russia and a wider area of cooperation in Europe'.[3] In the Commission's Wider Europe initiative of March 2003,[4] it was explained that the European Union must 'promote the regional and subregional cooperation and integration that are the preconditions for political

---

* Dr Wybe Th. Douma, Senior Researcher, T.M.C. Asser Institute, The Hague.

[1] Agreement on Partnership and Cooperation between the European Communities and their Member States and the Russian Federation, *OJ* 1997 L 327/3.

[2] PCA, Preamble.

[3] PCA, Art. 1.

[4] Communication from the Commission to the Council and the European Parliament, *Wider Europe – Neighbourhood: A New Framework for Relations with our Eastern and Southern Neighbours*, COM (2003) 104 final, Brussels, 11 March 2003. More recently, two more Communications were adopted: *Paving the way for a new Neighbourhood Instrument*, COM (2003) 193 final, Brussels, 1 July 2003, and *European Neighbourhood Policy Strategy Paper*, COM (2004) 373 final, Brussels, 12 May 2004.

The European Union: An Ongoing Process of Integration – Liber Amicorum Alfred E. Kellermann
© 2004, T.M.C. Asser Instituut, The Hague, and the authors

stability, economic development and the reduction of poverty and social divisions in our shared environment.' The neighbours to the east and south, including Russia, would need to be offered 'the prospect of a stake in the EU's Internal Market and further integration and liberalisation to promote the free movement of – persons, goods, services and capital.' This integration process is specifically aimed at countries 'that do not currently have the perspective of membership of the EU,' it is added. Integration is thus used to describe not only the process leading to membership, as it is in the Europe Agreements, but also as a way of describing the development towards closer relationships with third countries.[5] At the St Petersburg Summit of May 2003, it was agreed that the long term goals of EU-Russia cooperation would be the development of four 'common spaces' in Europe: a common economic space (with specific reference to environment and energy); a common space of freedom, security and justice; a space of cooperation in the field of external security; and one of research and education, including cultural aspects.[6]

The EU-Russia integration process constantly proves to be a demanding process for both sides. This became especially clear in the wake of the EU enlargement, as major differences of opinion existed on issues like the extension of the PCA to the new Member States, the EU conditions for Russia's WTO accession and Russia's failure to ratify the Kyoto Protocol. In this contribution, some aspects of these controversies and their alleged links will be examined against the background of the development of the EU-Russia relationship. One particular focus point will be the integration efforts in the field of environmental protection, an area where Alfred Kellermann and the author of this contribution cooperated in the framework of a Moscow-based TACIS project, in the role of team leader and senior legal expert respectively.

2.   HISTORICAL BACKGROUND

2.1   From non-recognition to the 1997 PCA

It took a while before the relationship between the Soviet Union and the European Communities (EC) could be formalised. The non-recognition of the EC by the

---

[5] In this respect, this PCA, which is similar to the ones concluded with other Eastern European and Central Asian countries, thus differs only slightly from the Europe Agreements, contrary to R. Petrov's suggestions in his contribution 'The Partnership and Co-operation Agreements with the Newly Independent States', in A. Ott and K. Inglis, eds., *Handbook on European Enlargement. A commentary on the enlargement process* (The Hague, T.M.C. Asser Press 2002) pp. 175-194 at p. 179.

[6] See section 3.2 below.

Council for Mutual Economic Assistance (CMEA, also referred to in the West as Comecon) and *vice versa* formed the main reason for this. Only in 1988 did the two sides formally recognise each other and open the possibility to conclude bilateral agreements between the EC and individual CMEA States.[7] The following year, a Trade and Cooperation Agreement was concluded between the USSR and the EC.[8] Shortly afterwards, however, the Soviet Union ceased to exist and a new instrument needed to be created. A PCA between the Russian Federation and the European Communities and their fifteen Member States was signed in Corfu on 24 June 1994. It entered into force on 1 December 1997.[9] The delay was caused by a number of circumstances, and was even temporarily suspended by the European Union, due to the Russian forces' military hostilities in Chechnya. With the start of peaceful negotiations in Chechnya, the ratification process was resumed. In October-November 1996, the PCA was ratified by the State *Duma* and the Federation Council, and in October 1997 its ratification was completed by the EU Member States.

With its 178 pages, the PCA forms an extensive and comprehensive agreement. It deals first and foremost with strengthening economic, political and trade relations between the parties, but protection of the environment forms an important issue throughout the PCA. Already in the preamble, it is mentioned that the parties are desirous of establishing close cooperation in the area of environmental protection taking into account the interdependence existing between the parties in this field. In Article 55, the parties recognise that an important condition for strengthening the economic links between Russia and the Community is the

---

[7] Joint Declaration on the establishment of official relations between the European Economic Community and the Council for Mutual Economic Assistance, Luxembourg, 25 June 1988, *OJ* 1988 L 157/35.

[8] Agreement between the European Economic Community and the European Atomic Energy Community and the Union of Soviet Socialist Republics on trade and commercial and economic cooperation, *OJ* 1990 L 68/3.

[9] Council and Commission Decision of 30 October 1997, *OJ* 1997 L 327/1-2. From this decision, the mixed character of the PCA becomes clear when looking at the multitude of legal bases mentioned there. The PCA indeed covers not only commercial policy and other EC policy areas, but also EU matters, for instance, in the field of the Common Foreign and Security Policy. See further C. Hillion, 'Institutional aspects of the Partnership and Cooperation Agreement between the European Union and the Newly Independent States of the former Soviet Union: case studies of Russia and Ukraine', 5 *CMLRev.* (2000) pp. 1211-1235. The Treaty establishing a Constitution for Europe, agreed upon in June 2004, introduces a single legal basis for PCAs in Art. I-56 ('The Union and its immediate environment'): '1. The Union shall develop a special relationship with neighbouring States, aiming to establish an area of prosperity and good neighbourliness, founded on the values of the Union and characterised by close and peaceful relations based on cooperation. 2. For this purpose, the Union may conclude specific agreements with the countries concerned. These agreements may contain reciprocal rights and obligations as well as the possibility of undertaking activities jointly. Their implementation shall be the subject of periodic consultation.'

approximation of legislation. Russia promises that it shall 'endeavour to ensure'[10] that its legislation will be gradually made compatible with that of the Community, *inter alia*, in the areas of the environment and the protection of the health and life of humans, animals and plants.[11] In Article 57 on industrial cooperation, the promotion of public and private sector efforts to restructure and modernise industry under conditions ensuring environmental protection and sustainable development are mentioned. Article 61 stresses cooperation on the adoption and implementation of environmental legislation in the field of mining and raw materials. Article 69 deals with environmental cooperation and stresses among other things the need to improve laws to Community standards.[12]

2.2   The 1999 Common Strategy

From the side of the EU, a so-called Common Strategy[13] on Russia was adopted soon afterwards, namely at the Cologne European Council on 4 June 1999.[14] The document aims at strengthening the relationship with Russia on the basis of the PCA through 'binding orientations' and increased coherence of EU and Member States action. The main objectives of the Common Strategy are consolidation of democracy, the rule of law and public institutions in Russia, integration of Russia into a common European economic and social space, cooperation to strengthen stability and security in Europe and beyond and addressing common challenges on the European continent.

---

[10] The careful phrasing of this duty indicates that it constitutes an obligation to perform to the best of one's abilities rather than an obligation to ensure a certain result.

[11] Other areas mentioned include company law, banking law, company accounts and taxes, protection of workers in the workplace, financial services, rules on competition, public procurement, consumer protection, indirect taxation, customs law, technical rules and standards, nuclear laws and regulations, and transport.

[12] Other provisions in the PCA mentioning the environment are those on agriculture (Art. 64), energy (Art. 65), construction (Art. 68), the Coal and Steel Contact Group (Protocol 1) and the Joint Declaration in relation to Article 6 of Protocol 2.

[13] Common strategies set out overall policy guidelines for activities with individual countries. This instrument was introduced by the Amsterdam Treaty in 1999 (Art. 13(2) EU). They are decided by the European Council, on a recommendation from the Council, in areas where the Member States have important interests in common. Each strategy specifies its objectives, its duration and the resources that will have to be provided by the European Union and the Member States. The Council implements them by adopting joint actions (Art. 14(1) EU: joint actions address specific situations; they lay down their objectives, scope, the means to be made available to the Union, if necessary their duration, and the conditions for their implementation) and common positions (Art. 15 EU: common positions define the approach of the Union to a particular matter of a geographical or thematic nature; Member States are to ensure that their national policies conform to these common positions). See further A. Dashwood, 'External relations provisions of the Amsterdam Treaty', 5 *CMLRev.* (1998) pp. 1019-1045.

[14] *OJ* 1999 L 157/1. The Common Strategy was valid until 24 June 2003 and was extended without further amendment until 24 June 2004 (*OJ* 2003 L 157/68).

One of these common challenges is the environment, described as the common property of the people of Russia and the EU. The sustainable use of natural resources, management of nuclear waste and the fight against air and water pollution, particularly across frontiers, are described as priorities in this area. To this end, the EU pledges to support the integration of Russia into a wider area of economic cooperation in Europe, *inter alia*, by promoting progressive approximation of environmental legislation. The document also sets out that the EU is to cooperate with Russia to improve energy efficiency and energy conservation, by supporting the integration of environmental considerations in economic reform and the efforts to strengthen the enforcement of national environmental legislation, and finally by working with Russia, especially in areas adjacent to the enlarging Union, to reduce water and air pollution and to improve environmental protection.

2.3   Environmental aspects of the 2001 summits

The Joint Statements issued at the 2001 summits between Russia and the European Union confirmed that the environment remained a 'major priority' in their relations. In Moscow, on 17 May 2001, the leaders of Russia and the European Union even referred to cooperation on this issue as a 'key priority'. Particular attention was drawn to energy efficiency as a way to limit the growth in demand in this area and enhance environmental protection.[15] At the Brussels Summit of 3 October 2001, both sides welcomed 'the agreements on climate change reached by Ministers in Bonn on 23 July 2001 during the meeting of the Conference of Parties to the UN Framework Convention on Climate Change (UNFCCC)' and promised to 'work together for its full implementation with a view to early ratification and entry into force of the Kyoto protocol, particularly at the 7th meeting of the Conference of parties to the UNFCCC in Marrakech from 29 October to 9 November 2001.' It was also indicated that both sides 'believe that implementation of the Kyoto Protocol may help not only to reduce greenhouse gas emissions, but also to increase European investment in the energy sector in Russia in order to improve its energy efficiency and economic performance.' The European Union expressed that it was very favourably disposed towards the Russian proposal 'to host a world conference on climate change in 2003, which could be both the annual Conference of Parties to the Framework Convention on Climate Change and the first meeting of the Conference of Parties to the Kyoto Convention.'[16]

---

[15] See <http://www.eur.ru/en/p_239.htm>.
[16] See <http://www.eur.ru/en/p_238.htm>.

2.4   **Commission Communication on EU-Russia environmental cooperation**

In December 2001, a Communication on EU-Russia environmental cooperation[17] was released in which the Commission set out its ideas and proposals in order to work towards the objectives sketched at the two summits. *Inter alia*, the Commission argued that the time was ripe to develop a closer and more coordinated bilateral dialogue on environmental issues through the PCA, with a common strategic agenda and reinforced procedures, and stressed the importance of linking environmental, economic and social objectives in constructing a common European economic space that would be sustainable. In the view of the Commission, Russia would gain a lot from such cooperation. The economy would become more efficient and productivity would be raised, for instance by applying cleaner and more modern technology and management techniques and by reducing the wasteful use of energy, water and raw materials. Exports would be facilitated and the climate for foreign investment in Russia would improve, as investors want a clear, stable and efficiently enforced regulatory framework so that they can assess with confidence what their environmental responsibilities are. Last but not least, the health of those living in densely populated industrial areas would benefit from reductions in pollution. President Putin himself admitted that '[u]p to 15 percent of Russia's regions are in critical or near-critical condition.'[18]

3.   WORDS AND DEEDS ON THE ENVIRONMENT

3.1   **Kyoto, Johannesburg and Moscow**

Russia's promises from October 2001 concerning an early ratification of the Kyoto Protocol were not kept. One year later, the Protocol was still not ratified. At the Johannesburg World Summit on Sustainable Development in September 2002, Russia's Prime-Minister, Mikhail Kasyanov, did state that 'ratification will occur in the very near future.' At the same venue, Deputy Minister Mukhamed Tsikanov of the Economic Development and Trade Ministry indicated that there was a risk that Russia would not ratify because 'we don't have the economic stimulus, the economic interest in the Kyoto Protocol.' He did add that, for the moment, the plan in Moscow was still to ratify. By March 2003, however, this had still not occurred, prompting a visit to Moscow by EC Environment Commissioner Margot Wallström and the Greek and Italian Environment Ministers to

---

[17] COM (2001) 772 final, Brussels, 17 December 2001.
[18] 'Putin calls for overhaul of environmental policy', *Moscow Times*, 5 June 2003.

encourage Russia to follow through on its pledges. 'The world is waiting for Russia to demonstrate that it is ready and willing to become a major player in the multilateral efforts to combat climate change,' Ms Wallström stated ahead of her visit.[19]

At the same time, the protection of the environment in general was receiving less and less attention in Russia. In 1996, the part of the Ministry of Environmental and Natural Resources dealing with environmental protection had been transformed into a State Committee. This Committee was abolished in 2000, and its functions relegated to the Ministry for Natural Resources (MNR). The main function of the MNR is to provide the national economy with resources. On top of that, a steep reduction of staff in the territorial bodies of the former environmental enforcement and permitting authority was undertaken. Inspectors became responsible for ever larger areas as their colleagues were dismissed.[20]

Authorities dealing with issuing permits and licences are part of the public administration in relation to which Russia itself recognises that major improvements are necessary. Such improvements are to be achieved via administrative reform, as this is a key factor to combat widespread corruption. Such reforms, announced in 2000 as being one of President Putin's key policy priorities, would need to tackle the very root of the problem, i.e. the bureaucratic over-regulation of economic activity, which creates the opportunity for corruption. As two Russian experts put it with regard to the area of Russian waste management: 'artificially created government control of the waste disposal activities leads to an unjustified concentration of the human and financial resources at the disposal of environmental authorities on the activities having negligent environmental impact. As a result, the industrial facilities worthy of special attention due to a major hazard they represent to the environment and human health are left unattended. An approach like that results in excessive financial expenditures to ensure the specified requirements and creates serious bureaucratic obstacles to productive activities, breeding mass corruption, however, in most cases causing no apparent influence on the state of the environment in a given region. An approach like that fully demonstrates the inefficiency of the whole system of government regulation.'[21] This opinion confirms the Commission's view on the investment climate in Russia as described above. Unfortunately, the efforts undertaken in the area of administrative reform have so far not lead to many

---

[19] Press release IP/03/322, Brussels, 5 March 2003.

[20] For a full overview of these developments, see Oleg Kolbasov and Irina Krasnova, 'Environmental Law of the Russian Federation', in *International Encyclopaedia of Law* (The Hague/London/New York, Kluwer Law International 2003).

[21] Valentin V. Lutsenko and Maxim V. Gratchev, 'Environmental permitting and enforcement in the Russian Federation', in Wybe T. Douma and Alfred E. Kellermann, eds., *Economic aspects of environmental policy in Russia* (Moscow 2004) p. 39.

concrete results.²² The consolidation and strengthened position of President Putin after his re-election in May 2004 might mean that more progress can be made in the future.

As for environmental legislation, a Federal Law on Environmental Protection was adopted in February 2002, but – due to a multitude of reasons – this law has failed to form a clear framework for achieving results and is often not applied in practice.²³ Stimulating Best Available Technologies (BAT) is possible under this law but also does not take place in practice. Likewise, the State Environmental Expertise system (a type of environmental impact assessment) has severe shortcomings.²⁴ As for the actual standards that are to be observed, a large number of them still stem from the former Soviet Union and are outdated, impractical, inflexible or uneconomic in today's Russian Federation.

In many respects, the legacy of the former planned economy still needs to be overcome. Natural resources are still significantly under-priced, obsolete production technologies use energy and resources in quantities significantly exceeding those used in Western Europe, there is a lack of environmental management systems, and ecologically clean and safe technologies are not stimulated. Incentives to modernise are as yet virtually non-existent. Thus, there is a clear need for movement towards a compliance-oriented approach, based on equitable and environmentally sound criteria.

Since 1991, through its Technical Assistance to the Commonwealth of Independent States (TACIS) programme, the European Union has tried to stimulate, *inter alia*, improvements in the field of environmental protection and energy efficiency. In the period from 1998 to 2003, numerous projects were supported.²⁵ One of these was a project entitled *Harmonisation of environmental standards –*

---

²² The overall responsibility for administrative reform lies with the Government Commission, headed by P.M. Kasyanov and set up in August 2001.

²³ See М.М. Бринчук и О.Л. Дубовник, *Федеральный закон 'Об охране окружающей среды': теория и практика*, Государство и Право, 2003, No. 3, pp. 30-41. For a detailed study in English and Russian of this law, see *Inception Report* of TACIS Project 'Harmonisation of Environmental Standards – Russia', Annex 1, Review of Legislative and Institutional Framework, and the final report of the same project, both available at <http://www.envharmon.msmu.ru>.

²⁴ See Aleg Cherp and Svetlana Golubeva, 'Environmental assessment in the Russian Federation: evolution through capacity building', in 22(2) *Impact Assessment and Project Appraisal* (2004) pp. 121-130; Konrad von Ritter and Vladimir Tsirkunov, *How Well is Environmental Assessment Working in Russia: A Pilot Study to Assess the Capacity of Russia's EA System* (Moscow/Washington, World Bank 2002).

²⁵ These included, *inter alia*, assistance to the Ministry of Natural Resources on water management (€2.4 million); assistance to the Ministry for Emergencies to improve industrial accident prevention (€3 million); the inclusion of an environmental protection element in the conversion of the chemical weapon industry (€4 million); continued institutional support to the State Committee for Environmental Protection (SCEP) and to regional authorities in the area of waste management (€2.5 million) and environment monitoring systems (€2.5 million).

Russia, which received 2 million euros in funding. It was aimed at supporting the State *Duma* in its efforts to align Russia's environmental legislation with the EU environmental *acquis*. The project resulted in Russian and international experts (among whom Alfred Kellermann and the author of this contribution) carrying out studies of the present Russian system and comparing it with the EU system, notably in the field of industrial pollution, and suggesting improvements. Initially, some of the Russian experts wondered how the European Union planned to approximate EU environmental legislation to that of Russia. Reference to the text of the PCA and studies highlighting that only some aspects of Russian environmental legislation are better than that of the European Union – on paper and certainly not in practice – convinced them that the focus should be on approximating Russia's environmental law to that of the European Union. A more persistent issue concerned the initial costs of cleaner production methods and the way in which these would harm Russia's economic growth – an issue that also recurs where the non-ratification of the Kyoto Protocol is concerned.

Draft conclusions were discussed with numerous stakeholders, including permitting and enforcement authorities, NGOs and industry, and were finalised taking their comments into account. The recommendations were also investigated and tested through case studies in three pilot regions.[26] The main recommendation thus developed was that Russia should introduce a system of integrated permitting based on BAT for those branches of industry that are the main polluters. This system would stimulate resource efficiency, innovation and more effective protection of human health and the environment. The final report in which this recommendation and others were laid down was offered to and accepted by the State *Duma* Committee on Environment in November 2003. Through awareness-raising actions during the start of 2004, the project team ensured that the newly elected *Duma* and others were provided with information on these recommendations, in order to ensure that future legislative changes can build on the recommendations. A follow-up TACIS project might smoothen the road towards actual implementation of the recommendations in practice, i.e. the actual adoption of amendments to the existing environmental legislation. As already indicated above, Russia is under no strict legal obligation actually to approximate its legislation to that of the European Union. In this respect, the view expressed by Commissioner Chris Patten on the extension of key parts of the EU single market comes to mind: 'It is not a matter of imposing EU legislation word for word on Russia, but of offering a model for economic and legislative integration.'[27]

---

[26] Moscow Oblast, Penza Oblast and Arkhangelsk Oblast.
[27] Chris Patten, speech at the European Business Club Conference: 'Investing in Russia', Brussels, 2 October 2001.

3.2   Four common spaces

At the St Petersburg Summit in May 2003, the European Union and Russia agreed to reinforce their cooperation in the framework of the PCA. As evident from the Joint Statement issued at the end of the summit,[28] it was agreed that the goal of common economic and social spaces set out in the 1999 Common Strategy would be expanded to four common spaces that would need to be created in the long term: a common economic space (in a new, broader sense); a common space of freedom, security and justice; a space of cooperation in the field of external security; and one of research and education, including cultural aspects.

The environment was one of the areas touched upon extensively in connection with the common economic space. It was made known in the Joint Statement that the two sides had agreed 'to make every necessary effort to ensure that the Kyoto Protocol becomes a real tool for solving the problems of global warming and to this end we shall seek its entry into force as soon as possible.' Russia and the European Union also confirmed their readiness to cooperate closely in preparing the World Conference on Climate Change, which was to be held in Russia later that year. The European Union asked Russia to submit the Kyoto Protocol to the *Duma* for ratification as soon as possible. At the Conference, President Putin explained how Russia interpreted 'as soon as possible'.

3.3   The World Conference on Climate Change and further Russian arguments

This Conference, convened between 29 September and 3 October 2003, was intended to be the first meeting of the parties to the Kyoto Protocol. Since Russia had not ratified, this was not possible. Instead, it was hoped that Russia would use this opportunity to announce when it would ratify. However, President Putin's opening speech dashed any hopes for a swift entry into force of Kyoto. 'Russia is being actively called on to ratify the Kyoto protocol as soon as possible. I am certain that these appeals will also be heard many times at your meeting. I want to say that the Government of the Russian Federation is carefully examining and studying this issue, studying the entire range of complex problems connected with this', Putin said. 'A decision will be made after this work is finished. And, of course, it will be made in accordance with the national interests of the Russian Federation.' The President later added during the forum: 'In Russia, you can often hear, either in joke or seriously, that for a northern country like Russia, it would be no big deal if it gets 2 or 3 degrees warmer. Maybe it would even better – we would spend less money on fur coats and other warm things, and agriculture

---

[28] See <http://www.eur.ru/en/p_234.htm>.

specialists say our grain production will increase, and thank God for that. All that is true. But we must also think about something else. We much think about the consequences of these possibly global climate changes.'[29]

Joke Waller-Hunter, the executive secretary of the UN Framework Convention on Climate Change, which also oversees the Kyoto Protocol, was diplomatic in her praise of Russia for its commitment to climate change issues. At the same time, she was frank in expressing her disappointment. 'We had hoped that [President Putin] would have been somewhat more specific on the date when he would expect the Russian ratification to take place,' she said. 'Last year in Johannesburg, the [Russian] prime minister announced Russia would ratify the Kyoto Protocol in the nearest future, and we had hoped the nearest future had come today and that we would have a clear signal.'[30]

The Conference itself definitely examined the issue of climate change and a very wide range of problems linked to it, but consensus on the benefits of Russia's ratification of the Kyoto Protocol was not reached. The opponents of Kyoto brought forward fierce arguments. Andrei Illarionov, economic adviser to President Putin, warned for instance that 'the Kyoto Protocol will stymie economic growth; it will doom Russia to poverty, weakness and backwardness', claiming that each percentage point of GDP growth is accompanied by a 2 per cent growth in CO_2 emissions.[31] Kyoto would thus stand in the way of reaching President Putin's 2003 goal of doubling Russia's GDP by the year 2010. As Russia's GDP grew by 7.3 per cent in 2003 and the forecast for 2004 is 6.6 per cent growth, average annual growth during the 2005-2010 period would need to be some 9.8 per cent in order to reach this goal – a highly unlikely scenario with or without ratification of the Kyoto Protocol. Such arguments did meet with opposition,[32] showing some of the mistakes in Illarionov's reasoning (notably with regard to the link between reductions in CO_2 emissions and GDP growth in many transition economies), but these counterarguments were far less catchy than the original messages of doom and received little attention in the Russian media.

One opinion piece by Vyacheslav Nikonov, Director of the Politika Foundation, argued that, with the United States out of the game, Russian gains from emissions trading would be much smaller than earlier projected. He further

---

[29] See <http://www.kremlin.ru/eng/text/speeches/2003/09/29/1942_53028.shtml>. See also S. Lambroschini, 'Putin remarks start off international climate conference on sour note', available at: <http://www.rferl.org/features/2003/09/29092003152837.asp>.

[30] See <http://unfccc.int/press/stat2003/stat_290903.pdf>.

[31] See <http://www.rusnet.nl/news/2003/10/07/print/commentary_01_5423.shtml>.

[32] For instance, by Bert Bolin (chair emeritus of IPCC) and others, who at the conference presented 'Answers to the questions raised by A.N. Illarionov during his talk "Anthropogenic factors in global warming: some questions" at the World Climate Conference 2003, prepared from material of the IPCC Third Assessment Report (TAR) by attending scientists. Document on file with author.

objected that the European Union had created its emissions trading scheme without consulting Russia, claiming that the scheme would not provide Russia with the kind of market that it had hoped for. In his view, this fairly closed scheme would lead to trade being focussed on the new EU Member States, which would benefit from the influx of money and new technology. Nikonov also pointed to concessions by the European Union in the area of trade that Russia had hoped for, but which had not been granted, including concessions with respect to WTO accession, visa-free entry and anti-dumping investigations. He warned that with a number of uncertainties surrounding the effects of the Protocol on Russia and the potential of the emissions trading market, we cannot 'sell our future economic growth for an unspecified price.'[33]

Later on, Illarionov even went as far as stating that 'The Kyoto Protocol is a death pact, however strange it may sound, because its main aim is to strangle economic growth and economic activity in countries that accept the protocol's requirements. At first we wanted to call this agreement a kind of international Gosplan, but then we realized Gosplan was much more humane and so we ought to call the Kyoto Protocol an international gulag.[34] In the gulag, though, you got the same ration daily and it didn't get smaller day by day. In the end we had to call the Kyoto Protocol an international Auschwitz.'[35] These verbal assaults seem to indicate that Russia was not aiming at a serious debate on these matters but rather that it was looking for concessions in other areas, like its WTO accession and the extension of the PCA. Before commenting on the likelihood of this hypothesis being true, some of the events on the eve of the enlargement of the European Union will be scrutinised.

3.4   Italian Alleingänge

From the point of view of a European common foreign policy, a rather disastrous general EU-Russia summit took place in Rome in November 2003. At a joint news conference with President Vladimir Putin, Prime Minister Berlusconi endorsed Kremlin policies ranging from the arrest of oil magnate Khodorosvsky to the war in Chechnya. The Commission and most Member States dissociated themselves from Berlusconi's statements.

In the Joint Statement, Russia and the European Union stated that they recognised their 'responsibility to tackle together and in the framework of relevant international organisations, instruments and fora, common environmental challenges and shared concerns regarding climate change', but did not refer to the

---

[33] Vyacheslav Nikonov, 'Costs of Kyoto', *The Statesman*, 21 September 2003.
[34] The Soviet labour camps where millions of people died.
[35] 'Illarionov likens Kyoto to Auschwitz', *Moscow Times* 15 April 2004.

Kyoto Protocol. While the two sides solemnly pledged to reinforce their strategic partnership, progress on the extension of the PCA, needed before the 1 May 2004 because of the imminent enlargement of the European Union, was also left unmentioned.[36]

In December 2003, Italian Environment Minister Altero Matteoli criticised the European Commission for wrongly using strong-arm tactics to try to get Russia to ratify Kyoto. In his opinion, softer methods would be more effective. He failed to spell out what was wrong with the Commission's tactics, and claimed that 'there has never been a declaration by Russia against Kyoto',[37] overlooking the numerous times at which Kyoto was condemned for standing in the way of economic growth by people like Andrei Illarionov.

3.5   The controversies surrounding extension of the PCA

On 14 January 2004, Russia presented a list of fourteen specific concerns with respect to the imminent EU enlargement. Among these concerns were issues like Russian agricultural exports to the new Member States, which would need to comply with stricter hygiene and sanitary standards, quantitative restrictions regarding export of Russian steel[38] and grain, and higher import tariffs on goods. Furthermore, Russia demanded the non-application of EU barriers against Russian exports of nuclear fuel materials to the trade in such materials carried out under agreements and contracts signed between Russia and the relevant acceding countries before 1 May 2004, as well as guarantees regarding the non-application of restrictions under EC directives on the diversification of energy supply sources regarding quantitative or other ceilings for energy imports from Russia.[39] Some Russians even put a price tag on all of these concerns, claiming that the enlargement process would cost Russia 150 million euros per year,[40] while Deputy Foreign Minster Vladimir Chizhov – in charge of relations with the European

---

[36] See <http://www.eur.ru/en/p_236.htm>.

[37] 'Italians assail treatment of Moscow over Kyoto', *Moscow Times* 10 December 2003.

[38] Under the June 2002 Agreement between the European Coal and Steel Community and the Russian Federation (*OJ* 2002 L 195/55-71), Russia could sell 1.3 million tons of steel roll to the European Union in 2004. Exports to the new Member States account for some 500,000 tons annually, so Russia would want the steel quota to be raised.

[39] The situation of the Russian-speaking communities in Latvia and Estonia was also raised (these countries should bring their legislation in the field of national minorities in line with the Framework Convention of the Council of Europe on the Protection of National Minorities), as was the extension of the EU visa regime to the new Member States and the application of EU aviation noise restrictions on flights of Russian aircraft to the acceding countries (a transition period was asked for) and Kaliningrad.

[40] According to Konstantin Kosachyov, head of the State *Duma*'s international affairs committee, in an interview with Interfax on Monday, 2 February 2004.

Union – even estimated that it would cost Russia 375 million dollars.[41] Consequently, Russia claimed that the enlargement of the European Union called for substantial changes to the content of the 1994 PCA.

These demands resulted in a sharp reaction from the European Union. In its conclusions of 23 February 2004, the External Relations Council confirmed that the 1994 PCA 'remains the essential cornerstone of the European Union's relations with Russia.' It emphasised that the PCA 'has to be applied to the EU-25 without pre-condition or distinction by 1 May 2004. To do so would avoid a serious impact on EU-Russia relations in general.' According to the Council, the timely extension of the PCA would allow Russia to benefit from the many advantages accruing to it from EU enlargement, including in the trade field. The European Union was open to discussing any of Russia's legitimate concerns over the impact of enlargement, but insisted that this should remain entirely separate from PCA extension.[42]

At the same meeting, an internal assessment of the Common Strategy for Russia was presented with recommendations to strengthen the partnership. The *Financial Times* revealed that the memo in question concluded that the European Union failed to speak with one voice and that it contained the following passage: 'Russia has often made use of differences among the Member States and EU Institutions and used a policy of linking often unrelated issues.'[43]

This assessment obviously did not lead to immediate improvements within the European Union. The following day, French President Jacques Chirac stated that the European Union should show more respect for Russia's national interests as Moscow adjusts to EU enlargement, and that the European Union had been too tough on Moscow in the past. 'Moscow is making an enormous effort to regain its rightful place in the world,' Chirac said. 'We must convince Russia that we regard its efforts with friendship.'[44]

Hectic negotiations followed right until the end of April, i.e. just before the actual EU enlargement. Only on 27 April 2004 was agreement reached to extend the 1994 PCA as the European Union had demanded. The Protocol in which this extension was laid down applies provisionally as of 1 May 2004 until all instruments of approval have been laid down.[45] A Joint Statement on EU Enlargement and EU-Russia Relations was adopted alongside the Protocol that affirmed the extension itself. The Statement deals with many of the concerns put forward by Russia. For instance, both sides acknowledged that the overall tariff level for the

---

[41] *Financial Times*, 23 February 2004.

[42] Conclusions of the External Relations Council, Brussels, 23 February 2004, 6294/04 (Presse 49).

[43] Judy Dempsey, 'EU report criticises relationship with Russia', *Financial Times*, 22 February 2004.

[44] Press conference in Budapest, see <http://www.eubusiness.com/afp/040224113650.18tdtxww>.

[45] Protocol, Art. 5. The texts of the Protocol and of the original PCA are available at: <http://www.eur.ru/en/p_243.htm>.

import of goods of Russian origin to the new Member States would decrease from an average of 9 per cent to around 4 per cent, due to the application by the enlarged European Union of the Common Customs Tariff to imports from Russia, as of 1 May 2004, leading to improved conditions for trade. Furthermore, the Statement underlined that agreement had been reached to adapt the EU-Russia agreement on trade in certain steel products to reflect traditional Russian exports to the acceding countries, resulting in an overall increase of the quota. Also, it was agreed that special measures concerning the most significant existing EU anti-dumping measures on Russian exports would be adopted. The purpose of these transitional special measures is to prevent a sudden sharp negative impact on traditional trade flows. As for agricultural concerns, Russia and the European Union confirmed their intention to complete the procedures to introduce new veterinary certificates for the export of products of animal origin from the European Union to Russia as soon as possible and to continue negotiations on a veterinary cooperation agreement to facilitate the trade in goods of animal origin between Russia and the enlarged European Union. Both sides committed them-selves to addressing outstanding issues with regard to the ongoing EU authorisation process for the import of Russian products and the certification requirements for EU exports of animal products to Russia, and reaffirmed their commitment to avoid any unnecessary disruption of trade in these products. The European Union confirmed that it will not impose any limits on the import of fossil fuels and electricity and recognised that long-term contracts have played and will continue to play an important role in ensuring the stable and reliable supply of Russian natural gas to the EU market. Other topics that were touched upon were Kaliningrad, noisy aircrafts[46] and visa requirements.[47]

3.6   WTO and Kyoto progress: EU-Russia Summit of 21 May 2004

If a country wants to join the WTO, it first needs to conclude bilateral agreements with any WTO member demanding this. As already explained, Russia's major

---

[46] The European Union noted that since 1 April 2002, after a ten-year phase-out period, Member States have been allowed to authorise, on a case-by-case basis, operations of noisy aircraft. This will continue following EU enlargement. The European Union confirmed that an additional phase-out period, until 31 December 2004, had been agreed for operations at Lithuania's Kaunas airport and in Hungary, as set out in the Accession Treaty.

[47] The importance of people-to-people contacts in promoting mutual understanding between citizens was underlined, and it was confirmed that the facilitated visa issuance regimes between Russia and the acceding countries that existed at the moment of EU enlargement would be preserved on a reciprocal basis after 1 May 2004, insofar as they are compatible with EU and Russian legislation. The intention is to facilitate visa issuance for Russian and EU citizens on a reciprocal basis and to launch negotiations in 2004 with a view to concluding an agreement. The conditions for visa-free travel as a long-term perspective will continue to be examined.

trading partner is the European Union, so it came as no surprise that the two sides
entered into negotiations on this issue. The European Union demanded, among
other things, that Russia would increase its energy prices for the internal market,
notably for gas. The discussions were long and hard. Prodi, thanking the negotiating team at the May 2004 summit where an agreement was finally struck, put it as
follows: 'They worked like hell.' A detailed discussion of the deal that was
eventually struck will need to wait for the 400 or so pages in which the deal is
laid down to become public, although some points were set out in a press
release.[48]

At the same time, progress was booked on Kyoto. President Putin stated that
'We will speed up Russia's movement towards ratifying the Kyoto Protocol.'[49]
Alas, a *caveat* appeared again, this time in the form of Putin stressing that
ratification is not an issue for him but for the Parliament to decide. He did
indicate that the process would be accelerated. Considering the overwhelming
support for Putin in the State *Duma* elected in December 2003, this might be true
on paper. In practice, however, the new *Duma* is effectively a rubber stamp that
will ratify if Putin urges it to do so – or decline to do so if no such request is
made. Thus, the proof of the pudding will be in the eating.

3.7   The missing link

Was there a link between the agreements on PCA extension, WTO accession and
Kyoto ratification? According to Sergey Yastrzhembsky, envoy of the Kremlin to
the European Union, there was. Shortly before the May 2004 summit, he stated
that the apparent breakthrough on Russian accession to the WTO could pave the
way for Russia to ratify the Kyoto Protocol by the end of 2004, and that a deal
could be done. 'We don't say no [to Kyoto],' he said, adding that Russia would
look for certain measures to be taken in return. 'We would like to see that our
interests are welcomed and satisfied in different spheres … for example, the

---

[48] Doc. IP/04/673. The Russian Federation committed itself to ensuring that its average tariff
level will not exceed certain fixed levels and tariff rate quotas. In services, Russia will be taking
commitments in a large range of sectors, including telecommunications, transport, financial services,
the environment and tourism. The agreement also solved a range of trade-related energy questions, in
particular on the question of the domestic price for industrial users of gas. This price is to cover
costs, profits and investment needed for exploitation of new fields, and is to be gradually increased
from its current level of $27-28 to $37-42 by 2006 and $49-57 by 2010, which is in line with
Russia's own energy strategy. Increasing domestic energy prices will encourage a more efficient use
of energy resources in Russia and is thus supportive of the Kyoto goals. Finally, agreement was
reached to revamp the system of charges currently applied to EU airlines overflying Siberia to make
it cost-based, transparent and non-discriminatory by 2013 at the latest.

[49] Press Conference following the EU-Russia Summit, 21 May 2004. Transcription available at:
<http://www.eur.ru/en/news_584.htm>.

WTO.'[50] At the summit itself, Prime Minister Bertie Ahern of Ireland also appeared to describe a link. He underlined that the WTO talks had brought new clarity and that this could simplify ratification of the Kyoto Protocol.[51] President Putin explained first of all that Russia did not link WTO accession and the Kyoto Protocol. He elaborated, saying that Russia had long since made its position clear: 'We are for the Kyoto process and we support it. We do have some concerns regarding the commitments we would have to take on. But one of the biggest concerns was that we had to face several issues all at once that imposed serious commitments on us and gave rise to a great number of risks: EU enlargement, Kyoto itself with its potential complications and consequences, and the process of our accession to the World Trade Organisation. The European Union has made some concessions on some points during the negotiations on the WTO. This will inevitably have an impact on our positive attitude to the Kyoto process. We will speed up Russia's movement towards ratifying the Kyoto Protocol.'[52] These elaborations indicate that in practice, a link did exist. They also show that Illarionov himself is distorting facts in the Kyoto debate. Asked by a journalist whether his fierce opposition to Kyoto reflected the Kremlin's position, Illarionov replied that 'Putin didn't say he supports the Kyoto Protocol, he said he supports the Kyoto process.'[53]

4.   CONCLUDING REMARKS

The European Union aims to integrate neighbouring countries like Russia into a 'Wider Europe' and in this way avoid new dividing lines. Also, the European Union wants to ensure that Russia approximates its legislation to that of the

---

[50] Interview with the EU Observer, 18 May 2004, available at: <http://www.euobserver.com>.

[51] Press Conference of 21 May 2004, see n. 42 above.

[52] Ibid. He also stated: 'We expressed concern that EU enlargement, the complications involved in the WTO negotiating process and our full adherence to the Kyoto process could give rise to problems for the Russian economy in the long and medium term. At any rate, there are a good number of potential unpredictable risks that we would face. This was our concern and it was listened to. I want to emphasise that we did not push our demands at all costs, but rather, we listened to each other and reached agreement on taking certain steps regarding EU enlargement.' President Putin further explained that the agreement on Russia's WTO accession 'reduces the risk for our economy in the medium term and it frees us to a certain extent to move faster to resolve the question of Russia joining the Kyoto process. I cannot tell you with 100 percent certainty exactly how this will proceed because ratification is the responsibility not of the President but of the Russian parliament. But we will speed up this process, as I already said.'

[53] 'Illarionov attacks Britain, vows to bury Kyoto', *Moscow Times* 12 July 2004. In the same article, Illarionov also is quoted as accusing British Prime Minister Tony Blair's government of declaring 'all-out and total war on Russia' and using 'bribes, blackmail and murder threats' to force Russia to ratify the Kyoto Protocol.

European Union, *inter alia*, in the field of environmental protection. In practice, achieving these goals turns out to be not such an easy task. The Kyoto Protocol and the example of the above-mentioned TACIS project, *Harmonisation of environmental standards – Russia*, show that it takes a lot of time and effort to persuade Russia to alter its environmental legislation. Other goals set out in joint statements and in EU communications, strategies, action plans, agreements, programmes and so forth were the creation of an open and pluralistic democracy in Russia, stimulation of the free press, the rule of law and judicial independence. It is common knowledge that progress towards achieving these goals has been slow and sometimes even completely absent.

The Helsinki European Council of December 1999 concluded that 'Common Strategies ... enable maximum coherence, added value and efficiency in the Union's external action' and that the Common Strategy on Russia 'strengthens the cohesion and effectiveness of action by the Union, the Commission and the Member States.'[54] In the light of the achieved results, it seems that these viewpoints were somewhat overly optimistic. The fact that the carrot of EU membership is missing in the EU-Russia relationship might be one complicating factor standing in the way of the European Union's ability to achieve progress. Experience also teaches that a coherent and effective approach was lacking at several instances, notably under the Italian Presidency. The Commission thus seems right in claiming that in order to reach results, a more coherent, consistent and effective approach is necessary.[55] In particular, it seems that the European Union, the Commission and the Member States need to coordinate their positions closely and speak with one voice, with a view to making progress towards agreed objectives. Furthermore, perseverance and increased coherency will be needed to achieve concrete results. As for TACIS projects aimed at legislative approximation, it should be kept in mind that Russia has an extensive system of laws and regulations in place that protects vested interests, notably in the bureaucracy. Any attempt to suggest changes needs to take this reality into account and needs to be built on extensive consultation with stakeholders. In order to ensure a sense of ownership, involvement of Russian experts who are willing to consider improvements is also recommended. Last but not least, the efficiency of TACIS projects would gain from making the results of earlier and parallel projects more readily available. Only with such increased efforts will a Wider Europe truly reflect European values in practice.

---

[54] *Bull. EU* 6-1999, Conclusions of the Presidency, point 79.

[55] Communication from the Commission to the Council and to the European Parliament, *On relations with Russia*, COM (2004) 106 final, Brussels, 9 February 2004.

THE EUROPEAN UNION'S TROUBLED RELATIONS WITH THE FEDERAL REPUBLIC OF YUGOSLAVIA (1991-2001)

Steven Blockmans*

1.   INTRODUCTION

A book paying tribute to Alfred Kellermann cannot be considered complete without a legal analysis of the European Union's relations with the countries of the Western Balkans.[1] While Fred's activities in this region have centred around the (pre-) accession of Croatia and Serbia and Montenegro to the European Union, this contribution will focus on a form of EU action during a phase which largely preceded the era of partnership and pre-accession[2]: efforts to stabilize the region through the imposition and implementation of sanctions. This paper specifically addresses the sanctions imposed by the European Union on the Federal Republic of Yugoslavia (FRY), the predecessor of the union of Serbia and Montenegro,[3] in the

---

* Researcher on the law of the European Union, T.M.C. Asser Institute, The Hague.

[1] As in the policy documents of the European Union, the term 'Western Balkans' will be used throughout this paper to indicate the south-eastern region of Europe composed of five countries: Albania, Bosnia-Herzegovina (BiH), Croatia, the former Yugoslav Republic of Macedonia (FYROM, alternatively Macedonia) and the union of Serbia and Montenegro (SaM) including Kosovo. The term 'Macedonia' is used here as an informal name. Greece believes that the name Macedonia should properly be applied to its own northern region with origins dating from the time of Alexander the Great. Similarly, the name 'Kosovo' is used here in spite of the Albanian and Serb appellations for the region, respectively 'Kosova' and 'Kosovo-Metohija'.

[2] On 22 March 2004, the Council adopted Regulation (EC) No 533/2004, *OJ* 2004 L 86/1, on the establishment of European Partnerships in the framework of the Stabilisation and Association Process (SAP) for all five countries of the Western Balkans. The European Partnerships, which were adopted by the Council in the middle of June 2004, identify priorities for action to enable the further integration of these countries into the European Union, in the light of criteria defined by the European Council. The Commission's proposal for the European Partnership for Croatia was published on 20 April 2004, at the same time as the Commission's positive *avis* on Croatia's application for EU membership. Macedonia submitted its application to join the European Union on 22 March 2004.

[3] The European Union forced a new Constitutional Charter and Implementing Law on Serbia and Montenegro. The Constitutional Charter was adopted and proclaimed on 6 February 2003 by the Parliament of Serbia and Montenegro. See GAERC Conclusions of 24 February 2003, 6604/03 (Presse 52). The Constitutional Charter is underpinned by the Belgrade Agreement of 14 March 2002. See W. van Meurs, 'The Belgrade Agreement: Robust Mediation between Serbia and Montenegro', in D. Lopandic and V. Bajic, eds., *Serbia and Montenegro on the Road to the European Union – Two Years Later* (Belgrade, European Movement in Serbia 2003) p. 192.

The European Union: An Ongoing Process of Integration – Liber Amicorum Alfred E. Kellermann
© 2004, T.M.C. Asser Instituut, The Hague, and the authors

period from 1991 to 2001. The analysis is limited to sanctions taken by the European Union autonomously, i.e. not as a derivative of the obligations resting upon the Member States to implement sanctions adopted at the level of the UN Security Council.[4] Sanctions taken by EU Member State governments individually, or collectively outside the framework of the European Union, fall outside the scope of this contribution.[5] This paper will focus primarily on an analysis of 'targeted' or so-called 'smart' sanctions. Sanctions in the commercial field will therefore be largely left aside.[6] As amply demonstrated in the scholarly literature, proving the effectiveness of smart sanctions in changing the behaviour of targeted authorities is fraught with difficulties of measurement, and will therefore also be left aside.[7] While the decisions to adopt sanctions will be briefly presented against their respective political backgrounds, the analysis of the sanctions will be strictly legal.

In principle, 'targeted sanctions' are restrictive measures that are designed and implemented in such a way as to affect only those (groups of) persons that are held responsible for breaches of the peace or threats to international peace and security.[8] The term is often used for measures such as arms embargoes, travel bans, visa restrictions and financial sanctions. However, arms embargoes may

---

[4] See, *inter alia*, S. Bohr, 'Sanctions by the United Nations Security Council and the European Community', 4 *EJIL* (1993) p. 256; K. Lenaerts and E. De Smijter, 'The United Nations and the European Union: Living Apart Together', in K. Wellens, ed., *International Law: Theory and Practice. Essays in Honour of E. Suy* (The Hague, Kluwer Law International 1998) p. 439; and D. Bethlehem, 'Regional Interface between Security Council Decisions and Member States Implementation: The Example of the European Union', in V. Gowlland-Debbas, ed., *United Nations Sanctions and International Law* (The Hague, Kluwer Law International 2001) p. 291.

[5] Examples of individual sanctions include various orders enacted by the United Kingdom to prohibit exports to SaM, including the *Serbia and Montenegro (United Nations Sanctions) Order 1992*, which covered broadly the same ground as Council Regulation (EEC) No 1432/92, *OJ* 1992 L 205/2, 22 July 1992, and Council Regulation (EEC) No 3534, *OJ* 1992 L 358/16, 8 December 1992.

[6] See P.J. Kuyper, 'Trade Sanctions, Security and Human Rights and Commercial Policy', in M. Maresceau, ed., *The European Community's Commercial Policy After 1992: The Legal Dimension* (Dordrecht, Martinus Nijhoff Publishers 1993) p. 387; and, more generally, P. Eeckhout, *The External Relations of the European Union – Legal and Constitutional Foundations* (Oxford, OUP 2004) pp. 422-464.

[7] For an analysis of the effectiveness of UN sanctions against Yugoslavia (1991-1995), see the Report of the Copenhagen Round Table on UN Sanctions in the Case of the Former Yugoslavia, UN Doc. S/1996/776. See also J. Devin and J. Dashti-Gibson, 'Sanctions in the Former Yugoslavia: Convoluted Goals and Complicated Consequences', in T. Weiss, et al., eds., *Political Gain and Civilian Pain: Humanitarian Impacts of Economic Sanctions* (Lanham, Rowman & Littlefield Publishers Inc. 1997) p. 149. For an attempt to reach some tentative conclusions with regard to the effectiveness of the European Union's targeted sanctions against the FRY because of the situation in Kosovo, see A. de Vries, 'European Union Sanctions Against the Federal Republic of Yugoslavia from 1998 to 2000: A Special Exercise in Targeting', in D. Cortright and G. Lopez, eds., *Smart Sanctions – Targeting Economic Statecraft* (Lanham, Rowman & Littlefield Publishers Inc. 2002) p. 87.

[8] Based on the definition used in the so-called Interlaken Process, the first comprehensive attempt to examine the feasibility of targeted financial sanctions, initiated by the Swiss Government in 1998. See *A Manual for Design and Implementation of Targeted Financial Sanctions – Contributions from the Interlaken Process* (2001), available at <http://www.watsoninstitute.org>.

withhold arms from both armed rebel groups and legitimate governments, flight bans may hit innocent travellers more heavily than members of the targeted regime and financial sanctions can also have strong effects on general commerce by denying the possibility of payment. It may thus be useful to add to the definition that targeted sanctions are intended not to hurt innocent parties or cause 'collateral' damage, or at least to minimize such effects, because they are concentrated on those (groups of) persons that are held accountable for the violation of international law.

2. DECISION MAKING WITH RESPECT TO EU SANCTIONS

The discussion on EU decision making in the field of sanctions, in particular the respective roles of the Community and its Member States, has mostly revolved around the implementation of UN Security Council resolutions. At present, these issues have been largely settled, following the incorporation of Article 301 into the EC Treaty:

> 'Where it is provided, in a common position or in a joint action adopted according to the provisions of the Treaty on European Union relating to the common foreign and security policy, for an action by the Community to interrupt or to reduce, in part or completely, economic relations with one or more third countries, the Council shall take the necessary urgent measures. The Council shall act by a qualified majority on a proposal from the Commission.'

The article accommodates the earlier practice of the foreign policy role of the Member States and the role of the Community as responsible for the common market in a satisfactory manner, by envisaging, first of all, that a common position or joint action will have been adopted according to the provisions of Title V TEU, i.e. a political decision providing for action by the Community to interrupt or reduce economic relations with one or more third States. The second stage is for the Community to take the action provided for by a measure adopted under Article 301 EC. Article 301 operates across the board of Community competences, without it being necessary to resort to another legal basis. While it is broad enough to include restrictions on the movement of capital and payments, a special provision has been included in the treaty chapter on capital and payments. Article 60 EC provides that

> '[i]f, in the cases provided for in Article 301, action by the Community is deemed necessary, the Council may, in accordance with the procedure provided for in Article 301, take the necessary urgent measures on the movement of capital and on payments as regards the third countries concerned.'

Therefore, if the measure includes restrictions on capital movements or payments, the measure will include Article 60 as a legal basis for action.[9] Article 60 is different from Article 301 in that it goes on to provide, in paragraph 2, that Member States 'may, for serious political reasons and on grounds of urgency, take unilateral measures against a third country with regard to capital movements and payments.' The Commission and the other Member States are to be informed of such measures by the date of their entry into force, and the Council may, acting by a qualified majority, decide that the Member State concerned should amend or abolish the measures it has taken. The reason for this provision is that it may be necessary for the Member State to take immediate action to prevent the removal of financial assets from its jurisdiction.

The European Union has only a very limited experience with the autonomous adoption and imposition of sanctions. Although individual Member States, in their capacity as permanent or temporary members of the Security Council, take part in the decision making of this UN organ, the input of those States is not generally the result of prior discussion and decision making within the framework of Title V TEU. Decision making within the European Union on the objectives and the means of sanctions often has an *ad hoc* character. Within the Secretariat General of the Council there is not even a dedicated unit entrusted with the conception and design of sanctions. Only a small permanent team exists within the Commission to assist with the coordination of sanctions issues, including the design thereof, the drafting of sanctions regulations and monitoring the application of sanctions by the Member States.[10]

3.   POLITICAL OBJECTIVES OF THE SANCTIONS AGAINST
          THE FRY

Sanctions were imposed on the republics of Serbia and Montenegro during two different episodes of the wars waged on the territory of the former Socialist Federal Republic of Yugoslavia. The first episode (between 1991 and 1996) saw the outbreak and escalation of hostilities in the wake of the declarations of independence of Slovenia, Croatia and (later) Bosnia-Herzegovina.[11] In the absence of direct initiatives or involvement from the United Nations, the United States, NATO and the CSCE at the outset of this period, the European Community assumed leadership and responsibility and hoped to leverage a ceasefire

---

[9] See, e.g., Council Regulation (EC) No 2471/94, *OJ* 1994 L 266/1, 15 October 1994.

[10] See A. de Vries, loc. cit. n. 7, at p. 89.

[11] For a historical and political account of the dissolution of Yugoslavia and the war in Bosnia, see L. Silber and D. Little, *The Death of Yugoslavia*, 2nd edn. (London, Penguin 1996) and M. Glenny, *The Fall of Yugoslavia*, 3rd edn. (London, Penguin 1996).

accord by threatening the belligerents that it would block trade and withdraw economic aid of which Yugoslavia was a major beneficiary.[12] On 5 July 1991, the Community imposed an arms embargo against Yugoslavia and appealed to others (the CSCE, the United States and the United Nations) to follow suit, which they did.[13] A pattern of negotiated ceasefires facilitated by EC mediation – mostly violated by Serbia, which was on the offensive in Croatia and Bosnia – was accompanied by EC threats to impose economic sanctions on Serbia and the possibility of recognition of the other republics seeking independence. In response to the failure of the factions to honour ceasefires and accept the EC peace plan tabled in The Hague in October 1991, the European Community on 11 November unilaterally suspended the 1980 EEC-Yugoslav Cooperation Agreement,[14] the generalized tariff preferences and PHARE assistance, food aid and financial cooperation.[15] It also restored quantitative restrictions on imports of Yugoslav textiles.[16] On 2 December 1991, in a tangible demonstration of support for those republics in favour of the EC peace initiative, the European Community restored trade accord terms, GSP aid, and economic and financial aid to the Yugoslav republics, except Serbia and Montenegro.[17] Later in December, the European Community also invited those republics seeking diplomatic recognition (Slovenia, Croatia, Bosnia-Herzegovina and Macedonia) to submit applications by 24 December or else lose the opportunity to do so.[18] While the political impact of these measures on Serbia was significant, because EC action isolated and punished Belgrade, it also ended the sole EC stewardship of the international

---

[12] For an analysis of the political impact of the European Community (and later the European Union) on the conflicts in ex-Yugoslavia from 1991 to 1995, see R. Ginsberg, *The European Union in International Politics – Baptism by Fire* (Lanham, Rowman & Littlefield Publishers Inc. 2001) p. 57.

[13] UNSC res. 713 (1991) from 25 September 1991 and a similar decision of the CSCE in Prague on 9 September 1991. The Community's arms embargo was not the EEC's competence but that of the Member States. See D. Lopandic, 'The European Community and the Yugoslav Crisis (1989-1992) – Some Issues of International Law', 3 *Jugoslovenska Revija za Medunarodno Pravo* (1994) p. 311 at p. 316.

[14] The Cooperation Agreement between the EEC and the Socialist Federal Republic of Yugoslavia was signed in Belgrade on 2 April 1980 and approved on behalf of the Community on 24 January 1983. Council Regulation (EEC) No 341/83, *OJ* 1983 L 41/1, 14 February 1983. See D. Lopandic, 'Un exemple de sanctions économiques de la CEE: suspension/dénonciation de l'accord de coopération entre la CEE et la Yougoslavie', 2 *Revue des Affaires Européennes* (1992) p. 67.

[15] Council Decision 91/586/ECSC, EEC, *OJ* 1991 L 315/47, 15 November 1991; Council Decision 91/602/EEC, *OJ* 1991 L 325/23, 27 November 1991; Council Regulation (EEC) No 3300/91, *OJ* 1991 L 315/1, 15 November 1991; and Council Regulation (EEC) No 3302/91, *OJ* 1991 L 315/46, 15 November 1991.

[16] Council Regulation (EEC) No 3301/91, *OJ* 1991 L 315/3, 15 November 1991.

[17] Council Regulation (EEC) No 3567/91, *OJ* 1991 L 342/1, 12 December 1991.

[18] For the predetermined criteria for recognition by the European Community, see *Bull. EC* 12-1991, at 1. For a background to the creation, work and impact of the so-called 'Badinter Commission', see L. Silber and D. Little, op. cit. n. 11, at pp. 190-204; and R. Ginsberg, op. cit. n 12, at pp. 78-83.

effort to negotiate a peaceful settlement to the conflict in Croatia, because the European Community had to acknowledge the collapse of the peace talks at The Hague as well as Serbia's already confirmed distrust of the European Community as a mediator.

The United Nations (and later the Contact Group and NATO) built on the record and experience of EC mediation. All financial sanctions, visa and travel bans adopted during the remainder of the first episode of war in the former Yugoslavia were included in the multilateral efforts implemented by the United Nations against the Federal Republic of Yugoslavia (whose Constitution was promulgated on 27 April 1992). All restrictions were aimed at calling a halt to the breaches of international peace and security in the region and the unacceptable loss of human life and material damage. The measures adopted to this end were also aimed at dissuading the FRY from further violating the integrity and security of Bosnia-Herzegovina and at inducing the federation of Serbia and Montenegro to cooperate in the restoration of dialogue with the other parties to the conflict.

At the end of 1995, a controversial peace agreement reached after heavy American arm-twisting at the US air force base in Dayton and signed on 14 December at the Royaumont Palace in Paris ended the Bosnian war and therefore also the need for sanctions.[19] But while the UN arms embargo on the States of the former Yugoslavia was lifted in accordance with Security Council resolution 1021 (1995), the European Union continued its own arms embargo to ensure the safety of the international troops and civilian personnel stationed in the region.[20] It is the only example of autonomous EU action at the end of the first episode. One commentator has argued that, while all other restrictions on economic and financial relations with the FRY were indeed terminated by the European Union in December 1996, following the adoption of UN Security Council resolution 1074 (1996),[21] a whole 'outer wall of EU sanctions' remained in place: a set of political conditions for the normalization of relations between the FRY and the European Union, ranging from respect for the Dayton/Paris Accords and cooperation with the ICTY, and the introduction of democratic reforms and respect for human and minority rights, especially in Kosovo, to good neighbourly relations with the other countries from the former Yugoslavia and membership of the

---

[19] The present structure of the State of Bosnia-Herzegovina was established under the General Framework Agreement for Peace, initialled in Dayton on 21 November 1995 and signed in Paris on 14 December 1995, 35 *ILM* (1996) p. 75. See, *inter alia*, R. Holbrooke, *To End a War* (New York, Random House 1998) and S. Bose, *Bosnia After Dayton: Nationalist Partition and International Intervention* (London, Hurst & Co. 2002).

[20] Common Position 1996/184/CFSP, *OJ* 1996 L 58/1, 7 March 1996. The EU arms embargo remained in place, even after the beginning of the Kosovo crisis in 1998.

[21] Common Position 1996/708/CFSP, *OJ* 1996 L 328/5, 18 December 1996, and Council Regulation (EC) No 2382/96, *OJ* 1996 L 328/1, 18 December 1996.

Council of Europe and the WTO.[22] While the European Union surely gave the impression of paternalism by relying on a rigorous form of conditionality to 'normalize' relations with the FRY,[23] it is suggested here that these conditions cannot be qualified as sanctions. They should be seen as elements of the then new, more coherent EU strategy of engagement towards the countries of the former Yugoslavia, which accompanied the multilateral Royaumont Process for Stability and Good Neighbourliness in South-East Europe and formed the precursor of the Stabilisation and Association Process (SAP), the EU's regional approach to mutual cooperation among countries that did not qualify for Association Agreements (Europe Agreements).[24]

During the second episode of the wars in the former Yugoslavia, the European Union took a range of measures against the FRY because of its role in Kosovo.[25] The sanctions were not based on resolutions of the UN Security Council, but were taken autonomously by the European Union. Over time, the objectives of sanctions gradually shifted. Initially, the goal was to end the use of force against – and the continued oppression of – the Albanian population in Kosovo. Later, the goal was to convince the FRY regime to negotiate a political solution in Kosovo. Finally, the goal became to bring about a change in the regime in Belgrade to enable such a political solution and to create lasting stability in the whole Balkan region. The increasing severity of the sanctions was justified by the FRY regime's continued violation of international humanitarian law and fundamental human rights.

The initiative for most of these sanctions came from the so-called Contact Group on Yugoslavia, which consisted of the United States, France, the United Kingdom, Germany, Italy and Russia. While the Contact Group was very effective in getting Russia and the Western allies to work together in dealing with the war in Bosnia-Herzegovina, cooperation with respect to the Kosovo crisis was

---

[22] GAC conclusions of 29 April 1997 on the principle of conditionality governing the development of the EU's relations with certain countries of South East Europe, *Bull. EU* 4-1997, point 2.2.1. See B. Alendar, 'Conditions for the Normalization of Relations between FR Yugoslavia and the European Union – The Outer Wall of Sanctions of the European Union', 49 *Review of International Affairs* (1998) p. 7.

[23] Conditionality, entailing the possibility of sanctions, or making cooperation/assistance dependent on progress by a 'partner' was a strong feature in the EU-FRY relationship. See E. Lannon, K. Inglis and T. Haenebalcke, 'The Many Faces of EU Conditionality in Pan-Euro-Mediterranean Relations', in M. Maresceau and E. Lannon, *The EU's Enlargement and Mediterranean Strategies – A Comparative Analysis* (London, Palgrave 2001) p. 97.

[24] SEC(96)252 and COM(96)476 final, Brussels, 14 February 1996. For further reading on these action plans, see S. Blockmans, 'EU Conflict Prevention in the Western Balkans', in V. Kronenberger and J. Wouters, eds., *The European Union and Conflict Prevention* (The Hague, T.M.C. Asser Press 2004) p. 293.

[25] For a political narrative of the fight for Kosovo, see T. Judah, *Kosovo – War and Revenge*, 2nd edn. (New Haven, Yale University Press 2002).

less effective, because Russia disagreed on the sanctions policy. The Contact Group nevertheless continued to function, even after Russia had more or less given up on this format. The problem which the EU members of the Contact Group faced was that they could not implement most of the sanctions themselves. They had to act through the European Union and therefore needed to obtain the agreement of the other Member States. That agreement was in most cases reached by keeping the wording of the common positions vague and/or ambiguous, leaving it to the European Commission to find a more precise interpretation that would form the basis for the directly applicable EC legislation.[26]

In the spring of 1999, the policy of using sanctions to coerce the FRY regime into compliance with the demands of the Contact Group was replaced by a policy of using military force. In the declaration on Kosovo of the Cardiff European Council of 15 June 1998, conditions were imposed on President Milosevic and a declaration was issued stating that, unless the regime responded without delay,

'... a much stronger response, of a qualitatively different order, will be required from the international community to deal with the increased threat to regional peace and security. The European Council welcomed the acceleration of work in international security organisations on a full range of options, including those which may require an authorisation by the UN Security Council under Chapter VII of the UN Charter.'[27]

The failure of the Rambouillet negotiations at the end of 1998 and the serious deterioration of the situation in Kosovo in early 1999 led to the announced stronger response (i.e. the NATO intervention occurring between March and June 1999), which was conducted without the authorization of the UN Security Council.

As a means of supporting the military intervention, existing sanctions were strengthened and an oil embargo was imposed. Financial sanctions were reinforced and investments were banned, but these measures took effect only in June 1999, just after the FRY Government had agreed to withdraw its army from Kosovo and NATO military air raids had stopped. At that time, the objectives of the sanctions became more oriented towards reaching lasting regional stability in the Balkans, as indicated in the Common Position of 10 May 1999.[28] Following the September and December 2000 electoral victories of the democratic opposition in the FRY and the end of President Milosevic's rule, most of the sanctions were lifted. The arms embargo and the ban on the sale and supply of equipment

---

[26] See A. de Vries, loc. cit. n. 7, at pp. 90-91.

[27] *Bull. EU* 6-1998, point I-35.

[28] Common Position 1999/318/CFSP, *OJ* 1999 L 123/1, 13 May 1999.

that might be used for internal repression or terrorism remained in place until November 2001.[29]

4.   EU SANCTIONS AGAINST THE FRY

The EU sanctions imposed against the FRY can be divided into the following broad categories: an arms embargo, including a prohibition on equipment for internal repression and terrorism; travel restrictions, including visa and flight bans; an oil embargo; and financial sanctions, including a ban on new investment.

4.1   Arms embargo

In Security Council resolution 1021 (1995), the UN Security Council lifted the arms embargo against the FRY (and the other republics formerly belonging to the Socialist Federal Republic of Yugoslavia) that had been imposed in 1991 and maintained throughout the war in Bosnia. The European Union continued its arms embargo, however, and did not remove its previous restrictions on weapons exports to the FRY.[30] In the beginning of 1998, in view of the Kosovo crisis, the UN Security Council imposed a new arms embargo against the FRY. The arms embargo targeted the FRY regime as well as the Kosovar organizations that used arms to promote their causes. Since the previous EU arms embargo remained in place, there was no need for the European Union to take new measures. In April 1998, the European Union imposed a prohibition on the export to the FRY of equipment that could be used for internal repression and terrorism.[31] Here again, parties on both sides in the FRY were targeted. After long discussions, the Council of Ministers agreed on a list of prohibited equipment used for internal repression and terrorism. The list did not contain dual-use goods, however, and Member States were therefore free to decide whether or not to authorize the export of dual-use goods to the FRY.

On 10 September 2001, The UN Security Council adopted resolution 1367 (2001) terminating the prohibition on selling or supplying arms to the FRY. The European Union considered that its arms embargo and ban on supplying equipment that might be used for internal repression or terrorism had thereby also become redundant. Both sets of sanctions were lifted on 7 November 2001, it being understood that, with respect to arms exports to the FRY, the Member

---

[29] Common Position 2001/719/CFSP, *OJ* 2001 L 268/49, 9 October 2001, and Council Regulation (EC) No 2156/2001, *OJ* 2001 L 289/5, 6 November 2001.

[30] Common Position 1996/184/CFSP, *OJ* 1996 L 58/1, 7 March 1996.

[31] Council Regulation (EC) No 926/98, *OJ* 1998 L 130/1, 1 May 1998.

States would strictly apply the EU Code of Conduct for Arms Exports adopted on 8 June 1998.[32]

4.2   Visa restrictions

A visa ban with respect to persons who had been identified as having clear security responsibilities and other senior FRY and Serbian representatives responsible for repressive action in Kosovo was adopted by the European Union on 19 March 1998.[33] An initial list of ten persons was published, on which President Milosevic himself did not appear. It was announced that other senior FRY and Serbian representatives would be added to the visa ban list if the authorities failed to respond to the demands of the international community. A second list of nineteen persons was issued in December 1998. This list contained the names of persons deemed to have played a major role in diminishing and curtailing the role of the independent media, thereby violating recognized international norms and showing further lack of respect for democratic princi-ples.[34] Again, President Milosevic was not listed.

Only in May 1999, when hope was abandoned that he would ever agree to a negotiated resolution of the conflict, was Milosevic himself subjected to the visa ban, together with his family, all ministers and senior officials of the FRY and Serbian Governments, and persons close to the regime whose activities supported President Milosevic.[35] This latter category included a number of military leaders, as well as directors and other chief executives of companies and organizations. After January 2000, members of the police and security forces and of the judici-ary were also added to the list. Between May 1999 and August 2000, the list of persons grew from about 280 to almost 800 names.[36]

The selection of the persons to be included on the list was mostly based on reports from diplomatic representatives of the Member States and the Commis-sion in Belgrade. In January 2000, a common position was adopted identifying the categories of persons against whom visa restrictions would be imposed:

---

[32] Art. 2 of Common Position 1998/240/CFSP was repealed by Common Position 2001/719/CFSP, *OJ* 2001 L 268/49, 9 October 2001. Council Regulation (EC) No 2156/2001, *OJ* 2001 L 289/5, 6 November 2001 repealed Council Regulation (EC) No 926/98 altogether.

[33] Common Position 1998/240/CFSP, *OJ* 1998 L 95/1, 27 March 1998.

[34] Common Position 1998/725/CFSP, *OJ* 1998 L 345/1, 19 December 1998.

[35] Common Position 1999/318/CFSP, *OJ* 1999 L 123/1, 13 May 1999, and Council Decision 1999/319/CFSP, *OJ* 1999 L 123/3, 13 May 1999.

[36] See Council Decisions 1999/424/CFSP, *OJ* 1999 L 163/86, 29 June 1999; 1999/612/CFSP, *OJ* 1999 L 242/32, 14 September 1999; 2000/177/CFSP, *OJ* 2000 L 56/2, 1 March 2000; 2000/348/CFSP, *OJ* 2000 L 122/7, 24 May 2000; 2000/370/CFSP, *OJ* 2000 L 134/1, 7 June 2000; and 2000/495/CFSP, *OJ* 2000 L 200/1, 8 August 2000.

- persons indicted for crimes as defined in Articles 1 to 5 of the [ICTY] statute;
- the following persons: President Milosevic, his family and all Ministers and senior officials of the Federal and Serbian Governments;
- persons whose activities support President Milosevic politically and/or financially (including publishers, editors-in-chief and SPS party members);
- leaders of the military and police forces and those responsible for intelligence or security services;
- persons involved in repression activities.[37]

These categories were rather broad, and a considerable degree of discretionary power and political compromise was necessary to keep the list restricted to those who really counted. In the same common position, the Council also indicated that persons to whom the criteria were no longer applicable would be deleted from the list.[38]

Following the democratic elections that ousted Milosevic from the Presidency, the ban on the issue of visas was confined to Milosevic and the natural persons associated with him.[39] While the black list was considerably reduced, it still contained a substantial number of persons earmarked for non-admission to the European Union.[40] After the free and fair legislative elections in Serbia in December 2000, the Council further confined the visa restrictions to only Milosevic, his family and persons indicted by the ICTY (thirteen persons in all).[41]

4.3 Flight ban

Following the deterioration of the situation in Kosovo, the European Union complemented the sanctions it had adopted during the course of 1998 by means of Regulation (EC) No 1901/98 of 7 September 1998, imposing a flight ban against the FRY.[42] While the Council had already decided in June 1998 to ban all flights

---

[37] Common Position 2000/56/CFSP, *OJ* 2000 L 21/4, 26 January 2000, Art. 1(2).

[38] Ibid., Art. 1(3). Still, the burden of proof was left with the person listed and there was no recourse to judicial authorities within the European Union. On these issues, see S. Blockmans, 'De EU toont haar melktanden. Het instellen en implementeren van gerichte sancties ter handhaving of herstel van de internationale vrede en veiligheid', in T.M.C. Asser Instituut, *Veiligheid en het recht van de Europese Unie* (The Hague, T.M.C. Asser Press 2002) p. 85 at pp. 91-96. Article 1(7) of the Common Position also stated that '[i]n exceptional cases, exemptions may be made if this would further vital Union objectives and be conducive to political settlement...'.

[39] Common Position 2000/696/CFSP, *OJ* 2000 L 287/1, 14 November 2000.

[40] Council Decision 2000/697/CFSP, *OJ* 2000 L 287/2, 14 November 2000. Some 330 persons remained listed.

[41] Common Position 2001/155/CFSP, *OJ* 2001 L 57/3, 27 February 2001.

[42] *OJ* 1998 L 248/1, 8 September 1998. See generally S. Karaggianis, 'Sanctions internationales et droit communautaire. A propos du règlement 1901/98 sur l'interdiction de vol des transporteurs yougoslaves', 35 *Revue Trimestrielle de Droit Européen* (1999) p. 363; D. Wibaux, 'A propos de quelques questions juridiques posées par l'interdiction des vols des compagnies yougoslaves', 44 *AFDI* (1998) p. 262.

by Yugoslav carriers between the FRY and the European Union,[43] the delay in rendering the decision effective was caused by the fact that the flight ban might constitute a violation of the bilateral air services agreements that several Member States had concluded with the FRY. Greece and the United Kingdom initially agreed that the flight ban could only take effect after the end of the obligatory notification period for terminating their agreements (respectively six and twelve months). In September, the United Kingdom rallied to the position of the other thirteen Member States and the Commission that the flight ban did not necessitate a termination of the bilateral air services agreement, but was justified as a countermeasure against the breaches by the FRY of its *erga omnes* obligations[44]:

> 'Whereas the Government of the FRY has not stopped the use of indiscriminate violence and brutal repression against its own citizens, which constitute serious violations of human rights and international humanitarian law, and has not taken effective steps to find a political solution to the issue of Kosovo through a process of peaceful dialogue with the Kosovar Albanian Community in order to maintain the regional peace and security.'

The flight ban did not apply to EU carriers or to those of third countries.[45] In the same regulation, a symbolic but nevertheless important exemption was made for charter series flights between Leipzig and Tivat by Montenegro Airlines. In January 1999, the scope of this exemption was broadened to cover all individual or charter series flights by Montenegro Airlines between Montenegro and the European Union, on the condition that conclusive evidence was provided by the Montenegrin Government to the Commission that neither the Serbian nor the FRY authorities would benefit, directly or indirectly, from the revenues resulting from the flights authorized.[46] Primarily aimed at JAT (*Jugoslovensko Aviontransport*), a State-owned company and the Yugoslav national flag carrier, the flight ban was a targeted measure intended to deprive the FRY regime of revenues from air traffic services.[47] The European Union clearly broke new ground in adopting

---

[43] Common Position 98/426/CFSP, *OJ* 1998 L 190/3, 4 July 1998.

[44] *Barcelona Traction, Power & Light Co.* case, ICJ Rep. (1970) para. 33. While there may be a question as to which particular human rights obligations are truly *erga omnes*, gross breaches of certain fundamental human rights and humanitarian law obligations seem to be covered at least.

[45] Another exemption related to emergency landings on the territory of the Community and ensuing take-offs. See Art. 3 of Council Regulation (EC) No 1901/98.

[46] Council Regulation (EC) No 214/99, *OJ* 1991 L 23/6, 30 January 1999.

[47] See Art. 1 of Council Regulation (EC) No 1901/98. However, JAT was allowed to make flights over the European Union. Not allowing these overflights, it was feared, would lead the FRY to deny EU carriers the right to fly over the FRY, which would impose significant costs on these EU carriers.

this flight ban as a countermeasure by relying on the violation of *erga omnes* obligations by the FRY.[48]

When the NATO intervention began in 1999, the flight ban was extended to cover all flights between the European Union and the FRY.[49] An exemption was made for strictly humanitarian flights.[50] In the fall of 1999, the Council decided to expand the existing exemptions for flights to and from the Republic of Montenegro and the Province of Kosovo, and for Montenegro Airlines.[51] These two exemptions to the flight ban were clearly intended to support the opposition of the Montenegrin Government to the FRY regime in Belgrade.

A six-month suspension of the flight ban was decided in March 2000 and was later extended for another six months in August 2000.[52] This suspension was officially presented as a concession to the Yugoslav opposition, which claimed that the flight ban was hitting innocent Yugoslavs harder than members of the regime.[53] It was assumed that the visa ban would be sufficient to prevent FRY ruling elites from using air traffic services. The flight ban was completely lifted in the first half of October 2000.[54]

---

[48] The measure has not been challenged before the CFI and/or the ECJ, either by way of direct action against the institutions or via a preliminary ruling from a national court. However, the ban was challenged in Belgian courts, where JAT requested provisional measures. The Cour d'Appel de Bruxelles rejected the request on several grounds. In considering the legality of Regulation (EC) No 1901/98 itself, it was considered to fulfil the following conditions: 'ces mesures répondent à une violation antérieure du droit international; cette violation autorise les contre-mesures; ces contre-mesures ne sont pas d'une illicéité absolue; elles sont proportionnées à la violation initiale du droit international; leur mise en oeuvre est précédée d'une sommation adressée à l'État responsable de mettre fin à la violation initiale du droit international.' Cour d'Appel de Bruxelles (9ème Chambre), Case 1998/KR/528 *Jugoslovensko Aerotransport* v. *l'État Belge*, JT 1999, 693. See generally, P. Palchetti, 'Reactions by the European Union to Breaches of Erga Omnes Obligations', in E. Cannizzaro, ed., *The European Union as an Actor in International Relations* (The Hague, Kluwer Law International 2002) p. 219.

[49] Common Position 1999/318/CFSP, *OJ* 1999 L 123/1, 13 May 1999, and Council Regulation (EC) No 1064/1999, *OJ* 1999 L 129/27, 22 May 1999.

[50] See Art. 3(2) and (3) of Council Regulation (EC) No 1064/1999 and section 4.4 of this paper for the consultation procedure on the basis of which the Commission could monitor, on a case-by-case basis, the authorization of flights by the Member States.

[51] Common Position 1999/604/CFSP, *OJ* 1999 L 236/1, 7 September 1999, and Council Regulation (EC) No 2151/1999, *OJ* 1999 L 264/3, 12 October 1999, imposing a ban on flights between the territories of the Community and the Federal Republic of Yugoslavia other than the Republic of Montenegro or the Province of Kosovo, and repealing Council Regulation (EC) No 1064/1999.

[52] Common Position 2000/176/CFSP, *OJ* 2000 L 56/1, 1 March 2000, and Council Regulation (EC) No 607/2000, *OJ* 2000 L 73/4, 22 March 2000; Common Position 2000/454/CFSP, *OJ* 2000 L 183/1, 22 July 2000, and Council Regulation (EC) No 1746/2000, *OJ* 2000 L 200/24, 8 August 2000.

[53] This does not exclude the fact that strong lobbying from the European business community, notably the EC air carriers, also helped to convince the Council to suspend this type of sanction.

[54] Common Position 2000/599/CFSP, *OJ* 2000 L 255/1, 9 October 2000, and Council Regulation (EC) No 2227/2000, *OJ* 2000 L 255/2, 9 October 2000.

4.4   Oil embargo

In April 1999, when NATO was already engaged in air strikes in Kosovo, the Council decided to impose an oil embargo on the whole of the FRY in order to deprive the FRY army of essential supplies of petroleum and petroleum products.[55] The EU oil embargo against the FRY initially also covered the Republic of Montenegro (with its oil import facilities in the ports of Bar and the Bay of Kotor) and Kosovo. For the selection of products to be embargoed, the Commission proposed to copy the list of petroleum and petroleum products that was prepared for the implementation of the UN Security Council oil embargoes imposed on Angola and Sierra Leone. This was done to avoid protracted technical debates in the Council. The proposal was adopted without discussion.[56]

Exemptions from the oil embargo were approved for sales, supplies or exports for verified and strictly humanitarian purposes, in particular for the needs of internally displaced persons and returnees. With a view to avoiding different interpretations by the Member States of the term 'strictly humanitarian', a specific consultation system was set up.[57] Another exception concerned sales, supplies, and exports to diplomatic and consular missions of the Member States and to the international military peacekeeping presence within the FRY. The latter was necessary to allow the aircraft involved in the NATO air strikes to 'import' fuel into the FRY. An initiative from some Member States to allow NATO naval forces to check and search ships in the international waters of the Adriatic Sea failed to obtain the necessary support.[58]

---

[55] Common Position 1999/273, *OJ* 1999 L 108/1, 27 April 1999, and Council Regulation (EC) No 900/1999, *OJ* 1999 L 114/7, 1 May 1999.

[56] See A. de Vries, loc. cit. n. 7, at p. 95.

[57] Commission Regulation (EC) No 1084/1999, *OJ* 1999 L 131/29, 27 May 1999, as amended by Commission Regulation (EC) No 1971/1999, *OJ* 1999 L 244/40, 16 September 1999, established a list of competent authorities that could authorize the sale, supply or export of petroleum and petroleum products for the purposes and under the conditions laid down in Art. 2(1) of Council Regulation (EC) No 900/1999 and that should receive notifications referred to in Art. 2(2) of that Regulation. Before any Member State could authorize a sale, supply, or export of petroleum or petroleum products to the FRY, it had to notify its intention to do so to the other Member States and the Commission. If the Commission or any other Member State questioned the strictly humanitarian character of the intended sale, supply, or export, it needed to notify the other Member States and the Commission of its objection to the authorization within one working day. In such a case, the Commission would convene a meeting with all Member States to discuss the character of the transaction. Only after such a meeting took place could the Member State that intended to grant an export authorization do so, on the condition that, if it did, it had to report to the Commission and the other Member States why it still considered the transaction to be serving strictly humanitarian purposes.

[58] See A. de Vries, loc. cit. n. 7, at p. 95.

The oil embargo was continued after the end of the military intervention. In September 1999, a common position was adopted calling for exceptions for the Republic of Montenegro and for the Province of Kosovo.[59] A Council regulation to this effect entered into force in October 1999.[60] The delay of the partial lifting of the embargo was needed for the Commission to create a system whereby the exceptions would not create loopholes through which petroleum and petroleum products could slip into the rest of the FRY. The Commission cooperated with the competent authorities within the Republic of Montenegro to establish a control mechanism that would guarantee the effectiveness of the EU oil embargo. A similar agreement could not be reached with the UN administration in Kosovo because its mandate did not authorize cooperation with third parties on an oil embargo against the FRY. As a result, petroleum exports from the European Union to Kosovo could only take place if the competent authorities within the European Union obtained conclusive evidence that the products sold, supplied or exported stayed within the province. Under the circumstances, such evidence was very difficult to obtain. The oil embargo was partially suspended in March 2000 and then lifted in October 2000, following the electoral victory of the democratic opposition in the FRY and the end of President Milosevic's rule.[61]

4.5 Financial sanctions

The first financial sanction imposed against the FRY was a March 1998 prohibition against the provision or use of government or other official financial support for trade with or investment in the Republic of Serbia. A ban was also imposed on the provision or use of government or other official financing for the privatization of State-owned firms in the Republic of Serbia.[62] The prohibition on financing for privatization was intended to deny financial benefits to the FRY/Serbian Governments as the owners of the companies to be privatized. But of course the general denial of trade or investment support hurt all companies in Serbia. The Republic of Montenegro was exempted from this measure. These sanctions were lifted in November 2000.[63]

---

[59] Common Position 1999/604/CFSP, *OJ* 1999 L 236/1, 7 September 1999.

[60] Council Regulation (EC) No 2111/1999, *OJ* 1999 L 258/12, 5 October 1999, prohibited the sale and supply of petroleum and certain petroleum products to certain parts of the FRY and repealed Council Regulation (EC) No 900/1999.

[61] Council Regulation (EC) No 607/2000, *OJ* 2000 L 73/4, 22 March 2000, followed by Common Position 2000/599/CFSP, *OJ* 2000 L 255/1, 9 October 2000 and Council Regulation (EC) No 2228/2000, *OJ* 2000 L 255/3, 9 October 2000.

[62] Common Position 98/240/CFSP, *OJ* 1998 L 95, 27 March 1998 and Council Regulation (EC) No 926/98, *OJ* 1998 L 130, 1 May 1998.

[63] Common Position 2000/599/CFSP, *OJ* 2000 L 255, 9 October 2000 and Council Regulation (EC) No 2488/2000, *OJ* 2000 L 287, 14 November 2000.

In June 1998, by means of Regulation (EC) No 1295/98,[64] the Council ordered that all funds held outside the territory of the FRY and belonging to the Government of the FRY and/or the Government of the Republic of Serbia were to be frozen. EU financial institutions were prohibited from making funds available, directly or indirectly, to or for the benefit of those governments. The funds to be frozen or denied were narrowly defined in Article 1 of the Regulation: 'funds of any kind, including interest, dividends or other value accruing to or from any such funds.'

When it was realized that this narrow approach did not cause real financial problems for the FRY/Serbian regime, the Commission was asked in the fall of 1998 to report on ways to increase the effectiveness of the financial sanctions. In May 1999, the Council decided to strengthen the financial sanctions by extending the range of targets and the scope of funds to be frozen. According to Council Regulation (EC) No 1294/1999, the targets of financial sanctions included not only the Governments of the FRY and the Republic of Serbia, but all

'... agencies, bodies or organs, companies, undertakings, institutions and entities owned or controlled by that Government, including all financial institutions and State-owned and socially-owned entities organized in the Federal Republic of Yugoslavia as of 26 April 1999, any successors to such entities, and their respective subsidiaries and branches, wherever located, and any persons acting or purporting to act for or on behalf of any of the foregoing.'[65]

At the same time, the scope of the assets to be frozen and prohibited was expanded to include:

'... financial assets and economic benefits of any kind, including, but not necessarily limited to, cash, cheques, claims on money, drafts, money orders and other payment instruments; deposits with financial institutions or other entities, balances on accounts, debts and debt obligations; publicly and privately traded securities and debt instruments, including stocks and shares, certificates representing securities, bonds, notes, warrants, debentures, derivatives contracts; interest, dividends or other income or value accruing from or generated by assets; credit, right of set-off, guarantees, performance bonds or other financial commitments; letters of credit, bills of lading, bills of sale; documents evidencing an interest in funds or financial resources, and any other instrument of export-financing.'[66]

---

[64] Council Regulation (EC) No 1295/98, *OJ* 1998 L 178/33, 23 June 1998.
[65] Council Regulation (EC) No 1294/1999, *OJ* 1999 L 153/63, 19 June 1999, Art. 1(2).
[66] Ibid., Art. 1(3).

The Government of Montenegro and all its agencies, bodies and organs at any level, as well as the UN administration in Kosovo, were excluded from these sanctions.

It was the Council's intention to safeguard the Yugoslav private sector from the financial sanctions insofar as persons in that sector did not act on behalf of or for the benefit of the FRY or Serbian Governments. To highlight this aspect of the sanctions regime, the Commission proposed to attach a so-called 'white list' to the Regulation that would contain the names and other relevant data of companies that would not be subjected to the sanctions. Initially, the Council did not adopt this proposal for fear that publicizing the identity of such companies would make them targets for ownership or control by the FRY or Serbian Governments. But not providing such a list meant that only the most conspicuously targeted companies in the FRY were subject to the freeze of funds. This situation prevailed until April 2000, when the Council finally adopted the necessary amendments in Regulation (EC) No 723/2000 in order to better target the freeze of funds and enhance the effectiveness of the existing financial sanctions.[67]

This was done, *inter alia*, by closing loopholes and improving enforcement. In this Regulation, the Council established a 'white list' of companies in Serbia (minus the Province of Kosovo and the Republic of Montenegro) that were deemed not to be owned or controlled by the FRY/Serbian Governments, directly or indirectly. To qualify for this white list, companies in the FRY had to submit evidence to that effect. If a company in Serbia was not listed, it was deemed to fall within the scope of one or more of the four so-called 'black lists' that were also included in the Regulation to target the freeze of funds of companies, undertakings, institutions or entities that were owned or controlled by the FRY/Serbian Governments.[68] By reversing the burden of proof, it was expected that better targeting would be possible.[69] Article 1(6)(2) of Regulation (EC) No 723/2000 stipulated that a company, undertaking, institution or entity in Serbia would be presumed to be 'white' if it fulfilled any of the following criteria:

---

[67] *OJ* 2000 L 86/1, 7 April 2000. Because most Member States were not able to execute the screening of FRY companies within the foreseen deadline, the most relevant articles dealing with the increased targeting of the FRY/Serbian regime entered into force only on 1 July 2000 by way of Council Regulation (EC) No 1059/2000, *OJ* 2000 L 119/1, 20 May 2000.

[68] For the text of the white and black lists, see Art. 1(3) of Council Regulation (EC) No 723/2000, *OJ* 2000 L 86/1, 7 April 2000.

[69] This reversal of the burden of proof did not apply to the Republic of Montenegro and the Province of Kosovo. Indeed, in those two areas the sanctions were alleviated to the extent that only companies deemed to be owned or controlled by the FRY/Serbian Governments were put on a black list. If not on the black list, any company in the Republic of Montenegro or the Province of Kosovo would be considered to be 'white'.

- [being] able to withhold from the Government of the FRY and the Government of the Republic of Serbia, its revenues obtained from transactions with natural or legal persons within the Community;
- [being] engaged in transactions with natural or legal persons within the Community not exceeding, on a monthly basis, a value of EUR 100,000; [or]
- [not being active in] the following sectors: banking and financial services, energy and fuel supply, production of or trade in military or police equipment, transport, petrochemicals, iron and steel.

The first and, as it turned out, last list of about 190 'white' companies was published on 1 July 2000.[70] The financial sanctions against companies were already lifted in November 2000, as a consequence of the democratically held presidential elections of 24 September 2000.[71]

The strengthened financial sanctions of June 1999 also applied to individuals. Annex 1 to Regulation (EC) No 1294/1999 contained a list of names of individuals to whom the assets freeze would be applied. This list was identical to the list drawn up for the visa ban. It was regularly updated in conformity with the updates of the visa ban list, although the criteria for being listed were oriented to involvement in economic and financial activities rather than police, security, military or judicial activities. The assets freeze against individuals was the only financial sanction that was not lifted in November 2000, although the list of persons to whom it applied was significantly reduced, mostly by deleting a large number of military officials.[72] In June 2001, the Commission further reduced the number of persons listed in Annex I in order to bring it in line with the list that was used to deny Milosevic, his family and persons indicted by the ICTY admission to the EU Member States.[73]

4.6   Investment ban

In July 1998, Council Regulation (EC) No 1607/98 imposed a general ban on new investments in the Republic of Serbia.[74] However, the prohibition concerned only

---

[70] Commission Regulation (EC) No 1440/2000, *OJ* 2000 L 161/68, 1 July 2000.

[71] Common Position 2000/599/CFSP, *OJ* 2000 L 255/1, 9 October 2000 and Council Regulation (EC) No 2488/2000, *OJ* 2000 L 287, 14 November 2000.

[72] Common Position 2000/696/CFSP, *OJ* 2000 L 287/1, 14 November 2000, and Council Regulation (EC) No 2488/2000, *OJ* 2000 L 287/19, 14 November 2000. Annex I still listed 37 persons against whom a freeze of funds was maintained: Slobodan Milosevic, five of his family members, and 31 members of the FRY Government as on 9 October 2000.

[73] Commission Regulation (EC) No 1205/2001, *OJ* 2001 L 163/14, 20 June 2001.

[74] *OJ* 1998 L 209, 25 July 1998. The Regulation was based on Common Position 1998/374/CFSP, *OJ* 1998 L 165/1, 10 June 1998. Earlier on, Common Position 1998/240/CFSP, *OJ* 1998 L 95/1, 27 March 1998, and Council Regulation (EC) No 926/98, *OJ* 1998 L 130/1, 1 May

the transfer of funds or other financial assets to Serbia 'insofar as such funds or other financial assets are transferred for the purposes of establishing a lasting economic link with the Republic of Serbia, including the acquisition of real estate there.' An exemption was made for the transfer of funds used solely for projects in support of democratization, humanitarian and educational activities, and independent media. A year later, the investment ban was strengthened in Regulation (EC) No 1294/1999, which prohibited any participation in or ownership or control of any real estate, company, undertaking, institution or entity located, registered or incorporated within the Republic of Serbia or, wherever else located, registered or incorporated, owned or controlled by the Government of the FRY or the Government of the Republic of Serbia.[75] The ban concerned not only State-owned or State-controlled companies but also private companies in Serbia. The above-mentioned exemption with respect to certain projects was maintained. Investments in the Republic of Montenegro were also exempted, although this exemption only applied to companies that were not owned or controlled by the FRY or Serbian Governments. In principle, the investment ban covered the Province of Kosovo, but investments in that province could be authorized to avoid serious damage to an EU company or industry or to the interests of the Community itself.[76] The investment ban was lifted in November 2000.[77]

5.   CONCLUDING REMARKS

From 1991 until the end of the war in Bosnia, the European Community/Union, much as other international actors, was pre-occupied with attempts to contain and ultimately end the violent conflicts in the Western Balkans. Despite a number of mostly reactive and punitive initiatives against the Former Republic of Yugoslavia, no coherent EC/EU sanctions policy existed in its own name. In fact, most of the sanctions imposed by the European Community/Union on the FRY were a derivative of obligations that originated at UN level and were terminated once the UN Security Council decided thus. The only exceptions thereto, and thus the only examples of autonomous EU action in this period, were the precursors to the multilateral sanctions in 1991 (the EC arms embargo of July and the unilateral

---

1998, had already prohibited (a) 'the provision and/or use of government and/or other official financial support, insurance and/or guarantees in respect of new export credit for trade with or investment in the Republic of Serbia...', and (b) 'the provision or use of government and/or other official financing for privatizations in the Republic of Serbia...'.

[75] *OJ* 1999 L 153/63, 19 June 1999, in Art. 4(1). The Regulation was based on Common Position 1999/318/CFSP, *OJ* 1999 L 123/1, 13 May 1999.

[76] Ibid., Art. 8.

[77] Common Position 2000/599/CFSP, *OJ* 2000 L 255, 9 October 2000, and Council Regulation (EC) No 2488/2000, *OJ* 2000 L 187, 14 November 2000.

withdrawal of trade preferences in November) and the continuation of the EU arms embargo after the UN arms embargo on the countries of the former Yugoslavia was lifted in 1995.

The second episode of the wars waged by the FRY shows a distinctively more ambitious development of the European Union's own sanctions policy. When studying the EU sanctions against the FRY as a reaction to the war in Kosovo, one notices a development from very narrow targeting of the FRY and Serbian Governments in the first half of 1998, to a broader range of measures extending the impact to a larger group of persons and entities, becoming almost non-targeted in the case of the oil embargo and the flight ban in mid-1999. After that, the sanctions were narrowed again to the Belgrade regime, diminishing the impact on non-targeted sectors of the population, although in the summer of 2000 the financial sanctions impacted severely on many non-targeted companies and entities. After the elections of 24 September 2000, most of the sanctions were lifted, although a limited visa ban and assets freeze affecting approximately 600 individuals remained in place as of January 2001. The need for unanimity to adopt common positions that had allowed the more reluctant Member States to limit the scope and severity of the initial sanctions in 1998 gave the Member States that favoured stronger sanctions the leverage in 2000 to trade off the suspension of the flight ban and mitigation of the oil embargo for a strengthening of the financial sanctions. Of course, such divergences in opinion within the Council put the Commission in a difficult spot with respect to the design and execution of sanctions. This lack of conviction and the resulting inaction in the implementation of sanctions may have allowed the FRY regime to ignore the sanctions.

In a time where the European Union is actively seeking to increase its capacity to master international conflicts on its own, or to be an equal partner with other countries, notably the United States, concrete steps need to be taken to ensure that the military and non-military means and procedures can be deployed rapidly and effectively to manage crises and prevent conflicts. One would expect that the sanctions described in this paper, as non-military coercive instruments, would have a place in the arsenal of the European Union. But they apparently do not sit well with most Member States. Not even the beginning of a discussion on the role of sanctions as instruments of the Common Foreign and Security Policy has taken place yet. If that remains the case, the probability is that any new sanctions taken by the European Union will display the same characteristics as the sanctions against the FRY.

BIBLIOGRAPHY ALFRED E. KELLERMANN

EDITOR AND CO-AUTHOR OF THE FOLLOWING BOOKS

A.E. Kellermann, *Colloquium of law teachers on European law* (The Hague, T.M.C. Asser Instituut 1972).

A.E. Kellermann, J.J.M. Tromm, J.S. de Jongh and R. Winter, eds., *Guide to EEC Legislation* (Amsterdam, North Holland 1979, updated periodically).

A.E. Kellermann, *EEC-Comecon relations* (The Hague, T.M.C. Asser Instituut 1980).

A.E. Kellermann, J.J.M. Tromm, J.S. de Jongh and R. Winter, eds., *Guide to EC Court Decisions* (Amsterdam, North Holland 1982, updated periodically).

A.E. Kellermann, *Technological Development and Cooperation in Europe – Legal Aspects* (The Hague, T.M.C. Asser Instituut 1987).

H.G. Schermers, C.W.A. Timmermans, A.E. Kellermann and J. Stewart Watson, eds., *Article 177 EEC: Experiences and Problems* (Amsterdam, North Holland 1987).

H.G. Schermers, C. Flinterman, A.E. Kellermann, J.C. van Haersolte and G.-W. van de Meent, eds., *Free Movement of Persons in Europe* (Dordrecht, Martinus Nijhoff Publishers 1993).

T. Heukels, A.E. Kellermann, J.J.M. Sluys and V.P. Verkruissen, *De kwaliteit van EG-regelgeving: aandachtspunten en voorstellen – rapport van de Werkgroep kwaliteit en EG-regelgeving* (The Hague, Ministerie van Justitie 1996).

J.A. Winter, D. Curtin, A.E. Kellermann and B. de Witte, eds., *Reforming the Treaty on European Union – The Legal Debate* (The Hague, Kluwer Law International 1996).

A.E. Kellermann, G.C. Azzi, S.H. Jacobs and R. Deighton-Smith, eds., *Improving the Quality of Legislation in Europe* (The Hague, Kluwer Law International 1998).

A.E. Kellermann, K. Siehr and T. Einhorn, eds., *Israel among the Nations –
International and Comparative Law Perspectives on Israel's 50th Anniversary*
(The Hague, Kluwer Law International 1998).

A. Petchsiri, A.E. Kellermann, C. Tingsabadh and P. Watananguhn, eds.,
Strengthening ASEAN Integration: Lessons from the EU's Rule of Law (Bangkok,
Centre for European Studies at Chulalongkorn University 2001).

A.E. Kellermann, J.W. de Zwaan and J. Czuczai, eds., *EU Enlargement: The
Constitutional Impact at EU and National Level* (The Hague, T.M.C. Asser Press
2001).

W.Th. Douma and A.E. Kellermann, eds., *Economic Aspects of Environmental
Policy in Russia* (Moscow, ERM 2004).

D. Curtin and A.E. Kellermann, *The EU Constitution: The best way forward?*
(The Hague, T.M.C. Asser Press, forthcoming).

A.E. Kellermann, J. Czuczai, S. Blockmans and A. Albi, *Hopes and Fears of New
Member States and (Pre-)Candidate Countries – Their Views on the European
Constitution* (The Hague, T.M.C. Asser Press, forthcoming).

EDITOR AND CO-AUTHOR OF THE FOLLOWING ASSER COLLOQUIA
PROCEEDINGS (IN DUTCH)

Uitvoering Gemeenschapsrecht in de Nederlandse rechtsorde (The Hague,
T.M.C. Asser Instituut 1972).

*Het onderwijs in het Recht van de Europese Gemeenschappen aan de Nederlandse
Universiteiten en Hogescholen* (The Hague, T.M.C. Asser Instituut 1973).

Onderwijs Europees Recht (The Hague, T.M.C. Asser Instituut 1974).

Rechten van de mens (The Hague, T.M.C. Asser Instituut 1975).

*Plaats en taak van een Europees Parlement bij een verdere beleidsintegratie op
sociaal-economisch gebied in Europa* (The Hague, T.M.C. Asser Instituut 1976).

Externe betrekkingen van de Europese Gemeenschappen (The Hague, T.M.C.
Asser Instituut 1977).

De Europese Politieke Samenwerking (The Hague, T.M.C. Asser Instituut 1979).

Uitvoering van het Gemeenschapsrecht in Nederland (The Hague, T.M.C. Asser Instituut 1981).

Europeesrechtelijke aspecten van consumentenbescherming (The Hague, T.M.C. Asser Instituut 1982).

De rol van de Europese Gemeenschappen in een Nieuwe Internationale Economische Orde (The Hague, T.M.C. Asser Instituut 1983).

EEG-Handelspolitiek en beschermende maatregelen tegen de invoer uit derde landen (The Hague, T.M.C. Asser Instituut 1984).

Gedifferentieerde integratie in de Europese Gemeenschappen (The Hague, T.M.C. Asser Instituut 1985).

Europees milieurecht: praktische problemen bij de totstandkoming en uitvoering (The Hague, T.M.C. Asser Instituut 1989).

Fraude in de Europese Gemeenschappen (The Hague, T.M.C. Asser Instituut 1990).

De economische en sociale samenhang in de EG – de Europese Structuurfondsen (The Hague, T.M.C. Asser Instituut 1991).

Een Economische en Monetaire Unie (EMU) in Europa – juridische en constitutionele consequenties (The Hague, T.M.C. Asser Instituut 1991).

Onderwijs Europees Recht in Nederland (The Hague, T.M.C. Asser Instituut 1993).

De BV Nederland op de interne markt (The Hague, T.M.C. Asser Instituut 1993).

Externe bevoegdheden van de Europese Unie (The Hague, T.M.C. Asser Instituut 1994).

Diversiteit van de besluitvorming van de Europese Unie (The Hague, T.M.C. Asser Instituut 1995).

Rechtsbescherming in de Europese Gemeenschap (The Hague, T.M.C. Asser Instituut 1997).

Art. 90 EG en de privatisering van Nederlandse publieke ondernemingen (The Hague, T.M.C. Asser Instituut 1998).

Flexibiliteit en het Verdrag van Amsterdam (The Hague, T.M.C. Asser Press 1999).

Europees Kartelrecht gedecentraliseerd? – Het Witboek (The Hague, T.M.C. Asser Press 2000).

Europees Recht en de decentrale overheid in Nederland en België (The Hague, T.M.C. Asser Press 2002).

'Veiligheid' en het recht van de Europese Unie (The Hague, T.M.C. Asser Press 2003).

Europees Burgerschap (The Hague, T.M.C. Asser Press 2004).

CONTRIBUTIONS AND ARTICLES IN THE FOLLOWING PUBLICATIONS AND PERIODICALS

'Les directives de la CEE dans l'ordre juridique neerlandais', 5 *Cahiers de Droit Européen* (1969) pp. 247-312.

'Nietigverklaring van een Raadsverordening door het Hof van Justitie der Europese Gemeenschappen en Uitvoering van een Hofarrest door de Raad van Ministers', in T.M.C. Asser Instituut, *Tien jaren T.M.C. Asser Instituut 1965-1975* (The Hague, T.M.C. Asser Instituut 1975) pp. 91-97.

'Betekenen de uitspraken van het Hof van Justitie van 14 januari 1981 een uitholling van het fiscale discriminatieverbod van artikel 95 EEG-Verdrag?', in R. Barents, ed., *In Orde – Liber Amicorum Pieter VerLoren van Themaat* (Deventer, Kluwer 1982) pp. 143-154.

'The Netherlands in Face of its Community Obligations', 20 *Common Market Law Review* (1983) pp. 297-333.

'Good Faith in the Decisions of the Court of Justice of the European Communities', 38 *Bulletin IAJL* (1987) pp. 12-16.

'Bronnen voor juridische informatie inzake Europees recht', in VNO-NCW, *Beleidsbeïnvloeding en Rechtsbescherming, Ondernemen in Brussel* (1989) pp. 101-104.

'Supremacy of Community Law in the Netherlands', 14 *European Law Review* (1989) pp. 175-185.

with F.H. Possen, 'Court of Last Instance in Matters of Trade and Industry (CBB)', in J. Korte, ed., *Primus Inter Pares: The European Court and National Courts. The Follow-up by National Courts of Preliminary Rulings ex Art. 177 of the Treaty of Rome: A Report on the Situation in the Netherlands* (Florence, EUI 1990) pp. 37-45.

with J.A. Winter, 'Dutch Report', in J. Schwarze, I. Govaere, F. Hélin and P. Van den Bossche, eds., *The 1992 Challenge at National Level* (Baden-Baden, Nomos 1990) pp. 523-555.

'Council of State', in J. Korte, ed., *Primus Inter Pares: The European Court and National Courts. The Follow-up by National Courts of Preliminary Rulings ex Art. 177 of the Treaty of Rome: A Report on the Situation in the Netherlands* (Baden-Baden, Nomos 1991).

with S. Mol, and J.A. Winter, 'Netherlands', in J. Schwarze, U. Becker and C. Pollak, eds., *The 1992 Challenge at National Level* (Baden-Baden, Nomos 1991) pp. 355-397.

'Legal Impact of Procedural Irregularities in the Decision-Making of the Council of Ministers of the EC', in M. Sumampouw, L. Barnhoorn, J.A. Freedberg-Swartzburg, J. Tromm and J.A. Wade, eds., *Law and Reality – Essays on National and International Procedural Law in Honour of Cornelis Carel Albert Voskuil* (Dordrecht, Martinus Nijhoff Publishers 1992) pp. 149-155.

with J.A. Winter and A. Baas, 'Netherlands', in J. Schwarze, U. Becker and C. Pollak, eds., *The 1992 Challenge at National Level* (Baden-Baden, Nomos 1993) pp. 351-388.

'Ratification Processes of the Treaty on European Union – Viewpoint of the Dutch Government', 18 *European Law Review* (1993) pp. 243-247.

'The Quality of Community Legislation Drafting', in D. Curtin and T. Heukels, eds., *Institutional Dynamics of European Integration – Essays in Honour of Henry G. Schermers*, Vol. II (Dordrecht, Martinus Nijhoff Publishers 1994) pp. 251-262.

'Institutional Problems of Enlargement of the European Union', in W.P. Heere, ed., *Contemporary International Law Issues: Conflicts and Convergence* (The Hague, T.M.C. Asser Instituut 1996) pp. 169-174.

'Asser College Europe: A Network for European Integration', *On Our Way to a New Europe, Asser College Europe Alumni 1989-1999* (The Hague, T.M.C. Asser Instituut 1999) pp.13-24.

'Proposals for Improving the Quality of European and National Legislation', 1 *European Journal of Law Reform* (1999).

'Adaptation of Law and Economy to the Principle of Non-Discrimination on Grounds of Nationality, in particular in Areas of Right of Establishment and Free Movement of Services and Capital – Institutional and Constitutional Aspects', in J. Swierkocki, ed., *Accession Negotiations – Selected Results* (Lodz, European Institute 2001) pp. 337-372.

'Application of Community Law by National Courts', 10 *EMP* (2002) pp. 4-9.

'The Growing Impact of Principles of Good and Corporate Governance Strengthening the Rule of Law', in A. Petchsiri, P. Sutthisripok and P. Thontiravong, eds., *Comparative Regional Integration – ASEAN and the EU*, Monograph Series, Vol. 2 (Bangkok, Interdisciplinary Department of European Studies of Chulalongkorn University 2002) pp. 59-81.

'Application of Community Law by National Courts; Direct Effect and Supremacy', in A. Petchsiri, P. Sutthisripok and P. Thontiravong, eds., *Comparative Regional Integration – ASEAN and the EU*, Monograph Series, Vol. 2 (Bangkok, Interdisciplinary Department of European Studies of Chulalongkorn University 2002) pp. 135-149.

'EC-ASEAN Cooperation Agreement versus Europe (EAs), Stabilization and Association (SAAs) and Partnership and Cooperation Agreements (PCAs)', in A. Petchsiri, P. Sutthisripok and P. Thontiravong, eds., *Comparative Regional Integration – ASEAN and the EU*, Monograph Series, Vol. 2 (Bangkok, Interdisciplinary Department of European Studies of Chulalongkorn University 2002) pp. 205-216.

'Conclusion: Summing Up and Suggestions', in A. Petchsiri, P. Sutthisripok and P. Thontiravong, eds., *Comparative Regional Integration – ASEAN and the EU*, Monograph Series, Vol. 2 (Bangkok, Interdisciplinary Department of European Studies of Chulalongkorn University 2002) pp. 217-222.

'Preparation of National Constitutions of Candidate Countries for Accession', 2 *Romanian Journal of European Affairs* (2002) pp. 74-81.

'The growing impact of the principles of good governance in strengthening the application of the rule of law in European context', in W.P. Heere, ed., *From Government to Governance, The Growing Impact of Non-State Actors on the International and European Legal System* (The Hague, T.M.C. Asser Press 2004) pp. 83-93.

'Direct Effect of Europe Agreements in the Pre-Accession Period', 2 *Revista Romana de Drept Comunitar* (2004, forthcoming).

'The Impact of EU Enlargement on the Russian Federation', 4 *Romanian Journal of European Affairs* (2004, forthcoming).

INDEX